D0276378

THE CHILD AT SCHOOL

What is the nature of children's social life in school? How do their relationships and interactions with peers, teachers, and other school staff influence their development and experience of school? This book, written by leading researchers in educational and developmental psychology, provides answers to these questions by offering an integrated perspective on children's social interactions and relationships with their peers and teachers in school. Peer interactions in school have tended to be underestimated by educationalists, and this book redresses the balance by giving them equal weight to teacher–child interactions.

This second edition has been extensively revised on the basis of many years of research and teaching experience. The authors highlight common misconceptions about children, their social lives, and school achievement which have often resulted in ineffective school policy. The book covers a number of important topics relating to the child at school, including:

- The significance of peer-friendships
- The nature and importance of play and break-times
- Aggression and bullying
- Peer relations and learning
- The classroom environment and teacher–pupil interaction
- The influence of gender on children's learning
- Advantages and disadvantages of different methodological approaches for studying children in school settings
- Policy implications of current research findings.

The Child at School will be essential reading for all students of child development and educational psychology. It will also be an invaluable resource for both trainee and practising teachers and teaching assistants, as well as clinical psychologists and policy makers in this area.

Peter Blatchford is Professor of Psychology and Education at the UCL Institute of Education, UK.

Anthony D. Pellegrini is Emeritus Professor at the University of Minnesota, USA.

Ed Baines is Senior Lecturer in Psychology and Education at the UCL Institute of Education, UK.

NCI LIBRARY WITHDRAWN FROM STOCK

Luimneach

International Texts in Developmental Psychology

Series editor: Peter K. Smith, Goldsmiths College, University of London, UK.

This volume is one of a rapidly developing series in *International Texts in Developmental Psychology*, published by Routledge. The books in this series are selected to be state-of-the-art, high level introductions to major topic areas in developmental psychology. The series conceives of developmental psychology in broad terms and covers such areas as social development, cognitive development, developmental neuropsychology and neuroscience, language development, learning difficulties, developmental psychopathology and applied issues. Each volume is written by a specialist (or specialists), combining empirical data and a synthesis of recent global research to deliver cutting-edge science in a format accessible to students and researchers alike. The books may be used as textbooks that match on to upper level developmental psychology modules, but many will also have cross-disciplinary appeal.

Each volume in the series is published in hardback, paperback and eBook formats. More information about the series is available on the official website at: http://www.psypress.com/books/series/DEVP, including details of all the titles published to date.

Published Titles

Aging and Development: Social and Emotional Perspectives, Second edition
By Peter Coleman and Ann O'Hanlon

Childhood Friendships and Peer Relations: Friends and Enemies, Second edition
By Barry Schneider

Children's Literacy Development: A Cross-Cultural Perspective on Learning to Read and Write, Second edition
By Catherine McBride

Child Development: Theories and Critical Perspectives, Second edition
By Rosalyn H. Shute and Phillip T. Slee

The Child at School: Interactions with Peers and Teachers, Second edition
By Peter Blatchford, Anthony D. Pellegrini and Ed Baines

THE CHILD AT SCHOOL

Interactions with Peers and Teachers

Second Edition

*Peter Blatchford, Anthony D. Pellegrini
and Ed Baines*

Routledge
Taylor & Francis Group

LONDON AND NEW YORK

Second edition published 2016
by Routledge
27 Church Road, Hove, East Sussex BN3 2FA

and by Routledge
711 Third Avenue, New York, NY 10017

Routledge is an imprint of the Taylor & Francis Group, an informa business

© 2016 Peter Blatchford, Anthony D. Pellegrini and Ed Baines

The right of Peter Blatchford, Anthony D. Pellegrini and Ed Baines to be
identified as the authors of this work has been asserted by them in accordance
with sections 77 and 78 of the Copyright, Designs and Patents Act 1988.

All rights reserved. No part of this book may be reprinted or reproduced or
utilised in any form or by any electronic, mechanical, or other means, now
known or hereafter invented, including photocopying and recording, or in any
information storage or retrieval system, without permission in writing from the
publishers.

Trademark notice: Product or corporate names may be trademarks or registered
trademarks, and are used only for identification and explanation without intent
to infringe.

First edition published by Hodder Education 2000

British Library Cataloguing in Publication Data
A catalogue record for this book is available from the British Library

Library of Congress Cataloging in Publication Data
Pellegrini, Anthony D.
  The child at school : interactions with peers and teachers / Peter Blatchford,
Anthony D. Pellegrini and Ed Baines. — [Second edition].
    pages cm
  Includes bibliographical references and index.
  1. Child development. 2. School children—Psychology. 3. Social
interaction in children. I. Blatchford, Peter. II. Baines, Ed. III. Title.
  LB1115.P44 2015
  372.18—dc23   2015002739

ISBN: 978-1-84872-299-6 (hbk)
ISBN: 978-1-84872-300-9 (pbk)
ISBN: 978-1-315-72695-3 (ebk)

Typeset in Bembo
by Keystroke, Station Road, Codsall, Wolverhampton

Coláiste
Mhuire Gan Smál
Luimneach

Class	372.18
Suff	BLA
MI	15001237

MIX
Paper from
responsible sources
FSC
www.fsc.org   FSC® C013056

Printed and bound in Great Britain by
TJ International Ltd, Padstow, Cornwall

PB: to the memory of Irene Blatchford
AP: to the memory of Ann Pellegrini
EB: to Evan and Orla, my fantastic children. I am enjoying your childhood very much and hope that when you are older, you will remember it fondly too!

CONTENTS

CONTENTS

FIGURES AND TABLES

Figures

Tables

1

AN INTRODUCTION TO *THE CHILD AT SCHOOL*

A personal introduction

The idea for this book began almost 25 years ago when one of us (AP) was spending the year at Sheffield University conducting research on children's behaviour on the school playground. AP and PB had been invited to participate in a symposium at the university on bullying and aggression on the playground. After that day, and the subsequent evening in the pub, we each recognized the fact that children's social lives in schools were both very important and very understudied.

Since that time we have collaborated on a number of projects, including a project on children's games and their social relations, funded by the Spencer Foundation. Most centrally, our work has taken a developmental orientation on children's social behaviour and relationships in schools. Over the past number of years we have participated in a number of symposia on both sides of the Atlantic and written numerous journal articles for psychological and education journals addressing the role of children's social behaviour, especially during breaktime, in the lives of children at school.

Since the first edition, the authors have conducted extensive further research. PB has extended his work on peer interaction by co-directing a large-scale project in which a programme of collaborative group work in schools was developed and evaluated (the SPRinG project). We draw on this project and also two other large projects directed by PB, one on the effects of class size in schools (e.g., Blatchford, 2003) and another on the role and impact of Teaching Assistants in schools (e.g., Blatchford et al., 2012). PB and EB also directed a follow-up survey of breaktimes in schools, which we draw on in the book.

AP has also been extending his work in the areas of play, aggression, and development more generally. Specific to his work in play, he has helped to further clarify how object play is different from other forms of object use, such as construction, exploration, and tool use, and how play may actually affect phylogeny. His work on aggression and bullying has demonstrated how some bullies are socially competent, not deficient in social information processing, and how some forms of aggression relate to group stability, in the form of dominance hierarchies.

AP and PB are pleased that EB has joined us in writing this second edition of the book. He first joined us on the Spencer project and then subsequently worked with PB on the group work projects at the Institute of Education and also national surveys of breaktime/recess in UK schools.

The second edition has been substantially revised to reflect the many developments in the fields covered and to reflect material and insights from our research projects. The authors also draw on many years of teaching at undergraduate, masters and doctoral levels, as well as professional development work with teachers. We draw on these experiences and the feedback we received to further refine what we consider to be key applications of the research on the academic and social world of children and their peers at school.

Our 'developmental' orientation

Our orientation to the study of children in schools draws extensively from the sub-fields of developmental, social, educational and evolutionary psychology. As we explain below it seems to us that research in these different traditions has tended to be conducted separately, and not always with knowledge of research in other areas. It is our aim in this book to offer a unifying perspective on interactions that draws on developmental, but also educational and social psychology, in order to inform both adult–child and peer interactions and relationships.

In this second edition we have expanded our discussion of development, per se, and consequently have drawn extensively from the evolutionary biological literature. Specifically, we stress a developmental perspective on children in schools because children are qualitatively different from adults and this perspective captures this distinction most directly. Below, we make a number of points about the way the term 'development' is understood and used. First though, we identify some other main themes in the book.

As the book's subtitle states, an important theme of the book is a focus on interactions and relationships between and among people. We feel that interactions in school have tended to be considered by researchers in a fragmented way; for example, interactions between teachers and pupils have tended to be considered quite separately from research on interactions between children. Often the two types of interaction have been studied from very different theoretical perspectives and even disciplines.

It is probably true to say that developmental psychologists are not as familiar as they might be with research on classroom interactions – but, in turn, educational psychologists tend not to be familiar with developmental research on parent–child interactions and peer interactions. This is unfortunate because there are many conceptual and methodological overlaps between the two kinds of research, and much that each can learn from the other. Pianta (2006, in Hamre & Pianta, 2010) makes the strong assertion that the study of development in classrooms offers as much for developmental theory as it does for educational practice. He argues that the classroom environment should be of particular interest to developmental psychologists because: (1) there are important effects of daily interactions with adults and peers in schools on children's development – after all, they are in schools for the majority of the day; (2) interactions in schools are as important as interactions with parents and in the home because they are intended to bring about developmental change; and (3) classrooms are often the location within which intervention programmes are implemented. Despite Pianta's call, it is a salutary fact that the recent two-volume *Oxford Review of Developmental Psychology* (2013) does not have any chapters which examine pupils in classroom or school contexts.

Nevertheless it is possible to take the application of developmental psychology to schools too far. Hamre and Pianta (2010) have shown how, particularly in the USA, recent research on classrooms has drawn on research on processes in home settings, working on the assumption that there are underlying processes driving development, e.g., in the application of research on maternal sensitivity and effective parenting to research on teacher sensitivity and effectiveness. But Hamre and Pianta also point out that one needs to be careful about taking this application to an extreme because the home and the classroom are very different environments with very different dynamics, culture and interactions. In classrooms the driving rationale is the need to consider interactions in relation to school academic progress. So although the more recent interest of developmental psychologists in classrooms is, from the point of view of this book, very timely, it is important not to lose sight of the earlier longstanding research on classrooms and the interactions that take place there.

There is another reason why we feel the classroom is an important site for research in its own right. In preparing this edition it has become apparent that there has if anything been a decline over the past 20 years or so in close observational studies of what goes on in classrooms. Given the rich tradition of classroom studies, on which we draw in this book, this more recent trend is unfortunate and perhaps reflects the way school policy has become driven by econometric concerns with academic performance rather than close attention to the details of pedagogy and teacher–pupil talk. One aim of this book, therefore, is to champion the value of observational studies of children and their interactions in schools.

Observational methods are important because they enable us to describe in a systematic and rich way the everyday interactions children have with their social and physical environments. As we show in this book, the authors have possibly a uniquely extensive experience of direct systematic observational methods for studying children in different school settings such as the playground or the classroom (e.g., Pellegrini, 2012).

One thing that strikes anyone interested in interactions and relationships in school settings is that there is also a large literature that extends well beyond the realms of psychology, e.g., sociological, ethnographical and linguistic. This book differs from other texts which have focused on interactions in school contexts, because our approach is concerned with the psychological dimensions of these interactions and relationships.

But we are very mindful that all too often research and reviews of research situate themselves in silos of discrete subject knowledge, even when they are essentially interested in the same phenomena. It is probably beyond the space available to conduct a fully integrated text across disciplines, but in this book, despite the psychological orientation, we seek wherever we feel it is helpful to integrate material from different approaches, e.g., with regard to teacher–pupil interactions and sex differences in classroom interaction.

Children's interactions and relationships with peers and adults are complementary. It seems to us that peer interactions in schools have tended to be underestimated, and sometimes discouraged by educationalists, and one aim of this book is to give equal weight to peer–peer and teacher–child interactions. In this book we seek to point out ways in which these two types of behaviours and relationship affect children in different ways. So, for example, adults may be effective at helping a child plan a shopping trip, but peers are much better at affording opportunities for children to use diverse functions of language. When preschoolers are playing, they use a wide variety of functions of language (Pellegrini, 1983) but when children are interacting with the teacher they typically are in the role of responder and reciter.

As well as the developmental approach, a main theme of this book is the adoption of a contextual approach. One widely known theoretical tradition seeks to interpret learning and development within ecologically meaningful environmental contexts (Bronfenbrenner, 1979; Weinstein, 1991). Peer relations will take place in different contexts – out of school, e.g., at home or outside the home, as well as in school. Within the 'microsystem' of a school, there will be smaller within-school contexts, in particular the classroom and playground, which have qualitatively distinct sets of relationships, rules and dynamics that promote or hinder learning and social development. As we shall see there are also within-class settings, especially small groups of pupils, that can also be considered as distinct contexts with particular features and effects.

School environments are often considered purely in terms of settings for academic development. Of course, the classroom is a prime place for interaction, at least between children and teachers, and these interactions have a specific role in children's academic development. But interactions between teachers and pupils have been considered in much research as if existing in a vacuum. In contrast, we consider some of the particular ways in which the classroom context can affect the nature of interactions between teachers and children. We also believe that other contexts in schools are important. In particular we have each spent much time researching children's behaviour on school playgrounds, and consider this a neglected but important area. Indeed, we consider the school playground, and school breaktime, as one of the best places to study children's social behaviour. Additionally, we also show how breaktime, and social behaviour on the playground, can be important to children's academic and social skills.

Children can also be seen to interact with 'context' as well as with people. In this book we discuss ways in which contexts affect children; for example, when children are given doctor props with which to play, they typically engage in play which has a medical theme. On a more global level, children are embedded in classrooms and schools which have different levels of structure. In less structured, 'open field' situations, children may be free to choose their activities and partners. In this sort of context, children are likely to choose a friend with whom to interact and their interaction is likely to be cooperative, rather than disruptive.

Additionally, interactions with friends, compared with other classmates, around academic tasks are likely to be sophisticated and result in high performance. In more structured, 'closed field' situations, children do not have such a choice, and their interactions are less cooperative and in many cases less productive (Hartup, 1996). We also recognize that children affect contexts. By this we mean that children choose contexts which are consistent with their personality; for example, aggressive children choose other aggressive youngsters to play with, while shy children choose other shy children. As children continue to interact with each other they tend to re-enforce this similarity.

This interest in contexts for development has a broader connection with policy. Children may, for example, have a school friendship network which is quite separate from their out of school network. For some pupils it may be difficult to meet their school friends out of school. At secondary school level, students may travel some distance to school, often by car, and are unlikely to meet school friends, unless visits are arranged. This situation may be becoming more common with more market-led policies in education, when the encouragement of parental choice of schools can result in long journeys to the desired school, rather than the automatic choice of the nearest, local school.

There is another kind of context – this time not spatial but historical. Peer relations, and the contexts within which they occur, may be very different to the situation 10 or 25 years ago. There have been many complex social cultural changes over time and these will inevitably affect peer relations. To give an example: peer relations are now the focus of much media interest usually because of the widespread reporting of bullying, anti-social behaviour and violence between gangs in inner cities. There is a widespread sense of risk and threat from criminality and bad behaviour when children and young children meet when unsupervised. There is a general sense that behaviour has got worse in recent years (Blatchford & Baines, 2010). A recent submission to the Children's Society national inquiry in the UK (2007) indicated that the number of teenagers with no best friends had increased over the past 16 years, while those who reported being assaulted or threatened by a peer had increased.

There are signs that these negative views about peer interactions affect parents of school-aged pupils and their decisions concerning the movements of their sons and daughters. It also affects school policies on pupil behaviour. There are signs, for example, that in the USA, the UK and Australia, children of primary school age (5–11 years) have fewer opportunities out of school for interacting freely with peers and thus developing friendships and social skills. For example, a survey in the early 1990s showed that one important venue for peer interaction is disappearing: students are now far less likely to walk to school, in comparison to 30 years ago, and have far less independence out of school (Hillman, 1993). A survey by the Home Office and the DCSF in 2003 found that two-thirds of 8–10 year olds and nearly a quarter of 11–15 year olds had never been to the park or shops on their own (Home Office and DCSF, 2005). In addition, a third of 8–10 year olds had never played out with their friends without an adult present. A survey of pupil views (Blatchford & Baines, 2006) found that nearly a third of 8–15 year olds rarely met friends outside of school.

To return to our treatment of development, we will also discuss the effects of, or consequences of, interactions and relationships in schools – for example in terms of the consequences of having/not having friends in school, of being rejected by their peers, of receiving different kinds and quantities of interactions from their teachers, and of teachers having low expectations of children in their class. These effects can be seen in the short term and the long term; for example, difficulties in interactions with peers can be considered in terms of immediate effects, but can also be considered in relation to long-term effects on personal adjustment (e.g., Parker & Asher, 1987).

Attention to the effects of interactions and relationships is consistent with our developmental approach, and is also connected to a concern with the role or function of interactions in different school contexts, e.g., relationships, such as friendships, in school, interactions on playgrounds, interactive teaching in class-rooms, and different interactions of boys and girls in classroom and playground. A broad approach to effects is useful because the value of interactions in some school contexts can be overlooked and underestimated, with sometimes unfor-tunate consequences. The way schools in the USA and the UK are limiting or eliminating breaktime (Baines & Blatchford, 2011; Pellegrini & Bohn, 2005) may be misguided if breaks during the school day have an important social function (Blatchford, 1998), improve achievement (Pellegrini & Smith, 1998) and posi-tively impact children's adjustment to school. Further, the social cognitive skills used in the playground have important implications for achievement (Pellegrini & Bohn, 2005).

We stress the fact that different relationships have different consequences. As noted above, when children interact with friends rather than acquaintances, their interactions are often more complex. For example, they are both more likely to disagree and resolve their disagreements (Hartup, 1996). Relatedly, when children make the transition from preschool to primary school with a friend in their classroom, they adjust to school more successfully than children without friends (Ladd & Price, 1987). Importantly, friends, relative to acquaintances, also facilitate higher levels of performance on cognitive tasks (Jones & Pellegrini, 1996; Pellegrini et al., 2002; Zajac & Hartup, 1997). These sorts of comparisons between different types of peers are particularly important because they are often the opposite of what gets done in schools; for example, teachers often separate friends because they think it will interfere with engagement.

Another theme of this book is a concern with differences between children. This will be evident in two main ways. First, the differences between children in their social relations in terms of rejected vs. popular, friendless vs. befriended, high vs. low expectation, etc. Secondly, we will be interested throughout in group differences, mainly male vs. female, e.g., in relation to interactions with teachers. As we shall see in several chapters, it can also be important to examine ways in which gender and ethnicity are connected.

We cover the advantages and disadvantages of qualitative and quantitative approaches to observation research. We situate ourselves in the longstanding debates between different educational research traditions. In general, our view of the long-running debate (sometimes the term 'war' has been applied) between different research paradigms is that it is often both unproductive and artificial. Specifically, the scientific enterprise consists of both inductive processes, as is primary in ethnography and ethology, and deductive processes (Russell, 1931/1959), as is typified in experimental psychology. For example, in our use of observational methods, we, like some ethnographers and ethologists, stress the importance of inductive categories. Similarly, like some branches of ethnography, we talk about the transaction between children and their contexts. Yet we also, in contrast to some working from a qualitative or ethnographic framework, see value in quantifying our observations, and deductively testing hypotheses experimentally generated from the inductions. In the tradition of ethological studies of children's development and children in school (Blurton Jones, 1972), we too agree that children should be studied in their natural habitats to maximize our understanding. This is one reason why we were drawn to the school playground as a research site, but why we also think observations in the classroom are very valuable.

Correspondingly, we recognize the value of using experimental analogues of naturalistic settings. The field experiments of Smith and Connolly (1972), Pellegrini, Hubert and Jones (1995) and Baines et al. (2007) are examples of the ways in which experiments can be conducted in schools to understand more closely the nature of things. After all, teachers often 'experiment' with different techniques of teaching – this is not much different. But we also comment critically on the use of experimental methods, for example, as used to study teacher expectations and class size differences. Experimental methods are usually seen as the 'gold standard' for addressing causality, and we discuss studies that have used such designs. But there are also alternatives which may, for some purposes, be more valid, and we discuss these as well; for example, the use of regression analyses which control statistically for potentially confounding factors, as in research on the effects of class-size differences in school (see Chapter 8).

Consistent with our developmental orientation, we recognize and stress the role of longitudinal research. Indeed the only way in which development per se can be studied is longitudinal, for developmental research is concerned with the 'process' of change. Cross-sectional studies of different age groups do not meet that criterion. Neither do they, nor can they, examine the ways in which children address transitions in development, such as from preschool to primary school or from primary to middle school. Longitudinal research embedded in a naturalistic design is a very powerful tool in understanding children in schools, and one that researchers of all stripes should aspire to.

Although we take a developmental perspective, in this book we do not seek to cover extensively areas such as cognitive and emotional development and learning, even though they are clearly related to social behaviour. Rather the focus is on the interactive and social nature of school life, involving peers and adults.

What do we mean by 'development'?

The term 'developmental' is used in many different ways by those interested in children. Most basically, the term has its origins in biology (recall that Piaget was trained as a biologist), and from embryology more exactly, and it addresses the process of differentiation that living organisms undergo from conception until death (i.e., ontogeny). The construct 'development' is also of interest to those of us interested in children in schools. Even at the level of public educational policy, the notion of 'development' is evoked: some states in America have 'Developmental Kindergartens'; 'development' in such cases is defined implicitly as 'remedial' classrooms for children. Also in terms of applications to schooling, development is used in terms of curricula and evaluation procedures for children as being 'developmentally appropriate'. Here 'development' means that curriculum and evaluation procedures should be congruent with the children's level of competence. For example, in the area of evaluation, because preschool and kindergarten children's motivation in assessment situations is highly variable (e.g., affected by the sex and/or race of the tester), more naturalistic approaches of evaluation (e.g., observation of behaviour) are developmentally appropriate for this period. Similarly, if peer relations are a hallmark of the preschool and early school years (Waters & Sroufe, 1983), developmentally appropriate practice should therefore involve opportunities for children to interact with each other in a variety of settings.

Different views of development

It should be clear that the term 'developmental' has wide and disparate uses. Here we present our view of 'development' as it applies to children's development in the context of schools and contrast it with another, more commonly held position. The first, and probably more common and familiar, model considers the child as an unfinished or incomplete adult. This view is represented in the theories of Piaget and Vygotsky (see Pellegrini & Smith, 1998). For Piaget (1969, cited in Gould, 1977), especially, ontogeny represents a progression towards human adulthood, perhaps reflecting his not so implicit view that human cognitive development recapitulated phylogeny. For example, he suggested that by studying children's thinking we could gain insight into thinking of 'primitive man' and, correspondingly, that children's acquisition of logico-mathematical thought parallels the history of Western science (Piaget, 1969, cited in Gould, 1977). From this view, the less mature stages represent 'lower forms', relative to adulthood. Relatedly, this view of development is often seen as something controlled by a genetic problem, possibly related to distant phylogeny, with minimal 'plasticity', or changeability, in response to genetic mutation, epigenesis, and environmental perturbations (Bateson & Gluckman, 2011). Importantly – and as we will expand upon later – changes in one's environment from conception through adulthood can impact on individual development.

Most developmental theories under this heading assume the existence of an extended period of childhood in terms of training for adulthood. Thus children's behaviour is understood in terms of adults' more advanced behaviour (e.g., pre-operational thought is deficient relative to formal operational thought) and early behaviours are seen in terms of how they are 'transformed' into mature behaviours. In Piaget's terms, the end point is formal operational thought. The thought and behaviour of preschool children is thus considered to be 'less developed' than formal operational thought or merely a means to the end of operational thought. It is the job of the developmentalist to chart the course from infancy and early childhood, through adolescence, to adulthood. Typically, and as exemplified by Piaget's model, one developmental pathway is specified. Piaget's discussion of egocentricism is a good example of this 'unfinished' orientation. The egocentric child, in this model, has neither the ability nor the desire to take another person's perspective. This limitation is 'overcome' through repeated clashes with the social world. In short, egocentricism is a liability to be overcome.

The educational implications of this view are that we present children with materials and activities at their 'developmentally appropriate' levels but the importance of these tasks is considered in terms of the ways in which they contribute to operational thought. Further, we often consider the specified pathways as the only ways in which children can reach desired outcomes. For example, we may think that all children must engage in symbolic play if they are to develop into competent adults. Alternative pathways to competence are not typically considered.

Related to the notion of continuous progress towards adulthood, is the stress on early experiences. If development is continuous, the argument goes, disturbances in the early processes should have important, and sometimes irreversible effects. It is these early experiences upon which subsequent development is based. Viewing infancy and early childhood as a 'critical period' is an example of this perspective.

A second, and preferred, view, however, considers development as much more plastic and sensitive to the individual's ecology, and thus proceeds through 'epigenesis' (Bateson & Gluckman, 2011). Though the term 'epigenetics' was coined by Waddington (1957) in his prescient discussion of epigenetic landscape, it currently refers to the molecular processes by which genetic traits can persist without changing the sequenced DNA through processes that result in the silencing or activation of gene expression (Bateson & Gluckman, 2011). From this position, development is not the mere unfolding of the DNA inherited from one's parents or as a result of gene mutation. Instead, there is transaction between the organism and the environment such that each influences the other over the course of development. In the case of individuals influencing their environments, they can change environments to make them safer, warmer, cooler, etc. In the other case, a very well-known example involves the effect of mothers' nutrition on foetal and subsequent development. Babies born to mothers experiencing poor nutrition will be smaller than if the mother were well nourished. On the other hand, if this same baby, after birth, was to be reared in a richer environment, with an abundance of nutrients, this individual, as an adult, would be more prone to insulin deficiency and high blood pressure.

Also following from this position, 'childish' behaviours are not considered to be imperfect and something to be overcome, but as important responses to the niche of childhood. This view of development assumes that individuals use strategies at different points in development and in different ecological niches so as to maximize benefits and minimize costs, similar to views represented in the theories of Bateson (1978). So, for example, in some contexts it might 'pay' for children to learn how to use tools through play, while for others a better strategy would be to learn them directly from a more competent adult (Bock, 2005). Obviously, these two views have very different, and important, implications for the ways in which we interact with children in schools.

According to this second view, and as noted above, developmental processes can be viewed as responses to the specific demands of specific niches in development, such as childhood. So, specific behaviours, such as egocentric responses and pretend play, are not viewed as immature versions of adult behaviour but as adaptive responses to the special needs of the niche of childhood. Take the example of very young children's limited locomotor capabilities. These could be viewed in immature, unfinished terms or could be viewed as adaptive, in that this limited mobility results in children staying closer to their caregivers, which, in turn, fosters children's learning new skills (Bjorklund & Green, 1992; Gould, 1977). Educationally, this stance also stresses the need for 'developmentally appropriate' practice, but stress is placed on the role of these activities for the specific needs of childhood, rather than as preparation for adulthood.

This view of development also has implications for our views on the continuity of developmental pathways. Accordingly, we suggest that individual children may take many different pathways to developmental competence in different periods (Bateson & Gluckman, 2011; Kagan, 1983). This is very different from the first view of development that implied that the developmental route is related to phylogenetic history. The second view of development assumes that there is no one royal road to competence. The road taken is a result of children's individual differences and a result of different niches. Suffice it to say for now that we have two views of development, one stressing the child as an incomplete version of adults, and the other viewing childhood as having its own integrity. Correspondingly, the behaviours and cognitions characteristic of childhood have value for that period and a specific context. Because of the important and we feel neglected role of peers we now offer some introductory comments on the role of peers in development.

The role of peers in development

There is an ambivalent view about peer relations stemming from psychological theory and research. On the one hand there is a well-established position that peer relations have particular value for social and even cognitive development. In an influential book, Youniss (1980) adapted the theories of Piaget and Sullivan to show how peer relations differed from adult–child relations by showing equality, cooperation, reciprocity and mutuality – all of which make a contribution to social development. This positive view has been given an added dimension with a theory of socialization which downplays the role of parents and other adults in favour of the important role of the group and particularly the peer group in development (Harris, 1995). On the other hand, as we shall see in the chapters that follow, much psychological research on peer relations has been concerned with difficulties experienced with peer relations in terms of, for example, peer rejection, bullying, victimization and withdrawal.

One general theme that underpins discussion of peer relations is the overall importance of peer relations in development. Hartup (1996) has argued that the evidence is not strong because much is correlational, that is, features of peer relations are related to later outcomes, but not necessarily in a causal way. There are two basic models recognized in many papers concerning the role of peer relations and friendships in social development. In the first model, peer relations and friendship relations play a direct role in development; for example, low peer acceptance causes peer developmental outcomes. However, a second model does not assume that peer relations directly affect developmental outcomes. Rather, underlying individual differences and behavioural/social difficulties lead to poor peer and friendship relations and hence poor developmental outcomes. Low peer acceptance is therefore a symptom of the underlying disturbance (personality traits/behavioural problems). So, according to this model, poor peer relations do not cause maladjustment, but are a reflection of it. An allied debate involves the extent to which peer relations can be considered a developmental 'advantage' or 'necessity'. Hartup (1992) tends to favour the first of these two models, while

Harris (1995) and Newcomb and Bagwell (1996) argue that the friendships of children and adolescents have a special place in development.

An excellent discussion of the role of peer relations in development can be found in Howe (2010). In our view we need to move beyond basic and simple models of the role of peer relations in development to focus on the complex multivariate dynamic between individual characteristics, peer relations, the quality and nature of relationships and the socializing influence of peers, and a host of other variables including family factors, background (SES, ethnicity and so on).

This book

In this volume, therefore, we view the child in school as a developmental being, interacting with his/her social and physical environments. From this view we can better understand those seemingly idiosyncratic behaviours of young children and help make schools more effective and happier places for children to live in. Importantly, we have pointed out how some common misconceptions about children, their social lives, and school achievement (e.g., regarding breaktime and friends) have resulted in ineffective school policy. We have identified some main themes in this book – its developmental perspective on interactions in schools, but also its concern with contextual factors and the effects of interactions, differences between children and research methods.

It has been 15 years since the first edition and in this second edition we have extensively revised and extended the text. We have tried to reflect newer research and understandings about the topics covered, and there are many ways in which the narrative has been restructured. As described above, we have also drawn heavily from our research work since the first edition. We now indicate the key changes we have made in the description of each chapter.

The book is divided into two halves. In the first half we look at peer interactions. In Chapter 2, we examine children's social competence and peer relations. Social competence is considered broadly and developmentally. While there are different demands in different developmental periods, the ability to adjust and contribute to one's context is a hallmark of competence. As Pellegrini's (2009) research has shown, dimensions of social dominance are included in social competence.

This is followed by a chapter on friendships in school (Chapter 3) which, in line with much research, summarizes how friendship relations develop with age, but concentrates on the significance of friendships in the school context. It also examines the school breaktime as a context for friendships, and highlights the group nature of social life and experiences with friends. The chapter also considers the value of friendship experiences for development and also the possible positive and negative psychosocial implications of having friends as well as the developmental implications for children that are friendless.

As mentioned above, the authors have championed research on children's play behaviour and experience on school playgrounds (e.g., Blatchford, 1998;

Blatchford, Baines & Pellegrini, 2003; Pellegrini, 1995), and we devote two chapters to research on play (Chapter 4) and breaktime/recess (Chapter 5). In our discussion of play, we define play from a number of different dimensions, outline different forms of play that are observed during childhood, and then make inferences about the value of each form for children. We examine the pro vs. anti breaktime debate, describe 'within-child' influences of gender, temperament and age on playground behaviour, and the influence of the timing of breaktime, and end with an examination of its cognitive and social implications.

In Chapter 6 we discuss a dark side of peer interaction in school – aggression. An aspect of peer aggression in schools, studied extensively, is bullying. For this reason our discussion will concentrate on problems of bullying and victimization. Bullying is defined as persistent negative behaviour directed at a specific child or group of children. Victims are typically weaker and more submissive than bullies, so there is also a power differential between bullies and victims.

Chapter 7 is a new chapter in which we bridge the gap between the world of peer relations and schools. This captures recent work on ways that peer relations and social networks are connected to: school attainment and academic adjustment; friendships and learning interactions; effects of school factors on peer relations; and the formal role of peer relations in classroom learning – specifically, research on collaborative and cooperative group work. There have been huge advances in understanding of groupings and collaborative group work, and the SPRinG project co-directed by PB and involving EB has taken place since the first edition. This was one of the biggest (and possibly *the* biggest) study worldwide on collaborative group work, and the book weaves key findings and implications into the text in this chapter.

In the second half of the book we turn to teacher–pupil interactions and influences on children's school performance. In Chapter 8 we examine research and conceptualizations of the classroom environment. The chapter has two parts: first, ways of conceiving contexts at the class level, in terms of the physical layout of classrooms, the number of pupils, allocation to classes on the basis of ability, social and psychological dimensions of the classroom; and, second, in terms of within-class contexts such as behavioural segments, tasks, activities, and within-class groupings. We further extend the chapter beyond the first edition by looking at more recent work including our own on class-size effects, on ability grouping/tracking, and within-class group arrangements in schools.

In Chapter 9 we turn to interactions with adults in the classroom. We extend the chapter to encompass work stemming from sociocultural and ethnographical approaches, including coverage of questioning, scaffolding and dialogic teaching. In addition – given that Teaching Assistants or paraprofessionals working in classrooms now make up a quarter of the workforce in schools in the UK, with signs that this is growing in other countries too – we also look at interactions between Teaching Assistants/Aides (TAs) and pupils, which was a key concern of recent projects directed by PB.

In Chapter 10 we examine teacher expectations. We believe this topic is very important, e.g., because it is a main process through which social psychological research has been insightful when applied to classrooms. We update this chapter, e.g., by reference to the wider school influences on expectations and also the clearer consequences for pupil progress. We make use of recent experiences in working through this topic with primary school trainee teachers.

In Chapter 11 we turn to sex differences in classroom interaction. We argue that better understanding of influences on the relative performance of boys and girls is a main challenge for educational research, with important theoretical and practical implications. As in the first edition, the chapter focuses on the role of teaching and classroom interactions, but we also look at ways in which other within-child factors such as self-perceptions, self-concept and motivational processes help inform gender differences in interaction and achievement. The literature review is updated and we again include coverage of ethnographical work, because of the insights it sheds on the role of peer relations and self-perceptions on sex differences.

Finally, in Chapter 12 we draw out some overarching points that we feel arise out of the book and stress the importance of this work for policy in schools.

In conclusion, our aim in this book is to stress the importance of research on interactions for educational as well as social policy. School policy and practice, like other aspects of social policy, should be based on our best available knowledge. In this book, we have provided what we see as the best knowledge on children's social lives in school. Further, in anticipation of unanswered and unasked questions, we provide a thorough exposition on methods for studying social processes in school.

References

Baines, E. & Blatchford, P. (2011). Playground games and activities in school and their role in development. In A.D. Pellegrini (Ed.), *The Oxford Handbook of the Development of Play*. New York: Oxford University Press.

Baines, E., Blatchford, P. & Chowne, A. (2007). Improving the effectiveness of collaborative group work in primary schools: effects on science attainment. *British Educational Research Journal*, 33, 663–680.

Bateson, P.P.G. (1978). How behavior develops. In P.P.G. Bateson & L. Klopfer (Eds), *Perspectives in Ethology, Vol 5* (pp. 55–66). New York: Academic.

Bateson, P. & Gluckman, P. (2011). *Plasticity, Robustness, Development, and Evolution*. Cambridge: Cambridge University Press.

Bjorklund, D.F. & Green, B.L. (1992). The adaptive nature of cognitive immaturity. *American Psychologist*, 47, 46–54.

Blatchford, P. (1998). *Social Life in School: Pupils' Experience of Breaktime and Recess from 7 to 16 Years*. London: Falmer Press.

Blatchford, P. (2003). *The Class Size Debate: Is Small Better?* Maidenhead: Open University Press.

Blatchford, P. & Baines, E. (2006). *A Follow-Up National Survey of Breaktimes in Primary and Secondary Schools* (Report to Nuffield Foundation Ref: EDV/00399/G). Retrieved

10 September 2009, from www.breaktime.org.uk/NuffieldBreakTimeReport–WEBVersion.pdf.

Blatchford. P. & Baines, E. (2010). Peer relations in school. In K. Littleton, C. Wood & J. Kleine Staarman (Eds), *Elsevier Handbook of Educational Psychology: New Perspectives on Learning and Teaching*. Bingley, UK: Emerald.

Blatchford, P., Baines, E. & Pellegrini, A. (2003). The social context of school playground games: sex and ethnic differences and changes over time after entry to junior school. *British Journal of Developmental Psychology*, 21, 481–505.

Blatchford, P., Russell, A. & Webster, R. (2012). *Reassessing the Impact of Teaching Assistants: How Research Challenges Practice and Policy*. Abingdon, UK: Routledge.

Blurton-Jones, N.G. (Ed.) (1972) *Ethological Studies of Child Behaviour*. Cambridge: Cambridge University Press.

Bock, J. (2005). Farming, foraging, and children's play in the Okavango Delta, Botswana. In A.D. Pellegrini & P.K. Smith (Eds), *The Nature of Play: Great Apes and Humans* (pp. 254–284). New York: Guilford.

Bronfenbrenner, U. (1979). *The Ecology of Human Development*. Cambridge, MA: Harvard University Press.

The Children's Society (2007). The Good Childhood national enquiry: evidence summary – friends. Retrieved 10 September 2007, from www.childrenssociety.org.uk/resources/documents/good%20childhood/Friends%20evidence%20summary_2721_full.pdf.

Gould, S.J. (1977). *Ontogeny and Phylogeny*. Cambridge, MA: Harvard University Press.

Hamre, B.K. & Pianta, R.C. (2010) Classroom environments and developmental processes: conceptualization and measurement. In Meece, J.L. & Eccles, J.S. (Eds), *Handbook of Research on Schools, Schooling and Human Development*. New York and London: Routledge.

Harris, J.R. (1995). Where is the child's environment? A group socialisation theory of development. *Psychological Review*, 102, 458–489.

Hartup, W.W. (1992). Friendships and their developmental significance. In H. McGurk (Ed.), *Childhood Social Development: Contemporary Perspectives*. Hove, UK: Lawrence Erlbaum Associates.

Hartup, W.W. (1996). The company they keep: friendships and their developmental significance. *Child Development*, 67, 1–13.

Hillman, M. (1993). One false move. In M. Hillman (Ed.), *Children, Transport and the Quality of Life*. London: Policy Studies Institute.

Home Office and DCSF (2005). 2003 Home Office Citizenship Survey: top-level findings from the children's and young people's survey. Retrieved 10 October 2007 from www.dcsf.gov.uk/research/data/uploadfiles/RW29.pdf.

Howe, C. (2010). *Peer Groups and Children's Development*. Chichester: Wiley-Blackwell.

Jones, I. & Pellegrini, A.D. (1996). The effects of social relationships, writing media, and microgenetic development on first grade students' narratives. *American Educational Research Journal*, 33, 691–718.

Kagan, J. (1983). Classification of the child. In W. Kessen (Ed.), *Handbook of Child Psychology, Vol 1* (pp. 527–560). New York: Wiley.

Ladd, G.W. & Price, J.M. (1987). Predicting children's social and school adjustment following the transition from preschool to kindergarten. *Child Development*, 58, 1168–1189.

Newcomb, A.F. & Bagwell, C. (1996). The developmental significance of children's friendship relations. In W.M. Bukowski, A.F. Newcomb & W.W. Hartup (Eds), *The Company They Keep: Friendships in Childhood and Adolescence*. Cambridge: Cambridge University Press.

Parker, J.G. & Asher, S.R. (1987). Peer relations and later personal adjustment: are low accepted children at risk? *Psychological Bulletin*, 102, 357–389.

Pellegrini, A. (1983). The sociolinguistic context of the preschool. *Journal of Applied Developmental Psychology*, 4, 397–405.

Pellegrini, A.D. (1995). A longitudinal study of boys' rough and tumble play and dominance during early adolescence. *Journal of Applied Developmental Psychology*, 16, 77–93.

Pellegrini, A.D. (2009). *The Role of Play in Human Development*. New York: Oxford University Press.

Pellegrini, A.D (2012). *Observing Children in their Natural Worlds,* Third Edition. New York: Taylor & Francis.

Pellegrini, A.D. & Bohn, K. (2005). The role of recess in children's cognitive performance and school adjustment. *Educational Researcher*, 34, 13–19.

Pellegrini, A.D., Huberty, P.D. & Jones, I. (1995). The effects of recess timing on children's playground and classroom behaviors. *American Educational Research Journal*, 32, 845–864.

Pellegrini, A.D., Melhuish, E., Jones, I., Trojanowska, L. & Gilden, R. (2002). Social contexts of learning literate language: the role of varied, familiar, and close peer relationships. *Learning and Individual Differences,* 12, 375–389.

Pellegrini, A.D. & Smith, P.K. (1998). Physical activity play: the nature and function of a neglected aspect of play. *Child Development,* 69, 577–598.

Russell, B. (1931/1959). *The Scientific Outlook*. New York: Norton.

Smith, P.K. & Connolly, K. (1972). Patterns of play and social interaction in pre-school children. In N. Blurton Jones (Ed.), *Ethological Studies in Child Behaviour* (pp. 65–96). London: Cambridge University Press.

Waddington, C.H. (1957). *The Strategy of the Genes*. London: Allen & Unwin.

Waters, E. & Sroufe, L.A. (1983). Social competence as developmental construct. *Developmental Review,* 3, 79–97.

Weinstein. R. (1991). The classroom as a social context for learning. *Annual Review of Psychology,* 42, 493–525.

Youniss, J. (1980). *Parents and Peers in Social Development: A Sullivan–Piaget Perspective*. Chicago: University of Chicago Press.

Zajac, R.J. & Hartup, W.W. (1997). Friends as coworkers: research review and classroom implications. *The Elementary School Journal,* 98, 1, 3–13.

2

CHILDREN'S SOCIAL COMPETENCE AND PEER RELATIONS

Introduction

It is current practice in many, if not most, schools in the UK, USA, and much of the rest of the industrialized world, to be concerned with children's academic achievement, typically defined in terms of children's performance in the traditional areas of literacy, mathematics, and science. These same assessments are used, in turn, to rank schools within countries and compare countries with each other. While we do not disagree with the importance of academic progress, in the present book we take a broader and more developmental view of children and schooling. Correspondingly, and also central to the orientation of the book, children's social experiences, with peers, siblings, and adults, are crucial not only to healthy and optimal development but also to their performance on traditional measures of academic achievement.

As we argued in the first chapter, young children are qualitatively different from teenagers and teens are, again, different from adults. Further, and perhaps more importantly, each of the stages in development have integrity within themselves and are not imperfect variants of adulthood. From this position there are different 'developmental tasks' (Waters & Sroufe, 1983) for different periods of development. For example – and as we'll expand upon later – infants' seeking and maintaining proximity to an adult caregiver is a hallmark for that period, but that same behaviour would not be an appropriate developmental task during middle childhood or adolescence. Consequently, there is little direct continuity in behavioural indicators of competence across ontogeny – and thus highlights the notion that stages are qualitatively different from each other. In cases where continuity may be observed, the homologous behaviours may have different functions at different periods. On the other hand, a developmental orientation also entails continuity across periods. Social competence appears to be such a complex construct, and if schools are to be effective they should recognize both the importance of social competence and the developmental integrity of different developmental periods. In this chapter, we first make a case for the centrality of social interaction in schools. Next we define 'social competence', the organizational construct around which this chapter will be organized.

The centrality of social interactions for children in schools

It is not controversial to state that humans are social animals and that they spend much of their time interacting with peers and in mixed age groups, throughout their life spans. While the exact nature of the behaviours and interactions change, with time, many of these interactions and relationships are in the service of them securing resources in their environments and, with development and transition across different niches, the nature and abundance of resources change, and so too should corresponding interactions. For example, in infancy, individuals are typically well-provisioned, protected, and dependent on the almost constant care from adults with whom they form attachment relationships (Sroufe, 2005). Attachment relationships, in turn, are the basis for subsequent relationships: friendships beginning in childhood, and romantic relationships, beginning at puberty (e.g., Dunn, 1993).

The way in which children learn to interact with peers and form relationships is a result of, among other things, opportunities to do so. To state the obvious (though sometimes ignored) point, children do not learn to cooperate, compromise, and assert themselves in a social vacuum; lots of opportunities are necessary to hone these interactional and relationship skills (Harlow & Zimmerman, 1959; Sroufe, 2005; Suomi & Harlow, 1972). This is our reason for putting a premium on affording opportunities for children's social interactions and relationships in schools: school is where children in the industrialized world learn to interact and form relationships with others. While opportunities exist in most preschools, this changes very abruptly when children enter formal schooling (at around 5 years of age in many industrialized countries). Indeed, and certainly in many American and UK primary schools, social interaction and 'talking' to peers during most of the school day is frowned upon, if not formally sanctioned.

Why this change? Speculatively, it may be the case that educators and adults naively see the job of schooling as teaching children 'basic skills' in the form of reading, arithmetic, and science, and interaction with peers is something that interferes with this mission, when in fact they are inter-correlated and complementary (e.g., Coie & Dodge, 1998; Parker & Asher, 1987).

To take an interesting (and troubling) case study, many university educational psychology departments in the United States are marginalizing social and developmental courses and personnel, and adding to a more cognitive and STEM (science, technology, engineering, and mathematics) orientation. The not so implicit assumption is that social interactions and relationships interfere with the more important job of learning more important subject matter. Correspondingly, in many American schools, 'talking' between children is characterized as something 'bad', often sanctioned, and social interaction between students, beginning in and continuing through secondary schools, is limited to break/ recess times (where they too have not been eliminated) or lunch breaks. In a similar way, in Chapters 3 and 5 we show how teachers often separate friends in classrooms because they believe that friends will talk and distract each other, while the research evidence is clear that the quality of working relations between friends can be more productive than that between non-friends.

There are islands of enlightenment, however. The province of British Columbia has recently recognized the importance of peer interaction to children's school adjustment by labelling social responsibility a 'foundational skill' in schools, equivalent to a fourth 'R' (British Columbia Performance Standards, 2001; we acknowledge Shelley Hymel, at the University of British Columbia, for this information).

In support of our claim of the importance of social interaction in schools, numerous longitudinal studies have documented the importance of children's peer relations in their adjustment to elementary school. For example, Ladd and colleagues (Ladd et al., 1996; Ladd, Price & Hart, 1988) have shown that successful transition from preschool to primary school is fostered when children make the transition with a friend. As we show in Chapter 3, friends provide important social emotional support for each other in the new and stressful environment of primary school. Further, longitudinal research has also shown that young children's lack of social competence predicts disaffection with school, poor grades, and eventually, dropping out of school (Coie & Dodge, 1998). In short, social competence, not academic achievement, drives certain measures of school effectiveness, like dropping out, and to ignore or minimize its importance is short-sighted, at best.

In primary school, social interactions and relationships with peers often develop in the context of social games, such as tag, soccer, and jump rope games. As Piaget (1962) argued, games are a modal form of interaction for primary school-age children and thus an appropriate developmental task for children of this age. Our longitudinal research (Pellegrini et al., 2002) has documented empirically the importance of games for children's, and especially boys', adjusting to the first mandatory year of primary school. In this work, inner-city Minneapolis first graders (in two schools) were observed on their playgrounds at recess and assessed on varying aspects of social competence and adjustment to school. We found that children, but especially boys, used their facility with games (ball games, chase, and jumping or singing games) as a way to achieve and maintain social competence with their peers and adjust to very early schooling (as assessed by self-report and teacher ratings). Game facility was measured by aggregating teacher ratings, peer nominations, and observations of time spent in games and levels of game sophistication. Game facility predicted unique and significant variance in children's end-of-year social competence (measured by teacher rating scales and peer nominations of social preference), beyond that predicted by beginning-of-year social competence. Similarly, game facility predicted unique and significant variance in end-of-year adjustment, beyond beginning-of-year adjustment (see Chapter 5 for more on this).

These findings are consistent with results showing the reciprocal effects of peer relations and success in early schooling (Coie & Dodge, 1998) and also extend earlier work on peer relationships and adjustment to school (e.g., Ladd et al., 1988) to the extent that the majority of the students in our study were low-income children (75% of our sample of children were on free or reduced price lunch, and Spanish was the first language for 40% of the children). It is well known that children, and especially boys, from economically disadvantaged groups have difficulty adjusting to and succeeding in school (e.g., Heath, 1983). We demonstrated that their success in one part of the first-grade school day (games at recess) could predict more general school adjustment.

Social competence as a developmental construct

Social competence is a difficult construct to define, and definitions range from relatively discrete behavioural descriptions (e.g., Dodge, 1986) to more broad, organizational conceptions (Waters & Sroufe, 1983). In this chapter we take the latter approach because it is consistent with our developmental orientation in that it can account for continuities as well as discontinuities across developmental epochs. Further, these two properties enable us to treat each developmental period with integrity such that there will be different indicators of social competence at different periods of development. Correspondingly, these within-stage indicators are treated as adaptive to each period and not as imperfect variants of adult behaviour.

From this orientation, articulated by Sroufe and colleagues (Sroufe, 2005; Waters & Sroufe, 1983) and Vaughn and colleagues (e.g., Vaughn et al., 2009), we define social competence as children's ability to coordinate affect, cognition, and behaviour in achieving personal social goals and accessing resources in their specific developmental niches (Vaughn et al., 2009; Waters & Sroufe, 1983). Thus, social, affective, and cognitive processes are integrated to access and maintain resources across development, thus providing underlying continuity to the construct. Correspondingly, the specific behaviours and indicators of social competence at different periods used in the service of resource control will vary across development. For example, crying is a competent strategy for infants to employ to access food from their parents but not for primary school children. In the latter case either asking an adult for help or getting food themselves from a storage area are more appropriate.

The choice of behaviours used to access and maintain resources will, of course, vary in different niches and across different developmental periods. Individuals will marshal their social, cognitive and affective skills and strategies to assess the value of the resources and the associated costs of the behaviours used to access and maintain the resources (Pellegrini, 2008). When resources are scarce and there is relatively high competition for them, individuals may have to use assertive and sometimes agonistic strategies. By way of evidence, Smith and Connolly (1972, p. 130), in their magisterial experimental studies of preschool environments and behaviour, found that object disputes and aggression increased when the number of toys was diminished. When resources are abundant, and everyone gets a share (i.e., scramble competition), then strategies are more likely to be cooperative than aversive; costs associated with using aversive strategies would be too high given the abundance of resources (Pellegrini & Hou, 2011).

In short, there are different indicators of social competence in different ecologies at different ages, so there are different hallmarks for children at different ages. By implication, the hallmarks for toddlers should not be considered as unfinished or incomplete versions of adult behaviour; they represent adaptability to that specific developmental niche. Our conception of social competence, following Waters and Sroufe (1983), considers competence as 'an integrated concept which refers broadly to an ability to generate and coordinate flexible, adaptive responses to demands in the environments' (Waters & Sroufe, 1983, p. 80).

Waters and Sroufe further specify their definition of social competence by listing some of its subcomponents for the preschool period by which children can secure and maintain resources. First, individuals must contribute to situations. Responding to others (e.g., answering questions) or making one's own contributions to conversations (e.g., asking questions) are ways of contributing. Second, children must recognize the opportunity or demand to respond. For example, in conversation children are obligated by the rules of social discourse to respond to questions. Third, children should possess a repertoire of response alternatives. For example, children should have an array of responses to others' discourse; they can ask for questions to be clarified, change the topic, or answer the question. Fourth, they should be able to choose alternatives that are appropriate to specific situations. Importantly, children's ability to assess costs and benefits associated with different strategies in relation to the value of different situations should determine strategy choice. (We'll expand more on this point later in this chapter.) Fifth, children should be motivated to respond. That is, children should want to engage in social discourse or interact with materials. As such, children should want to interact with different forms of stimuli; they should be active not passive. Sixth, children should persist at their interactions and change their responses to meet situational demands. For example, children's play with their peers should be sustained. Individual children may have to alter their social responses (e.g., sharing toys) in order for the interaction to be sustained. Last, children's responses should be fine-tuned. That is, children should be able to decide quickly when to use certain types of behaviour. In addition, they should be adept at using them in different areas.

How do these individual processes relate to specific developmental hallmarks? Waters and Sroufe (1983) have listed social competence hallmarks through childhood, and they are displayed in Table 2.1. The issues presented in this table

TABLE 2.1 Salient issues in child development (adapted from Waters and Sroufe, 1983)

Age	Issue
0–3 months	Physiological regulation
3–6 months	Tension management
6–12 months	Establishing effective attachment relationship
12–18 months	Exploration and mastery
18–30 months	Autonomy
30–54 months	Impulse management, sex role identification, peer relations
Middle childhood	Form loyal friendships
	Sustain relationships
	Function in stable groups
	Coordinate friendships, groups, and relationships
Adolescence	Form intimate relationships
	Commitment in relationships and relationship network

are meant to highlight those specific competences that are appropriate for each age level. After mastery of one set of competencies, the child moves on to the next set of skills, each solving the problems germane to that specific period.

During middle childhood and adolescence, youngsters' social competence becomes concerned with investment in the peer worlds and integrating self and peer relationships, respectively. Specific to middle childhood, children are becoming more concerned with sustaining their relationships with peers at both the friend and group levels. With friends they are beginning to form loyal friendships (Hartup, 1996). Part of this process involves negotiating conflicts, tolerating a range of emotional experiences, while at the same time using relationships to enhance self. At the group level, individuals in middle childhood are learning to adhere to group norms and maintaining gender boundaries. In the end, of course, children must coordinate their friendships and group functioning.

In adolescence, relationships become more intimate as well as more varied. During this period, youngsters are just beginning to form intimate relationships in same- and cross-gender relationships (Collins & Sroufe, 1999). By way of exhibiting commitment in these relationships, they must learn to negotiate self-relevant conflicts. Successful relationships at this level of intimacy require management of one's emotional vulnerability, self-disclosure practices and self-identity. Adding to the complexity, this management must be accomplished across different relationships, both same- and cross-gender (Sroufe at al., 1993).

How to measure social competence

As one would expect for a construct with a wide variety of definitions, there are correspondingly numerous ways in which to measure it. From these different perspectives, we have two general approaches: a specific skills/behavioural indicator approach or a more molar, integrative approach. The benefit of a specific skills/behavioural approach is the perceived ease of measurement. So, for example, if we conceptualized social competence in terms of children's peer popularity and friendship, we could ask adults to rate children along those dimensions (e.g., Anderson & Messick, 1974; Dodge & Coie, 1987). As noted above, the disadvantage of this approach is that it assumes that peer popularity and friendship are equally important across developmental periods and that the indicators of each are the same, a position not consistent with our developmental approach. We know, for example, that the defining attributes of friendship change from preschool through primary school (Hartup, 1996 – discussed in Chapter 3).

Further, using a limited number of indicators minimizes the validity of the construct being assessed. That is, the validity of a construct is maximized when multiple indicators of that construct are used and thus minimizing measurement error (Cronbach, 1971; Cronbach & Meehl, 1955; Rushton, et al., 1983). Also, using a molar approach to construct definitions makes assessment of a construct across a developmental period more robust. Following this broad-band approach to social competence, it should be assessed from different perspectives (children themselves, peers, teachers and parents), using different formats.

The sceptical reader may ask: Why should we go through the extra time and costs of this multi-informant, multi-method approach? First, and as noted above, this approach maximizes construct validity by minimizing measurement error. Second and relatedly, cross-measure and cross-informant agreement for discrete measures of social competence are not very good. For example, among preschool children, Pellegrini and colleagues (2007) found a correlation of 0.22 between directly observed and teacher-rated social dominance (note that the amount of shared variance between these measures is 5%; that is, by squaring the correlation coefficient between these measures we find out how much overlap there is between the measures). In a meta-analysis of measures of social competence, Renk and Phares (2004) found the following inter-relationships (and amount of shared variance): parents and teachers, 0.38 (15%); peers and self, 0.21–0.31 (4%–9%); teachers and peers, 0.48 (23%). In short, individual measures, generally, account for very small amounts of the variance in social competence, even when the magnitudes of the correlation coefficients are statistically significant. The low level of variance accounted for in these studies is particularly important when assessments are used to make 'high stakes' decisions about children, such as assignment to special classes. In short, in order to capture individuals' social competence, or any construct for that matter, it is often helpful to use a multi-method, multi-informant methodology.

The role of adults, peers and props in social competence

As the low levels of cross-situational concordance of measures of social competence suggested, it is important to recognize that children's exhibition of social competence varies according to the context in which they are assessed. Specifically and within schools, we find that peers and adults – differentially – elicit, support and facilitate social competence. If we conceptualize competence as one's ability to marshal one's affective, cognitive and social capabilities to access and maintain resources in one's environment, then we should observe variation among competent and incompetent individuals in different environments.

The term 'peer' refers to individuals of equal status. We typically use the term 'peer' to refer to same-age children, though children may not be of equal status on measures such as popularity (e.g., being 'liked' a lot and not 'disliked' by peers – see Chapter 3), friendship, or dominance (i.e., ability to acquire and maintain resources). For Piaget (1962), peers were particularly important in spurring children's cognitive and social development. That is, in peer, relative to adult, contexts children experience views discrepant from their own (and thus resulting in 'dis-equilibration' of their extant concepts) and often adjust their views resulting in accommodation and 're-equilibration', and conceptual development. Specifically, peers are both more likely to conflict with each other than with an adult (Pellegrini, 1984) and correspondingly, accommodate to those disagreements (Hartup, 1996). It is probably the case that peers accommodate to each other more readily than they do to adults because they enjoy interacting with them more. From Piaget's theory, this dis-equilibration/re-equilibration cycle results in conceptual development, thus affecting children's behaviour and social competence.

Peers serve also as models and reinforcers for each other. Peers reinforce each other by giving positive attention and approval, affection and personal acceptance, and by submitting to each other's wishes. Peers also serve as models for each other. However, both positive and negative behaviours are modelled and subsequently learned from peers. Children tend to imitate those peers most similar to themselves (Hartup & Coates, 1967). Further, children are more likely to imitate those peers who are warm, rewarding and powerful (Hetherington & Parke, 1979). The notion of peer similarity and mutual reinforcement seems to be a powerful determinant of children's behaviour. In the chapter on friendship (Chapter 3) we will see how these dimensions also influence children's friendship choices and the stability of those friendships.

Consistent with Piagetian theory, environments that are highly structured by adults elicit low levels of competence from children of preschool and school age, relative to interactions with peers. Simply, when children and adults are together, adults often do most of the work that initiates and maintains social interaction. It may be for this reason that children with low levels of social competence choose to spend time with a teacher on the playground during recess rather than with peers: teachers probably initiate a conversation and keep it going whereas peers are probably less likely to do so (Pellegrini, 1992). This has been confirmed in a number of studies. For example, in an observational study of preschool children, Wright (1980) attempted to identify positive indicators of children's social competence. Her general definition of social competence, like others', was children's socially adaptive behaviour. She identified a number of naturally occurring behaviours which were related to various measures of social adaptability. More specifically, she first examined child–child and child–adult interactions. She then examined how these behaviours related to children's test scores; test scores were used as a measure of adaptability in preschool. She found, first, that the child–adult behaviours tend not to be related to measures of adaptability. Three types of peer interactions were, however, related to social adaptability: successful and positive seeking of peers' attention; successfully using peers as instrumental resources; and successfully leading peers. Children must exhibit higher levels of competence to secure resources around peers than around adults. Adults, it seems, do much of children's work for them.

Similarly, in both American preschools and primary schools we find that adults often inhibit exhibition of competence. For example, in a study of preschool children's use of a variety of functions of oral language, one of us found a negative correlation between the number of adults present and functional uses of language (Pellegrini, 1983). Relatedly, adult presence was negatively correlated with preschool children's levels of sophistication in interaction with their peers as well as social dramatic play (Pellegrini, 1984; Pellegrini & Perlmutter, 1989). Similar relations are found for primary school children, where there was a negative predictive correlation between the frequency of children's interaction with adults on the playground and their academic achievement (Pellegrini, 1992). These results support Waters and Sroufe's (1983) notion that social competence involves children seeking out social stimuli and having an effect on those stimuli.

These results are also important in terms of schools providing contexts which provide opportunities for children to learn and practise socially competent behaviours. To our knowledge, and as noted in Chapter 5, the playground at breaktime/recess is the context par excellence which does this. It is one of the very few places in school where there is minimal adult direction, where children can interact with each other on their own terms. We should note that minimal adult supervision does not mean neglect. Adults should be available to discourage aggression and help children in need, not to form and direct children's peer interactions. It is these peer contexts in which children learn so much about the consequences of their behaviours.

The role of props

The effects of peers on social competence, however, are moderated by the types of resources available to children. An early study by Johnson (1935) found that when the availability of toys was decreased, children experienced both more positive and more negative interactions. The specific types of toys with which children interact also affect their social behaviour. A number of naturalistic and experimental studies have shown that when children interact with art materials they engage in non-social and quasi-social behaviour (i.e., solitary and parallel interaction, respectively) (Pellegrini, 1984; Pellegrini & Perlmutter, 1989). When these same children interact with dramatic props (e.g., dress-up clothes) or blocks they more frequently exhibit social, or cooperative, interaction.

The effect of toys on children's behaviour is not a direct one, however. The ways in which children play with toys depend in part, on their age, sex, the sex of their playmates, and the level of sex-role stereotype of the toys. For example, when 3-year-old girls interact with a male-preferred toy, such as with large wooden blocks, their behaviour is more sophisticated than the play of 5-year-old girls with the same toys (Pellegrini & Perlmutter, 1989). Girls seem to learn at a young age that they should not exhibit competence with male-preferred toys. The lesson, here, is that toys do not have an effect, independent of personal variables, on children's behaviour. Research on the effects of toys on older children's behaviour is, generally, not available (Hartup, 1983). By the time children enter elementary school they are not expected to interact with toys during class time.

Training social skills and competence

A specific direction of work has concerned efforts to help children develop more effective social skills. The evidence that less popular children have less competence in general social skills, suggests that rejected children and neglected children (those that are neither liked nor disliked) could be helped by programmes of social skill training. One famous approach was developed by Spivak and Shure (1974), and aimed to help children become more effective in social problem solving, by analysing causes and generating solutions to social problems. There have been specific initiatives to encourage interpersonal relations, collaborative conflict resolution, peer counselling and assertiveness training, which have been used as part of preventive work to reduce conflict and bullying (Sharp & Cowie 1994; Sharp, Cooper & Cowie 1994). Roffey, Tarrant and Majors (1994), drawing on a wide range of applied work, offer many examples of action to help young pupils' social relations and friendships, including role-playing exercises, activities to learn and practise social skills, group-work strategies, and exercises to improve the classroom social climate. School initiatives in the UK, such as SEAL (Social and emotional aspects of learning) and PSHE (Personal, social and health education) lessons in schools, that deal with peer relations may be helpful. Berndt and Keefe (1995) feel that a combination of individual skills-based programmes and more general programmes directed at cooperation are likely to maximize the positive effect of friends.

In our view, however, it is probably simplistic to think that difficulties faced by some children are just to do with inadequacies in their social skills repertoire. It may, for example, have much to do with the more general aims and attitudes of children towards others. As a result of social skills training, children may be able to behave appropriately, but their underlying social orientation towards others may be unaltered – for example, they may still want to dominate others, or always want others to show they like them. Moreover, interventions predominantly based in classrooms (and sometimes in rooms away from the classroom context) will always be at best partially successful, because, as we have seen in this chapter, the classroom is only one school context within which children meet. Interventions addressing peer relations in classrooms will need to be aware of peer informal relations and culture – as seen during breaktime, for example (Blatchford, 1998).

Conclusion

In this chapter we have examined children's social competence and peer relations. We chose to examine social competence because the construct represents the processes children must use in order to be a functioning member of society. Further, the notion of social competence includes both social and cognitive behavioural measures. The construct 'social competence' is enormously important for educators to consider. As Zigler and Trickett (1978) noted more than a generation ago, educational programs for children should consider the whole child, not just cognitive dimensions, such as IQ and achievement. Broadly defined, social competence for primary school children certainly does include cognitive dimensions, such as achievement. It also includes other behaviours which are important in children's functioning in those institutions (school, families and neighbourhoods) in which they live. To that extent, it is also important for us to consider children's interactions with peers and adults in their lives. Children who exhibit maladaptive behaviour with peers and adults also have problems with achievement in school (Coie & Dodge, 1998). This constellation of behaviour leads to problems, such as juvenile delinquency, and substance abuse, in later life. Thus educators must pay more attention to social competence. In subsequent chapters we discuss, more specifically, the importance of two dimensions of peer relations: friendship and popularity.

References

Anderson, S. & Messick, S. (1974). Social competency in young children. *Developmental Psychology*, 10, 282–293.

Berndt, T. & Keefe, K. (1995). Friends' influence on adolescents' adjustment to school. *Child Development*, 66, 1312–1329.

Blatchford, P. (1998). *Social Life in Schools: Pupils' Experiences of Breaktime and Recess from 7 to 16 Years.* London: Falmer Press.

British Columbia Performance Standards (2001). *Social Responsibility: A Framework.* Retrieved from www.bced.gov.bc.ca/perf_stands/sintro.pdf.

Coie, J.D. & Dodge, K.A. (1998). Aggression and antisocial behavior. In N. Eisenberg (Ed.), *Manual of Child Psychology, Vol. 3, Social, Emotional, and Personality Development* (pp. 779–862). New York: Wiley.

Collins, W.A. & Sroufe, L.A. (1999). Capacity for intimate relationships: a developmental construction. In Furman, W., Brown, B.B. & Feiring, C. (Eds), *The Development*

Luimneach

1086107004

of Romantic Relationships in Adolescence (pp. 125–147). New York: Cambridge University Press.

Cronbach, L. (1971). Validity. In R.L. Thorndike (Ed.), *Educational Measurement* (pp. 443–507). Washington, DC: American Council on Education.

Cronbach, L.J. & Meehl, P.E. (1955). Construct validity in psychological tests. *Psychological Bulletin,* 52, 281–302.

Dodge, K.A. (1986). A social information processing model of social competence in children. In M. Perlmutter (Ed.), *Minnesota Symposium on Child Psychology* (pp. 18, 77–125). Hillsdale, NJ: Erlbaum.

Dodge, K.A. & Coie, J.D. (1987). Social information processing factors in reactive and proactive aggression in children's peer groups. *Journal of Personality and Social Psychology,* 53, 1146–1158.

Dunn, J. (1993). *Young Children's Close Relationships.* Beverly Hills: Sage.

Harlow, H. & Zimmerman, R.R. (1959). Affectional responses in the infant monkey. *Science,* 130, 421–432.

Hartup, W.W. (1983). Peer relations. In E.M. Hetherington (Ed.), *Handbook of Child Psychology,* Vol. IV (pp. 103–196). New York: Wiley.

Hartup, W.W. (1996). The company they keep: friendships and their developmental significance. *Child Development,* 67, 1–13.

Hartup, W.W. & Coates, B. (1967). Imitation of a peer as a function of reinforcement from the peer group and rewardingness of the model. *Child Development,* 38, 1003–1016.

Heath, S. (1983). *Ways with Words.* New York: Cambridge University Press.

Hetherington, E. & Parke, R. (1979). *Child Psychology.* New York: McGraw Hill.

Johnson, M. (1935). The effect and behavior of variation in the amount of play equipment. *Child Development,* 6, 56–68.

Ladd, G.W., Kochenderfer, B.J. & Coleman, C.C. (1996). Friendship quality as a predictor of young children's early school adjustment. *Child Development,* 67, 1103–1118.

Ladd, G.W., Price, J.M. & Hart, C.H. (1988). Predicting preschoolers' peer status from their playground behaviors. *Child Development,* 59, 986–992.

Parker, J.G. & Asher, S. (1987). Peer relations and later personal adjustment: are low accepted children at-risk? *Psychological Bulletin,* 102, 357–389.

Pellegrini, A. (1983). The sociolinguistic context of the preschool. *Journal of Applied Developmental Psychology,* 4, 397–405.

Pellegrini, A.D. (1984). The social cognitive ecology of preschool classrooms. *International Journal of Behavioral Development,* 7, 321–332.

Pellegrini, A.D. (1992). Kindergarten children's social cognitive status as a predictor of first grade success. *Early Childhood Research Quarterly,* 7, 565–577.

Pellegrini, A.D. (2008). The roles of aggression and affiliation in resource control: a behavioral ecological perspective. *Developmental Review,* 28, 461–487.

Pellegrini, A.D. & Hou, Y. (2011). The development of preschool children's (Homo sapiens) uses of objects and their role in peer group centrality. *Journal of Comparative Psychology,* 125, 239–245.

Pellegrini, A.D., Kato, K., Blatchford, P. & Baines, E. (2002). A short-term longitudinal study of children's playground games across the first year of school: implications for social competence and adjustment to school. *American Educational Research Journal,* 39, 991–1015.

Pellegrini, A.D. & Perlmutter, J. (1989). Classroom contextual effects on children's play. *Developmental Psychology,* 25, 289–296.

Pellegrini, A.D., Roseth, C., Milner, S., Bohn, C., Van Ryzin, M., Vance, N., Cheatham, C.L. & Tarullo, A. (2007). Social dominance in preschool classrooms. *Journal of Comparative Psychology,* 121, 54–64.

Piaget, J. (1962). *Play, Dreams and Imitation in Childhood* (C. Gattengno & F.M. Hodgson. Trans). New York: Norton. (Original work published 1951).

Renk, K. & Phares, V. (2004). Cross-informant ratings of social competence in children and adolescents. *Clinical Psychology Review,* 24, 239–254.

Roffey, S., Tarrant, T. & Majors, K. (1994). *Young Friends: Schools and Friendship.* London: Cassell.

Rushton, J., Brainerd, C. & Pressley, M. (1983). Behavioral development and construct validity: the principle of aggregation. *Psychological Bulletin,* 94, 18–38.

Sharp, S., Cooper, F. & Cowie, H. (1994). Making peace in the playground. In P. Blatchford & S. Sharp (Eds), *Breaktime and the School: Understanding and Changing Playground Behaviour.* London: Routledge.

Sharp, S. & Cowie, H. (1994). Empowering pupils to take positive action against bullying. In P.K. Smith & S. Sharp (Eds), *School Bullying: Insights and Perspectives.* London: Routledge.

Smith, P.K. & Connolly, K. (1972). Patterns of play and social interaction in pre-school children. In N. Blurton Jones (Ed.), *Ethological Studies of Child Behaviour* (pp. 65–96). London: Cambridge University Press.

Spivak, G. & Shure, M.B. (1974). *Social Adjustment of Young Children: A Cognitive Approach to Solving Real Life Problems.* San Francisco: Jossey-Bass.

Sroufe, L.A. (2005). Attachment and development: a prospective longitudinal study from birth to adulthood. *Attachment and Human Development,* 7, 349–367.

Sroufe, L.A., Bennett, C., Englund, M., Urban, J. & Shulman, S. (1993). The significance of cross-gender boundaries in preadolescence: contemporary correlates and antecedents of boundary violation and maintenance. *Child Development,* 64, 455–466.

Suomi, S. & Harlow, H. (1972). Social rehabilitation of isolate-reared monkeys. *Developmental Psychology,* 6, 487–496.

Vaughn, B.E., Shin, N., Kim, M., Coppola, G., Krzsik, L., Santos, A., Peceguina, I., Daniel, J.R., Verissimo, M., DeVries, A., Elphick, E., Ballentina, X., Bost, K., Newell, W., Miller, E., Snider, J. & Korth, B. (2009). Hierarchical models of social competence in preschool children: a multisite, multinational study. *Child Development,* 80, 1775–1796.

Waters, E. & Sroufe, L.A. (1983). Social competence as developmental construct. *Developmental Review,* 3, 79–97.

Wright, M. (1980). Measuring the social competence of preschool children. *Canadian Journal of Behavioral Science,* 12, 17–32.

Zigler, E. & Trickett, P. (1978). I.Q., social competence, and evaluation of early childhood intervention programs. *American Psychologist,* 33, 789–798.

3
PUPIL FRIENDSHIPS IN SCHOOL

One of the most taken-for-granted aspects of life is the everyday contacts we have with friends. We probably all value our friends, and our most enjoyable moments are in their company. Although we invest much in our friendships, and can be upset if we fall out, we usually do not examine them analytically. Yet the everyday encounters we have with friends depend on, and reveal, a bewildering and sophisticated set of skills and understandings. These are developed over the course of childhood. Making and maintaining friendships are major aspects of a child's life, and, as we shall see, friendship relations during childhood may be important for later social development and personal adjustment.

Although there are many occasions where children come into contact with friends – for example, in the home and at out-of-school clubs – one of the main settings within which children get a chance to meet friends is in school. In this chapter we examine friendships within the context of school. We will not seek to provide a comprehensive, general review of research on friendships (see Bagwell & Schmidt, 2011; Berndt & McCandless, 2009; Hartup, 1996; Howe, 2010; Rubin et al., 2013; Vitaro, Boivin & Bukowski, 2009); rather our aim will be to draw out particular features of friendships in school settings, show their positive as well as possible negative aspects, and consider whether they can be uniquely important contexts for children's development. A main feature of this chapter will be to examine the significance of friendships at school. This chapter will not examine peer relations and friendships in relation to learning, engagement and adjustment in the school classroom, as this will be discussed in Chapter 7.

In this chapter there are four main sections:

1. What is friendship?
2. Developmental trends in children's friendships

3. Contexts for friendship development
4. The significance of children's friendships for development and adjustment.

What is friendship?

We look first at the definition of friendships. The terms 'friend' or 'friendship' are widely used in our language in a range of different ways with different meanings. It is common for children and adults to talk about a close or best friend as someone that they have a special relationship with. On the other hand, parents often tell their children to 'go and play with their friends' – even when the other children present are only very vaguely acquainted. The nature of a friendship relation and what it means for an individual may thus vary between persons and contexts. Some children report having lots of friends whilst others are happy to report that they have just one very good friend. Similarly whilst some friendships appear very positive, reciprocal and intimate, others may involve conflict, emotional turmoil and even aggression. Many would question whether the latter characterization of friendship could actually be considered a friendship at all. Yet for the individuals involved, the relationship may be important, possibly the only friendship they have, and nevertheless be described as a friendship by one or both of the individuals involved. There is, therefore, an inherent subjectivity in the nature of and thinking about friendship relations, and this is evident from the surprise often experienced by parents when they find out whom a child considers to be his or her friend!

In seeking to identify the implications of friends and their possible influence on a child's development and adjustment to school, we need to try and pin down what a friend is and how to identify children who are friends. 'Friendship' is usually described as a dyadic relationship where the individuals, who are not family members or romantic partners, know and like each other – that is, liking is mutual. Hartup (1992) has drawn up a list of defining characteristics of friendships, suggesting that they: involve reciprocity (equality) and commitment; are affiliative rather than attachment-based; involve common interests; and are egalitarian. Other characteristics of friends are that they spend time together, know each other well, involve feelings of goodwill, intimacy or closeness, and trust and involve the provision of help when needed. Although, as noted already, the extent to which this is actually the case may vary, the general point is that friendships between children tend to be symmetrically and horizontally organized, as opposed to adult–child relations which are asymmetrical and vertically organized. The nature of friendships as involving affiliation and being between equals means that they normally require effort, sometimes negotiation, sensitivity and understanding of the other to enable them to be sustained. A friendship where one member is unsupportive, aggressive or selfish towards the other may be short lived!

A further complication in understanding the notion of friendship is that the nature and basis of the friendship varies across different age ranges. For example, it is unlikely that young children would report that they value intimacy and loyalty in their friendships, while these would be common characteristics reported as important amongst adolescents. In a study involving interviews with Scottish and Canadian children between the ages of 6 and 14, Bigelow and La Gaipa (1975) found that children of different ages had varied expectations about their 'best friends'. While young and older children alike mentioned the importance of spending time with friends in joint activities, liking one another and sharing, younger children tended to emphasize features that were rather more self-serving. Older children were more likely to highlight shared values, loyalty and reciprocity, and the oldest children highlighted increased sensitivity, mutual understanding and self-disclosure.

We need to distinguish friendship from notions of sociometric status such as popularity and social acceptance. These concepts are based on the notion of 'liking' (though see discussion of 'perceived popularity' in Parkhurst & Hopmeyer, 1998; Rubin et al., 2013) and thus are likely to be highly related. The traditional approach used to derive a child's sociometric status is to ask children in a class to nominate those children they like most (LM) to be with (or play with) and those children they like least (LL) to be with. These measures are often used as measures of 'peer acceptance' and 'peer rejection' respectively. Coie, Dodge and Coppotelli (1982) suggested that nominations for liking and dislike can be combined into a single measure to provide measures of 'social preference' (LM − LL) and 'social impact' (LM + LL). They further suggest that children can be classified on the basis of high and low scores on these dimensions into the categories of 'popular', 'rejected' and 'controversial' and 'neglected'. The remaining pupils are categorised as 'average'. Classification involves the use of a statistical threshold which is rather arbitrary and thus many studies prefer to stick with the continuous measures of acceptance and rejection or social preference and social impact. More recently, and in response to concerns about explicitly asking pupils to identify whom they do not like to be with, studies have increasingly used the full class roster with a rating scale (e.g., a 5-point Likert scale). This provides a reflection of the extent to which each child is liked by every other child (see Asher & Dodge, 1986; Maasen, Van Boxtel & Goossens, 2005). The benefit of a rating approach is that children must comment on all peers but it is more time-consuming than a peer nomination approach.

Although peer acceptance and rejection are largely reputation-based measures, rather than trait-like characteristics of individual children, there is good evidence of moderate stability in these measures in the short term, with test–retest correlation coefficients in the region of 0.6–0.8 (Schneider, 2000). Stability is slightly lower over the longer term. Hymel et al. (1990) reported a coefficient of 0.56 over 3 years during middle childhood. Estimates of stability over time of status classifications (i.e., into popular, controversial, etc.) tend to show low stability over time and highlight the value of continuous measures of peer acceptance and rejection (Schneider, 2000). It is important to note that studies that have examined stability in sociometric status over time have examined only situations where the whole peer group (however defined) remained intact, and that greater instability is likely when there are changes in context – for example, due to school transitions or mixing up of the composition of classrooms at the start of a new year.

Correlations between peer acceptance and the number of reciprocal friends are relatively high and one estimate suggests that this is of the order of 0.69 (Demir & Urberg, 2004). Though sociometrically popular children tend to have a lot of friends and, conversely, rejected children may have few friends (Nangle et al., 2003), they are still different aspects of social functioning. A child may be rejected and isolated, or neglected by others but may have a meaningful friendship. To know that a child is more or less popular does not necessarily tell us much about the closeness or strength of their friendship. Social acceptance and popularity are thus not sufficient conditions for success in friendship relations. (We return to the topic of peer acceptance in relation to learning in Chapter 7, and further discussion of research on sociometric status can be found in Howe, 2010; Ladd, 2005; and Rubin et al., 2013.)

Identifying friendships

Given the ambiguities in defining friendship and the possible different meanings and roles that friendships have in people's lives, it is no surprise that there are a range of approaches to identifying friendships. Different approaches have advantages and disadvantages. The main approach to the identification of friends and best friends is to ask people themselves. A reciprocal nomination, that is when two people identify each other as friends, is considered to provide the best evidence of the existence of a friendship (regardless of the quality of the relationship). This approach reduces the chance of including friendships that are desired by one child or those where there is a difference of opinion between the two persons. The approach captures the notion of reciprocity which is an important attribute of definitions of friendship but also preserves the inherent subjectivity. A way to remove this subjectivity might be to provide a definition of what a friendship is and is not (as is often the approach used in self-report bullying questionnaires – see for example Olweus, 1993) but friendships vary in nature and apparent function, context, and so on, and a more 'objective' approach to the study of friendships would lead to a very narrow understanding of the nature, value and variability of friendships. However the implication is that in order to examine the role of friendships there is also a need to understand the nature or quality of that relationship.

When asking children to identify their friends, some studies limit the possible number of responses allowed (for example, to three – see Berndt & McCandless, 2009), or restrict responses to one gender. Such decisions are made based on evidence that it is rare for children to identify a member of the opposite sex as a friend (Hartup, 1983), and for practical reasons associated with the scale of the research. But limiting the numbers of friends identified can be problematic.

Some children might feel a pressure to name more friends than they have while others are not in a position to identify all of their friends. In circumstances where children have a rich social life outside of school but not within school, children can wrongly appear that they have few friends. Making effective use of joint child and parent reports, some studies aim to capture all friendships that a child has within and outside of school (Fletcher et al., 2013). Whilst providing a more comprehensive understanding of all friendships, there are obvious difficulties with establishing whether friendships are reciprocal or not.

Researchers have also begun to consider treating friendship as a matter of degree and in terms of a continuum which differentiates acquaintances, just friends, good friends and close or best friends (Berndt & McCandless, 2009). This avoids dichotomous distinctions of persons either having friends or being friendless. Using such a continuum, longitudinal studies are better placed to capture the wax and wane of naturally occurring friendships over time; there are however few studies that adopt this approach.

There are times when children are not able to identify their friends (for example toddlers and young children with limited language) and so adults are sometimes asked or observations are carried out (e.g., Howes, 2009). However, when researchers have compared the responses of teachers and parents to those identified by children themselves, they have found only modest agreement (Fletcher et al., 2013; Gest, 2006; Neal et al., 2011). Friendship is a very personal and subjective experience and children themselves are thus the best sources of information about their own relationships.

Friendship quality

There is much recognition now that it is one thing to identify a friendship but friendships can vary quite markedly in terms of their nature and quality. There is now growing evidence that friendship quality is implicated in psychological adjustment, e.g., loneliness, depression, deviance and maladjustment, and complex models have evolved to show the place of friendship quality in this regard (e.g., Bagwell & Schmidt, 2011).

Researchers have therefore sought to measure the quality of the relationship between friends and have focused on both positive and negative features. Measures usually stem from questionnaires, though some use interviews, which can be completed by a child or adolescent in relation to a particular friend. Two such measures are the Friendship Qualities Scale from Bukowski, Hoza and Boivin (1994) and the Friendship Quality Questionnaire from Parker and Asher (1993). Measures try to describe features of the friendship such as companionship, intimacy, affection, help, security, conflict and conflict resolution, but each approach will not measure all of these and some overlap (Bukowski et al., 1994; Parker & Asher, 1993). An identified relationship with a friend is usually rated on a 5-point scale running from 'not at all true' to 'really true'. There have been attempts to develop a friendship quality assessment to be used with preschool children (Ladd, Kochenderfer & Coleman, 1996). The value of such an instrument may be uncertain since young children have difficulties estimating the quality of their relationship, may perceive friendships differently, and are likely to be limited in reflecting on them objectively.

Although there is agreement about some of the constructs that make up friendship quality, there is less agreement about others and the nature of the questions asked (see Bagwell & Schmidt, 2011). Some questions refer to what the friend does for the child (e.g., 'gives advice with figuring things out'), whilst others refer to what the children do together (e.g., 'help each other ...'). This brings into focus whether it is the behaviour of the friend that these measures should examine, the quality of the relationship itself or a combination of the two.

Some researchers argue that friendship quality may best be conceived in terms of two main dimensions, one that relates to positive aspects of the relationship and another that relates to the negative features (see Berndt & McCandless, 2009). To date there is limited inclusion of the negative features of friendship within measures of friendship quality. While most questionnaires include measures of conflict, there is increasing awareness that we also need to consider measuring constructs such as inequality in the relationship, aggression and/or dominance and, following the work of Hartup (1996) and Dishion et al. (1996), negative peer influence. On this last negative feature there is an increasingly large literature suggesting that friends and peers generally can influence each other in negative and sometimes positive ways, particularly during adolescence (see Altermatt, 2012; Prinstein & Dodge, 2008).

Since many studies only focus on the quality of a single friendship, it is difficult to establish whether this relationship is characteristic of all friendships that a child has. Furthermore, as friendship quality is based on a child's perceptions of the relationship it is no surprise, given the subjective nature of friendship, that there are studies showing only moderate agreement between friends in their perceptions about the quality of their friendship (Simpkins et al., 2006). Some individuals may over or underestimate the quality of their friendship, depending on the number of friends they have or the extent to which they are liked by others in the peer group. Children showing signs of depression were less positive about their friendships (Brendgen et al., 2002) while those that were overly positive about their friendship were more likely to have stable friendships (Brendgen et al., 2004).

Similarly, socially withdrawn and aggressive children have been found to interpret and respond to negatively oriented vignettes in different ways, depending on whether those involved are friends or non-friends (Burgess et al., 2006). The social information processing model from Crick and Dodge (1994) is a useful framework for considering individual differences in attributions and behaviours. This model suggests that different children perceive, interpret and respond to social behaviours in different ways, depending on particular characteristics of the individual child, and this may have important implications for peer relations and friendships.

Developmental trends in children's friendships

A lot of research on children's friendships has been concerned with charting developmental trends in friendship relations (see Parker & Gottman, 1989). An early developmental account was provided by Sullivan (1953). A central theme of Sullivan's approach is the value of close peer relationships in the development of the ability to empathize and sympathize with others. Friendship relations are therefore seen as important for later social development. The well-known developmental model of Selman (1980) has a number of similarities but is largely based on Piagetian stages, and links friendship relations to cognitive development. Other models have also been advanced. Maxwell (1990) has reviewed these and argues that there is a good deal of consensus about the main stages of progression:

1. At pre-school and early infant/elementary school, thinking about friends is egocentric, with superficial awareness of the friend as a person and low commitment to the relationship.
2. In the middle primary years, there is greater awareness of personal characteristics and views of others; the child is more committed to friendships and more selective.
3. From the later primary school years on, there is more intensity, sense of loyalty and commitment, more self-disclosure, intimacy and integrating of views, opinions and values.

(Maxwell, 1990, p. 179)

There is, then, some agreement about general developmental progression in friendship relations, though there are differences in views about underlying processes. Selman's view is consistent with the notion, which owes much to Piagetian thought, that developments in friendship relations reflect more general structural transformations in the child's understanding of the social and physical world. A somewhat different view is seen in the work of Youniss (1980), who sees friendships as developing through the elaboration of a single construct – social reciprocity. A third view sees friendship relations developing more on the basis of the accumulation of separate experiences such as common interests, intimacy, and commitment. Much of the empirical work supporting these early developmental models of friendship has tended to involve children's descriptions of friendship relations in the context of interviews or structured tasks. But more recent research has questioned this view, and this has to a large extent come about because of observation and study of children in real-life situations.

A number of such studies have shown that even young children can show in their day-to-day behaviour some of the friendship qualities and social skills previously expected only of older children. As long ago as the 1970s, one of the authors found on the basis of an observational study of dyads that there was a developmental progression of contacts over the first two years, and a surprising degree of reciprocity and interest in each other (Blatchford, 1979;

also Vandell & Mueller, 1980). Even young children can show understanding of, and sensitivity towards, others, and can maintain at least a degree of attachment, affection and intimacy in friendships (Dunn, 2004; Howes & Lee, 2006). Friendships from a young age can also show a degree of stability over time. Howes (1987, cited in Dunn, 1993) found that preschool children tended to maintain friendships over a two-year period and sometimes much longer. Another study, cited by Dunn (1993), found that more than two-thirds of preschool children had reciprocated friendships (Gershman & Hayes, 1983). Dunn (1993) found that the average time that 4-year-old children had been close friends was two years. Of course, these friendships between such young children will depend on living close or having ready access to each other but, as Dunn reminds us, and as parents know, this does not always guarantee that children will be friends.

Nevertheless it is important to remember that parents are instrumental in selecting the social context within which toddlers socialize and meet with peers. It is likely that children become friendly with the offspring of parents' friends and that parents will be active in choosing who they are happy for their child to play with. This probably continues from early childhood right the way through to middle childhood at least in the context of the home. In this way parents may influence early experiences of peers and set the activities and interests which influence future friendship formation. According to Kerns, Cole and Andrews (1998) parents who are proactive in initiating play dates and supervise play from a distance have children with more friends.

A particularly important aspect of friendship that children can become quickly aware of is the voluntary and affiliative nature of friendships. Dunn (1993) provides an example of the increasingly conscious understanding of this in children:

(5-year-old in Pennsylvania)

I: How about if your sister took a toy from you – would that be OK or not OK?

C: Not OK! I would be pissed off, and I would kick her!

I: Why?

C: Because she'd be taking something from me. Because she'd be stealing it. A CRIME!

I: What about if Jeff took something from you?

C: That would be OK ... because I wouldn't mind.

I: How about if you took a toy from Jeff?

C: I would never do it. Because he's my friend. My best, best, best, best friend!

I: What about if you took a toy from your sister? Would that be OK or not OK?

C: OK ... because she's my sister and I hate her guts ... Well I don't actually hate her, but ...

(Dunn, 1993)

The specific nature of friendship is significant here – it is different to the relationship between this boy and his sister! It may be the case, as noted by Hartup (1996), that friends, unlike siblings, operate in an 'open field', that is, they have an opportunity to leave the interaction at any time. This option maximizes children's need to resolve conflicts and ideally through compromise, to self-regulate their behaviour and language if they want to maintain the relationship.

Children are also proactive in trying to sustain, develop and manage their relationships. Ethnographic research by William Corsaro (2003) highlights that even preschoolers can collude to establish and protect their interaction and relationship with a friend by preventing others from participating in the joint play. Preventing others from joining the activity may help children to sustain the mutual interaction with a friend and to allow the dyadic relationship to develop. The addition of a third playmate can bring tensions and power games which can undermine friendships. Children may use friendship as an excuse or gambit to get their own way in a relationship, for example, by suggesting that they won't be a friend anymore, if the child does or doesn't do something.

It is no surprise that participating in interactions within which friendships develop often involves sophisticated social and cognitive skills. In a substantial study involving observations of young preschool and school-aged children whilst playing with a peer at home, Gottman (1983) identified a number of processes that occur during the formation of friendships. These processes included sharing of feelings, engaging in joint play, maintaining and elaborating of each other's involvement in play, communicating with each other involving asking and answering questions, and clarifying and resolving of conflict. If young children are well equipped with the cognitive, social and emotional skills to handle these processes well, they are more likely to be successful in establishing and sustaining friendships. It is not difficult to see how the presence of such skills can assist in their further development through the negotiation and renegotiation of relationships during playful interactions. There may also be overlaps with skills involved in school learning, as we will see in Chapter 7.

Contexts for friendship development

Research on children's friendships has tended to be non-specific about contexts within which friendship relations occur, and little is known about friendships in different contexts. However, research on friendship tends to be conducted within school settings and often relies on reports of friendship drawing on class and school rolls – it thus usually relates to friendships developed within the context of school.

Broadly speaking there are three main settings in children's lives where friendships have a chance to evolve. These are:

1. Out of school (this could be further sub-divided, for example, into after-school clubs and at home)

2. The classroom
3. The school playground at breaktime and the lunch room.

A possible fourth context might be the virtual context, involving the use of social networking sites and instant messaging. This context is receiving an increased amount of research attention and is an important feature of adolescent peer relationships and friendships but is also extending into the social lives of children during middle childhood. However, there is evidence that the virtual context is an extension of the day-to-day contexts in which children are situated and it is rare that friendships are established and sustained only within the context of online technology, at least at this age (Tokunaga, 2010), and thus will not be considered here further.

There is relatively little research on opportunities children have to develop and sustain friendships outside of school. Children may have a school friendship network which is quite separate from their out-of-school network and in some cases it may be difficult for children and adolescents to meet with friends outside of school. Research conducted by two of the authors suggested that over a quarter of English children aged 10, 13 and 15 years rarely met with friends outside of school (Baines & Blatchford, 2011). The rise in home entertainment, modern constraints such as increased traffic, pressure on space in cities, and policies and behaviours prompted by concerns about risk taking, bullying, and strangers can function to keep children inside the home. Parents are often discouraged from allowing their children unsupervised out of the home so they become unable to benefit from free play and socialization with peers and friends. Adolescents may, as a matter of course, travel some distance to school and are unlikely to meet school friends without prior arrangement. Surveys since the early 1990s show that students in the UK, at least, are less likely to walk to school, that large proportions of 8–10-year-olds have never been to a park, shops, or played out with their friends unsupervised (Baines & Blatchford, 2012; Shaw et al., 2013). An unlikely source of reduction in opportunities to socialize freely with peers and friends comes from the increase in adult-led after-school provision designed to provide care and/or additional learning opportunities while busy parents work. However, as others argue, these may be important occasions where children and young people come together with peers, and these may influence peer relationships (Fredricks & Simpkins, 2013).

Friendships in the classroom

We will be considering the role of peer relations in relation to classroom learning in Chapter 7 and so we will consider this only briefly here. Within classrooms there are likely to be contextual influences on friendship relations, e.g., proximity. As early as 1934, Moreno suggested that friendships will rarely come about unless the persons involved are physically near to each other. So it is highly likely that pupils who sit next to each other or are required to work together are more likely to become friends than students who are not seated together or who rarely come into contact. Some studies have suggested that the nature, stability and qualities emphasized in friendships may be affected by classroom organization, interaction, values, ethos and control (Hallinan, 1979; Solomon et al., 1988). Ability grouping, for example, can mean that children forge friendships within their ability groups in ways that sustain or facilitate disaffection and negative behaviours or positive and motivated approaches to learning (Dishion, Piehler & Myers, 2008; Hallinan & Sorenson, 1983; Hargreaves, 1967). Despite this work there is little knowledge about how the dynamics of classrooms affect friendship formation and development and in turn how these influence learning.

Friendships and the contexts of breaktime and meal times

A particular setting within school, where children meet their friends, is during breaktimes or recess and during meal times (see Chapter 5). For some children, these times may be just about the only setting within which friendships can form and develop. The important characteristic of breaktime is that it is the main 'open' setting in school, that is, a time when children are relatively free from adult supervision and where the rules of engagement are more their own (Blatchford, 1998). Meal times are more constrained yet there are often freedoms for children to decide who they will sit with to eat their meal. By their very nature, meal times offer more opportunity for sustained talk, the sharing of interests, gossip, stories and jokes and key interests in childhood culture (Baines & MacIntyre, in preparation). These times may be associated with developing understanding, intimacy and companionship and are important to children.

Friendship networks in class, breaktime and meal time contexts may not overlap exactly. It may be, for example, that in the classroom children will tend to be seated with children of similar ability and this may affect who they are friends with. However, breaktime friendship relations may have a different basis; for example, they may play with, and make friends with, children who enjoy similar games and activities. In Britain, a main playground activity – at least at primary level for boys – is soccer, and this can draw boys together, and sometimes seal friendships, though the boys may be academically at very different levels. Breaktime is implicated in the development of friendships in school because it is the main setting within which pupils, possibly not in the same class, have the opportunity to meet.

Playground games support initiation and development of friendship

Shared playground activities are a main site for the initiation and development of friendships and a context within which a wide range of social skills are developed. Playground games appear to serve different functions in friendship relations during different stages in school life (Blatchford, 1999). After entry to school, games draw children together and provide a framework for interaction through which friendships can develop. A child's suggestion of a game to play can be an opening gambit in emerging social relationships. Shared knowledge of play scripts and games may minimize the importance (at least initially) of other social skills necessary for competent interaction (Pellegrini & Blatchford, 2002). Once initiated, friendships then utilize and develop playful activities that are of joint interest, involving shared scripts, ways of playing and the development of new scripts thus enabling enhanced knowledge and opportunities for further developing friendships. The social function of games therefore may change from a role in the formation of friendship groups to one of supporting and maintaining them. Games played by friends can, in part at least, define them as a group, different to others. But one consequence of this increasing stability in friendship groups can be reduced opportunities to try new games. New trends and themes in child (and adult) culture, games and play objects provide novel frameworks which can lead to the initiation and development of new friendships (Baines & Blatchford, 2011). Davies (1982) has also commented on the connections between play and friendships, and has argued that much of the building of shared understandings that lies at the heart of friendships develops through play. She describes how the compulsive dynamic of a game can draw children in, aiding friendship formation, and providing access to a shared children's culture.

Friendships and peer groups at breaktime

Hartup (2009), like many others (e.g., Berndt, 1996), has set in place the assumption that childhood friendships are mainly dyadic in nature. Bukowski and Hoza (1989) in fact define friendships as 'the experience of having a close, mutual, dyadic relation'. However it is often the case that children meet and develop their relationships in the company of a group of friends and playmates engaged in playful interactions. These larger social contexts may significantly impact on dyadic friendships. For example, in our longitudinal research on children's friendships one group of three girls who were friends spent much of their time on the school playground together (nearly 100% of observations). However the friendship between two of the girls (which predated school) involved much conflict and they were often observed to fall out, yet the two girls sustained a positive friendship with the third girl. It was apparent that the conflict between the two girls may have arisen in the context of vying for the friendship of the third girl. When this third girl left school at the end of the school year, the relationship between the two girls disintegrated and they formed new friendships with other girls and groups in the class. What is interesting about this case is that the third girl may have been the reason why the two girls had a friendship high in conflict but also was the reason that kept them together as a group.

Since Moreno's (1934) early work there has been renewed interest in social groups and networks (Cairns, Xie & Leung, 1998; Kindermann, 2007). This has been informed by an ecological approach to the understanding and investigation of peer relationships in context (Kindermann & Valsiner, 1995).

Rather than providing a full review of this area (see Cairns et al., 1998; Gifford-Smith & Brownell, 2003; Rodkin & Hanish, 2007; Rubin et al., 2006), we thought it would be helpful for the reader if we drew on our observation data on the networks of pupils at breaktime (Blatchford et al., 2003; Pellegrini et al., 2002), to illustrate the overall group basis of school peer relations (see Baines and Blatchford, 2009, for further information).

Blatchford, Pellegrini, Baines and Kentaro undertook a longitudinal study over a year of classrooms in the USA and UK. The UK part of the research took place in four classrooms from four separate schools, involving data on friendships and observations of 119 children (7–8-year-olds) on the playground going about their daily business of socializing and engaging in playful activities. From the data collected at each of the two time points, children were found to form same-sex groups of different sizes with different levels of cohesion, roles within the group and variations in the overlap with friendships (see Baines & Blatchford, 2009). Figure 3.1 illustrates these structures with what is called a sociogram (a visual representation of the relationships within groups).

Figure. 3.1 shows the social groups from one of the classes involved in the study at the end of the year (a similar map is presented in Blatchford & Baines (2010) but using data collected at the start of the year). The interesting thing about this figure is that it is based on observational data (not the usual questionnaire data). The different shaded bubbles indicate males (black) and females (light grey). The different shaded arrows show different levels of relationship between students (e.g. the black lines indicate that students spend more than 50% of their time together). The different shaped bubbles represent different roles adopted within the group. Findings from the study show that some individuals and groups spend a lot of time together while others spend less time together. Groups are thus not necessarily discrete entities with a clear membership or boundary; some groups are more coherent and/or cohesive than others and of course they may change over time. It is of note that male groups were more highly interconnected as indicated by multiple links to many members within groups (within Figure 3.1), the female groups less so. There were also some girls (but no boys) not connected to groups. In the figure, one girl was an 'isolate' who rarely spent time with any of these children.

The groups were associated with particular breaktime activities. The close knit group of four girls engaged in a combination of chasing and fantasy activities, and the close knit triad of girls spent most of their time chatting and grooming each other. The large group of boys engaged in physical, sporty and sometimes competitive/cooperative team activities, while the smaller male group engaged exclusively in fantasy and rough and tumble play.

Consistent with previous research (Benenson, Apostoleris & Parnass, 1998; Maccoby, 1998) we found across the study that girls and boys tended to form distinct groups. Each class consisted of one large group of boys and a smaller group whilst there were a number of groups of girls. On average, boys' groups were larger than those of girls (6–7 vs. 2–4 members). Girls' networks were often

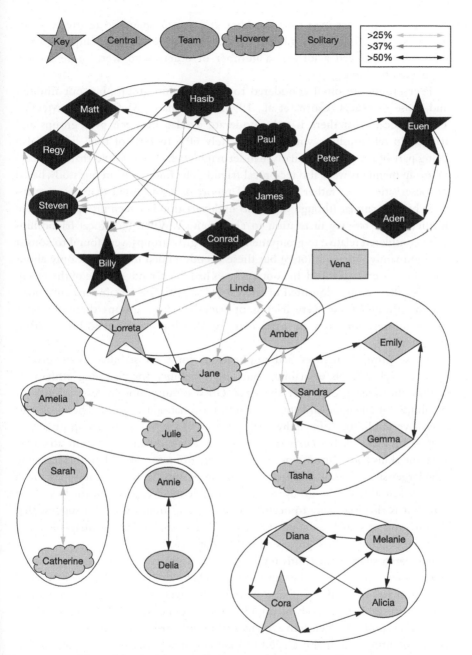

FIGURE 3.1 Map of the social networks in one class, resulting from systematic observation data

observed to interact over time together as a group, spending relatively equal amounts of time together, while boys' groups tended to contain a clique of a few boys who socialized a lot and a number of others who were more loosely connected to them.

Peer groups are often considered to be friendship groups, but our findings and those of others (Cairns et al., 1995; Kindermann, McCollam & Metzler, 1996) indicate that there is only moderate overlap between peer groups and friendship relationships, with approximately 60% to 80% of total friends also being part of the group. Similarly, Kindermann et al. (1996) found that only 26% of group members were also reciprocal friends. The findings from our study, based on observation data rather than verbal report data, suggested that the overlaps were broadly similar (though there was high variation between groups) but were further found to vary in relation to child gender. When reciprocal friendships were considered relative to group membership, girls' groups were found to consist predominantly of friends (66%) but these friends tended to represent only about half of the friends girls had. In contrast, boys had few friends outside of the group but also their groups consisted of friends (44%) with the remainder being non-friends (though these were friends of friends). These groups therefore offer opportunities, for boys in particular, to develop new friendships within the group.

These group structures had implications for their stability. Boys' groups showed higher levels of stability but also flexibility for changing affiliations within the large group over the year. Girls' groups showed less stability or flexibility for changing affiliations without terminating the group. These patterns may have implications for individual coping and the nature of group processes. Girls seem more likely to experience group break-up than boys and in turn may have the skills and relationships outside of the group to cope when this happens. The larger size of group and lack of friendships outside of the group may mean that exclusion from the group is a more problematic experience for boys than girls but is also less likely to occur. These different trends may also suggest that group processes such as conformity, harassment and tolerance may be more strongly evident in boys' groups than those of girls.

Research suggests that girls tend to aim for greater equality and exclusivity within their friendships and groups (Eder & Hallinan, 1978) and may be inclined to terminate a friendship if one member behaves in a way that emphasizes superiority or higher levels of popularity (see Benenson, 2014). Similarly, the greater levels of self-disclosure evident within girls' groups may indicate a greater need for intimacy and also a need to maintain smaller more personable groups that are more likely to disclose personal information to others. High levels of intimacy within girls' friendships may lead them to have higher expectations of their friends, so that when there is a breakdown in loyalty or a conflict of some sort, these expectations make the problems unresolvable. Boys, on the other hand, appear rather more tolerant of each other and accepting of dominance and hierarchy within their friendships and groups (Benenson & Alavi, 2004).

There may be greater tolerance of each other but boys are also less likely to seek and provide psychological support to a friend.

Many of these findings are consistent with what has become described as the 'two cultures perspective' (see Maccoby, 1998) which suggests that children from early childhood tend to socialize in same-sex groups which are very different in their structure, functioning and culture, and that many of the sex differences observed in behaviour and functioning arise as a result. Despite increased interaction between the sexes in adolescence, the same-sex focus of these groups may often continue into adulthood. A number of studies have questioned features of the two cultures theory (e.g. Thorne, 1993; Zarbatany, McDougall & Hymel, 2000) though the evidence remains broadly consistent with the basic model. Although our study found different sized groups, including larger groups of girls and small groups of boys with varying levels of apparent involvement (as indicated by time spent together), these groups were predominantly single-sex and it is likely that these peer groups have varying micro-cultures (partly illustrated by the different activities they engaged in) that may influence values, behaviour and development. Peer groups may therefore be more a case of *multiple* gendered cultures rather than *two* separate distinct cultures, as suggested by the model.

According to sociocultural perspectives (e.g. Harris, 1995) such peer groups (consisting of two members or more) may act as important contexts for development, since they are contexts within which social norms, attitudes and values are shared, shaped and developed via conformity and within-group preference. These views emphasize the possibility that the processes involved in children finding their place amongst peers can be a very powerful driver of socialization and development. Harris has gone so far as to suggest, though not without much critical review (see Collins et al., 2000; Howe, 2010), that peer groups (or extra-familial groups at least) may have a greater influence on development than parents.

Roles within groups

Another way of thinking about groups is in terms of the roles and status of members within the group. Studies have tended to focus on capturing the degree of 'centrality' of particular members within the group and many studies differentiate between members who are nuclear, secondary and peripheral (Gest et al., 2001). Adler and Adler (1998) also provide an interesting insight into the power struggles that take place between members in pre-adolescent groups. But group members may also be different in other ways and may take on complementary roles (Cairns, 1979). Little research has examined this notion of complementarity of roles within groups except in relation to bullying (e.g., see Salmivalli, 2010).

In Figure 3.1 we illustrate roles in terms of the notion of game involvement – that is, the extent to which children within the peer group are involved in organizing and engaging in joint activities on the playground. We identified five game involvement roles: key, central, team, hoverer and solitary. Key players and their assistants, central players, were often close friends and the main organizers of activities and games and they were verbally involved in the planning and playing of games. Key players were in particular the active and dominant voice. Team players were less involved in the organization of games but were engaged in playing them, and hoverers tended to leave games to observe or socialize with others. Solitary players would often play alone or not consistently socialize with a peer group.

We can connect the notion of game involvement roles to that of network centrality within the group (Ellis & Zarbatany, 2007; Gest, Graham-Bermann & Hartup, 2001). Key and central players are highly visible within the group and therefore might be considered 'nuclear' group members but even team players were stable and consistently involved members of groups. Team players and hoverers may be the behavioural equivalent of 'secondary' and 'peripheral' group members. However, there is little research on the behavioural correlates of network centrality roles within peer groups and even less relating peer group roles to friendship and best friend relations. Studies have however found that network centrality correlates well with the number of friendships, sociometric status and pro-social and antisocial behaviour (Gest et al., 2001) as well as leadership and athletic ability (Farmer & Rodkin, 1996). Friendship and friendship quality may be particularly important for establishing and changing group roles and it may be that close affiliations form the central figures around which peers come together to form peer groups. The wax and wane of friendships may therefore be reflected in the roles that children adopt within their groups.

The significance of children's friendships for development and adjustment

This last main section is an attempt to answer the key question: How important are friendships in development? This may appear straightforward – of course friends are good for you! Actually, there are as many dangers in a generalized view about the positive effects of friendships, as there are in overlooking the significance of friendships in development. Views on this vary on a continuum from little or no importance, through to useful but not essential, to a view (as advocated by Sullivan) that friendships are essential in development. But a main problem is that it is very difficult empirically to establish the developmental importance of friendship relations independently from other types of peer relations. A particular problem is that children need to have certain social skills in order to establish friendships in the first place. It is difficult therefore to determine how far friendships are important for further developing these skills or whether other overlapping peer relations constructs are more important. Another issue of importance is how friendship contributes to personal adjustment and wellbeing.

So what can we say about the importance of children's friendships? Hartup has concluded on the basis of his review of evidence that:

> Correlational studies show that children with friends are more socially competent than children who do not have friends, and that troubled children have difficulty in friendship relations. Causal models, tested with longitudinal data, suggest that friendship experience forecasts developmental outcome in conjunction with personal attributes and other experiences. Making friends, keeping them, and making new ones are all relevant. The current evidence suggests, however, that we can better argue that friendships are developmental advantages than argue that these relationships are developmental necessities.
>
> *(Hartup, 1992, pp. 200–201, our emphasis)*

This opinion qualifies the importance of friendship, though in practice there may be a very fine line between 'advantage' and 'necessity'. More recently and after nearly twenty years of research since Hartup's review, the conclusion, though perhaps more developed in terms of the importance of children's friendships, remains much the same. Bagwell and Schmidt (2011, p. 114) conclude: 'The evidence is clear that children with friends are better off than children without friends, especially in terms of social competence and psychosocial adjustment . . . Nevertheless, simply having a friend does not guarantee positive outcomes'. That is, friendships seem to offer distinct advantages but cannot be concluded to be a necessity for development and adjustment.

A starting point for a consideration of the importance of children's friendships is the well-established view that peer relations have particular value for social, emotional and cognitive development. In an influential book, Youniss (1980) adapted the theories of Piaget and Sullivan to show how peer relations were qualitatively different to adult–child relations. In contrast to adult–child relations, peer relations are characterized by equality, cooperation, reciprocity and mutuality – all of which make a contribution to social development. Youniss did not argue that adult–child and peer relations were better or worse than each other, rather that they served different functions and had different effects.

The following sections will consider first, whether friendships are important for the development of skills; second, whether they support psychological adjustment; and finally whether friends and friendlessness can have a negative effect on adjustment.

Context for the acquisition of social, cognitive and emotional skills

In a rather inelegant but useful phrase, friendships have been described as 'cooperative socialization contexts' (Hartup, 1999). Friendships may be particularly important socialization contexts because children tend to spend much more time with their friends, they know each other much better, they increasingly become aware of what may irritate and please each other, they often have much in common, and their affiliation may become stronger as time moves on. Overall, as we have seen, friendships support cooperation, reciprocity, effective conflict management, companionship, intimacy and commitment, and these begin early in life and extend into adolescence. All of these are important aspects of social relations and social skills, and all can have their roots in friendship relations.

Evidence for the important connection between friendship and social skills comes from studies which have compared the behaviour of children who differ in terms of whether they have friends or not. Much of the research suggests that children without friends are less socially skilled, playful and positive when interacting with peers and more disruptive and negative in their interactions (Newcomb & Bagwell, 1996).

Approaching this in a slightly different way, Howes (1988) in a study of young children found that social behaviour between stable friends was more competent, children were more successful in group entry, more complementary and reciprocal in their social play, more cooperative, and more likely to engage in pretend play. In a study comparing the interactions of friends and non-friends, Foot, Chapman and Smith (1977) found that friends who watched a funny film were more likely to be coordinated and reciprocal in their behaviour. Friends engaged in higher levels of smiling, laughing and touching, as well as talking. Thus there was a more obvious affective synchrony between friends. Studies of friends engaged in problem-solving activities also suggest that there is more coordination and collaboration in the completion of tasks and activities than between non-friends (Newcomb & Brady, 1982; Zajac & Hartup, 1997).

Maxwell (1990) describes friendships in terms of a socialization function – for example, through learning to self-regulate aggressive and other types of impulses in socially acceptable ways. He concludes: 'The peer group provides arguably the most efficient and highly motivating context for the learning and development of social skills which will ultimately enable children to live effectively as a member of adult society' (p. 171).

Friendships are also contexts where children learn to trust others, become socially sensitive, develop moral understanding about how to treat others as well as become aware of alternative perspectives and understandings. A particular feature of friendships, especially best friendships, is that they involve intimacy, which is a marked mutual affection and valuing of a friend and often involves self-disclosure and confiding in each other. The behavioural expression of intimacy changes with development and in adolescence there appears to be a marked increase in self-disclosure, particularly for girls (McNelles & Connolly, 1999, cited in Bagwell & Schmidt, 2011, p. 77). In early adolescence feelings of loyalty, security and emotional support and closeness in friendships may depend on intimacy.

In a study of intimacy in pre-adolescent and adolescent friendships Buhrmeister (1990, cited in Bagwell & Schmidt, 2011, p. 80) found similar levels of intimacy between the two age groups but also found that intimacy in adolescents' friendships was more strongly connected to social wellbeing through higher levels of self-esteem and sociability and lower levels of internalizing distress. However there is relatively little research that has looked at intimacy in children's friendships. Intimacy through self-disclosure and joint problem solving between friends may be important for resilience and adjustment to the new and increasing independence that children experience and desire during adolescence.

Friendships are also sites for disagreement and conflict. Research on disputes between young children in early childhood has highlighted that they are important sites for learning argumentation strategies involving explanation and justification (Baines & Howe, 2010; Howe & McWilliam, 2006). It may be surprising then that a number of studies have found that friends are more likely than non-friends to engage in conflict (Dunn & Cutting, 1999; Hartup et al., 1988). As children's social skills develop, the way they resolve disagreements changes (Laursen, Finkelstein & Betts, 2001) from initially physical strategies to strategies involving coercion (e.g. 'I'm bigger than you' or 'I won't be your friend if you don't let me') to strategies based on negotiation (e.g. 'you have a go this time and I will go next'). Of importance here, however, are indications that friends tend to be more cooperative in resolving disputes and use strategies that allow the friendship to continue (Dunn, 2004). Friends are more likely to resolve arguments through the use of disengagement, negotiation and compromise rather than dominance strategies. In contrast to conflicts with peers where those in conflict may have little to lose through the use of aggressive strategies, if conflicts between friends are not resolved to their mutual satisfaction then the friendship may be put at risk (Dunn, 2004). Conflicts may even lead to stronger and better quality friendships (Selman, 1980).

Another area where friendships may be important is in the development of emotional understanding and skills. Interactions between friends are times when they experience many emotions – amusement, laughter, frustration and anger. They can also lead to experiences of sadness and loss, for example when a close friend chooses to spend more time with someone else. It is very likely that children learn a lot about their own and others' emotions, and also how to control their own and others' feelings. Are friendships unique in this provision, beyond, for example, experiences with parents, teachers or peers more generally? There is limited evidence to help us answer this question, though the nature and quality of friendship relations may be important for children's developing social and emotional understanding (Dunn, 2011).

Research has largely emphasized the important role of the parents and particularly the mother in the development of emotions and emotional knowledge (Denham, Basset and Wyatt, 2007). But a number of studies suggest that emotional competence is associated with greater success and positive engagement with peers and friends. Young children (4-year-olds) who were more aware of others' emotions and views showed greater coordination during pretend play with friends (Dunn, 2004). Similarly 4–5-year-olds' emotional understanding of happy, sad and angry emotions was related to social interactive play with peers, though amongst boys only (Mathieson & Banerjee, 2011). Preschoolers who engage in more complex play interactions were more likely to understand mixed emotions three years later, aged 6 (Maguire & Dunn, 1997). Other research tells us rather more about the implications of emotional expression relative to current or future peer relations. On the whole this work indicates that children who are emotionally more positive have more friends and are better liked (Denham, Bassett & Wyatt, 2007). Those who openly express their negative emotions rather than regulating these emotions and putting on a 'brave face', are less liked (Saarni, 2008; Ladd et al., 1996). Similarly, those children who express enjoyment at another child's expense and/or endorse vengeful responses tend to have fewer friends and are more likely to argue with their friends (Arsenio, Cooperman & Lover, 2000; Rose & Asher, 1999). In a study of children new to school, Ladd et al. (1996) found that talk with friends about negative affect was associated with gains in loneliness over the school year. Thus dwelling on negative events and expressing negative emotions may discourage friendships with peers. In many cases children learn to control the expression of these feelings and to manage the impressions of peers. While much of the research in this area connects friendship and peer relations with emotional expression and understanding, it does not tell us whether friendships are unique contexts for the development of emotional understanding or greater emotional wellbeing.

In summary, the day-to-day interactions that take place between friends may offer relatively unique opportunities for the development and honing of certain types of social, cognitive and emotional skills that are of value in the future and for sustaining positive relationships with peers. It would be simplistic to assume however that all experiences of friendship will inevitably lead to an 'improvement' in skills and understanding. It is likely that certain types of friendship will lead to less positive social skills (e.g. the existence of a submissive friend may lead to a child being dominant) and social conduct, as we shall see later.

Friendships support psychological and school adjustment

As well as acting as important and possibly unique contexts for the development of a range of social, communicative, cognitive and emotional skills, friends may contribute to a child's social and psychological wellbeing (Majors, 2010; Rubin et al., 2013). There are a number of ways in which they may support adjustment, for example by acting as a friendly ear and a supportive emotional resource, by offering advice or emotional security or as a way in to develop other positive relationships with peers. We will explore some of these possibilities through the remainder of this section.

Friends as an emotional resource

One of the main potential benefits of friendships is that they may be an important emotional resource in times of difficulty. Friends can help in solving everyday problems, buffer stress (e.g., parental separation) and provide security when experiencing new things or new contexts and meeting new people. In a classic and poignant study, Freud and Dann (1951) studied six children who had spent their early years during the Second World War in close contact with each other but without stable care or attention from adults. Examination of the children after the end of the war, suggested that they were hypersensitive, restless, aggressive and difficult to handle but were not deficient, delinquent or psychotic. It appeared that continual contact with each other had ameliorated the effects of a terrible early life, including lack of contact with their parents or other adults.

In early, disturbing research by Harlow (1969) and Harlow and Harlow (1965), monkeys were reared in a variety of different environments. It was found that social contact between young peer monkeys was of paramount importance in the development of social and sexual relations later on in life. In one experiment, the long-term social adjustment of infant monkeys deprived of mother contact was bleak, but, when reared with contact with other infant monkeys, they were surprisingly unaffected. Interestingly, infant monkeys deprived of contact with other monkeys from the age of 4 to 8 months, but who experienced normal mothering, were found to be less affectionate with peers and more aggressive.

These two famous studies are indicative of the possible value of early peer relations and friendships as a resource in times of stress and difficulty. Studies since have examined whether friendships can make up for poor parenting or poor parent–child relationships. Overall findings suggest that having a friend can offer protection against poor quality family relationships, and having a high quality friendship is even more protective relative to feelings of self-worth and social competence (Gauze et al., 1996). In a 3-year longitudinal study of abused children, Bolger, Patterson and Kupersmidt (1998) found that friendships, particularly those of high quality, can attenuate the negative effects of chronic abuse on later self-esteem and may even function to improve it. A range of other studies also indicate that friendship may moderate the relationship between negative family environments and later adjustment outcomes. However, Bagwell and Schmidt (2011) argue that these studies only provide moderate evidence of a unique buffering effect of friendships. This is because in studies where a number of peer relations measures are examined, as well as friendship, these are also found to moderate the relationship between negative aspects of the family context relative to child outcomes such as externalizing problems (Criss et al., 2002). Nevertheless, certain aspects of peer relationships do seem to limit the effects of negative parenting and parent–child relationships on aspects of future adjustment.

There is clearly much more to this issue than the presence or not of friends, and further work in this area ought to consider the quality of the friendship and other peer relations variables. Is it the case that certain characteristics of peer relations enhance feelings of self-efficacy, self-esteem and confidence? Or is it that friends offer opportunities for positive interactions and the development of positive relationships, enhancing feelings of relatedness? Alternatively friendships may act as a source of therapy, allowing children to problem solve and overcome particular difficulties.

Friendship as protection

Friendships may have a protective role for children who become targets of harassment and dislike by the wider peer group. We know for instance that children who do not have a mutual friend are more likely to be victimized than those that do, and that victims are less likely to be nominated as friends and have difficulties developing and sustaining high quality friendships (Fox & Boulton, 2006; Mouttapa et al., 2004; Sijtsema, Rambaran & Ojanen, 2013). What this means is that those children that are victimized are likely to experience a decrease in victimization if they develop a good quality mutual friendship (Bowker et al., 2006). Supportive and non-aggressive friends can buffer against the negative effects of victimization on academic progress (Schwartz et al., 2008). A main difficulty here therefore is how children with difficulties can be encouraged to develop friendships when they put off so many people.

There are a number of ways in which friendship, once developed, may protect against victimization. The friend may stand up to others or act as a deterrent or witness. Alternatively they may act as a confidant and provide a child with confidence to extend their network of relationships with peers. What is less clear is whether the presence of a friend just stops the process of victimization and its effects from happening or whether the process is more complex, e.g. that interaction with the friend is therapeutic.

One way in which friends may act as an emotional resource is in terms of joint problem solving. Rose (2002) describes a process of conversational exchange, referred to as 'co-rumination', which often takes place within friendships. Co-rumination is the process of talking about problems and negative feelings. It involves self-disclosure and higher levels of intimacy within friendships. During such exchanges friends can offer useful advice on how to respond and react to conflicts and negative feelings (e.g. 'look on the bright side', 'I would ignore him, he's always like that') and engage in humorous exchanges to cheer up a friend. However excessive co-rumination has been found to be prospectively associated with higher levels of anxiety and depression, especially amongst girls (Rose, Carlson & Waller, 2007). It may also be the case, as noted earlier, that excessive co-rumination and talk about negative affect may lead to decreases in popularity, loss of friends and increased loneliness. A subsequent study of pre-adolescent girls found that although co-rumination correlated with depression and friendship quality it did not predict changes in depressive symptoms over time (Starr & Davila, 2009). It may be that in certain circumstances co-rumination has a positive effect but that in other particular forms of stressful events it may be negative. This highlights the importance of considering other factors and life experiences and the need for further research.

Adjustment to school

The importance of friendship as a support in adjusting to school has been the subject of much research, particularly in the USA (Ladd et al., 1996; Berndt & Keefe, 1995). There appears to be some consensus that friendships can improve children's social and academic adjustment to school. More supportive friendships can help children have more positive perceptions of school and help them behave better. Berndt and Keefe make the point that the success of friends in helping adjustment to school will depend on the quality of friendships involved. If based on mutual respect and collaboration, and if viewed positively, then they will help involvement in school, but if friendships are viewed more negatively then behaviour may become more disruptive.

On entry to a new school, pupils must adapt to new things including more formal organizational and working arrangements. A main change is in the social realm, where children are no longer the oldest in the school, they must re-establish old friendships and develop new friendships with unfamiliar peers, avoid being bullied, and find their place within the new social structure and culture (Bailey & Baines, 2012; Hargreaves & Galton, 2002). Disruption of the social realm may be unsettling for pupils at the key time between childhood and adolescence when peer relationships become increasingly important (Sullivan, 1953). During adolescence, students show an increased dependency on friendship support and identification, and conformity with peers also increases (Wentzel, 1991). Similarly, researchers suggest that many adolescents begin to value social goals over academic goals (Anderman, Maehr & Martin, 1994) and the socially disruptive nature of transfer may facilitate this.

For children about to go through the transfer to secondary school, being with or near friends is their most important consideration but is often less important for parents when selecting the new school (Evangelou et al., 2008). For children, friends offer familiarity, shared experiences, support and sympathy. Consistent with children's views, studies have indicated that children who already have a good friend on transfer to a new school are more likely to adapt socially to the new context than children who do not have a secure or stable friendship (Aikens et al., 2005; Berndt et al., 1999). Children who had a stable friendship were more likely to have higher levels of leadership and sociability, to be more popular, to hold positive perceptions of school, and to experience increased school adjustment, achievement and engagement. It is likely that stable and close friendships across transitions provide a secure base, enabling children to have the confidence to socialize with a wider range of peers and therefore develop positive new relationships with others in school. This in turn may make school enjoyable and engaging and thus lead to the observed effects on school engagement and adjustment. On the other hand, those who have few friendships of quality may struggle to adapt academically as well as socially to a new school. Particular friendships and social networks may 'socialize' children's attitudes, motivation and behaviour towards learning and thus may be important to whether adolescents 'tune' in or out of school (Farmer & Rodkin, 1996; Wentzel & Caldwell, 1997).

Other studies have also found that friends can have a positive effect when children are starting their first formal school. Ladd (1990) found that the more children a child knew in class on entry to school the better adjusted to school they were at the end of the year. Ladd et al. (1996) also studied children on entry to school and found that two features of friendship quality – validation and aid – predicted gains in perceptions of classroom peer support, and also children's perception of their own affect in school. Children who thought their friendships offered higher levels of aid tended to like school better as the school year progressed. So having friends who help with difficult social situations may enhance children's feelings of competence and security in school.

Can friends be bad for you? The importance of the identity of one's friends

So far we have been considering how friends and friendships can have a positive or protective influence on development. The possibility that friendships can have a darker side is starkly evident in the case of several high-profile crimes in both the USA and UK involving young friends. One example was the James Bulger case – where two friends Jon Venables and Robert Thompson kidnapped and killed the toddler in a city in the north of England. According to the press and evidence presented during the subsequent court case, both boys had antisocial backgrounds, were bullies but also the victims of bullying, and were socially rejected by many of their school mates. Another example was the Columbine school massacre which took place in Colorado, where thirteen students were killed and a further twenty-one injured at their high school by two teenagers, Eric Harris and Dylan Klebold, dressed in black trench coats. This attack was planned by the duo and there have been similar cases since. What is particular about these cases is that they are not committed by lone individuals but rather were carried out by young people who were friends. There are a range of similarities across the various cases in terms of characteristics of the youths involved, the nature of their family background and relationships and, importantly, their relationships with peers. In both cases mentioned above, the young people appear to have been socially rejected by their peers and had met and become friends.

These cases are extreme, but there are other more everyday examples, e.g., groups of children that victimize others (Juvonen & Galván, 2008; Salmivalli, 2010) and friends filming each other engaged in delinquent activities to contribute to social networking websites. It is now well established that one cannot consider the developmental significance of friendships without first distinguishing at least two factors: the identity of a child's friends (e.g., their personality characteristics), and the quality of the friendship (Hartup, 1996).

Children tend to choose to be friends with others who are similar to themselves, and may also socialize each other and thus become more similar over time (Prinstein & Dodge, 2008). Children who associate with friends whose behaviour is antisocial, anti-school or delinquent may be influenced to also behave in these ways as well as adopt the attitudes and aspirations held (Kandel, 1978). This may be particularly the case when a child has been rejected by peers and the opportunity for friendships with more pro-social children is limited. According to Elliott, Huizinga and Ageton (1985), association with a deviant friend is the strongest predictor of adolescent delinquency and drug use, and peers are regularly implicated in onset and increases in nicotine, drug and alcohol use and early sexual intercourse (Rose et al., 1999; Pilgrim et al., 1999; Schulenberg et al., 1999).

Research has had difficulties distinguishing between selection and socialization effects, not least because socialization effects may reflect an aspect of a selection effect (e.g. a child who takes up smoking might already be inclined to do this possibly because the child enjoys rebelliousness or risk-taking activity). It is likely that in many cases similarities between friends in attitudes, behavioural tendencies and interests are a main feature that leads to socialization in related areas. That is, a friend may be somewhat 'primed' to be influenced in a particular way on account of similar views, interests and values. On the other hand, some children may try to become more similar to peers in order to befriend them and thus a certain level of peer influence/socialization may precede selection similarity (Bukowski, Velasquez & Brendgen, 2008).

Other complications include the possibility of a joint influence on the friendship dyad such that it is not the effect of the friend but something the two have in common (Hartup, 1999; Poulin et al., 1999). This would apply, for example, if the friends are part of the same peer group/clique and are jointly influenced by another member of the group or the micro-culture within the group or the way the group is treated by other groups (e.g., see Adler & Adler, 1998). Similarly, information on the friend who does the influencing is often based on the perceptions of the individual who is influenced (Ryan, 2001) rather than more objective measurements. This means that sometimes peer influence is more about the individual's perception of the friend and norms than the friend's actual characteristics.

One of the main limitations of work in this field has been the lack of research on the actual socialization processes that may underpin peer influence. It is all very well to show on the basis of questionnaire data at two points in time that a person has become more similar to a friend but there needs to be some sort of account of *how* this change takes place. Most models of peer influence (e.g., Heilbron & Prinstein, 2008; Brown et al., 2008) involve mechanisms that are likely to be indirect. For example, a child who witnesses the teasing of another child by a friend for wearing particular clothes might in future avoid wearing anything that is also likely to get him or her teased. But it is likely that there are also more direct attempts to influence a peer through coercion, teasing and taunting and reinforcement of certain behaviours and attitudes.

One socialization process that has received substantial attention is the notion of 'deviancy training'. Deviancy training is the process whereby members of deviant groups reinforce and elevate the status of deviant behaviour and activities through laughter, approval and positive reactions to rule-breaking discussions (Dishion et al., 1996). A good example of this style of talk was observed by one of the authors who lived on a street corner in London much frequented by groups of teenagers. These groups often sat on the low-level wall just outside the sitting room window. On one occasion one boy was overheard recounting to his two friends how he had instigated a fight with a particular other boy (who they all clearly disliked). His story, recounted in an excited and at times very animated way with actions to illustrate, was met with laughter, aggressive language, excited gleeful responses and high fives. Such experiences involve excitement, reinforcement and expressions of support and may function to make friends and group members feel closer, establish a joint identity and attitude towards others. It may also function to reinforce an individual's status within the group.

Deviancy training has been found to be a powerful predictor of peer influence in terms of delinquent behaviour, violence, and involvement with police between early and late adolescence (Dishion et al., 1996; Granic & Dishion, 2003) and in the development of conduct problems between early and later childhood (Snyder et al., 2005). In a study of 10-year-old boys' relationships with friends who were identified as aggressive, it was found that those boys who showed moderate levels of aggressiveness seemed to be affected most by their disruptive friends such that they showed similarly high levels of delinquency later in adolescence (Vitaro et al., 1997).

Peers and friends may play an important role in influencing attitudes towards school, as well as the nature of classroom engagement, motivation and learning (Kindermann, 2007; Ryan 2001). Kindermann (2007), in a strong longitudinal study carried out over a school year that controlled for parent and teacher effects as well as peer selection effects, found relatively modest, yet significant, effects of peer socialization on teacher-rated engagement. There is an increasing sense that many children and young people may try to 'manage' peer expectations and influences by managing the way they are perceived by others. For example, young people and particularly boys may manage the effort (actual and apparent) that they put into school study so as not to appear like 'geeks' and to become rejected and the target of teasing or bullying (e.g., see Robinson (2013) reporting on how high-attaining black Afro-Caribbean boys manage their relationships with peers).

Children without friends

According to Sullivan, although new relationships are never exact copies of old ones, formative friendships can in a sense be 'templates' or models used in constructing future relationships (Hartup, 1992). Main features of 'chumship' in adolescence (e.g., loyalty, mutual support, intimacy, etc.) meet an overall need to avoid loneliness and an increasing capacity to achieve intimacy which can become translated into later romantic relationships. But what happens when children do not have friends, and what are the longer-term effects of friendships on later relationships and wellbeing? Are friendships necessary for positive future psychological adjustment? This has been an issue of interest for some years now but it is only recently that studies have the methodological rigour to enable some answers.

According to Rubin et al. (2013) estimates are that between 15% and 20% of children do not have a mutual friend. Early reviews of evidence suggested strong support for an association between peer adjustment, in terms of aggressiveness and low peer acceptance, and later maladjustment in terms of dropping out of school and criminality (Bagwell et al., 1998; Parker & Asher, 1987). However much evidence was correlational, that is, some features are related to later outcomes, but not necessarily in a causal way. These reviews highlighted the need for longitudinal studies to take account of a range of possible alternative variables as well as friendship, including initial child personal characteristics and other relationships with peers and others. By measuring all the relevant variables over time it is possible to identify their unique, combined and overlapping effects on various outcomes, like school adjustment. By controlling for the effects of other variables, studies can identify the unique contribution of friendship.

One longitudinal study that took this approach compared thirty adults with an enduring friendship during pre-adolescence with thirty adults who were friendless during pre-adolescence. Taking account of peer acceptance, the study found that stable friendship involvement at pre-adolescence uniquely predicted a more positive self-image and fewer symptoms of depression on reaching adulthood (Bagwell, Newcomb & Bukowski, 1998). A more recent longitudinal study of children from middle childhood to early adolescence that took account of peer rejection and a range of personal characteristics found that feelings of depression and loneliness, but not delinquency, were predicted by the number of years of friendlessness (Pedersen et al., 2007). However, other studies have failed to find long-term effects of friendship quality on mental health outcomes (Giordano et al., 1998).

These studies focus on effects during adolescence and adulthood but there are other studies that focus on childhood. It is of note that prior to the age of 4 or 5 many children may not have friends or regular playmates because they do not attend preschool or nursery settings that often. Friendships or regular playmates may thus play a relatively limited role during early childhood relative to later adjustment and relationships. It is likely that many of the reasons for having friends (e.g. companionship, intimacy, and so on) are met by other members of the family. As Bagwell and Schmidt (2011) suggest, "it is difficult to imagine that there is anything developmentally *necessary* about a relationship that many children simply do not have" (p. 70).

However there are some studies that suggest that friendships and competence in interactions with friends in early childhood may be related to later competence in later friendships. For example longitudinal research by Carollee Howes and colleagues found that a high quality relationship with a best friend at age 9 was predicted by the formation of close friendships during preschool at 4 years of age (Howes, Hamilton & Philipsen, 1998). Similarly, Dunn (2004) found that characteristics of friends in terms of their ability to understand alternative perspectives predicted the quality of subsequent friendships, suggesting benefits to good quality early friendships. On the other hand, when young children are socially reticent or when their friendships are of poor quality, then social difficulties and later adjustment may be affected. Although children who appear shy and withdrawn from peers during kindergarten have not been found to be less adjusted, studies indicate that these children tend to befriend similarly withdrawn children, that the relationship is less positive and does not provide the buffer against victimization that other friendships experience (Ladd & Burgess, 1999; Rubin et al., 2006).

Studies of friendlessness in childhood also highlight connections with loneliness. In their study of children 8 to 12 years of age, Nangle et al. (2003) found a connection between poor friendship relations, loneliness and feelings of depression, particularly for those children that were less popular. Research by Ladd and Troop-Gordon (2003) indicates that children without friends (chronic or sustained friendlessness) between first and third grade (6–9 years) were more likely to experience internalizing difficulties at age 10. This was the case even when chronic rejection and victimization were taken into account. The effect was partially mediated by children's self-beliefs, indicating that friendship is really important for bolstering feelings of self-worth, which in turn reduces feelings of loneliness.

One short-term longitudinal study found that different types of peer relationship (acceptance, friendship and victimization) were related to preschoolers' school and personal adjustment in shared and unique ways (Ladd, Kochenderfer & Coleman, 1997). Acceptance and friendship both predicted loneliness but their contribution overlapped markedly, whilst victimization uniquely predicted loneliness. This indicates that loneliness may be associated with low levels of acceptance and/or friendships, but that victimization seems to have an additional and unique relationship with loneliness. It may be that the absence of acceptance and/or the absence of friends make children feel lonely, but victimization is especially likely to make children feel lonely. There is clearly a need for such studies to provide a more nuanced and refined understanding of how friends and peer relations may relate to psychological adjustment.

To summarize this section, there is increasingly good longitudinal evidence that often takes account of a range of peer-relations measures that indicates that friendlessness or poor quality friendship can have a deleterious effect on social functioning and later wellbeing, and particularly on feelings of loneliness. There are a number of possible explanations for these results. The most likely may be that friendlessness means that individuals are less likely to have positive feelings about themselves and may lack supportive protection that can help protect against negative social experiences.

Conclusions

We have seen through this chapter that research on friendship has a rich history, and that ideas and understanding about the nature of friendship and how it is captured have developed and changed. The methodological sophistication of recent studies that control for a range of potentially confounding variables has substantially contributed to our understanding and shows that we are beginning to comprehend the importance of friendship in children's development for their wellbeing and social lives within and outside of school. Longitudinal and multivariate studies are beginning to model the effects of different aspects of peer relationships as well as friendship to provide a picture of how these interconnect to relate to future outcomes.

Research findings clearly suggest that in many cases having friends can offer support and protection and enhance psychological adjustment. Friendships can lay the foundations for future relationships and that most notably they can be contexts for the development of a wide range of social, cognitive and emotional skills or competences.

There is a strong sense however that these relationships, experiences, skills and outcomes will vary from individual to individual. Not all children have friendships, not all children have the very positive relationships that we normally expect of friendships, and not all friendships offer the same experiences. It is likely that even those friendships that are very positive, intimate and comfortable for children may not provide the best contexts for social adjustment. If children fall out with their friends then it may help them develop the skills for managing conflicts better in the future. On the other hand they may become more withdrawn and likely to be victimized. Friendships are likely to be unique contexts for development and the research field is increasingly taking account of individual differences (Bagwell & Schmidt, 2011).

Returning to Hartup's distinction between developmental 'advantages' and 'necessities', it seems that having good quality relationships with friends who are in themselves well-adjusted offers a distinct developmental advantage. Furthermore friendlessness can have important negative implications for future relationships, adjustment to school and psychological adjustment and loneliness, thus reinforcing friendship as a developmental advantage. On the other hand, having friendships with less well-adjusted peers can lead to problems and negative outcomes. Whether friendships are necessities relates to whether they are unique contexts for the development of particular skills and for adjustment. On this point it is harder to reach a clear consensus. Bagwell and Schmidt (2011) argue that the voluntary, reciprocal, equal and affiliative nature of friendships makes them significant. The question remains however whether the skills that these relationships contribute to are exclusively developed in these contexts. It is very likely that children develop some of the same social skills through their interactions with family members (including siblings, cousins, parents) or with non-friends (e.g., we have to amicably resolve arguments with others as well as with friends) and that adjustment may be related to affiliation, acceptance and intimacy with the range of people that are most important to the child. Friendships therefore may be part of a range of social contexts that are important for children.

Much research carried out on friendships has tended to consider them in rather abstract terms and away from the day-to-day contexts in which they take place. However studying friendships in context and the interactions between friends provides an important window into the processes underpinning these relationships (as we have seen from research on deviancy training) and how they may affect children's lives. However there is an absence of such research and much more needs to be done to examine the processes and interactions between peers and friends within the context of peer groups and their implications for relationships and adjustment in the short and longer term.

References

Adler, P.A. & Adler, P. (1998). *Peer Power: Preadolescent Culture and Identity*. New Brunswick, NJ: Rutgers University Press.

Aikins, J.W., Bierman, K.L. & Parker, J.G. (2005). Navigating the transition to junior high school: the influence of pre–transition friendship and self–system characteristics. *Social Development,* 14, 42–60.

Altermatt, E.R. (2012). Children's achievement-related discourse with peers: uncovering the processes of peer influence. In A.M. Ryan & G.W. Ladd (Eds), *Peer Relationships and Adjustment at School* (pp. 109–134). Charlotte, NC: Information Age Publishing.

Anderman, E. Maehr, M. & Martin, L. (1994). Motivation and schooling in the middle grades. *Review of Educational Research,* 64, 287–309.

Arsenio, W., Cooperman, S. & Lover, A. (2000). Affective predictors of preschoolers' aggression and peer acceptance: direct and indirect effects. *Developmental Psychology,* 36, 438–448.

Asher, S. & Dodge, K. (1986). Identifying children who are rejected by their peers. *Developmental Psychology,* 22, 444–449.

Bagwell, C.L., Newcomb, A.E. & Bukowski, W.M. (1998). Preadolescent friendship and peer rejection as predictors of adult adjustment. *Child Development,* 69, 140–153.

Bagwell, C.L. & Schmidt, M.E. (2011). *Friendships in Childhood & Adolescence*. New York: Guilford Press.

Bailey, S. & Baines, E. (2012). The impact of risk and resiliency factors on the adjustment of children after the transition from primary to secondary school. *Educational and Child Psychology, Special Edition on Psychological Perspectives on Transition,* 29(1), 47–63.

Baines, E. & Blatchford, P. (2009). Sex differences in the structure and stability of children's playground social networks and their overlap with friendship relations. *British Journal of Developmental Psychology,* 27, 743–760.

Baines, E. & Blatchford, P. (2011). Playground games and activities in school and their role in development. In A.D. Pellegrini (Ed.), *The Oxford Handbook of the Development of Play*. New York: Oxford University Press.

Baines, E. & Blatchford, P. (2012). Children's independent mobility and travel to school. Retrieved 8 January 2014 from: www.breaktime.org.uk/Publications.htm.

Baines, E. & Howe, C. (2010). Discourse topic management skills in 4-, 6- and 9-year-old peer interactions: developments with age and the effects of task context. *First Language,* 30(3/4), 508–535.

Baines, E. & MacIntyre, H. (in preparation). Children's social experiences with peers and friends during school meal times.

Benenson, J.F. (2014). *Warriors and Worriers: The Survival of the Sexes.* New York: Oxford University Press.

Benenson, J.F. & Alavi, K. (2004). Sex differences in children's investment in same-sex peers. *Evolution and Human Behavior,* 25, 258–266.

Benenson, J.F., Apostoleris, N.H. & Parnass, J. (1998). The organisation of children's same sex peer relationships. In W. Bukowski & A. Cillessen (Eds), *Sociometry Then and Now* (New Directions for Child Development no. 80). San Francisco: Jossey-Bass.

Berndt, T.J. (1996). Exploring the effects of friendship quality on social development. In W.M. Bukowski., A.F. Newcomb. & W.W. Hartup (Eds), *The Company They Keep: Friendships in Childhood and Adolescence.* Cambridge: Cambridge University Press.

Berndt, T., Hawkins, J. & Jiao, Z. (1999). Influences of friends and friendships on adjustment to junior high school. *Merrill-Palmer Quarterly,* 45(1), 13–41.

Berndt, T. & Keefe, K. (1995). Friends' influence on adolescents' adjustment to school. *Child Development,* 66: 1312–1329.

Berndt, T.J. & McCandless, M.A. (2009). Methods for investigating children's relationships with friends. In K.H. Rubin, W.M. Bukowski & B. Laursen (Eds), *Handbook of Peer Interactions, Relationships and Groups* (pp. 63–81). New York: Guilford Press.

Bigelow, B. & La Gaipa, J. (1975). Children's written descriptions of friendship: a multidimensional analysis. *Developmental Psychology,* 11, 857–858.

Blatchford, P. (1979). The development of social interaction between infants. Unpublished PhD thesis, University of Surrey, UK.

Blatchford, P. (1998). *Social Life in Schools: Pupils' Experiences of Breaktime and Recess from 7 to 16 Years.* London: Falmer Press.

Blatchford, P. (1999). Friendships at school: the role of breaktimes. *Education 3–13,* 27, 1, 60–65.

Blatchford, P. & Baines, E. (2010). Peer relations in school. In K. Littleton, C. Wood & K. Staarman (Eds), *Elsevier Handbook of Educational Psychology: New Perspectives on Learning and Teaching.* New York: Elsevier.

Blatchford, P., Baines, E. & Pellegrini, A. (2003). The social context of school playground games: sex and ethnic differences, and changes over time after entry to junior school. *British Journal of Developmental Psychology,* 21, 481–505.

Bolger, K., Patterson, C. & Kupersmidt, J. (1998). Peer relationships and self-esteem among children who have been maltreated. *Child Development,* 69, 1171–1197.

Bowker, J., Rubin, K., Burgess, K., Booth-LaForce, C. & Rose-Krasnor, L. (2006). Behavioral characteristics associated with stable and fluid best friendship patterns in middle childhood. *Merrill-Palmer Quarterly,* 52, 671–693.

Brendgen, M., Vitaro, F., Turgeon, L. & Poulin, F. (2002). Assessing aggressive and depressed children's social relations with classmates and friends: a matter of perspective. *Journal of Abnormal Child Psychology,* 30, 609–624.

Brendgen, M., Vitaro, F., Turgeon, L., Poulin, F. & Wanner, B. (2004). Is there a dark side of positive illusions? Overestimation of social competence and subsequent adjustment in aggressive and nonaggressive children. *Journal of Abnormal Child Psychology,* 32, 305–320.

Brown, B., Bakken, J., Ameringer, S. & Mahon, S. (2008). A comprehensive conceptualization of the peer influence process in adolescence. In M. Prinstein & K. Dodge (Eds), *Understanding Peer Influence in Children and Adolescents* (pp. 17–44). London: Guilford Press.

Buhrmeister, D. (1990). Intimacy of friendship, interpersonal competence, and adjustment during preadolescence and adolescence. *Child Development,* 61, 1101–1111.

Bukowski, W.M. & Hoza, B. (1989). Popularity and friendship: issues in theory, measurement and outcome. In T.J. Berndt & G.W. Ladd (Eds), *Peer Relationships in Child Development.* New York: Wiley.

Bukowski, W.M., Hoza, B. & Boivin, M. (1994). Measuring friendship quality during pre- and early adolescence: the development and psychometric properties of the friendship qualities scale. *Journal of Social and Personal Relationships,* 11, 471–484.

Bukowski, W.M., Velasquez, A.M. & Brendgen, M. (2008). Variations in patterns of peer influence: considerations of self and other. In M. Prinstein & K. Dodge (Eds), *Understanding Peer Influence in Children and Adolescents* (pp. 125–140). London: Guilford Press.

Burgess, K.B., Wojslawowicz, J.C., Rubin, K.H., Rose-Krasnor, L. & Booth-LaForce, C. (2006). Social information processing and coping strategies of shy/withdrawn and aggressive children: does friendship matter? *Child Development,* 77, 371–383.

Cairns, R. (1979). *Social Development: The Origins and Plasticity of Interchanges.* San Francisco: Freeman.

Cairns, R.B., Leung, M-C., Buchanan, L. & Cairns, B.D. (1995). Friendships and social networks in childhood and adolescence: fluidity, reliability, and interrelations. *Child Development,* 66, 1330–1345.

Cairns, R.B., Xie, H. & Leung, M-C. (1998). The popularity of friendship and the neglect of social networks: toward a new balance. In W. Bukowski & A. Cillessen (Eds), *Sociometry Then and Now* (New Directions for Child Development, no. 80) (pp. 25–53). San Francisco: Jossey-Bass.

Coie, J.D., Dodge, K.A. & Coppotelli, H. (1982). Dimensions and types of social status: a cross age perspective. *Developmental Psychology,* 18, 557–570.

Collins, W.A., Maccoby, E.E., Steinberg, L., Hetherington, E.M. & Bornstein, M.H. (2000). Contemporary research on parenting: the case for nature and nurture. *American Psychologist,* 55(2), 218–232.

Corsaro, W.A. (2003). *"We're Friends, Right?": Inside Kids' Culture.* Washington, DC: Joseph Henry Press.

Crick, N.R. & Dodge, K.A. (1994). A review and reformulation of social-information processing mechanisms in children's social adjustment. *Psychology Bulletin,* 115, 74–101.

Criss, M.M., Pettit, G.S., Bates, J.E., Dodge, K.A. & Lapp, A.L. (2002). Family adversity, positive peer relationships, and children's externalizing behavior: a longitudinal perspective on risk and resilience. *Child Development,* 73, 1220–1237.

Davies, B. (1982). *Life in the Classroom and the Playground: The Accounts of Primary School Children.* London: Routledge & Kegan Paul.

Demir, M. & Urberg, K. (2004). Friendship and adjustment among adolescents. *Journal of Experimental Child Psychology,* 88, 68–82.

Denham, S., Basset, H. & Wyatt, T. (2007). The socialisation of emotional competence. In J.E. Grusec & P.D. Hastings (Eds), *Handbook of Socialisation: Theory and Research* (pp. 614–637). New York: Guilford Press.

Dishion, T., Piehler, T. & Myers, M. (2008). Dynamics and ecology of adolescent peer influence. In M. Prinstein & K. Dodge (Eds), *Understanding Peer Influence in Children and Adolescents* (pp. 72–93). London: Guilford Press.

Dishion, T., Spracklen, K., Andrews, D. & Patterson, G. (1996). Deviancy training in male adolescent friendships. *Behavior Therapy*, 27, 373–390.

Dunn, J. (1993). *Young Children's Close Relationships: Beyond Attachment*. Newbury Park, CA: Sage.

Dunn, J. (2004). *Children's Friendships: The Beginnings of Intimacy*. Malden, MA: Blackwell.

Dunn, J. (2011). Mind-reading, emotion understanding and relationships. In M. Killen & R.J. Coplan (Eds), *Social Development in Childhood and Adolescence: A Contemporary Reader* (pp. 118–122). Chichester, UK: Wiley-Blackwell.

Dunn, J. & Cutting, A. (1999). Understanding others and individual differences in friendship interactions in young children. *Social Development*, 8, 201–219.

Eder, D. & Hallinan, M. (1978). Sex differences in children's friendships. *American Sociological Review*, 43, 237–250.

Elliott, D.S., Huizinga, D. & Ageton, S.S. (1985). *Explaining Delinquency and Drug Use*. Beverly Hills, CA: Sage.

Ellis, W.E. & Zarbatany, L. (2007). Peer group status as a moderator of group influence on children's deviant, aggressive and prosocial behaviour. *Child Development*, 78, 1240–1254.

Epstein, J.L. (1989). The selection of friends: changes across the grades and the different school environments. In T.J. Berndt & G.W. Ladd (Eds), *Peer Relationships in Child Development*. New York: Wiley.

Evangelou, M., Taggart, B., Sylva, K., Melhuish, E., Sammons, P. & Siraj-Blatchford, I. (2008). *Effective Pre-School, Primary and Secondary Education 3–14 Project (EPPSE 3–14). What Makes a Successful Transition from Primary to Secondary School? Research Report No. DCSF-RR019*. London: DCSF.

Farmer, T.W. & Rodkin, P. (1996). Antisocial and prosocial correlates of classroom social positions: the social network centrality perspective. *Social Development*, 5, 174–188.

Fletcher, A.C., Blair, B.L., Troutman, D.R. & Madison, K.J. (2013). Identifying children's friendships across diverse contexts: maternal and child perspectives. *Journal of Social and Personal Relationships*, 30, 858–880.

Foot, H., Chapman, A. & Smith, J. (1977). Friendship and social responsiveness in boys and girls. *Journal of Personality and Social Psychology*, 35, 401–411.

Fox, C. & Boulton, M. (2006). Friendship as a moderator of the relationship between social skills problems and peer victimisation. *Aggressive Behavior*, 32, 110–121.

Fredricks, J.A. & Simpkins, S.D. (2013). Organized out-of-school activities and peer relationships: theoretical perspectives and previous research. (Special issue on Organized out-of-school activities: settings for peer relationships.) *New Directions for Child and Adolescent Development*, 140, 1–17.

Freud, A. & Dann, S. (1951). An experiment in group upbringing. In R. Eissler, A. Freud, H. Hartmann & E. Kris (Eds), *The Psychoanalytic Study of the Child* (Vol. 6). New York: International Universities Press.

Gauze, C., Bukowski, W., Aquan-Asee, J. & Sippola, L. (1996). Interactions between family environment and friendship and associations with self-perceived well-being during early adolescence. *Child Development*, 67, 2201–2216.

Gershman, E. & Hayes, D. (1983). Differential stability of reciprocal friendships and unilateral relationships among preschool children. *Merrill-Palmer Quarterly*, 29, 169–177.

Gest, S.D. (2006). Teacher reports of children's friendships and social groups: agreement with peer reports and implications for studying peer similarity. *Social Development*, 15, 248–259.

Gest, S.D., Graham-Bermann, S.A. & Hartup, W.W. (2001). Peer experience: common and unique features of number of friendships, social network centrality, and sociometric status. *Social Development*, 10, 23–40.

Gifford-Smith, M. & Brownell, C. (2003). Childhood peer relationships: social acceptance, friendships, and peer networks. *Journal of School Psychology*, 41, 235–284.

Giordano, P., Cernkovich, S., Groat, H., Pugh, M. & Swinford, S. (1998). The quality of adolescent friendships: long–term effects? *Journal of Health and Social Behaviour*, 39(1), 55–71.

Gottman, J. (1983). How children become friends. *Monographs of the Society for Research in Child Development*, 48(2) (Serial No. 201).

Granic, I. & Dishion, T.J. (2003). Deviant talk in adolescent friendships: a step toward measuring a pathogenic attractor process. *Social Development*, 12, 314–334.

Hallinan, M.T. (1979). Structural effects on children's friendships and cliques. *Social Psychology Quarterly*, 42, 43–54.

Hallinan, M.T. & Sorenson, A.B. (1983). The formation and stability of instructional groups. *American Sociological Review*, 48, 838–851.

Hargreaves, D.H. (1967). *Social Relations in a Secondary School*. London: Routledge & Kegan Paul.

Hargreaves, L. & Galton, M. (2002). *Transfer from the Primary Classroom: 20 Years on*. London: Routledge-Falmer.

Harlow, H. (1969). Age-mate or peer affectional system. In Lehrman, D.S. (Ed.), *Advances in the Study of Behaviour* (Vol. 2). New York: Academic Press.

Harlow, H. & Harlow, M. (1965). Effects of various mother–infant relationships on Rhesus monkey behaviours. In B.M. Foss (Ed.), *Determinants of Infant Behaviour IV*. London: Methuen.

Harris, J.R. (1995). Where is the child's environment? A group socialisation theory of development. *Psychological Review*, 102, 458–489.

Hartup, W.W. (1983). Peer relations. In P.H. Mussen & E.M. Hetherington (Eds), *Handbook of Child Psychology* (Vol. 4). Socialization, personality and social development (pp. 103–196). New York: Wiley.

Hartup, W.W. (1992). Friendships and their developmental significance. In H. McGurk (Ed.), *Childhood Social Development: Contemporary Perspectives*. Hove, UK: Lawrence Erlbaum Associates.

Hartup, W.W. (1996). The company they keep: friendships and their developmental significance. *Child Development*, 67, 1–13.

Hartup, W.W. (1999). Constraints on peer socialization: Let me count the ways. *Merrill-Palmer Quarterly*, 45, 172–183.

Hartup, W.W. (2009). Critical issues and theoretical viewpoints. In K.H. Rubin, W.M. Bukowski & B. Laursen (Eds), *Handbook of Peer Interactions, Relationships and Groups* (pp. 3–19). New York: Guilford Press.

Hartup, W.W., Laursen, B., Stewart, M.I. & Eastenson, A. (1988). Conflict and the friendship relations of young children. *Child Development*, 59, 1590–1600.

Heilbron, N. & Prinstein, M.J. (2008). Peer influence and adolescent nonsuicidal self-injury: a theoretical review of mechanisms and moderators. *Applied and Preventive Psychology*, 12, 169–177.

Howe, C. (2010). *Peer Groups and Children's Development*. Oxford: Blackwell.

Howe, C. & McWilliam, D. (2006). Opposition in social interaction between children: why intellectual benefits do not mean social costs. *Social Development*, 15, 205–231.

Howes, C. (1988). Peer interaction of young children. *Monographs of the Society for Research in Child Development*, 53(1) (Serial No. 217).

Howes, C. (2009). Friendship in early childhood. In K.H. Rubin, W.M. Bukowski & B. Laursen (Eds), *Handbook of Peer Interactions, Relationships and Groups* (pp. 180–194). New York: Guilford Press.

Howes, C., Hamilton, C. & Philipsen, L. (1998). Stability and continuity of child-caregiver and child peer relationships. *Child Development,* 69, 418–426.

Howes, C. & Lee, L. (2006). Peer relations in young children. In L. Balter & C. Tamis-LeMonda (Eds), *Child Psychology: A Handbook of Contemporary Issues* (pp. 135–152). Hove, UK: Psychology Press.

Hymel, S., Rubin, K.H., Rowden, L. & LeMare, L. (1990). Children's peer relationships: longitudinal predictions of internalizing and externalizing problems from middle to late childhood. *Child Development,* 61, 2004–2021.

Juvonen, J. & Galván, A. (2008). Peer influence in involuntary peer social groups: lessons from research on bullying. In M. Prinstein & K. Dodge (Eds), *Understanding Peer Influence in Children and Adolescents* (pp. 225–244). London: Guilford Press.

Kandel, D. (1978). Homophily, selection, and socialization in adolescent friendships. *American Journal of Sociology,* 84, 427–436.

Kerns, K., Cole, A.K. & Andrews, P.B. (1998). Attachment security, parent peer management practices and peer relationships in preschool. *Merrill-Palmer Quarterly,* 44, 504–522.

Kindermann, T.A. (2007). Effects of naturally existing peer groups on changes in academic engagement in a cohort of sixth graders. *Child Development,* 78, 1186–1203.

Kindermann, T.A., McCollam, T.L. & Metzler, B. (1996). A composite social-cognitive map of natural peer group networks in a cohort of 6th graders. Poster presented at the ISSBD conference, Quebec, Canada.

Kindermann, T.A. & Valsiner, J. (1995). *Development of Person-Context Relations.* Hillsdale, NJ: Erlbaum.

Ladd, G.W. (1990). Having friends, keeping friends, making friends and being liked by peers in the classroom: predictors of children's early school adjustment. *Child Development,* 61, 1081–1100.

Ladd, G.W. (2005). *Children's Peer Relations and Social Competence: A Century of Progress,* New Haven, CT: Yale University Press.

Ladd, G.W. & Burgess, K. (1999). Charting the relationship trajectories of aggressive, withdrawn, and aggressive/withdrawn children during early grade school. *Child Development,* 70, 910–929.

Ladd, G.W., Kochenderfer, B.J. & Coleman, C.C. (1996). Friendship quality as a predictor of young children's early school adjustment. *Child Development,* 67, 1103–1118.

Ladd, G.W., Kochenderfer, B.J. & Coleman, C.C. (1997). Classroom peer acceptance, friendship, victimization: distinct relational systems that contribute uniquely to children's school adjustment? *Child Development,* 68, 1181–1197.

Ladd, G.W. & Troop-Gordon, W. (2003). The role of chronic peer difficulties in the development of children's psychological adjustment problems. *Child Development,* 74, 1344–1367.

Laursen, B., Finkelstein, B. & Betts, N. (2001). A developmental meta-analysis of peer conflict resolution. *Developmental Review,* 21, 423–449.

Maassen, G.H., van Boxtel, H.W. & Goossens, F.A. (2005). Reliability of nomination and two-dimensional rating scale methods for sociometric status determination. *Journal of Applied Developmental Psychology,* 26, 51–68.

Maccoby, E.E. (1998). *The Two Sexes: Growing Up Apart, Coming Together.* London: Harvard University Press.

Maguire, M. & Dunn, J. (1997). Friendships in early childhood, and social understanding. *International Journal of Behavioral Development,* 21, 669–686.

Majors, K. (2010). Friendships: the power of positive alliance. In S. Roffey (Ed.), *Positive Relationships: Evidence Based Practice Across the World* (pp. 127–143). London: Springer.

Mathieson, K. & Banerjee, R. (2011). Peer play, emotion understanding, and socio-moral explanation: the role of gender. *British Journal of Developmental Psychology,* 29, 188–196.

Maxwell, W. (1990). The nature of friendship in the primary school. In C. Rogers & P. Kutnick (Eds), *The Social Psychology of the Primary School.* London: Routledge.

Moreno, J. (1934). *Who Shall Survive? A New Approach to the Problem of Human Interrelations.* Washington DC: Nervous and Mental Disease Publishing Co.

Mouttapa, M., Valente, T., Gallaher, P., Rohrbach, L. & Unger, J. (2004). Social network predictors of bullying and victimization. *Adolescence,* 39(154), 315–335.

Nangle, D., Erdley, C., Newman, J., Mason, C. & Carpenter, E. (2003). Popularity, friendship quantity, and friendship quality: interactive influences on children's loneliness and depression. *Journal of Clinical Child and Adolescent Psychology,* 32, 546–555.

Neal, J.W., Cappella, E., Wagner, C. & Atkins, M.S. (2011). Seeing eye to eye: predicting teacher-student agreement on classroom social networks. *Social Development,* 20, 376–393.

Newcomb, A.F. & Bagwell, C.L. (1996). The developmental significance of children's friendship relations. In W. Bukowski, W. Newcomb & W. Hartup (Eds), *The Company They Keep: Friendship in Childhood and Adolescence.* Cambridge: Cambridge University Press.

Newcomb, A.F. & Brady, J.E. (1982). Mutuality in boys' friendship relations. *Child Development,* 53, 392–395.

Olweus, D. (1993). *Bullying at School: What We Know and What We Can Do.* Oxford: Blackwell.

Parker, J.G. & Asher, S.R. (1987). Peer relations and later personal adjustment: are low-accepted children at risk? *Psychological Bulletin,* 102, 357–389.

Parker, J.G. & Asher, S.R. (1993). Friendship and friendship quality in middle childhood: links with peer group acceptance and feelings of loneliness and social dissatisfaction. *Developmental Psychology,* 29, 611–621.

Parker, J.G. & Gottman, J.M. (1989). Social and emotional development in a relational context: friendship interaction from early childhood to adolescence. In T.J. Berndt & G.W. Ladd (Eds), *Peer Relationships in Child Development.* New York: Wiley.

Parkhurst, J.T. & Hopmeyer, A. (1998). Sociometric popularity and peer-perceived popularity: two distinct dimensions of peer status. *Journal of Early Adolescence,* 18, 125–144.

Pedersen, S., Vitaro, F., Barker, E. & Borge, A. (2007). The timing of middle childhood peer rejection and friendships: linking early behaviours to adolescent adjustment. *Child Development,* 78, 1037–1051.

Pellegrini, A. & Blatchford, P. (2002). The developmental and educational significance of breaktime in school. *The Psychologist,* 15, 59–62.

Pellegrini, A., Kato, K., Blatchford, P. & Baines, E. (2002). A short-term longitudinal study of children's playground games across the first year of school: implications for social competence and adjustment to school. *American Educational Research Journal,* 39, 991–1016.

Pilgrim, C., Luo, Q., Urberg, K.A. & Fang, X.Y. (1999). Influence of peers, parents, and individual characteristics on adolescent drug use in two cultures. *Merrill-Palmer Quarterly,* 45, 85–107.

Poulin, F., Dishion, T. & Haas, E. (1999). The peer influence paradox: friendship quality and deviancy training within male adolescent friendships. *Merrill-Palmer Quarterly,* 45, 42–61.

Prinstein, M.J. & Dodge, K.A. (2008). Current issues in peer influence research. In M.J. Prinstein and K.A. Dodge (Eds), *Understanding Peer Influence in Children and Adolescents.* New York: Guilford Press.

Robinson, T. (2013). Exploring the narratives of African Caribbean high attaining boys: perceived peer influences in education. Unpublished Doctoral (DEdPsy) thesis, Institute of Education, University of London.

Rodkin, P. & Hanish, L. (2007). Social network analysis and children's peer relationships. *New Directions for Child and Adolescent Development,* 118.

Rose, A. (2002). Co-rumination in the friendships of girls and boys. *Child Development,* 73, 1830–1843.

Rose, A. & Asher, S. (1999). Children's goals and strategies in response to conflicts within friendship. *Developmental Psychology,* 35, 69–79.

Rose, A., Carlson, W. & Waller, E. (2007). Prospective associations of co-rumination with friendship and emotional adjustment: considering the socioemotional trade-offs of co-rumination. *Developmental Psychology,* 43, 1019–1031.

Rose, J.S., Chassin, L., Presson, C.C. & Sherman, S.J. (1999). Peer influences on adolescent cigarette smoking: a prospective sibling analysis. *Merrill-Palmer Quarterly,* 45, 62–84.

Rubin, K.H., Bowker, J. McDonald, K. & Menzer, M. (2013). Peer relationships in childhood. In P.D. Zelazo (Ed.), *The Oxford Handbook of Developmental Psychology, Vol. 2: Self and Other.* Oxford: Oxford University Press.

Rubin, K.H., Bukowski, W. & Parker, J.G. (2006). Peer interactions, relationships, and groups. In W. Damon, R.M. Lerner & N. Eisenberg (Eds), *Handbook of Child Psychology: Vol. 3, Social, Emotional, and Personality Development* (6th edn). New York: Wiley.

Rubin, K.H., Wojslawowicz, J.C., Rose-Krasnor, L., Booth-LaForce, C. & Burgess, K.B. (2006). The best friendships of shy/withdrawn children. *Journal of Abnormal Child Psychology,* 34, 143–157.

Ryan, A. (2001). The peer group as a context for the development of young adolescent motivation and achievement. *Child Development,* 72, 1135–1150.

Saarni, C. (2008). The interface of emotional development with social context. In M. Lewis, J. Haviland-Jones & L. Barrett (Eds), *Handbook of Emotions* (3rd edn). New York: Guilford Press.

Salmivalli, C. (2010). Bullying and the peer group: a review. *Aggression and Violent Behavior,* 15, 112–120.

Schneider, B.H. (2000). *Friends and Enemies: Peer Relations in Childhood.* London: Arnold.

Schulenberg, J., Maggs, J.L., Dielman, T.E., Leech, S.L., Kloska, D.D., Shope, J.T. & Laetz, V.B. (1999). On peer influences to get drunk: a panel study of young adolescents. *Merrill-Palmer Quarterly,* 45, 108–142.

Schwartz, D., Gorman, A.H., Dodge, K.A., Pettit, G.S. & Bates, J.E. (2008). Friendships with peers who are low or high in aggression as moderators of the link between peer victimization and declines in academic functioning. *Journal of Abnormal Child Psychology,* 36(5), 719–730.

Selman, R. (1980). *The Growth of Interpersonal Understanding: Developmental and Clinical Analyses.* New York: Academic Press.

Shaw, B., Watson, B., Frauendienst, B., Redecker, A., Jones, T., with Hillman, M. (2013). *Children's Independent Mobility: A Comparative Study in England and Germany (1971 to*

2010). Policy Studies Institute, London. Retrieved 5 February 2013 from: www.psi.org.
uk/images/uploads/Briefing-Childrens_Independent_Mobility_v4_3.pdf.

Sijtsema, J.J., Rambaran, J.A. & Ojanen, T.J. (2013). Overt and relational victimization and
adolescent friendships: selection, de-selection, and social influence. *Social Influence,* 8,
177–195.

Simpkins, J., Parke, R., Flyr, M. & Wild, M. (2006). Similarities in children's and early
adolescents' perceptions of friendship qualities across development, gender and
friendship qualities. *Journal of Early Adolescence,* 26, 491–508.

Snyder, J., Schrepferman, L., Oeser, J., Patterson, G., Stoolmiller, M., Johnson K. & Snyder,
A. (2005). Deviancy training and association with deviant peers in young children:
occurrence and contribution to early-onset conduct problems. *Development and
Psychopathology,* 17, 397–413.

Solomon, D., Watson, M., Delucchi, K., Schaps, E. & Battistich, V. (1988). Enhancing
children's prosocial behavior in the classroom. *American Educational Research Journal,*
25, 527–554.

Starr, L. & Davila, J. (2009). Clarifying co-rumination: associations with internalizing
symptoms and romantic involvement among adolescent girls. *Journal of Adolescence,* 32,
19–38.

Sullivan, H.S. (1953). *The Interpersonal Theory of Psychiatry.* New York: Norton.

Thorne, B. (1993) *Gender Play: Girls and Boys in School,* Buckingham: Open University
Press.

Tokunaga, R.S. (2010). Following you home from school: a critical review and synthesis
of research on cyberbullying victimization. *Computers in Human Behavior,* 26,
277–287.

Vandell, D. & Mueller, E. (1980). Peer play and friendships during the first two years.
In H. Foot, A. Chapman & J. Smith (Eds), *Friendship and Social Relations in Children*
(pp. 191–208). London: Wiley.

Vitaro, F., Boivin, M. & Bukowski, W.M. (2009). The role of friendship in child and
adolescent psychosocial development. In K.H. Rubin, W.M. Bukowski & B. Laursen
(Eds), *Handbook of Peer Interactions, Relationships and Groups* (pp. 568–588). New York:
Guilford Press.

Vitaro, F., Tremblay, R., Kerr, M., Pagani, L. & Bukowski, W.M. (1997). Disruptiveness,
friends' characteristics, and delinquency in early adolescence: a test of two competing
models of development. *Child Development,* 68, 676–689.

Wentzel, K. (1991). Relations between social competence and academic achievement in
early adolescence. *Child Development,* 62, 1066–1078.

Wentzel, K. & Caldwell, K. (1997). Friendships, peer acceptance and group membership:
relations to academic achievement in middle school. *Child Development,* 68,
1198–1209.

Youniss, J. (1980). *Parents and Peers in Social Development: A Sullivan-Piaget Perspective.*
Chicago: University of Chicago Press.

Zajac, R.J. & Hartup, W.W. (1997). Friends as coworkers: research review and classroom
implications. *The Elementary School Journal,* 98, 3–13.

Zarbatany, L., McDougall, P. & Hymel, S. (2000). Gender-differentiated experience in
the peer culture: links to intimacy in preadolescence. *Social Development,* 9, 62–79.

4

CHILDREN'S PLAY

Introduction

The study of play has long been of interest to developmental psychologists (e.g., Piaget, 1962) as well as scholars from a variety of disciplines – from anthropology (e.g., Bock, 2005; Lancy, 1996), through education, history (e.g., Cross & Walton, 2005), philosophy (Schiller, 1795/1967), psychology (Smith, 1982, 2009; Sutton-Smith, 1997) to zoology (e.g., Burghardt, 2005). In keeping with this diverse interest, scholars' assessments as to what constitutes play and what, if any, purpose it serves also vary. For example, some students of play suggest it is impossible to define (e.g., Wilson, 1975) while others have attempted to empirically validate dimensions of play behaviour (e.g., Smith & Vollstedt, 1985).

Correspondingly, hypotheses about functions of play also encompass the spectrum. Some behavioural psychologists (e.g., Scholsberg, 1947) have suggested that the construct was so unimportant that it should be relegated to the trash bin of science. At the other end of the continuum, some students of children's play (e.g., Singer, Golinkoff & Hirsch-Pasek, 2006) posit that children's play has benefits in a wide variety of social, emotional, and cognitive areas. A more middling, though sceptical, position has been taken by Martin and Caro (1985) who suggest that the value of play is probably minimal, given the relatively weak empirical connection between play and functions in a variety of species.

In this chapter we propose a definition of play. We then describe the ontogeny of locomotor, object, social, and pretend play, and also examine possible functions of each. We will argue that some forms of play do indeed serve a function, especially during childhood, and may, in fact, be at the vanguard of phylogenetic change.

What is play?

Virtually all students of play acknowledge the difficulty of trying to define it (e.g., Burghardt, 2005; Fagen, 1981; Wilson, 1975). Indicative of this problem is the fact that the term 'play' is often used to label most forms of children's social and nonsocial behaviour, regardless of whether it meets operational definitions of play. From this position, virtually anything that children do can be defined as play. For example, Mildred Parten (1932) in her seminal work categorized children's social participation as solitary *play*, parallel *play*, and cooperative *play* (all our emphases), which could include forms of peer interaction that might not be play, according to many operational definitions. Labelling the social behaviour of preschool children as 'play' continues to the present; for example, describing as 'play' the social interaction in sex-segregated peer groups (e.g., Fabes et al., 2003).

The explicit efforts made to define play (Burghardt, 2005; Wilson, 1975) have been contentious, akin to encountering a 'hornets' nest' (Bekoff & Byers, 1981). For example, Robert Fagen (1981), in his important volume, *Animal Play Behaviour*, has a five-page appendix listing definitions and criteria of play. In the child development literature a list of play attributes has also been proffered by Rubin and colleagues (1983) in their *Handbook of Child Psychology* chapter on play. Specifically, they defined play according to Piagetian-based observable behaviours (functional, symbolic, and games), dispositional attributes (intrinsic motivation, attention to means over ends, differentiation between play and exploration, relation to instrumental behaviour, freedom from external rules, and active engagement), and context (familiarity, free choice, minimal adult intrusion, and stress-free).

Rubin and colleagues further suggested that behaviours should not be treated categorically, as either play or not play, but instead continuously, from more to less playful, depending on the number of criteria met. The more criteria met, the more playful the behaviour, which implicitly assumes that all attributes have equal weight in contributing to playful behaviour. For example, a behaviour meeting four criteria (e.g., free choice, stress-free, freedom from external rules, and minimal adult intrusion) should be more playful than a behaviour meeting three criteria (e.g., non-instrumental, symbolic, and attention to means). The four-criteria behaviour might characterize a child taking a nap while the three-criteria behaviour could involve a child using a pencil as a rocket ship. Most observers would consider the second example to be play and the first not, despite the difference in the number of criteria met.

A more principled approach to defining play has been advanced by Burghardt (1984, 2005), a long-time student of play. Rather than taking a continuous approach, Burghardt views play more categorically, suggesting that there are core criteria, all of which must be present, for a behaviour to be categorized as play: the behaviour must be voluntary, observed in a 'relaxed field', the behaviour is not functional in the observed context, the behaviours are repeated but the behavioural elements are exaggerated, segmented, and non-sequential in relation to the functional behaviour. A relaxed field is one where the individual is safe, healthy, and well fed. Further, the child should choose to, voluntarily, engage in some social, locomotor, fantasy, or object-directed activity that is not directly or immediately functional, such as engaging in a wrestling bout whose function is not to hurt or defeat his/her peer. The nature and sequence of these behaviours would not resemble those in a functional context. For example, the child would use an exaggerated 'play face' to announce playful intent as he approaches a peer and in the course of wrestling the players would switch roles. These criteria can be realized in the four domains of play: locomotor (e.g., rolling down a hill), object (e.g., piling blocks in different configurations), social (e.g., play-fighting), and pretend (e.g., enacting domestic roles). Further, each of these domains, with the obvious exception of social play, can be either social or solitary

The voluntary component of this definition of play provides the motivation necessary for children to persevere at an activity, trying out a variety of behavioural routines where the means-over-ends, non-functional criterion has children not being concerned with doing something 'right', resulting in behaviours that are typically more exaggerated, non-sequential, and segmented, relative to their functional variants. From this definition, play behaviours are not imperfect attempts to copy, or accommodate to, functional behaviours but are instead creative, or behaviourally flexible, encounters with their worlds. (See the Piaget, 1962 and Sutton-Smith, 1966 debate on this point.) The behavioural flexibility characteristic of play, we suggest, is, in turn, crucial for the functional importance of play.

Antecedent conditions and gender differences

The structural aspects of children's play, such as exaggerated and segmented motor patterns, are remarkably similar to those of other primates, most notably, great apes (Lewis & Barton, 2006; Wrangham, 1987). Given this homology, we examine both distal (phylogenetic past) and proximal (hormonal and socialization events) antecedents of play, in order to maximize our understanding of this nettlesome construct (Tinbergen, 1963).

This continuity in social behaviour between great apes, especially chimpanzees, and humans may be due to similarities in the social organization of both species, especially that females migrate from their natal group and males take on multiple mates (exogamy) (Wrangham, 1987). This social organization results in males, relative to females, being more competitive and aggressive and having peer groups organized hierarchically in terms of social dominance. These effects, in turn, are translated into differences in male and female hormonal events that further differentiate boys' and girls' nervous systems, brains, and morphology. Androgens are especially important in predisposing males, more than females, to be physically larger, active, competitive, and physically aggressive (Hines & Shipley, 1984; Pellegrini, 2004). These hormonal events, in turn, are related to the size of the amygdala (Lewis & Barton, 2006), which plays an important role in enabling individuals to recognize and generate emotional displays of the sort used to mark play bouts. Prenatal hormonal events differentiate males' and females' brains and nervous systems and are also implicated in their morphology and social behaviour, with males, generally, being physically bigger, stronger, more active, and more competitive (Pellegrini & Archer, 2005). These differences are important precursors to children's segregation into same-sex peer groups (Pellegrini, 2004; Pellegrini et al., 2007) where their sex roles and associated behaviours get socialized through play in sex-segregated peer groups. For example, boys' play is not only more physically active than that of girls but their play themes are more quasi-agonistic and competitive (Pellegrini, 2004). By contrast, girls' groups are less active and typically involve enactment of domestic themes and are less competitive (Garvey, 1990; Pellegrini et al., 2007).

Though these early biological differences are important in children's social sex segregation (e.g., Campbell & Eaton, 1999; Martin & Fabes, 2001), sex-role socialization practices may moderate the role of physical activity in segregation and peer play. For example, according to Eagly (1997), male roles in contemporary society, relative to females', are higher status, so males may be more reluctant to integrate than girls. Girls, on the other hand, are more willing than boys to interact with opposite-sex peers because of boys' relatively higher status. By extension, individual differences within each sex and differing socialization events impact sex segregation (Fabes, 1994; Maccoby & Jacklin, 1987; Pellegrini et al., 2007). That is, some boys and girls are more or less active than their same-sex peers and these differences impact their sex segregation. Highly active children of both sexes are biased to interact with each other relatively early in the history of group formation because of behavioural compatibility (Bohn-Gettler et al., 2010; Pellegrini et al., 2007; Ruckstuhl, 1998; Serbin et al., 1994) but this bias changes, with time, due to socialization pressure.

Our research supports this claim (Bohn-Gettler et al., 2010; Pellegrini et al., 2007). Specifically, we examined the interaction between socialization and activity bias by observing children in their preschool classrooms across one academic year and found that boys' and girls' peer groups were generally segregated. However, segregation was affected by the sex of the child and their trait-like levels of physical activity as well as time of the year. Specifically, boys at all levels of physical activity remained at relatively stable levels of segregation across the duration of the school year. That high and low activity boys' level of segregation was stable is consistent with social role theory, which suggests generally that higher status adult roles relate to the differential treatment of males and females (Eagly, 1997). Thus, boys interacted with each other, rather than with girls, because of their relatively high status and girls' low status.

In short, biological and socialization events shape children's social and play behaviour, in the context of sexually segregated peer groups. In these segregated groups, children enact play themes that have both immediate and deferred benefits.

Different models of the function of play: deferred, immediate, and both deferred and immediate benefits

The putative beneficial consequences, or functions, of play can be staggering. For some psychologists, play is said to benefit children's early literacy, self-regulation, mathematics, uses of technology, and emotion learning (e.g., Singer et al., 2006). Function, for biologists, means something much more specific – it means adaptive functioning and naturally selected benefits associated with reproductive fitness and survival (Burghardt, 2005; Tinbergen, 1963). Following Darwin's theory of evolution by natural selection, evolutionary biologists examine how behaviours and strategies at different periods during individuals' life histories are either favoured or not favoured by natural selection. A behaviour or strategy will be favoured by natural selection, and be functional, if the associated benefits outweigh associated costs (Martin & Caro, 1985). Existence of costs, from this position, is also evidence of function.

Biologists also note that natural selection operates on all periods of development – not only adulthood (Martin & Caro, 1985). Consequently, it is important to view children's play as integral, and functional, to the juvenile period, not only as beneficial to some mature variant of that behaviour. To this end evolutionary biologists typically examine the relative costs and benefits associated with play with regards to growth and maintenance during childhood (Stearns, 1992) and the ways in which different strategies maximize benefits and minimize costs, at all periods of development. If, for example, one is concerned with the function of preschool boys' social play and its relation to their social dominance, we probably should not be immediately concerned with its role in reproductive behaviour as they are many years from sexual maturity. Instead, we might look at the costs of the behaviours associated with social play, such as the caloric expenditure, and the benefits associated with the growth of muscular and skeletal systems during the juvenile period (Byers & Walker, 1995; Pellegrini, 2008). The development of muscular and skeletal systems during the juvenile period should, in turn, be related to survival and later reproductive success.

In short, putative benefits of play can be deferred until maturity, as proposed by most theories of play (e.g., Piaget, 1962), or more immediate to the period during which they are observed (e.g., Bateson, 2005), or serve both immediate and deferred benefits (Pellegrini, 2009). In this section, we review three models of play: play serving deferred, immediate, and both immediate and deferred functions. Most generally, we propose that play during childhood may afford opportunities to develop behavioural flexibility.

Play serving deferred benefits

The classical view of play is that it is practice for adulthood. For example, Piaget's (1962, 1983) view of development was that young children's behaviour and thought were imperfect variants of adult operational thought. Play, from this view, is a form of 'autistic' thought by which children can assimilate new information into extant cognitive structures, with the goal of progressing towards mature, operational thought. This orientation of play as practice for adulthood goes back to at least Groos (1901) and has been restated in the contemporary developmental (Smith, 1982, 2009) and ethological (Fagen, 1981) literatures. While this view assumes that play during the juvenile period has no immediate purpose, it does afford individuals opportunity to master and practise in play those behaviours and skills associated with their more functional variants. This has been labelled the 'conventional' model of play (Martin & Caro, 1985).

One can conceive of the development of play in terms of one trajectory for the development of a serious behaviour with play and one trajectory for development without play. The two trajectories co-occur during childhood and the behaviours/skills developed in play during childhood may lead to improved serious behaviour at maturity. For example, the skills learned and developed in rough-and-tumble play during childhood, such as learning to land accurate blows, avoid attacks, and recognize dominant as well as subordinate conspecifics, will be useful in adult, serious fighting (Smith, 1982). Juveniles who engage in rough-and-tumble play should, as adults, be better fighters, relative to those who did not engage in rough-and-tumble play as juveniles (though see Sharpe, 2006 for counter evidence). Pat Bateson (1981) has characterized this as a 'scaffolding' model of play: play is used in the assembly of a skill, such as fighting, and when it is completed, the scaffolding is removed. It is an example of a behaviour being used in development (Bateson, 1976). There are, however, few data supporting the deferred benefits of play model (e.g., Martin & Caro, 1985; Sharpe, 2006).

Postponing benefits until adulthood for costs borne during childhood can be, however, very risky. The time from birth to maturity and adulthood is rife with survivorship risks, such as accidental death and loss of thermoregulation and nutrition. The high rates of mortality in play-related contexts, such as drowning, during infancy and childhood, relative to later in life, are a testament to these risks (National Vital Statistic Report, 2004). Given these risks, behavioural ecological theory predicts that a deferred benefits model would not be observed in all subsistence and more severe ecologies (Blurton Jones, 1993). In more abundant and safe ecologies, there are fewer survivorship risks, relative to more severe niches, and a higher likelihood of reaping deferred benefits; thus, costs associated with play in these contexts should be higher, as is the case in most industrial societies today.

Play serving immediate benefits

In contrast to the more common conventional, deferred benefit model, an immediate benefits model of play (Martin & Caro, 1985) posits that the benefits of play are reaped at that period during which the costs are incurred. In further contrast with the conventional model, the immediate benefits model posits that the play behaviours observed during the juvenile period are beneficial to the niche of childhood, specifically; they are not imperfect variants of adult behaviour (Bekoff, 1978; Bjorklund & Green, 1992). Bateson (1981) has labelled this the 'metamorphic' view of play: Play is beneficial to the juvenile period, but not beyond.

A case can be made for the immediate benefits of pretend play, such that pretence in childhood should increase children's efficacy associated with enacted social roles (Bjorklund & Green, 1992). For example, pretending to be a powerful adult or a superhero may afford opportunities for children to try out a number of different roles that, in reality, are not available to them. It is also probably the case that play during childhood affords specific opportunities associated with behavioural flexibility. For example, enacting pretend and social roles from a variety of perspectives leads to social problem-solving flexibility (Pellegrini, 1992) as well as the ability to take a variety of social perspectives (Burns & Brainerd, 1979).

Both immediate and deferred benefits: play and the role of behavioural flexibility in phylogeny

Behavioural plasticity in the expression of genotype is correlated with the variety of environments that a species inhabits (Hollander, 2008) – the more varied, the more plastic the expression. That humans, and a variety of other primates, are dispersed into incredibly varied niches suggests that their behavioural repertoires too should be varied if they are to adapt to those niches. Play during the juvenile period may be one strategy used to develop such a repertoire. Scholars from psychology (e.g., Bruner, 1972; Sutton-Smith, 1997; Pellegrini, 2013) and biology (e.g., Bateson, 2005; Burghardt, 2005; Fagen, 1981) have posited links between play and creative responses to the environment for over forty years. The role of play in the development of innovation was formalized by Špinka and colleagues (2001) in their 'training for the unexpected hypothesis'. The gist of the hypothesis is that in the safe context of play, characteristic of species with an extended juvenile period, animals place themselves into unconventional and often disorienting positions. These novel behavioural situations afford opportunity for them to experiment with a variety of routines in relatively safe circumstances and generate novel, and possibly adaptive, responses to their environments. With repeated play experiences, individuals become facile at enlisting these processes and thus they become more accessible in times of need, such as during an emergency.

We suggest that because play affords opportunities for the generation of new responses to novel environments, it is an excellent candidate as an exemplar of behaviour affecting evolutionary processes, what Bateson (2005) calls the 'adaptability' driver. The position that experiences during ontogeny affect phylogeny is broadly derived from theory dating back to Spalding (1873, cited in Bateson, 2005), Baldwin (1896) and the 'Baldwin Effect', and Lloyd Morgan

(1896). More recently epigenetic theory has been advanced to formalize the ways in which genes and the environment affect each other, suggesting that immature organisms, especially, are responsive to environmental perturbations and adjust their behaviours in response to these changes (Bateson & Gluckman, 2011; Gottlieb, 1998). The importance of play in impacting evolution relates to it being a relatively low-cost way in which to develop alternative responses to new and challenging environments (Bateson, 2005; Burghardt, 2005; Fagen, 1981). By 'low cost' we mean one that has low risk and is likely to be incorporated into the behavioural repertoire and eventually into the genotype. Specifically, it is probably less costly, and consequently more likely to spread through the population if it is accomplished in childhood through play (Bateson, 2005; Burghardt, 2005). Organisms, especially complex ones like humans, are especially sensitive to environmental perturbations early in development. Novel behavioural responses to these environments lead them to develop new, and more flexible, phenotypes, than less flexible conspecifics.

During infancy, mothers afford opportunities to learn and develop new phenotypes (Bjorklund, 2006), as demonstrated in Suomi's research with nonhuman primates (2005). During the juvenile period, this is likely to occur through peer play (Suomi & Harlow, 1972). That play during periods of immaturity is less costly than other strategies during other periods of development is predicated on organisms having surplus resources, such as being provisioned and protected (Burghardt, 2005). These conditions afford opportunities to develop novel behaviours early in ontogeny and these new behaviours, in turn, influence subsequent development. The ease (or low cost) with which play spreads through the population should be related to it being naturally selected. Innovative behaviours associated with play during the juvenile period should be especially prone to this process because of the protection and provisioning associated with play during the juvenile period. Later periods in development are not typically characterized by 'surplus resources' (Burghardt, 2005); thus at these stages of the life cycle, play would be less effective in skill learning than a more direct strategy, such as observational learning.

In each of the sections below, we will first describe four different forms of play (locomotor, social, object, and fantasy) and then proffer both immediate and deferred benefits for each, with specific reference to behavioural flexibility.

Different forms of play: locomotor, object, social, and pretend

Locomotor play

Locomotor play, like other forms of play, is multi-dimensional and may have a symbolic dimension, as in the case of boys enacting a superhero theme involving running, chasing, and jumping, and a social/solitary dimension (Pellegrini, 2009). The distinguishing behavioural features of locomotor play are a playful orientation (i.e., non-instrumental and a means-over-ends orientation) combined with a moderate to vigorous physical activity (Pellegrini & Smith, 1998). In this chapter, unlike in some of our earlier work (Pellegrini & Smith, 1998), we no longer consider rough-and-tumble a type of locomotor play. Instead rough-and-tumble will be treated as social play, as it has been by behavioural biologists (e.g., Fagen, 1981) and anthropologists (e.g., Fry, 2005). Like most forms of play, rough-and-tumble is multifaceted and can have object, locomotor and social dimensions, yet it is primarily social. Further, we label the form of play under discussion in this section as 'locomotor play', not physical activity, as we have in the past (Pellegrini & Smith, 1998). This re-labelling is an effort to keep labels in the human and behavioural biology literatures consistent.

Locomotor play, like all other forms of play, follows an inverted-U developmental course. It begins in early infancy, peaks during childhood, then declines during adolescence and more rapidly in adulthood (Fagen, 1981). The trends in locomotor play in humans appear to show two successive peaks, reflecting two types of locomotor play, probably with different functions: rhythmic stereotypies and exercise play (Pellegrini & Smith, 1998). In this chapter we discuss only exercise play as it is characteristic of school-age children.

Exercise play

By 'exercise play' we mean gross locomotor movements in the context of play, such as functionless swinging, jumping/climbing, splashing and swimming, marked by positive affect; it can be solitary or social, with parents or peers. In fact, much of the research on parent–infant play does not distinguish between exercise play and rough-and-tumble, as in the case of describing 'rough physical play' (e.g., Roopnarine et al., 1993). Unlike rough-and-tumble, it can be solitary and when it is social, exercise play does not involve fight-like motor patterns.

Relatively low rates of American parent–infant physical play have been reported by MacDonald and Parke (1984), with rates peaking at around 4 years of age. A few cases of infant exercise play without parents have been reported. Konner (1972), for example, reported that the !Kung, a one-time foraging group in Africa, encouraged infants to chase after and catch large insects.

Exercise play with peers increases from the toddler to preschool period and then declines during the primary school years, with a likely peak at around 4 to 5 years. Specifically, for 2-year-olds, Rosenthal (1994) reports that it accounts for about 7% of behaviour observed in day-care settings. For children 2 to 4 years of age, Field (1994) reports exercise play accounting for 10% of all day-care behaviour. Similarly, Bloch's (1989) observations of children in a Senegal fishing village found that gross motor activities, not all of which was play, accounted for 11% and 13% of children's play in the home at 2 to 4 years of age and 5 to 6 years of age, respectively. In one observational study in a British nursery school, McGrew (1972) found that approximately 20% of

4-year-olds' activity was physically vigorous, such as run, flee, and wrestle (a component of rough-and-tumble play). Similarly, in Smith and Connolly's (1980) British sample, with a mean age of 43 months, vigorous activities, such as run, chase, and climb (but also including rough-and-tumble play), accounted for 21% of their behaviour.

For children aged 6 to 10 years, exercise play declines, accounting for only 13% of all outdoor behaviour observed during school recess periods (Pellegrini, 1990). One of us (Blatchford, 1996) described the general levels of English primary school children's activity on the school playground and found that most (60%) of the children are engaged in some form of physically active play or games during their daily break times, which lasted between 65 and 75 minutes. Declines in exercise play in primary school are probably moderated by the school context in which they are observed.

In general, then, exercise, and possibly exercise play, is quite common in early/middle childhood, and appears to peak in the preschool and early primary grades, although more evidence is certainly needed to clarify exactly when the age peak occurs. In these studies, rough-and-tumble play as well as non-play forms of physical activity were probably included with exercise play, thus slightly inflating estimates.

Males engage in exercise play at higher rates than females. Eaton and Enns's (1986) meta-analysis of ninety studies of gender differences in motor activity level reported a significant difference in favour of males, with the effect size tending to increase from infancy to mid-adolescence. Part of this sex difference may be due to differential maturation rates. Eaton and Yu (1989) found that relative maturity (percent of estimated adult height attained) interacted with gender, being negatively related to activity level, with girls being both less active and more physically mature than boys. These results are consistent with sexual selection theory (Darwin, 1871) which posits that males' and females' reproductive roles determine morphology and behaviour. Thus males, because they compete with each other for mates, are bigger, more aggressive, and more active than females. These differences in physical activity form an important basis for the existence of segregated sex peer groups, as noted above, which begin in preschool and wane in early adolescence (Bohn-Gettler et al., 2010; Maccoby, 1998; Pellegrini et al., 2007; Pellegrini & Long, 2007).

Functions of locomotor play

As a first step in establishing the functional importance of locomotor activity play during childhood, we present evidence from a small number of play-deprivation studies, either natural or experimental. The logic behind deprivation studies is that if play is functional, individuals' levels and rates of locomotor play should increase after the deprivation, the assumption being that immature organisms will, after deprivation, attempt to compensate for lost opportunities (Burghardt, 2005). With this said, the use of deprivation study to determine the effects of play, more generally, has a long and interesting history in the animal literature. Deprivation studies, and especially social play deprivation studies (Einon, Morgan & Kibbler, 1978), are, however, often plagued by play deprivation being confounded with other sorts of deprivation, such as social interaction more generally (though see Pellis & Pellis, 2006). Locomotor play deprivation studies are less prone to this problem (Müller-Schwarze, 1968). Two sets of field experiments have looked at deprivation of locomotor play during childhood. Smith and Hagan (1980) studied English preschool children (3–4 years) who were deprived of vigorous exercise by varying the amount of time they remained in their classrooms engaged in sedentary seatwork. After deprivation periods, they played outdoors. On the long, compared to short, deprivation days, children's play was more vigorous in the immediate post-deprivation period. Utilizing a similar deprivation paradigm with American primary school children (5–9 years), Pellegrini and colleagues (Pellegrini, Horvat & Huberty, 1998) replicated Smith and Hagan's results: long, compared to short, deprivation periods resulted in higher levels of physical activity. Predictably, however, deprivation interacted with sex of the child; boys, compared to girls, were especially active after long deprivation.

These results support the following generalization: if children are deprived of opportunities for locomotor play, they will, when given the opportunity, engage in more intense and longer bouts of locomotor play than they would have done if not so deprived, suggesting that locomotor play serves some developmental function, possibly related to physical conditioning and skeletal and muscular development (Byers & Walker, 1995; Gunter et al., 2008; Pellegrini & Smith, 1998).

With the onset of locomotion, a developmental course may begin, as evidenced by the correspondence between exercise play and muscle differentiation, strength, and endurance. Byers and Walker (1995), in a thorough review of the animal play and motor training literatures, evaluated the issue of immediate or deferred benefits of exercise play for three aspects of motor training: endurance, strength, and skill and economy of movement. They suggest that exercise play may improve skill and economy of movement due to the effects of exercise on muscle fibre differentiation and cerebellar synaptogenesis. They also present developmental data from house mice, rats, and cats and conclude that physical activity in the juvenile period, beginning in the early postnatal period and declining at mid-lactation, is a sensitive period in the development of these functions. Exercise play during this period has a lasting effect on subsequent economy and skill of movement.

In children, exercise play may help shape the muscle fibres used in later physically vigorous activities. This could improve the economy and skill of movement along the lines suggested by Byers and Walker in other species, although we know of no direct evidence for this. However, the evidence suggests that endurance and strength may be developed through sustained exercise bouts. The age course of exercise play also corresponds to the growth of arm and leg muscles and bones during the preschool period (Tanner, 1970). Consistent with this claim, an experimental, longitudinal study of children documented the relation between one form of exercise play, jumping, and bone mineral content (Gunter et al., 2008). Exercise play during the school years and beyond might continue to benefit muscle and bone remodelling and strength, and endurance training.

An interesting, and provocative hypothesis for the role of locomotor play in the development of behavioural flexibility has been put forth by Povinelli and Cant (1995) who provide an example of the role of an uncertain environment in the evolution of behavioural flexibility. They compared the degree of behavioural flexibility in long-tailed macaques (*Macaca fascicilaris*) and orang-utans (*Pongo pygmaeus*). Their hypothesis was that behavioural flexibility (i.e., having a variety of non-stereotyped locomotor behaviours in their repertoires) was a result of encountering uncertain environments on which to move (in these cases, arboreal clambering). Orang-utans are physically larger than macaques, thus the niche of the orang-utans is relatively unpredictable. For example, an animal the size of an orang-utan (~ 40 kg) clambering from tree to tree will experience tree limbs and vines that are relatively unpredictable because they bend extremely or could break. In order to locomote successfully in these areas, orang-utans had to develop a very flexible behavioural repertoire so as to adjust to their unpredictable environment. Macaques, by contrast, are much smaller (~ 5 kg) and their locomotor repertoire through a similar environment is more predictable. Their weight does not perturb their travel as it does with orang-utans; consequently their behavioural repertoire related to locomotion is much more stereotyped than the larger orang-utan. With regard to children, it would be interesting to know the degree to which they seek out unpredictable motor experiences, such as walking balance beams and climbing trees, and subsequent motor facility.

In summary, exercise play, in the preschool years especially, seems sufficiently frequent that it can serve an immediate function for endurance and strength training. It may also improve skill and economy of movement, although specific evidence for this is lacking. This hypothesized set of functions is consistent with the age curve for exercise play (Tanner, 1970).

Object play

Given the centrality of object use in child developmental theory, it is surprising how little descriptive information there is about the varied ways in which children use objects in their natural habitats (see Pellegrini, 2013 for a review). Perhaps most commonly, in the child development literature, where efforts have been made to address the different types of object use and play exhibited by children, researchers have often conflated object play with different forms of object use. Specifically, much of the study of children's interactions with objects during childhood has been influenced by Smilansky's (1968) adaptation of Piaget's (1962) theory of play and the ways that she categorized behaviours directed at objects. In her influential monograph, Smilansky included 'constructive play' as a category to account for children's interactions with objects. Constructive play for Smilansky was an ends-oriented activity with objects, where something was built. Piaget, in contrast, did not consider construction to be play because of its ends, not means, orientation. This misuse of the term 'play with objects' by Smilansky is representative of the frequently loose use of the term 'play' in the developmental psychological literature. To remediate this, we will discuss each form of object use, in the order in which they occur in ontogeny.

Exploration

Exploration is the behaviour exhibited when individuals first encounter unfamiliar objects; they manipulate, or explore, their properties and attributes (Hutt, 1966; West, 1977). Through exploration, children find out that objects, for example, are flat or rounded, long or short, used for drinking or for covering one's head. While often conflated with play with objects (which will be defined below), the two differ behaviourally (Hutt, 1966; McCall, 1974). Specifically, exploration, relative to play, is characterized by elevated heart rate, low distractibility, and negative/flat affect. By contrast, children playing with objects have lower heart rates, are highly distractible, and display positive affect (Hutt, 1966). Further, exploration precedes other forms of object use, including play, in human ontogeny (Belsky & Most, 1981; McCall, 1974), as well as in other animals. In an important study of young children, Belsky and Most (1981) found that exploration of toys was the predominant activity of the youngest children (7.5–10.5 months), with no instances of pretend play with objects. From around 9 to 10.5 months, children named objects as they manipulated them. At 12 months, pretend play with objects appeared, co-occurring with exploration and naming of the objects, and then pretend displaced exploration. And, like Hutt (1966), Belsky and Most noted that exploration of an object precedes play with that object. These trends are consistent with a view that the processes involved in exploring are precursors to play with objects. By the time children are of preschool age, exploration accounts for a relatively small portion of their object time budgets, between 2% and 15% of children's total behaviour (Pellegrini & Hou, 2011; Pellegrini & Gustafson, 2005). In the case of the high end of the range, exploration spikes when children are exposed to novel objects, such as when they return to their preschool classrooms after their winter holidays. Given the relative infrequency of exploration during the preschool years, there are few documented age differences for directly observed exploration (Pellegrini & Gustafson, 2005).

There are reported sex differences in exploration, where boys exhibit more than girls (Bornstein, Haynes, O'Reilly & Painter, 1996; Pellegrini & Hou, 2011), though experimental studies of infants' and preschoolers' exploration do not consistently test for sex differences (e.g., Belsky & Most, 1981; Ross, Rheingold & Eckerman, 1972).

Exploration of objects occurs in both social and solitary contexts. Piaget (1962) described how solitary infants, as well as young children, explored objects, yet children's exploration can be facilitated by parental presence (Rheingold & Eckerman, 1970) and involvement (Belsky, Goode & Most, 1980). Adult facilitation continues through early childhood (~ 5.5 years of age), where adult encouragement significantly increases exploration (Henderson, 1984). However, we find that when children explore objects in preschool classrooms, they tend to do so in solitary contexts (Pellegrini, unpublished data) and it does not attract their peers' attention (Pellegrini & Hou, 2011).

Play with objects

Following our earlier stated definition of play, object play typically involves pretending with an object. Using objects in pretend play initially entails children simulating someone else's use of those objects. With experience, children learn to have other, more abstract, objects represent other objects. Correspondingly, children's play with objects is typified by them using objects in novel and varied ways (Pellegrini & Hou, 2011). For example, they can have a pencil representing a hammer. This begins in the context of parent–child interactions and then interaction with peers (Lillard, 2006; Tomasello, 1999). Indeed, of all the ways in which children use objects, play with objects is most highly related to creative uses of objects (Pellegrini & Hou, 2011).

Establishing an accurate time budget for play with objects during childhood is difficult because object play has typically been conflated with other forms of object use. In those few cases where object play was clearly differentiated from other forms of object use, it begins at around one year (Belsky & Most, 1981) and increases among 3–5-year-olds in American and UK preschool settings 18%–30% of children's time budgets (McGrew, 1972; Pellegrini & Gustafson, 2005; Pellegrini & Hou, 2011), and then declines, following the classic inverted-U trajectory of all forms of play.

Sex differences in object play are equivocal and not consistent with the more general literature on pretend play where girls, relative to boys, exhibit more and more sophisticated pretending (see Pellegrini, 2009, and Rubin et al., 1983, for reviews). In an observational study of ninety-two preschoolers' object use (i.e., exploration, construction, object play, and tool use) across one year using growth curve modelling, object play was not influenced by sex (Pellegrini & Hou, 2011). It may be that in this study girls' general facility with pretence was diluted by their interactions across a wider variety of objects (beyond replica toys) while boys' play with some forms of objects (such as using a rake for a pretend gun) increased, thus attenuating sex differences. For example, boys, more than girls, pretend that objects are weapons (Pellegrini & Gustafson, 2005), while girls more frequently use replica objects (e.g., dolls, dishes, pots) in more domestically themed roles (Pellegrini, 2009).

Object play, like pretend play more generally, becomes increasingly social with age (Rubin et al., 1983). For example, less than 2% of preschool and kindergarten children's object play, *generally defined*, is solitary, while 12% and 28% of preschoolers' and kindergarteners', respectively, is social (Rubin, Watson & Jambor, 1978). Thus, not only does object play increase across childhood but it also becomes increasingly social.

Construction

Much of what we know about construction is subsumed under the Smilansky-inspired label of 'constructive play', which, according to Smilansky, has the child using objects to construct, create, or build something (1968, p. 6). The above definition given by Smilansky, and subsequently revised by Rubin (Rubin et al., 1976; Rubin et al., 1978), includes a diverse constellation of goal-directed and non-goal-directed uses of objects. For example, using blocks to build steps might be considered constructive or pretend play. The same act, however, might also actually be considered 'tool use' if a child uses the steps to enhance his or her reach (Amant & Horton, 2008).

Further, 'constructive games' according to Piaget (1962) was considered not play per se as it represents a position between play and adaptive intelligence (Piaget, 1962). Thus, for Piaget and others (e.g., Pellegrini, 2013; Smith et al., 1985), construction is more accommodative and concerned with the end product of activity – the construction *per se* – while play is more assimilative and concerned with the activity, or means, than with the end, and consequently is not play *per se* (Piaget, 1962; Rubin et al., 1983; Smith et al., 1985; though see Burghardt, 2005). In further support of the claim that construction is not a form of play, it does not follow the typical inverted-U age-related trajectory (Smith et al., 1985).

Taking 'constructive play' as defined by Smilansky and Rubin and colleagues, it accounts for between 40% (Rubin et al., 1976) and 51% (Rubin et al., 1976) of all observed behaviour subsumed under Rubin's matrix. When construction is defined consistently with the definition in this chapter, we found that construction accounted for between 15% (Pellegrini & Gustafson, 2005) and 17% (Pellegrini & Hou, 2011) of behaviour. The very different figures derived from the Rubin and Pellegrini studies may reflect the fact that what Rubin and colleagues coded as constructive play probably included other forms of object use, such as tool use and perhaps solitary object play.

In terms of sex differences for 'constructive play', defined according to Smilansky and Rubin, it is reported that females engage in it more than males (Johnson & Ershler, 1981; Johnson, Ershler & Bell, 1980; Rubin et al., 1976). However, boys' constructions tend to be more complex than girls' (Erickson, 1977, cited in Rubin et al., 1983, q.v. for a summary), and boys, relative to girls, tend to be more facile with objects as indicated by their performance on the block-design portion of the Wechsler Preschool and Primary Scale of Intelligence

(Caldera et al., 1999). Data from two naturalistic studies of preschoolers' object use using the differentiated categories proffered here help to clarify this confusion. Beginning with an observational study with a limited sample, girls, relative to boys, spend more time in construction but boys spend more time than girls in object play (Pellegrini & Gustafson, 2005). In the other, larger observational study using growth curve modelling, there were no moderating effects of sex on construction (Pellegrini & Hou, 2011).

Possible functions of object use

In this section we cover only functions of object play, not the other forms of object use described above. A fuller treatment of object use can be found in Pellegrini (2013). Making inferences about the function of a behaviour can be defined in terms of its beneficial consequences and in terms of 'ultimate function', or reproductive fitness (Darwin, 1859/2006; Hinde, 1980). Perhaps the most frequently cited efforts to determine functions of object play in the developmental psychological literature involve looking for beneficial functions, through experimental manipulations where children are 'trained' to play with objects and then they are given similar, or different, objects in convergent or divergent problem-solving tasks.

Convergent experimental tasks associated with children's object use are often modelled after Köhler's (1924) famous experiments of a chimpanzee using objects to solve problems, such as putting together sticks to reach bananas hung above its head. In the paradigmatic child development experiment in this mould Sylva and colleagues (Sylva, Bruner & Genova, 1976) presented children with disassembled components of a tool (i.e., sticks and clamps) that had to be assembled in order to retrieve a lure, such as a toy. Children in different conditions were given opportunities to either play with the unassembled sticks, observe an adult assemble the sticks, or watch an adult use the clamp non-functionally (a control condition). Children in each condition were then asked to use the sticks to retrieve a lure. One experimenter saw children in both pre- and post-test conditions, thus confounding the results with experimenter bias. Using the same experimenter pre-post biases the results to the extent the knowledge of a child's status on the pre-test could affect the way they treat the child on the post-test. Results indicated that children in the play condition, relative to other conditions, were more systematic in their problem solving, moving from simple to complex moves and using information from hints and failures more effectively. These findings, however, do not replicate when experimenter bias is controlled, or under double-blind experimental conditions (Simon & Smith, 1983; Smith, 1988; Smith & Simon, 1984; Vandenberg, 1980).

Using objects in divergent problem-solving situations, or tasks for which there is no one correct answer, is also very common in the child development literature (Sutton-Smith, 1966). Specifically, Dansky and Silverman's (1973, 1975) frequently cited experimental studies examining the effects of 'play' with objects on children's associative fluency, or creative uses for objects. In the first study, Dansky and Silverman (1973) provided children with conventional, but unfamiliar, objects. In one condition they were asked to play with the objects; in others they observed an adult manipulating the objects or were exposed to a control condition. These sessions lasted less than ten minutes. Children were then asked to list all the uses possible for one of the objects to which they were exposed. For example, creative uses for a matchbox might include using it as a pretend boat. One experimenter interacted with children during both treatment and testing conditions. They found that children in the play condition generated the greatest number of creative responses, relative to children in the other conditions, possibly due to both testing and scoring biases.

In the second experiment by Dansky and Silverman (1975), children were assigned to similar conditions to those in the experiment described above, but then asked to generate creative uses for objects with which they did *not* interact in their respective treatments. Similar to their earlier studies, the same experimenters (in this case two, not one, experimenters were used) saw the same children in both treatment and testing conditions. Again, they found that children in the play condition, relative to the other conditions, were the most creative. They argued that these effects were due to an induced 'play set', a temporary, creative orientation to objects presented.

While being widely cited, these studies of associative fluency, like the Sylva and colleagues study, do not replicate when double-blind procedures are used (Smith & Whitney, 1987). The results in both types of studies, then, were probably due to experimenter bias, or testing bias specifically. As noted earlier, these studies also suffered from very limited experimental treatment durations. Furthermore, and especially in light of the limited time of the treatment and relative unfamiliarity of the experimental props, children may have been more likely to have been exploring the objects, not playing with them.

Time budget of object play and possible functions

Given these results, one could rightfully question the efficacy of an experimental treatment of ten minutes or so on children's behaviour. That the experimental literature on object play and problem solving has not consistently shown effects may be more due to these very limited treatments than to the lack of efficacy of the role of play or exploration with objects. An alternative, and perhaps more valid, approach to documenting the role of object play in tool use would involve documenting the time children spend in different object play situations across a relatively long period of time in their natural ecologies, and then regressing those values on to children's performance in different object use tasks (Pellegrini & Gustafson, 2005). This larger corpus of observations should provide a more robust, and valid, indicator of children's facility with objects, relative to the relatively short-term studies cited above.

By way of combining the first and second notions of function, Martin and Caro (1985) suggest that if play, or any other form of object use, is to be naturally selected, benefits associated with the construct should outweigh the costs. An important first step in establishing function from this perspective is to document costs and then relate those costs to a beneficial consequence, fitness, or both. Specifically, time spent in different types of activities with objects during childhood can be framed in this study in terms of behavioural ecology theory (e.g., van Schaik et al., 1999). From this position, descriptions of the 'costs' associated with an activity serve as an indicator of its importance, or possible function. For example, high cost behaviours should correspond to outcomes with high payoffs (Caro, 1988; Martin & Caro, 1985). Costs are typically documented in terms of the resources (time, energy, and survivorship, or risk of injury and death) expended to acquire or learn a skill. Time in an activity is typically expressed as the portion of the total time budget spent in that activity (e.g., Martin & Caro, 1985) and energy is typically expressed in terms of caloric expenditure in that activity relative to the entire caloric budget (e.g., Pellegrini, Horvat & Huberty, 1998).

The logic of this level of analysis is as follows. Learning and developing specific skills involve different trade-offs between costs and benefits, and individuals tend to adopt the most 'efficient', or optimal, strategies to solve different problems at specific points during ontogeny (Krebs & Davies, 1997; Stephens & Krebs, 1986). For example, in learning to use tools during childhood, trade-offs are made between different opportunities (e.g., playing with objects vs. learning to use an object through observation or direct instruction) in light of the finite amount of time and calories available. From this view, there should be a correspondence between time budgets and the benefits associated with expenditures in each activity.

To our knowledge there are very few time and energy budget studies of children's play, generally (though see Haight & Miller, 1993, for pretend play, and Pellegrini et al., 1998, for locomotor play), and fewer still for object play (though see Bock, 2005; Pellegrini & Gustafson, 2005; Pellegrini & Hou, 2011). The problem with documenting costs of object use and object play is compounded with the use of very loose and inconsistent terminology surrounding object use, as discussed above. Consequently, we will use data from the two Pellegrini studies (Pellegrini & Hou, 2011; Pellegrini & Gustafson, 2005) because they used definitions consistent with those presented here and they were put in time budget terms. In two short-term longitudinal studies of novel and creative object use, Pellegrini and colleagues (Pellegrini & Gustafson, 2005; Pellegrini & Hou, 2011) took relatively large assays of children's object use as well as their creative and novel uses of objects by sampling each set of constructs across an entire school year. In the later study, they also documented the social context (i.e., solitary, parallel, or social interaction and attention structure) of each type of object use.

In the first study, Pellegrini and Gustafson (2005) directly observed a modest sample of preschool children in their classrooms across one school year. The aim was to use children's object use sampled across the year to predict the use of objects to solve divergent and convergent object-related problems. A sub-sample of children were also asked to participate in three types of object-use tasks (two convergent and one divergent tool tasks) as well as a spatial IQ task (the Block design score of the Wechsler Preschool and Primary Scales of Intelligence, Object Design Test).

The divergent problem-solving task − associative fluency − involved asking children to generate novel uses for ordinary household objects. The first of the two convergent retrieval tasks involved *selecting a tool* (i.e., a plastic toy hoe, a plastic rake head without a handle, and a plastic toy rake handle without the rake head) with which to retrieve a toy dinosaur that had been placed out of reach of the child. In the second convergent task, children were asked to *make a tool* from Tinker Toy parts and then use it to retrieve a toy, similar to Sylva and colleagues (1976).

On the whole, there was a paucity of predictive relations between observed object uses and performance on the associative fluency task and on the connected and unconnected lure-retrieval tasks, when spatial IQ was controlled. Specifically, observed play did not predict problem solving on any of the three tasks. Given the paucity of relations between object uses and performance on any of the problem-solving tasks, we might question the often-trumpeted value of play for both convergent and divergent problem-solving tasks with objects, at least as measured in associative fluency and lure-retrieval tasks. This is similar to the argument made by Smith (1988) and colleagues in reference to the questionable role of play in lure-retrieval performance (Simon & Smith, 1983, 1985) and associative fluency (Smith & Whitney, 1987).

While this may be true for lack of effects on the lure-retrieval tasks, which involve making tools, it is also possible that the task of making tools to retrieve lures is simply too complex for preschool-age children. Specifically, children do not exhibit unassisted tool-making facility until well into middle childhood (Mounoud, 1996), even though they are capable of choosing the correct tool at a much younger age. As for the lack of relations for divergent, creativity tasks, it may be, again, that the choice of the task itself is inadequate. We might be better served by redefining creative uses of objects in terms of behavioural 'modules', as defined above, and the social learning implications of others observing novel behavioural modules, as defined by Bruner (1973) and West-Eberhardt (2003). Specifically, in object play individuals learn and practise at combining and disaggregating behavioural modules with varied objects to solve problems. Take, for example, a boy engaged in object play with pipe cleaners where he connects and bends two separate pipe cleaners into a pretend 'tunnel' for him to drive his toy car through. This specific module of connecting and bending could then be used on similar materials to solve a problem, such as, connecting and bending pipe cleaners to be used to retrieve a lure in a restricted physical space. Correspondingly, modules developed in play can be applied to very different types of objects; for example, attaching to lengths of rope to make it long enough to pull a wagon.

Further and perhaps more crucially, the social status implications of generating novel object use may be the most important function of object play, though it has been virtually ignored in the play literature, with Pat Bateson (2011) being a notable exception. He has suggested that the behavioural flexibility developed in play may be an evolutionary driver, and at the leading edge of evolutionary change. (More will be said about the role of innovative object in evolution later in this chapter.) According to Bateson, novel behaviours could be generated in play because of its high intrinsic motivation and its lack of concern for instrumentality. Those novel behaviours that out-compete alternatives will spread through the population and become dominant, in what we label the 'seeding hypothesis of play' (Pellegrini, 2013). These novel uses should, in turn, attract the attention of peers (Pellegrini & Hou, 2011) and may spread through the population, depending on their usefulness. This hypothesis is consistent with early work with chimpanzees (Menzel, Davenport & Rogers, 1972), where they gauged peer responses to individuals' novel and varied uses of objects by documenting 'attention structure', or the number of chimpanzees looking at chimpanzees as they used objects in different ways. It also may be the case that copiers of innovative object users accrue benefits.

From this argument, Pellegrini and Hou (2011) directly observed a relatively large sample (N = 92) of young children's object use (3–5 years of age) across a school year in university nursery school classrooms. Object use was coded as: exploration, play, construction, and tool use; each use was also independently scored for novelty and variety. Consistent with claims that object play is a mechanism for generating novel behaviour, they, like Hutt and Bhavnani (1972), found that only object play, not other forms of object use, significantly predicted novelty. In terms of the discriminant validity to the claim that play is a novelty generator, exploration, a convergent activity, was negatively and significantly correlated with novelty.

That this study found a relation between object play and novel uses of objects may be due to the fact that it sampled novel behaviours more widely than experimental studies, which typically used a single, short-term, contrived task. Aggregating across a large number of behavioural indicators probably maximized the validity of the construct 'novelty' (Cronbach, 1971; Rushton, Brainerd & Pressley, 1983). Of course the data from the Pellegrini and Hou study are correlational, not experimental, thus causal inferences should be minimized.

This evidence is, however, consistent with the 'seeding hypothesis'. Specifically, Pellegrini and Hou also found that only novel and creative uses of objects correlated significantly with peer attention structure. Further and consistent with the notion that innovation is a basis for attention, novel and creative uses of object play observed during the first quarter of the school year predicted peer attention structure of children using objects creatively in the final quarter of the year, with attention structure from the earlier period statistically controlled. Thus, the benefit associated with innovating in a social context and being observed is that innovators gain social dominance status, as measured by attention structure

(Chance, 1967; Pellegrini et al., 2007), in their groups and, correspondingly, have prioritized access to resources in their niches, in much the same way that socially dominant individuals have access to resources (Pellegrini, 2008). Specifically, dominance can be achieved by a variety of means, with the means chosen depending on the cost of using a specific strategy in relation to the value of the resources. So, in an ecology, such as Western preschools, where the costs of using an agonistic strategy are very high (e.g., likely and high sanction by both teachers and peers) in relation to benefits (e.g., most preschools are typically resource-rich so the benefit of access to objects is relatively low), status is gained by more prosocial and academically-oriented means, such as innovative facility with objects – a value advocated in many Western preschools (Smith, 1988).

Social play

Social play takes the form of interaction between children and adults and between children and adolescents themselves. The earliest forms of social play occur between children and adults, typically parents (Power, 2000). For example, a mother playing peek-a-boo with her infant is one of the earliest, and pan-cultural, forms of social play (Bruner & Sherwood, 1976; Fernald & O'Neil, 1993). In peek-a-boo play, mothers and babies engage in routinized interactions typified by unpredictability (for the baby at least) in vocalizations, expectations, and facial expressions (Fernald & O'Neill, 1993) and high positive affect. Similar structural features typify the social play between peers, whether that play revolves around play-fighting or pretend, domestic themes.

A problem associated with the study of social play, similar to the case of object play, is that many writers do not differentiate social interactions which are 'play' as defined in this chapter, from more general, non-play, social interactions, especially with peers. As noted above, in one of the foundational studies of preschoolers' social behaviour, Parten (1932) explicitly refers to her categories of social interaction among peers as reflecting children's *social participation* yet she also sometimes substitutes the word *play* to describe some of these behaviours. For example: 'The child *plays* (emphasis ours) in a group that is organized for the purpose of making some material product, or striving to attain some competitive goal, or of dramatic situations of adult or group life, or of playing formal games' (p. 251). From these examples one can see that *play* is being used colloquially as all behaviours children exhibit, not in a more exact sense. This inexact word choice to describe peer interaction continues currently (Fabes et al., 2003; Martin & Fabes, 2001), perhaps reflecting an implicit assumption that most forms of juvenile behaviour are 'play' (Martin & Caro, 1985). In this section we will limit the discussion to peer interactions which are clearly play in the form of rough-and-tumble play during childhood and into adolescence.

Rough-and-tumble play was first used in the social and behavioural sciences by Harlow (1962) in his discussion of the social play of rhesus monkeys, where rough-and-tumble play resembled 'play-fighting'. Following Harlow, Blurton

Jones (1972) defined children's rough-and-tumble play structurally in terms of: 'play face', physically vigorous behaviours, exaggerated movements, and soft, open handed hits or kicks, a pattern clearly different from aggression. Rough-and-tumble play is also characterized by reciprocal role taking and self-handicapping, such that players alternate between dominant and subordinate roles – for example, alternating between being on top and on bottom and between being the aggressor and being the victim (Pellegrini & Smith, 1998).

That players reciprocate roles and self-handicap has led to the so-called 50:50 rule, whereby in play-fighting each animal gains advantage in about 50% of the contests (Altman, 1962). The implication of the 50:50 is that play is 'fair' and cooperative to the extent that no individuals have unfair advantage over others and that the play bouts themselves are mechanisms by which individuals in group establish group cohesion – one of the primary, hypothesized, benefits of social play (e.g., Fagen, 1981). If the 50:50 is not followed, and some players unfairly exploit the playful tenor of rough-and-tumble play for their own advantage, or 'cheat', then rough-and-tumble play would be used to establish or maintain social dominance (Pellegrini, 2008). Play-fighting, to be motivating to players, should, however, combine elements of *both* cooperation (following the 50:50 rule) and competition (not following the rule) (Pellis, Pellis & Reinhart, 2013). Serge Pellis and colleagues (2013) propose that the 50:50 rule should be violated in situations where social dominance is unclear, such as in the early stages of group formation, a proposition supported with both preschool children (Pellegrini et al., 2007) and adolescents (Pellegrini & Long, 2002).

Rough-and-tumble play also follows the play-typical developmental, inverted-U, curve (Pellegrini & Smith, 1998), accounting for about 4% of all behaviour during the preschool period, peaking during the primary school years at around 10%, and declining again in early adolescence to around 4%. These data, like the time and caloric costs documented in the animal literature (e.g., Fagen, 1981), suggest that the time costs associated with rough-and-tumble play are modest.

There are also robust sex differences in the rough-and-tumble play of many animals (Meaney et al., 1985), including humans (Pellegrini & Smith, 1998). For example, year-long observations of 8-year-olds on their English school playgrounds found that males engaged in rough-and-tumble play at a rate three times that of females (Blatchford et al., 2003). Similarly, in a group of 13-year-old American middle school pupils, males' rough-and-tumble play was close to double that of females (Pellegrini, 2003).

Functions of rough-and-tumble play

Traditional accounts for the functions of rough-and-tumble play (e.g., Smith, 1982) posit that it affords safe opportunity to practise for fighting and hunting skills that will be useful in later life. There is, however, no direct evidence supporting this hypothesis (Martin & Caro, 1985; Sharpe, 2006). In terms of benefits associated with adult–child play, research by Parke and colleagues indicates that the ability to encode and decode play signals is facilitated in the vigorous play between parents (primarily fathers) and their children (primarily sons) beginning in infancy and continuing through early childhood (e.g., Parke et al., 1992). For example, children's ability to decode happy play signals, such as happy and sad faces, related positively to bout length of peer play (Parke et al., 1992).

A number of researchers (Pellegrini et al., 2007; Pellis & Pellis, 2006; Špinka et al, 2001) posit that a motivating factor in social play is its unpredictability, as presented in the 50:50 rule: Will I win or will I lose? Even with this uncertainty, there is a modicum of safety in play, and children are willing to take chances in this context. Children who engage in social play, from this argument, should be less fearful of uncertainty in the play context and behaviourally more flexible in responding to novel events, relative to less playful contexts (Pellegrini et al., 2007; Špinka et al., 2001). The only direct evidence to test this hypothesis, to our knowledge, showed a positive and significant relation between varied social play (indexed in terms of the variety of subcategories of rough-and-tumble observed) and novel responses to social problems (Pellegrini, 1992). Related work in the area of children's imaginary companions and subsequent behavioural flexibility is promising in this regard (e.g., Carlson & Taylor, 2005).

Rough-and-tumble play may also relate to social affiliation/cohesion benefits for boys during childhood (though see Sharpe, 2006). Most basically, rough-and-tumble play typically occurs in sexually segregated male groups that are typified by high activity and rough behaviour (Fabes, Martin & Hanish, 2003; Pellegrini et al., 2007). The behavioural compatibility hypothesis holds that children's sex-segregated groups are held together by the similarity of children's behaviour. That most boys enjoy rough-and-tumble play and most girls do not may be reason enough for them to bind as a group (Fabes et al., 2003), though the relative frequency of physically vigorous behaviour that is not rough-and-tumble play is also very important (Pellegrini et al., 2007).

Rough-and-tumble play may be related to another dimension of social affiliation, social dominance (de Waal, 1985), where dominance is defined as winning and holding resources at the relationship and group levels (Hinde, 1978). At the dyadic, relationship, level, individual A is dominant to B if in a contest for resources, he or she accesses those resources. These dyadic relationships, in turn, can be used to order individuals within a group hierarchically; for example, A>B>C. Cheating at rough-and-tumble play, or exploiting its playful tenor to exploit advantage, can be used to defeat an opponent and access resources. Even without cheating, children say they can determine their own as well as peers' strength from these encounters (Smith et al., 1992), though the 50:50 rule appears to be followed. So, children may use rough-and-tumble play in an indirect way to display their physical prowess, without using aggression, or blatantly cheating.

This picture changes in adolescence where rough-and-tumble and aggression co-occur. Neill's (1976) pioneering factor-analytic study of 12- to 13-year-old boys' playground behaviour found that rough-and-tumble play and aggression often co-occurred, a finding supported by Humphreys and Smith (1987) who found that at 11 years, but not at 7 and 9 years, dominance was a factor in partner choice in rough-and-tumble play bouts. For the older children, dominant youngsters initiated rough-and-tumble play with less dominant youngsters, or in asymmetrical groups. Results from a study of adolescents by Pellegrini (1995) support this view. In a longitudinal study of adolescent boys, he found that asymmetrical choices for rough-and-tumble play were observed during the first year of middle school (12 years), but not the second (13 years), and rough-and-tumble play was significantly and positively related to peer-rated dominance in both years. Thus, in adolescence, in contrast to childhood, youngsters' use of rough-and-tumble play corresponds to using aggression as a way in which to control resources.

The animal literature (e.g., Pellis & Pellis, 2006) has also demonstrated that social play can resemble sexual behaviour and it is hypothesized that the design features of this form of play, such as mounting, relate to adult mating behaviour. Perhaps not surprisingly, social play and sexual behaviour has not been widely studied, except in the psycho-analytically oriented literature (e.g., Isaacs, 1933/1972, though see Lamb & Coakley, 1993 and Thorne & Luria, 1986). More recently, however, we (Pellegrini, 2003) examined adolescents' inter-sexual rough-and-tumble play, in the context of 'push and poke' courtship (Maccoby, 1998; Schofield, 1981) whereby boys and girls use playful and ambiguous behaviour, resembling rough-and-tumble play, to initiate heterosexual interaction. These acts are sufficiently ambiguous that if the initiator is rebuffed he or she would not lose face among his or her peers. If, on the other hand, the behaviour is reciprocated, successful heterosexual interaction was initiated.

To more directly test this hypothesis, we videotaped males and females engaging in rough-and-tumble play and showed the films to boys and girls who were participants in those events they were viewing and to their non-participating classmates (Pellegrini, 2003). Results supported the hypothesis: female participants saw the bouts as playful, not aggressive, because they were experiencing rough-and-tumble play in the context of playful push and poke courtship. Non-participating females, on the other hand, had little experience in these matters and saw rough-and-tumble play as aggressive.

In summary, there may be two functions of rough-and-tumble play during childhood and two in adolescence. First, it may be primarily a competitive construct where children exploit peers and practise their fighting skills in same-sex groups. Second, it may be primarily a cooperative affair where children learn social skills which in turn relate to group cohesion. It may be, however, that these two options are complementary such that rough-and-tumble play, even if it co-occurs with aggression, could in fact relate to group cohesion if it were used in the context of *establishing* a dominance relationship. This should be the case when rough-and-tumble play is used in contests in the initial stages of group formation, as social dominance relationships are being sorted out. In adolescence, rough-and-tumble play between boys is directly related to aggression and social dominance. However, inter-sexual rough-and-tumble play may be used as a gambit to establish heterosexual contact.

Pretend play

Pretend play, also labelled symbolic play, fantasy play, and dramatic play, is arguably the most thoroughly studied aspect of human play behaviour. As noted earlier, pretend has been used as *the* defining attribute of children's play and considered a paradigm example of children's play (McCune-Nicolich & Fenson, 1984). For example, Rubin and colleagues (1983) included pretend as a dispositional criterion in defining play. This was reinforced empirically in an interview study conducted by Smith and Vollstedt (1985) where pretend was *the* most important defining attribute of play.

For Piaget (1962) symbolic play is an extension of the representational process where children recognize that one thing stands for another, and through repeated engagement of pretend play children practise having one thing representing another and separating the symbol from its referent. This ability, in turn, is important for children's more general representational competence, such as learning that words represent objects. The pretence of very young children is pretend in the sense that their actions are decontextualized, or taken out of their real and functional context, and that one thing substitutes for another (Fein, 1981).

Engaging in pretence, however, may not actually have children 'representing' in the strict sense that they are representing others' mental states when they play (Harris, 1991). Instead, Harris posits that young children 'simulate' the actions of others in their pretend play and this early form of pretence does not involve young children's representing the mental states of their co-players. From Harris's view, when young children simulate a pretend world, they assume that their simulations are the same as their playmates'. Through repeated social interactions in pretend play with peers, children, by the time they are about 3 years of age, come to recognize that this assumption is not correct, recognizing that they and their peers sometimes do not share the same view of a scenario that is being enacted. At this point, children put their own beliefs and desires about the scenario aside and try to imagine the beliefs and desires of their peers. With this accomplished, children will go back to their original simulation and try to understand it from the points of view of their peers. In the early phases of this process, children's understanding of others' simulations is a mixture of their imagined views of their peers and their own egocentric perspective. By 4 or 5 years of age children understand that they have different beliefs from others. Correspondingly, understanding others' points of views depends on the accuracy of children's simulations, not on the accuracy of their representation of others' beliefs and desires.

From solitary to social pretend play

Solitary behaviour and solitary play have been studied extensively by Rubin and colleagues (e.g., Coplan et al., 2001; Rubin et al., 1983). In naturalistic observation of preschoolers, typically conducted in university laboratory school, solitary pretend behaviours account for 1%–5% of all coded *play* behaviour (Rubin et al., 1983). We do not know, however, the ratio of solitary pretend play to other, *non-play* forms of behaviour.

A close adult–child relationship, such as the mother–child relationship, is central to the beginnings of social pretend play (Howes & Hamilton, 1992). Mothers seem to deliberately teach their infants to differentiate pretend from non-pretend behaviour, teach them to extend their play themes, and under certain conditions reinforce children's pretend enactments. Current evidence (e.g., Lillard, 2006) suggests that mothers actually guide children's play to more abstract levels. Correspondingly, Tomasello (1999; Tomasello & Call, 1997) also stresses the importance of mother–infant interaction in the development of very young children's understanding of the mental states of others. From Tomasello's position, that infants check to see if mothers are responding to their efforts to direct attention suggests that they, the infants, are beginning to view others as intentional agents.

Also important for the development of the symbolization processing in both pretend play and language is the realization by children that their imitations of adults can be used to solve social problems. Thus, they recognize that adults are using gestures and vocalizations to get something done (i.e., recognizing adults' intentions) and they use those same strategies to attain a goal (Tomasello et al., 1999). They come to realize that adults use symbols, language and gestures, to direct their attention. Correspondingly, by the second year of life, children recognize when adults use objects in pretence, indicative of also recognizing adults' intentionality. Continued experiences with adults and peers extend children's ability to understand that others have different views of situations and symbols than they do.

At around 1.5–2 years of age, pretence becomes more peer oriented and peaks in the preschool years, around 5 years of age (Rubin et al., 1983). The transition to pretend play with peers is a hallmark of preschool children's social cognitive and linguistic development. Because social pretend play involves the communication and coordination of abstract meaning between people, there is a possibility for ambiguity and the breakdown of interaction (Pellegrini, 1982). To avoid such breakdowns, children must use decontextualized oral language. By decontextualized language we mean language where meaning is conveyed primarily through linguistic means, rather than with shared knowledge assumptions or gestures (Bernstein, 1960; Olson, 1977; Heath, 1983; Pellegrini, 1982). It is also through these sorts of cooperative peer interactions that preschoolers come to recognize that their views of pretend play bouts and those of their peers differ (Moll & Tomasello, 2007).

There are at least two very different types of peer configurations that would support sophisticated social pretend play and oral language. First, and following the collaborative work of the sociologist, Basil Bernstein (1960), and linguist, Michael Halliday (1969–1970), children will use decontextualized oral language when they are engaged in pretence with peers with whom they share little background and thus will have to cognitively de-centre, or take another's point of view, and use explicit language to convey meaning. By contrast, close peer relationships, like friendships, might also support play and decontextualized oral language because in these relationships, relative to other configurations, friends are more likely to disagree, resolve that disagreement, and then de-centre (Hartup, 1996). This process, in turn, should support the enactment of sustained, abstract pretend play bouts.

In two experiments, Ed Melhuish and Pellegrini (Pellegrini et al., 2002) examined which of these two peer configurations was the more effective facilitator of decontextualized language and pretence in 5-year-olds in Cardiff, Wales. In the first experiment, dyads of previously unacquainted children were assigned to one of two conditions. In the unfamiliar/varied condition, individuals were paired with a different, previously unfamiliar peer in each of four observations. In the second, unfamiliar/acquaintance condition, initially unfamiliar children interacted with the same peer across all four observations. In both conditions, children were read a different narrative each time by an experimenter. After the reading, they were given toys, paper, crayons, and pen and told to play about then draw/write about the story that was just read to them. We found that in the unfamiliar/acquaintance condition, relative to the other condition, children's play was more sophisticated and they used more decontextualized language, especially about language about language (e.g., Monsters can't *talk*) and language about emotions (Look, she's very *sad*) across time. This suggests that the formerly unacquainted children established a relationship over time and the language they used reflected their willingness to talk about emotions and also to reflect upon the verbal processes by which they interacted.

In the second experiment, we used the same design with similar age Cardiff children and compared friendship dyads with an unfamiliar/acquaintance condition, like the second condition used in the first experiment. While friends used more decontextualized language, emotion terms, and 'meta-language' than the other group, these differences decreased significantly with time, again, supporting the hypothesis that the children in the unfamiliar/acquaintance condition established a relationship with time, not unlike a friendship. Thus, friends and familiarity maximize children's pretend play and decontextualized language, possibly due to the fact that friends provide emotional support for each other.

The general picture sketched here is of pretend play becoming more social and more complex with age. After beginning in the context of mother–child interaction at around 1.5–2 years of age, pretence becomes more social and peaks in the preschool years, around 5 years of age. During the preschool years pretence becomes more dependent on children's uses of rather sophisticated forms of language in order for it to be sustained.

Functions of pretend play

In this section, we will be limited to discussing the benefits of pretend play for early literacy as many have been proffered elsewhere (e.g., Lillard et al., 2013;

Singer et al., 2006). It should also be noted that Lillard (Lillard et al., 2013) has shown, like Smith (1988) earlier, that the numerous benefits claimed for pretend play should be tempered.

In terms of the benefits of pretence during childhood, we (Pellegrini & Galda, 1991) examined different forms of social pretence in preschool children and their subsequent relations to measures of emergent reading and writing. We argued that social pretence predicts early literacy because they both share the design features of being representational, realized in decontextualized language, and having narrative structure (Heath, 1983; Galda, 1984). In our longitudinal work, the level of representation in children's pretence (object transformations, such as feeding a doll, or ideational transformations, such as defining a role as Daddy) predicted children's early writing performance, while use of meta-linguistic terms in pretence predicted their subsequent reading, with verbal IQ controlled, findings that were replicated by Dickinson and Moreton (1991). These results support the hypothesis that the ambiguity inherent in negotiating meaning in social pretence affords opportunities to verbally explicate meaning and become adept at manipulation of different symbolic systems.

Conclusion

In this chapter we have covered fairly broad ground in examining the role of play in human development, concluding that some forms of play have immediate benefits, others, deferred benefits, and some both immediate and deferred. In each case play is implicated in behavioural plasticity where it may not only help shape adaptation to the juvenile or adult periods but also, and more provocatively, may help shape evolution. In this final section we speculate on the ways in which play might be beneficial, both during the juvenile period as well as later, impacting phylogenetic development.

That play is observed primarily during the juvenile period suggests that the extended juvenile period is crucial to the role of play in developmental plasticity and to assembling the complex set of skills necessary for survival and reproduction. Specifically, and as discussed above, the juvenile period is characterized by 'surplus resources', such as provisioning and protection, and thus affords opportunity for immature organisms to experiment with a variety of strategies that might be useful for future development in that specific niche. When faced with a relatively novel or uncertain, but safe, environment, play affords opportunities for behavioural and cognitive innovation and subsequent practice of newly developed behaviours and strategies.

With this said, we must also ask why should children play to learn or develop innovative behaviours and strategies when they might more efficiently learn them through direct adult tuition or, less directly, through observational learning. Part of the answer to this is that actual adult tuition has been rare in human history, until recent times (e.g., Lancy, 1996; Gosso et al., 2005). More fundamentally, however, adult tuition and observation of adults will only transmit existing practices. The possible benefit of play, relative to adult-directed strategies, is that behaviours generated in the context of play can be more innovative and most suitable to the varied niches inhabited by humans. For example, juveniles can take the behaviours they have observed and then, in play, recombine elements of these behaviours into novel routines (Bateson, 2005; Bruner, 1972; Fagen, 1981; Pellegrini, 2013; Sutton-Smith, 1966). In support of the innovative potential of peer play, levels of children's symbolic functional play are more varied and complex when adults are absent, relative to when they are present (Pellegrini, 1983). The degree to which children's play is more innovative in a solitary (Fagen, 1981) or peer context (Pellegrini, 1983) needs more study, however.

More generally, play is a relatively low cost and low risk way to learn new behaviours during periods of immaturity and thus likely to impact subsequent evolutionary processes (Bateson, 2005). The safety inherent in a protected and prolonged juvenile period supports the sort of innovations in play that could lead to solutions to abrupt environmental changes and thus be copied by peers as well as adults. Exploration and play in one's niche may enable individuals to forecast what their developmental niche will be, a strategy that may be especially important in novel environments. Successful innovations would, in turn, be naturally selected. From this position, play occurs primarily during the juvenile period when resources are abundant, but the benefits may be reaped then or later in development, possibly impacting phylogeny.

References

Altmann, S.A. (1962). Social behavior of anthropoid primates: analysis of recent concepts. In E.L. Bliss (Ed.), *Roots of Behavior* (pp. 277–285). New York: Harper.

Baldwin, J.M. (1896). A new factor in evolution. *American Naturalist,* 30, 441–451, 536–553.

Bateson, P.P.G. (1976). Specificity and the origins of behavior. In J. Rosenblatt, R. Hinde, E. Shaw & C. Beer (Eds), *Advances in the Study of Behavior* (pp. 6, 1–20). New York: Academic.

Bateson, P.P.G. (1981). Discontinuities in development and changes in the organization of play in cats. In K. Immelmann, G. Barlow, L. Petrinovich, and M. Main (Eds), *Behavioral Development* (pp. 281–295). New York: Cambridge University Press.

Bateson, P.P.G. (2005). Play and its role in the development of great apes and humans. In A.D. Pellegrini & P.K. Smith (Eds), *The Nature of Play: Great Apes and Humans* (pp. 13–26). New York: Guilford.

Bateson, P. (2011). Theories of play. In A. Pellegrini (Ed.), *The Oxford Handbook of the Development of Play* (pp. 41–47). New York: Oxford University Press.

Bateson, P. & Gluckman, P. (2011). *Plasticity, Robustness, Development, and Evolution.* Cambridge: Cambridge University Press.

Bekoff, M. (1978). Social play: structure function and the evolution of a co-operative social behavior. In G.M. Burghardt and M. Bekoff (Eds), *The Development of Behavior: Comparative and Evolutionary Aspects* (pp. 367–383). New York: Garland.

Bekoff, M. & Byers, J.A. (1981). A critical re-analysis of the ontogeny and phylogeny of mammalian social and locomotor play. In K. Immelmann, G. Barlow, L. Petronovich, and M. Main (Eds), *Behavioural Development* (pp. 296–337). Cambridge: Cambridge University Press.

Belsky, J., Goode, M.K. & Most, R.K. (1980). Maternal stimulation and infant exploratory competence: cross-sectional, correlational, and experimental analyses. *Child Development,* 51, 1168–1178.

Belsky, J. & Most, R. (1981). From exploration to play: a cross-sectional study of infant free-play behavior. *Developmental Psychology,* 17, 630–639.

Bernstein, B. (1960). Language and social class. *British Journal of Sociology,* 1, 217–227.

Bjorklund, D.F. (2006). Mother knows best: epigenetic inheritance, maternal effects, and the evolution of human intelligence. *Developmental Review,* 26, 213–242.

Bjorklund, D.F. & Green, B.L. (1992). The adaptive nature of cognitive immaturity. *American Psychologist,* 47, 46–54.

Blatchford, P. (1996). A national survey of break time in English schools. Paper presented at the annual October meeting of the British Educational Research Association, Lancaster.

Blatchford, P., Baines, E. & Pellegrini, A. (2003). The social context of school playground games: sex and ethnic differences, and changes over time after entry to junior school. *British Journal of Developmental Psychology,* 21(4), 481–505.

Bloch, M.N. (1989). Young boys' and girls' play in the home and in the community: a cultural ecological framework. In M.N. Bloch and A.D. Pellegrini (Eds), *The Ecological Context of Children's Play* (pp. 120–154). Norwood, NJ: Ablex.

Blurton Jones, N.G. (1972) (Ed.), *Ethological Studies of Child Behaviour.* Cambridge: Cambridge University Press.

Blurton, Jones, N. (1993). The lives of hunter-gatherer children: effects of parental behavior and parental reproductive strategy. In M.F. Pereira and L.A. Fairbanks (Eds), *Juvenile Primates: Life History, Development, and Behaviors* (pp. 309–326). New York: Oxford University Press.

Bock, J. (2005). Farming, foraging, and children's play in the Okavango Delta, Botswana. In A.D. Pellegrini and P.K. Smith (Eds), *The Nature of Play: Great Apes and Humans* (pp. 254–284). New York: Guilford.

Bohn-Gettler, K., Pellegrini, A.D., Dupuis, D., Hickey, M., Hou, Y., Roseth, C. & Solberg, D. (2010). A longitudinal study of preschool children's (*Homo sapiens*) sex segregation. *Journal of Comparative Psychology,* 124, 219–228.

Bornstein, M.H., Haynes, O.M., O'Reilly, A.W. & Painter, K. (1996). Solitary and collaborative pretense play in early childhood: sources of individual variation in the development of representational competence. *Child Development,* 67, 2910–2929.

Bruner, J. (1972). The nature and uses of immaturity. *American Psychologist,* 27, 687–708.

Bruner, J.S. (1973). Organization of early skilled action. *Child Development,* 44, 1–11.

Bruner, J. & Sherwood, V. (1976). Peekaboo and the learning of role structures. In J. Bruner, A. Jolly & K. Sylva (Eds), *Play: Its Role in Development and Evolution.* Harmondsworth: Penguin (pp. 277–285).

Burghardt, G.M. (1984). On the origins of play. In P.K. Smith (Ed.), *Play in Animals and Humans* (pp. 5–41). New York: Blackwell.

Burghardt, G.M. (2005). *The Genesis of Animal Play: Testing the Limits.* Cambridge, MA: MIT Press.

Burns, S.M. & Brainerd, G.J. (1979). Effects of constructive and dramatic play on perspective rating in very young children. *Developmental Psychology,* 15, 512–521.

Byers, J.A. & Walker, C. (1995). Refining the motor training hypothesis for the evolution of play. *American Naturalist,* 146, 25–40.

Caldera, Y.M., Culp, A.M., O'Brien, M., Truglio, R.T., Alvarez, M. & Huston, C. (1999). Children's play preferences, constructive play with blocks, and visual-spatial skills: are they related? *International Journal of Behavioral Development,* 23, 855–872.

Campbell, D.W. & Eaton, W.O. (1999). Sex differences in the activity level of infants. *Infant and Child Development,* 8, 1–17.

Carlson, S.M. & Taylor, M. (2005). Imaginary companions and impersonated characters: sex differences in children's fantasy. *Merrill-Palmer Quarterly,* 51, 93–118.

Caro, T.M. (1988). Adaptive significance of play: are we getting closer? *Trends in Ecology and Evolution,* 3, 50–54.

Chance, M.R.A. (1967). Attention structure as the basis for primate rank orders, *Man,* 2, 503–518.

Coplan, R.J., Gavinski-Molina, M.-H., Lagace-Seguin, D.G. & Wichmann, C. (2001). When girls versus boys play alone: nonsocial play and adjustment in kindergarten. *Developmental Psychology,* 37, 464–474.

Cronbach, L.J. (1971). Test validation. In R.L. Thorndike (Ed.), *Educational Measurement* (2nd edn). Washington, DC: American Council on Education.

Cross, G. & Walton, J. (2005). *The Playful Crowd.* New York: Columbia University Press.

Dansky, J. & Silverman, I.W. (1973). Effects of play on associative fluency in preschool-age children. *Developmental Psychology,* 9, 38–43.

Dansky, J. & Silverman, I.W. (1975). Play: a general facilitator of associative fluency. *Developmental Psychology,* 11, 104.

Darwin, C. (1859/2006). *The Origin of Species: By Means of Natural Selection of the Preservation of Favoured Races in the Struggle for Life.* Mineola, NY: Dover.

Darwin, C. (1871). *The Descent of Man, and Selection in Relation to Sex.* London: John Murray.

DeWaal, F.B.M. (1985). The integration of dominance and social bonding in primates. *Quarterly Review of Biology,* 62, 459–479.

Dickinson, D. & Moreton, J. (1991). *Predicting* specific kindergarten literacy skills from three-year-olds' preschool experiences. Paper presented at the April meeting of the Society for Research in Child Development, Seattle.

Eagly, E.A. (1997). Sex differences in social behavior: comparing social role theory and evolutionary psychology, *American Psychologist,* 52, 1380–1383.

Eaton, W.C. & Enns, L.R. (1986). Sex differences in human motor activity level. *Psychological Bulletin,* 100, 19–28.

Eaton, W.C. & Yu, A.P. (1989). Are sex differences in child motor activity level a function of sex differences in maturational status? *Child Development,* 60, 1005–1011.

Einon, D., Morgan, M. & Kibbler, C. (1978). Brief periods of socialization and later behavior in the rat. *Developmental Psychobiology,* 11, 213–224.

Fabes, R.A. (1994). Physiological, emotional, and behavioral correlates of gender segregation. In C. Leaper (Ed.), *Childhood Gender Segregation: Causes and Consequences* (pp. 19–34). San Francisco: Jossey-Bass.

Fabes, R.A., Martin, C.L. & Hanish, L.D. (2003). Young children's play qualities in same-, other-, and mixed-sex peer groups. *Child Development,* 74, 921–932.

Fagen, R. (1981). *Animal Play Behavior.* New York: Oxford University Press.

Fein, G.G. (1981). Pretend play in childhood: an integrative review. *Child Development,* 52, 1095–1118.

Fernald, A. & O'Neill, D.K. (1993). Peekaboo across cultures: how mothers and infants play with voices, faces, and expectations. In K. MacDonald (Ed.), *Parent–Child Play* (pp. 259–286). Albany, NY: State University of New York Press.

Field, T.M. (1994). Infant day care facilitates later social behavior and school performance. In E.V. Jacobs and H. Goelman (Eds), *Children's Play in Child Care Settings* (pp. 69–84). Albany: State University of New York Press.

Fry, D.P. (2005). Rough-and-tumble social play in children. In A.D. Pellegrini and P.K. Smith (Eds), *The Nature of Play: Great Apes and Humans* (pp. 54–88). New York: Guilford.

Galda, L. (1984). Narrative competence: play, storytelling and comprehension. In A. Pellegrini and T. Yawkey (1984), *The Development of Oral and Written Language in Social Context* (pp. 105–119). Norwood, NJ: Ablex.

Garvey, C. (1990). *Play* (2nd edn). Cambridge, MA: Harvard University Press.

Gosso, Y., Otta, E., Morais, M., Ribeiro, F. & Bussabb, V. (2005). Play in hunter-gatherer society. In A.D. Pellegrini and P.K. Smith (Eds), *Play in Great Apes and Humans* (pp. 213–253). New York: Guilford.

Gottlieb, G. (1998). Normally occurring environmental and behavioral influences on gene activity: from central dogma to probabilistic epigenesis. *Psychological Review*, 105, 792–802.

Groos, K. (1901). *The Play of Man*. New York: Appleton.

Gunter, K.B., Baxter-Jones, A.D.G., Mirwald, R.L., Almstedt, H., Fuchs, R.K., Durski, S. & Snow, C. (2008). Impact exercise increases BMC during growth: an 8-year longitudinal study. *Journal of Bone and Mineral Research*, 10, 1359.

Haight, W.L. & Miller, P.J. (1993). *Pretending at Home: Early Development in a Sociocultural Context*. Albany: SUNY Press.

Halliday, M.A.K. (1969–1970). Relevant models of language. *Educational Review*, 22, 26–37.

Harlow, H. (1962). The heterosexual affection system in monkeys. *American Psychologist*, 17, 1–9.

Harris, P.L. (1991). Natural simulation of mental states. Paper presented in the March symposium on 'Developmental processes underlying the acquisition of concepts of mind', at the biennial meetings of the Society for Research in Child Development, Seattle.

Hartup, W.W. (1996). The company they keep: friendships and their developmental significance. *Child Development*, 67, 1–13.

Heath, S. (1983). *Ways with Words*. New York: Cambridge University Press.

Henderson, B.B. (1984). Social support and exploration. *Child Development*, 55, 1246–1251.

Hinde, R.A. (1978). Dominance and role: two concepts with two meanings. *Journal of Social Biology Structure*, 1, 27–38.

Hinde, R.A. (1980). *Ethology*. London: Fontana.

Hines, M. & Shipley, C. (1984). Prenatal exposure to diethylstilbestrol (DES) and the development of sexually dimorphic cognitive abilities and cerebral lateralization. *Developmental Psychology*, 20(1), 81.

Hollander, J. (2008). Testing the grain-sized model for the evolution of phenotypic plasticity. *Evolution*, 62, 1381–1389.

Howes, C. & Hamilton, C.E. (1992). Children's relationships with caregivers: mothers and child care teachers. *Child Development*, 63, 859–866.

Humphreys, A.P. & Smith, P.K. (1987). Rough-and-tumble play, friendship, and dominance in school children: evidence for continuity and change with age. *Child Development*, 58, 201–212.

Hutt, C. (1966). Exploration and play in children. *Symposia of the Zoological Society of London*, 18, 61–81.

Hutt, C. & Bhavnani, R. (1972). Predictions from play, *Nature*, 237, 171–172.

Isaacs, S. (1972/1933). *Social Development in Young Children*. New York: Schocken.

Johnson, J.E. & Ershler, J. (1981). Developmental trends in preschool play as a function of classroom program and child gender. *Child Development,* 52, 995–1004.

Johnson, J.E., Ershler, J. & Bell, C. (1980). Play behavior in a discovery-based and a formal education preschool program. *Child Development,* 51, 271–274.

Köhler, W. (1924). *The Mentality of Apes.* Oxford: Harcourt, Brace.

Konner, M.J. (1972). Aspects of the developmental ethology of a foraging people. In N. Blurton Jones (Ed.), *Ethological Studies of Child Behaviour* (pp. 285–304). London: Cambridge University Press.

Krebs, J.R. & Davies, N.B. (1997). The evolution of behavioural ecology. In J.R. Krebs and N.B. Davies (Eds), *Behavioural Ecology: An Evolutionary Approach* (pp. 3–18). New York: Wiley.

Lamb, S. & Coakley, M. (1993). 'Normal' childhood sexual play and games: differentiating play from abuse. *Child Abuse & Neglect,* 17, 515–526.

Lancy, D.F. (1996). *Playing on the Mother-Ground.* New York: Guilford.

Lewis, K.P. & Barton, R.A. (2006). Amygdala size and hypothalamus size predict social play frequency in nonhuman primates: a comparative analysis using independent contrasts. *Journal of Comparative Psychology,* 120, 31–37.

Lillard, A.S. (2006). Guided participation: how mothers structure and children understand pretend play. In A. Göncü and S. Gaskins (Eds), *Play and Development* (pp. 131–154). Mahwah, NJ: Erlbaum.

Lillard, A.S., Lerner, M.D., Hopkins, E.J., Dore, R.A., Smith, E.D. & Palmquist, C.M. (2013). The impact of pretend play on children's development: a review of the evidence. *Psychological Bulletin,* 139, 1–34.

Lloyd Morgan, C. (1896). On modification and variation. *Science,* 5, 139–155.

Maccoby, E. (1998). *The Two Sexes: Growing Up Apart, Coming Together.* Cambridge, MA: Harvard University Press.

Maccoby, E. & Jacklin, C. (1987). Gender segregation in childhood. *Advances in Child Development,* 20, 239–287.

MacDonald, K. & Parke, R.D. (1984). Bridging the gap: parent–child play interactions and peer interactive competence. *Child Development,* 55, 1265–1277.

Martin, P. & Caro, T. (1985). On the function of play and its role in behavioral development. In J. Rosenblatt, C. Beer, M. Bushnel & P. Slater (Eds), *Advances in the Study of Behavior* (pp. 15, 59–103). New York: Academic Press.

Martin, C.L. & Fabes, R.A. (2001). The stability and consequences of young children's same-sex peer interactions. *Developmental Psychology,* 37, 431–446.

McCall, R.B. (1974). *Exploratory Manipulation and Play in the Human Infant.* Monographs of the Society for Research in Child Development, 39 (No. 155).

McCune-Nicolich, L. & Fenson, L. (1984). Methodological issues in studying early pretend play. In T.D. Yawkey and A.D Pellegrini (Eds), *Child's Play* (pp. 81–104). Hillsdale, NJ: Erlbaum.

McGrew, W.C. (1972). *An Ethological Study of Children's Behaviour.* London: Methuen.

Meaney, M.J., Stewart, J. & Beatty, W.W. (1985). Sex differences in social play. In J. Rosenblatt, C. Beer, M.C. Bushnel, and P. Slater (Eds), *Advances in the Study of Behavior* (pp. 2–58). New York: Academic Press.

Menzel Jr, E.W., Davenport, R.K. & Rogers, C.M. (1972). Protocultural aspects of chimpanzees' responsiveness to novel objects. *Folia Primatologica,* 17(3), 161–170.

Moll, H. & Tomasello, M. (2007). Cooperation and human cognition: the Vygotskian hypothesis. *Philosophical Transactions of the Royal Society,* 362, 639–648.

Mounoud, P. (1996). A recursive transformation of central cognitive mechanisms: the shift from partial to whole representation. In A.J. Sameroff & M.M. Haith (Eds), *The Five* to *Seven Year Shift: The Age of Reason and Responsibility* (pp. 85–110). Chicago: Chicago University Press.

Müller-Schwarze, D. (1968). Play deprivation in deer. *Behaviour,* 31, 144–162.

National Vital Statistic Report (2004). See www.data360.org/graph_group.aspx? Graph_Group_Id=347.

Neill, S. (1976). Aggressive and non-aggressive fighting in twelve-to-thirteen year old pre-adolescent boys. *Journal of Child Psychology and Psychiatry,* 17, 213–220.

Olson, D.R. (1977). From utterance to text: the bias of language in speech and writing. *Harvard Educational Review,* 47, 257–281.

Parke, R.D., Cassidy, J., Burks, V., Carson, J. & Boyum, L. (1992). Familial contributions to peer competence among young children: the role of interactive and affective processes. In R.D. Parke and C. Ladd (Eds), *Family-Peer Relationships* (pp. 107–134). Hillsdale, NJ: Erlbaum.

Parten, M. (1932). Social participation among preschool children. *Journal of Abnormal and Social Psychology,* 27, 243–269.

Pellegrini, A.D. (1982). Explorations in preschoolers' construction of cohesive test in two play contexts. *Discourse Processes,* 5, 101–108.

Pellegrini, A. (1983). The sociolinguistic context of the preschool. *Journal of Applied Developmental Psychology,* 4, 397–405.

Pellegrini, A. (1990). Elementary school children's playground behaviour: implications for children's social-cognitive development. *Children's Environment Quarterly,* 7(2), 8–16.

Pellegrini, A.D. (1992). Rough-and-tumble play and social problem solving flexibility. *Creativity Research Journal,* 5, 13–27.

Pellegrini, A.D. (1995). A longitudinal study of boys' rough and tumble play and dominance during early adolescence. *Journal of Applied Developmental Psychology,* 16, 77–93.

Pellegrini, A.D. (2003). Perceptions and functions of play and real fighting in early adolescence. *Child Development,* 74, 1552–1533.

Pellegrini, A.D. (2004). Sexual segregation in childhood: a review of evidence for two hypotheses. *Animal Behaviour,* 68, 435–443.

Pellegrini, A.D. (2008). The roles of aggressive and affiliative behaviors in resource control: a behavioral ecological perspective. *Developmental Review,* 28, 461–487.

Pellegrini, A.D. (2009). *The Role of Play in Human Development.* New York: Oxford University Press.

Pellegrini, A.D. (2013). Object use in childhood: development and possible functions. *Behaviour,* 150, 813–843.

Pellegrini, A.D. & Archer, J. (2005). Sex differences in competitive and aggressive behavior: a view from sexual selection theory. In B.J. Ellis and D.J. Bjorklund (Eds), *Origins of the Social Mind: Evolutionary Psychology and Child Development* (pp. 219–244). New York: Guilford.

Pellegrini, A.D., Dupuis, D. & Smith, P.K. (2007). Play in evolution and development. *Developmental Review,* 27, 261–276.

Pellegrini, A.D. & Galda, L. (1991). Longitudinal relations among preschoolers' symbolic play, metalinguistic verbs, and emergent literacy. In. J. Christie (Ed.), *Play and Early Literacy Development* (pp. 47–68). Albany, NY: SUNY Press.

Pellegrini, A.D. & Gustafson, K. (2005). Boys' and girls' uses of objects for exploration, play, and tools in early childhood. In A.D. Pellegrini and P.K. Smith (Eds), *The Nature of Play: Great Apes and Humans* (pp. 113–138). New York: Guilford.

Pellegrini, A.D., Horvat, M. & Huberty, P.D. (1998). The relative cost of children's physical activity play. *Animal Behaviour,* 55, 1053–1061.

Pellegrini, A. & Hou, Y. (2011). The development of preschool children's (*homo sapiens*) use of objects and their roles in peer group centrality. *Journal of Comparative Psychology, 125,* 239–245.

Pellegrini, A.D. & Long, J.D. (2002). A longitudinal study of bullying, dominance, and victimization during the transition from primary to secondary school. *British Journal of Developmental Psychology, 20,* 259–280.

Pellegrini, A.D. & Long, J.D. (2007). An observational study of early heterosexual interaction at middle school dances. *Journal of Research in Adolescence 17,* 613–638.

Pellegrini, A.D., Long, J.D., Roseth, C., Bohn, K. & Van Ryzin, M. (2007). A short-term longitudinal study of preschool children's sex segregation: the role of physical activity, sex, and time. *Journal of Comparative Psychology, 121,* 282–289.

Pellegrini, A.D., Melhuish, E., Jones, I., Trojanowska, L. & Gilden, R. (2002). Social contexts of learning literate language: the role of varied, familiar, and close peer relationships. *Learning & Individual Differences, 12,* 375–389.

Pellegrini, A.D. & Smith, P.K. (1998). Physical activity play: the nature and function of a neglected aspect of play. *Child Development, 69,* 577–598.

Pellis, S.M. & Pellis, V.V. (2006). Play and the development of social engagement: a comparative perspective. In P.J. Marshall and N.A. Fox (Eds), *The Development of Social Engagement: Psychobiological Perspectives* (pp. 247–274). New York: Oxford University Press.

Pellis, S.M., Pellis, V.V. & Reinhart, C.J. (2013). *The Evolution of Social Play*. In C. Worthman, P. Plotsky, and D. Schechter (Eds), *Formative Experiences: The Interaction of Caregiving, Culture, and Developmental Psychobiology* (pp. 404–432). New York: Cambridge University Press.

Piaget, J. (1962). *Play, Dreams, and Imitation in Childhood* (trans. C. Gattengno & F.M. Hodgson). New York: Norton (original work published 1951).

Piaget, J. (1983). Piaget's Theory. In W. Kessen (Ed.), *Handbook of Child Psychology: History, Theory and Methods* (pp. 103–128). New York: Wiley.

Povinelli, D.J. & Cant, J.G.H. (1995). Arboreal clambering and the evolution of self-conception. *Quarterly Review of Biology, 70,* 393–421.

Power, T.G. (2000). *Play and Exploration in Children and Animals*. Mahwah, NJ: Erlbaum.

Rheingold, H.L. & Eckerman, C.O. (1970). The infant separates himself from his mother. *Science, 168,* 78–83.

Roopnarine, J.L., Hooper, F., Ahmeduzzaman, A. & Pollack, B. (1993). Gentle play partners: mother-child and father-child play in New Delhi, India. In K. MacDonald (Ed.), *Parent–Child Play* (pp. 287–304). Albany: State University of New York Press.

Rosenthal, M.K. (1994). Social and non-social play of infants and toddlers in family day care. In E.V. Jacobs and H. Goelman (Eds), *Children's Play in Child Care Settings* (pp. 163–192). Albany: State University of New York Press.

Ross, H.S., Rheingold, H.L. & Eckerman, C.O. (1972). Approach and exploration of a novel alternative by 12-month-old infants. *Journal of Experimental Child Psychology, 13,* 85–93.

Rubin, K.H., Fein, G. & Vandenberg, B. (1983). Play. In E.M. Hetherington (Ed.), *Handbook of Child Psychology: Vol. IV. Socialization, Personality and Social Development* (pp. 693–774). New York: Wiley.

Rubin, K., Maioni, T. & Hornung, M. (1976). Free play in middle and lower class preschoolers: Parten and Piaget revisited. *Child Development, 47,* 414–419.

Rubin, K., Watson, K. & Jambor, T. (1978). Free play behaviours in preschool and kindergarten children. *Child Development, 49,* 534–536.

Ruckstuhl, K.E. (1998). Foraging behaviour and sexual segregation in bighorn sheep. *Animal Behaviour, 56,* 99–106.

Rushton, J.P., Brainerd, C.J. & Pressley, M. (1983). Behavioral development and construct validity: the principle of aggregation. *Psychological Bulletin*, 94(1), 18.

St.Amant, R. & Horton, T.E. (2008). Revisiting the definition of tool use. *Animal Behaviour*, 74(4), 1199.

Schiller, F. (1795/1967). *On the Aesthetic Education of Man*. London: Oxford University Press.

Schlosberg, H. (1947). The concept of play. *Psychological Review*, 54, 229–231.

Schofield, J.W. (1981). Complementary and conflicting identities: images and interactions in an inter-racial school. In S.R. Asher & J.M. Gottman (Eds), *The Development of Children's Friendships* (pp. 53–90). New York: Cambridge University Press.

Serbin, L.A., Moller, L.C., Gulko, J., Powlista, K.K. & Colburne, K.A. (1994). The emergence of gender segregation in toddler playgroups. In C. Leaper (Ed.), *Childhood Gender Segregation: Causes and Consequences* (pp. 7–17). San Francisco: Jossey-Bass.

Sharpe, L.L. (2006). Playfighting does not affect subsequent fighting success in meerkats. *Animal Behaviour*, 69, 1023–1029.

Simon, T. & Smith, P.K. (1983). The study of play and problem solving in preschool children. *British Journal of Developmental Psychology*, 1, 289–297.

Simon, T. & Smith, P.K. (1985). Play and problem solving: a paradigm questioned. *Merrill-Palmer Quarterly*, 31, 265–277.

Singer, D., Golinkoff, R.M. & Hirsch-Pasek, K. (Eds) (2006). *Play = Learning*. New York: Oxford University Press.

Smilansky, S. (1968). *The Effects of Sociodramatic Play on Disadvantaged Preschool Children*. New York: Wiley.

Smith, P.K. (1982). Does play matter? Functional and evolutionary aspects of animal and human play. *The Behavioral and Brain Sciences*, 5, 139–184.

Smith, P.K. (1988). Children's play and its role in early development: a re-evaluation of the 'play ethos'. In A.D. Pellegrini (Ed.), *Psychological Bases for Early Education* (pp. 207–226). Chichester: Wiley.

Smith, P.K. (2009). *Children and Play: Understanding Children's Worlds*. London: Wiley-Blackwell.

Smith, P.K. & Connolly, K. (1980). *The Ecology of Preschool Behaviour*. London: Cambridge University Press.

Smith, P.K. & Hagan, T. (1980). Effects of deprivation on exercise play in nursery school children. *Animal Behaviour*, 28, 922–928.

Smith, P.K., Hunter, T., Carvalho, A.M.A. & Costabile, A. (1992). Children's perceptions of playfighting, playchasing and real fighting: a cross-national interview. *Social Development*, 1, 211–229.

Smith, P.K. & Simon, T. (1984). Object play, problem-solving and creativity in children. In P.K. Smith (Ed.), *Play in Animals and Humans*. Oxford: Basil Blackwell.

Smith, P.K., Takhvar, M., Gore, N. & Vollstedt, R. (1985). Play in young children: problems of definition, categorization, and measurement. *Early Child Development and Care*, 19, 37–54.

Smith, P.K. & Vollstedt, R. (1985). On defining play: an empirical study of the relationship between play and various play criteria. *Child Development*, 56, 1042–1050.

Smith, P.K. & Whitney, S. (1987). Play and associative fluency: experimenter effects may be responsible for previous positive findings. *Developmental Psychology*, 23, 49–53.

Špinka, M., Newbury, R.C. & Bekoff, M. (2001). Mammalian play: can training for the unexpected be fun? *Quarterly Review of Biology*, 76, 141–168.

Stearns, S. (1992). *The Evolutions of Life Histories*. London: Oxford University Press.

Stephens, D.W. & Krebs, J.R. (1986). *Foraging Theory*. Princeton, NJ: Princeton University Press.

Suomi, S.J. (2005). Genetic and environmental factors influencing the expression of impulsive aggression and serotonergic functioning in rhesus monkeys. In R.E. Tremblay, W.W. Hartup & J. Archer (Eds), *Developmental Origins of Aggression* (pp. 63–82). New York: Guilford.

Suomi, S. & Harlow, H. (1972). Social rehabilitation of isolate-reared monkeys. *Developmental Psychology*, 6, 487–496.

Sutton-Smith, B. (1966). Piaget on play: a critique. *Psychological Review*, 73, 111–112.

Sutton-Smith, B. (1997). *The Ambiguity of Play*. Cambridge, MA: Harvard University Press.

Sylva, K., Bruner, J. & Genova, P. (1976). The role of play in the problem-solving of children 3–5 years old. In J. Bruner, A. Jolly, and K. Sylva (Eds), *Play: Its Role in Development and Evolution* (pp. 244–261). New York: Basic Books.

Tanner, J.M. (1970). Physical growth. In P.H. Mussen (Ed.), *Manual of Child Psychology* (3rd edn) (pp. 1, 77–156). New York: Wiley.

Thorne, B. & Luria, Z. (1986). Sexuality and gender in children's daily worlds. *Social Problems*, 33, 176–190.

Tinbergen, N. (1963). On the aims and methods of ethology. *Zeitshrift für Tierpsychologie*, 20, 410–413.

Tomasello, M. (1999). *The Cultural Origins of Human Cognition*. Cambridge, MA: Harvard University Press.

Tomasello, M. & Call, J. (1997). *Primate Cognition*. New York: Oxford University Press.

Tomasello, M., Striano, T. & Rochat, P. (1999). Do young children use objects as symbols? *British Journal of Developmental Psychology*, 17, 563–584.

Vandenberg, B. (1980). Play, problem solving, and creativity. In K. Rubin (Ed.), *Children's Play* (pp. 49–68). San Francisco: Jossey-Bass.

van Schaik, C.P., Deaner, R.O. & Merrill, M.Y. (1999). The conditions for tool use in primates: implications for the evolution of material culture. *Journal of Human Evolution*, 36(6), 719–741.

West-Eberhardt, M.J. (2003). *Developmental Plasticity and Evolution*. Oxford: Oxford University Press.

Wilson, E.O. (1975). *Sociobiology: The New Synthesis*. Cambridge, MA: Harvard University Press.

Wrangham, R. (1987). The significance of African apes for reconstructing human social evolution. In W.G. Kinzey (Ed.), *The Evolution of Human Behavior: Primate Models* (pp. 51–71). Albany, NY: SUNY Press.

5

BREAKTIME/RECESS IN SCHOOLS

The psychologist interested in peer relations during primary and secondary childhood is hard pressed to find a venue to observe naturally occurring peer interactions. One of the few, yet understudied, places where this can be done, with relative efficiency, is on the school playground during the breaktime, or the recess period as it is labelled in North America (Hart, 1993). The recess period is similar to free play time for preschool children. In both places we have a relatively large sample of children, located in one place, engaging in spontaneous and minimally directed peer interactions. Further, in both places children develop and learn important social skills.

In light of this it is interesting that the school recess period is currently being drastically eliminated or cut from the school day across North America and the UK, as will be discussed in the next section. The typically stated reason for this policy is that recess is counter-productive to traditional educational aims. From this position, it is often stated that having recess takes time away from teaching more basic skills in an already very limited and crowded school day. Thus, limiting recess time and re-allocating that time to instruction, on the assumption that this will maximize school performance, is one proffered solution to limited instructional time.

The orientation of this book is quite the opposite. We view social interaction and social relationships as integral to the educational enterprise. Thus, in this chapter we will argue that the recess period actually maximizes social and cognitive dimensions of school performance. Further, the recess period affords opportunities for children to learn and develop skills associated with two key 'developmental tasks' of middle childhood (Waters & Sroufe, 1983): peer relations and adjustment to full-day, formal schooling. But first, we provide a brief historical and theoretical background to the debate surrounding the role of recess and breaks from work during the school day.

Some historical and theoretical debate

Work is good. Play is bad

Questioning the role of recess in the primary school educational process is similar, we think, to the ways in which children's play has been questioned by some educators. Play, like what goes on at recess, is often seen as a force opposing work. Work is viewed as good and play is not. Some trace this dichotomy to the Puritan/Calvinistic ethic in America and much of the Anglo Saxon world (e.g., Sutton-Smith, 1997; Tawney, 1969/1926). Break times, leisure, and play are viewed as 'slothful'. Sloth, remember, is one of the seven deadly sins, portrayed in many Medieval (*before* the Reformation, per se) and Renaissance paintings. Thus, we cannot 'blame' Calvinism or the Protestant work ethic, primarily, for devaluing play and leisure in relation to work.

The positive role of labour and work was certainly stressed by explicitly anti-Christian theorists – most notably Karl Marx (1867/1906). Marx stated that one's labour, realized as one's place in the means of production, defined and formed one's consciousness. Further, benefits accrued without engaging in labour were frowned upon in Marx's notion of the 'unearned increment'. By extension, the benefits of manual labour were stressed by Mao Tse-tung, especially during the Cultural Revolution. The virtues of manual labour were stressed over the enterprise of intellectual activity. Those individuals in Mao's China who engaged in activities of the mind were 're-educated'. In short, the value of work over less visibly 'productive' activities has a long history and has had appeal to a very wide audience. Bertrand Russell (1932/1972) referred to this bias as the 'cult of efficiency'.

While Russell's argument is not aimed at children and schools per se but at the role of leisure and breaks from work for adults in modern industrial society (early twentieth century), his notion of 'idleness' is close to our definition of play and what goes on at recess – 'a capacity for light-heartedness and play' (p. 24). His larger point is that leisure does have benefits, and in his specific case to the economic wellbeing of society. Specifically, he suggested that the work day be reduced (remember this was published in 1932) so that people would have more time to spend in leisure activities, such as playing games, dancing, listening to music, and going to the cinema. The benefit associated with this extension of leisure, for Russell, was that people might choose to learn more about their professions, such as teachers or physicians, learning more about allied fields, or volunteer in public causes. All of this would, he argued, make the world a better *and* more productive place.

There are also developmental implications of Russell's view of leisure. Specifically, and as will be explicated later in this chapter, the view advanced by Russell was that the benefits associated with leisure and play were 'immediate' – not deferred until a later developmental period. That is, leisure, like play during childhood, is beneficial to that period of development where the leisure activities were exercised; they are not postponed to a later period.

By contrast, a more common stance, at least in much of developmental psychology, is to attribute importance to 'early experience' and posit that the benefits associated with play and leisure during childhood are 'deferred' until adulthood; e.g., the roles that children enact in dramatic play are practice for the skills associated with those roles in adulthood. A non-psychological variant of this notion can be found in Thomas Hughes's (1895) praise for the moral instruction afforded by game playing in childhood. In his book, *Tom Brown's School Days*, Hughes (echoing Wellington after helping to defeat Napoleon at Waterloo in 1815) talked about the moral and social lessons learned when young boys engaged in games played on the fields of Rugby School. The timeliness of his opinion is expressed in this frequently cited quote:

> You say you don't see much in it all; nothing but a struggling mass of boys, and a leather ball, which seems to excite them to a great fury, as a red rag does a bull. My dear sir, a battle would look much the same to see, except that the boys would be men, and the balls iron; but a battle would be worth your looking at for all that, and so is a football match. You can't be expected to appreciate the delicate strokes of play, the turns by which the game is lost and won − it takes an old player to do that, but the broad philosophy of football, you can understand if you will.
>
> *(Hughes, 1895, p. 99)*

From Hughes's view, the social skills learned while playing games are similar to those of leading men in battle. The lessons learned on the playing fields at Rugby were generalized to Waterloo. This view is very similar to the view of play espoused by ethologists who suggest that the function of play-fighting during the juvenile period is to provide opportunities to learn and practise skills associated with adult hunting and fighting (Pellegrini & Smith, 1998; Smith, 1982).

The realist might say (and rightly so) that discussions of play and school recess must be conducted in light of the world of real school policy. That is, parents, educators, and politicians are concerned about children's academic achievement as well as their safety in schools. Where they raise concerns that recess may interfere with safety and learning, those concerns must be addressed. This concern has led to recess being diminished or eliminated in the USA, England and Australia (Evans, 1990; Patte, 2006; Pellegrini, 2005).

The place of recess in the school day

Documentation of the place of recess in the school day is very patchy, possibly reflecting the low regard for recess in both the school and academic community. One early US 'national survey' was conducted by the National Association of Elementary School Principals (NAESP) in 1989. This survey was sent to the state superintendents of education of all fifty states plus the District of Columbia.

Responses from 47 states were received. Results indicated that 'recess', in some form, was held in 90% of the cases and of those cases, 96% had one or two recess periods daily. In 75% of the cases, recess lasted 15–20 minutes each. Importantly, we do not know the form that recess took. It could have been a physical education class or a more traditional free play period on the playground. Data from this survey should be interpreted very cautiously, given the limitations associated with the selectivity of the sample and the unknown psychometric properties of the survey.

In 1999 another survey was conducted by the US Department of Education, but only data on kindergartens was available (see Pellegrini, 2005). (We acknow-ledge Ithel Jones of Florida State University for providing these data.) At this point, 71% of American kindergartens reported having recess; 14.6% and 6.7% had, respectively, recess three or four times a week and 7.7% had no recess period. In terms of recess duration, 27% of the respondents said they had 30 minutes of recess, 67.4% had 16–30 minutes, and 6% had less than 15 minutes. Interestingly, children attending private kindergartens were twice as likely to have recess (48%) than those attending public kindergartens (22%). This last finding parallels a more general finding across all the primary grades where children above the poverty level have almost twice the amount of time in the school day allocated to recess (7%), relative to those from below the poverty level (4.%) (Roth, Brooks-Gunn & Linver, 2003). We will return to the policy implications of this discrepancy later in this chapter.

A further US survey conducted by the Center on Education Policy during 2006/07 found that nearly one-fifth of districts had shortened recess by an average of 50 minutes per week (see Ramstetter, Murray & Garner, 2010). There were differences in recess provision depending on the age of the children involved, so although nearly 97% of children in first grade had a recess period, only 74% of other grades in schools had recess. Differences were also found by age group, with first graders experiencing on average 28 minutes of recess per day and sixth graders experiencing 24 minutes on average. Schools where more than 75% of children received a free school lunch tended to have the shortest breaks.

In the UK the current situation is slightly better than in the US with most children experiencing a short morning break of approximately 15 minutes as well as a lunchtime of up to one hour, which includes time for eating lunch. However, two well-designed, nationally representative surveys of recess, or breaktime as it is called in England, in 1996 and in 2006 provide data on the changes in recess across the fifteen years between 1990/91 and 2005/06 (Blatchford & Baines, 2006; Blatchford & Sumpner, 1998). The surveys of a representative sample of 6%–7% of all primary and secondary schools in England and Wales found a growing trend for a reduction in the length of lunchtimes and virtual elimination of the afternoon recess from the school day in secondary schools and at upper primary level. Previously, longer lunchtimes and an afternoon recess were common. The 2006 survey showed that over a course of a week children in secondary school had on average 35 minutes less recess time, upper primary school children had 30 minutes less recess time and lower primary school children had 15 minutes less recess time than pupils had experienced in 1996. There are indications since 2006 that schools have shortened their breaktimes further, with the British government encouraging English schools to extend the school day and to introduce initiatives to improve the attainment outcomes of children from the poorest of backgrounds.

These data clearly indicate that recess holds a marginal place in the school curriculum. We, like Russell, argue that there is not enough leisure time in school in the form of recess. Quite apart from the opportunity that recess offers for tackling obesity and sedentary lifestyles – research suggests that at primary school it can contribute between 30% and 40% of children's recommended amount of daily physical activity (Ridgers, Stratton & Fairclough, 2006) – we will present developmental theory and data suggesting that recess time actually helps students adjust to school and learn, in the traditional sense.

Development in schooling: a metamorphic view

The idea that development can serve as a guide to schooling is, of course, not a new one. Perhaps the most visible translation of a developmental model for schools comes in the form of Developmentally Appropriate Practices from the National Association for the Education of Young Children (NAEYC, 1992). This document is a manifesto for the ways in which young children should be taught. Specifically, it lists instructional practices for infants, toddlers, preschoolers, and primary school students – for example, that stress the importance of play for preschoolers and the foundational role of primary school experiences for subsequent learning.

In this approach to schooling, children are treated as 'imperfect adults' (Bateson, 1981, 2005; Kagan, 1971) and the role of education is to move children along the path to adulthood. This is not to say that children are not viewed as qualitatively different from adults. From this teleological view, children's thinking is described as a progression from less to more differentiated, or developed, and by what it is they cannot do. This view of development highlights the importance of early experience as a determinant of adult behaviour. The benefits of education from this orientation are conceptualized as 'deferred': a skill is built in childhood and the benefits are reaped in adulthood in the form of enhanced skill development.

A contrasting view has been presented by Pat Bateson (1981, 2005; see also Chapter 4 and Pellegrini, 2009), whose 'metamorphic' view of development considers those 'immature' behaviours characterizing childhood as advantageous to the niche of childhood, rather than something imperfect which needs to be overcome. Like the metamorphosis of a tadpole into a frog or a caterpillar into a butterfly, the characteristics and behaviours of the young child are well suited to the period of childhood per se and may not be especially relevant to adult related skills. The benefits reaped from these behaviours are immediate, rather than deferred. These behaviours are not something directly shaped into adult-relevant skills. For example, the sucking behaviour of infants is certainly relevant to feeding during infancy but not related to feeding behaviours later in life (Bateson & Martin, 1999).

The metamorphic view posits that 'immature' behaviours characteristic of childhood, like play, are important to childhood per se and the benefits of play are reaped during that period (Bateson, 2005; Bjorklund & Pellegrini, 2000; Pellegrini, 2009). The clearest example of such an 'immediate benefits' view of play relates to locomotor play. The cardio-vascular and physical fitness benefits of play in childhood are immediate and do not relate to adult cardio-vascular health (Pellegrini & Smith, 1998). Dave Bjorklund and Tony Pellegrini (Bjorklund & Pellegrini, 2000) applied the cognitive immaturity hypothesis to children's play – suggesting that these processes are not inferior variants of adult behaviour but instead specific adaptations to the niche of childhood that enable young children to effectively learn skills and behaviours important for that period, per se. For example, children's over-estimation of their own social skills enables them to persevere at tasks even though, by adult standards, they are not doing it very well. This perseverance may lead to self-perceived success which may, in turn, lead to higher self-perceived competence and help with learning complicated skills and strategies.

At root, this view of development highlights the importance of the notion, for the zoologist Pat Bateson, that natural selection works on different periods of development, not only on adulthood. After all, in order to live to reproduce in adulthood one must adapt to and survive childhood! The construct of a 'developmental task' is important in identifying those behaviours and skills which are crucial to each developmental period (Sroufe, Egelund & Carlson, 1999; Waters & Sroufe, 1983). Developmental tasks vary with age – for example, impulse control during the preschool period, and peer group membership and adjustment during the early primary school years. Mastering the skills necessary for membership in one's school peer group and feeling efficacious in this area should provide a basis for adjustment to school (Pellegrini et al., 2002). We suggest that children's facility with social games is a candidate for an important developmental task as children make the transition to formal schooling.

Recess and social development

In primary school, most children spend much of their time at recess engaged in games (Pellegrini, 2009). Children's games, like recess, surprisingly, have not received extended empirical attention from psychologists or educators for a number of years. We say 'surprisingly' because at least one influential theorist (Piaget, 1983) suggested that games have important implications for children's social and cognitive development. Correspondingly, there have been repeated calls over the last fifty years in the developmental literature for more research on games (e.g., Gump & Sutton-Smith, 1955; Hart, 1993; Rubin, Fein &

Vandenberg, 1983; Sutton-Smith, 1971). Yet, neither the 1998 nor the 2006 *Handbook of Child Psychology* volume on social and personality development (Eisenberg, 1998, 2006), has a single reference in the subject index to games or games with rules, down from the rather sparse six references in the 1983 Handbook (Hetherington, 1983)!

While there are a number of possible reasons for the recent neglect of research on children's games, it clearly is consistent with the theme that scholars, like many school systems in the USA and the UK, do not take the play and games of children seriously. Another reason for this neglect may relate to availability of and access to a research sample of young children at a time when they typically engage in games (i.e., primary school). Compare the ease with which infants and preschool children can be observed in university laboratory schools and the massive amount of research on the modal forms of play for children of these ages, sensorimotor and fantasy play. Primary school-age children, on the other hand, are less accessible for study and proffer fewer opportunities for observations of peer interaction, as much of the primary school day is tightly scheduled around regimens of solitary, sedentary and teacher-directed academic work (Baines, Blatchford & Kutnick, 2003).

Observations of children at recess are an excellent venue to examine children's competence because interaction with peers at recess is both motivating and demanding for children. These are two necessary conditions for reliable and valid assessment of social competence, where social competence is defined rather globally as children's adjustment to the various developmental tasks, such as developing control of one's emotions, learning to make friends, and adjusting to school across the life span (Waters & Sroufe, 1983). That is, children typically enjoy recess and games (Blatchford, 1998), and to successfully engage in games requires a fair level of social and cognitive sophistication (Piaget, 1965). For example, children must know the rules of the games and subordinate their personal views and desires to those rules and to the positions of their peers. That they enjoy these interactions (possibly because they are self-selected) motivates them to exhibit the high levels of competence required to participate in the games. Children's engagement in playground games with their peers then should provide opportunities to learn and develop social skills as well as provide valid insight into their competence (see Chapter 3 which examines this issue in relation to friendships and friendship groups).

Changes with age in breaktime activities

On the basis of pupil accounts (Blatchford, 1998) and pupil observations (Baines & Blatchford, 2011; Blatchford, Baines & Pellegrini, 2003) we found that breaktime had a role in the initiation and development of friendships in school, but the nature of this role changed with age. Friendships between primary-aged children were often manifested in, and supported by, active breaktime activities and playground games (Pellegrini & Blatchford, 2002). But gradually over time and initially amongst girls, friendships were furthered in the context of – in a sense – an absence of activity. In effect the high levels of physical and playful activity begin to be replaced by conversational interaction, often of the type seen at meal times where children share gossip and jokes, make plans, and talk about news and shared interests. By the time children are in secondary school (11 to 16 years) physical activity and games are almost completely replaced by sustained talk (Blatchford, 1998). It is relatively easy for adults to underestimate the value of 'hanging around' to pupils' social relations. Pupils at this age are more likely to make deliberate efforts to escape from adults, and keep interactions private. So in the school context there may be a special role for break and lunchtimes at secondary level, because it is the main school setting within which a degree of privacy and freedom from adults is possible.

Mixed-sex activities

There are times when boys and girls come together to engage in joint activities though these relationships may never reach the status of a same-sex friendship, at least not until adolescence. Research by Barrie Thorne (1993) draws attention to the way games and activities that bring together boys and girls can act to re-affirm single-sex groups but also represent covert interest in and learning about the opposite sex. Through such games children appear to be checking boundaries of what is permissible with the opposite sex. A kind of creativity in games can reflect developments in social relations between boys and girls. Thorne describes these activities as 'border work'. In this activity, boys or girls may act to disrupt the activities of the opposite sex (for example, boys disrupting a girls' game of skipping/jump rope or girls kicking a soccer ball as far away as possible to disrupt a boys' game of soccer). On the other hand boys' and girls' friendship groups may come together to play more provocative games such as 'kiss chase' or play at having 'boy friends' or 'girl friends' which involve teasing but also offer opportunities for affiliation and affection. These occasions may act to foster knowledge about and closer friendship relations between members of the opposite sex. Such activities may become more common in secondary school as part of the development of early romantic relationships. For instance teasing, push and pull, tag and be tagged are some of the activities that young adolescents engage in within mixed-sex social groups. However, we know relatively little about encounters during 'border work', the persons involved and the social implications of participating in them, for example in relation to status with same-sex peers.

Playground games and school adjustment

Before proceeding, it is important to differentiate play and games as they are sometimes confused, possibly because they share some design features. For example, both play (e.g., fantasy play) and games (e.g., soccer) are rule-governed.

The rules governing games, however, are to a point a-priori and codified, whereas the rules governing play are flexible, negotiated by players in different ways, and not set in advance. For example, in a play episode where two children are pretending to cook a meal, they can negotiate rules and roles regarding what is to be cooked (e.g., 'Let's cook stew. No, let's make a cake') and how it is to be cooked ('I want to be the cook now'). Once these issues are agreed upon, play behaviour is consistent with the rules for the theme and the roles, until the rules or roles are challenged. At that time they are typically re-negotiated (Fein, 1981; Garvey, 1990). Indeed, more time is typically spent negotiating and re-negotiating roles and rules in play than in play itself (Garvey, 1990; Sachs, Goldman & Chaille, 1984).

Games, on the other hand, are guided by explicit rules that are set in advance, and violation of these rules usually results in some form of sanction, not re-negotiation (Garvey, 1990). So, for example, in a game of basketball, a child running with the ball without dribbling would be told by peers to forfeit the ball. Because games require following a-priori rules they are not typically observed in children until the primary school years. Nevertheless there are flexibilities in the rules that may be drawn on within a particular game and the interpretation and application of rules and compliance can become the focus of discussion. Some children, more than others, may be able to get away with flouting or manipulating the rules. However a child that tries to flout the rules without the necessary status or social competence might become less liked as a result (Baines & Blatchford, 2011). There are also reliable gender differences in games. Following Piaget (1965) and others, boys, more than girls, prefer to engage in competitive games outdoors (Harper & Sanders, 1975; Pellegrini, 1992a, 2004; Pellegrini et al., 2002; Thorne, 1993). While girls prefer to engage in verbal games, including games like jump rope (skipping in the UK), hopscotch and hand-clapping games, during middle childhood they appear to engage less readily in games than conversation and sedentary activity (Baines & Blatchford, 2011).

We present data from a longitudinal study of first graders attending two public schools in Minneapolis (Pellegrini et al., 2002). The sample consisted of 78 children (30 males and 48 females), with a mean age of 77 months. Most of the children in the sample were lower socioeconomic status (as judged by their receiving free or reduced lunch) and for approximately 40% of the sample, Spanish was the first language. A total of four research associates worked on this project, all of whom were female graduate students. Logistically, each of two research associates was assigned to separate schools to conduct behavioural observations. To minimize bias, research associates did not interview or test the children they observed.

We predicted that being facile with games on the school playground at recess should predict adjustment to the very earliest school years because game facility is an indicator of children's engagement in one important dimension of the school day. Being engaged in this context with peers should generalize to school adjustment in first grade because, as a developmental task for this period, it is an indicator of children's sense of efficacy in the very early grades of school. Children attribute great importance to having peers with whom to interact at recess. Being good at games at recess seems to be an important part of enjoying school and peers at school.

Game facility was defined here (Pellegrini et al., 2002) using multiple informants and formats. These individual measures were aggregated to maximize construct validity (Cronbach, 1971). First, and most generally, game facility was also defined observationally as the percent of total time observed engaged in games across the entire school year, where games were generally coded as chase games (e.g., tag), verbal games (e.g., jump rope/chanting), and ball games (e.g., basketball). Second, and also using direct observations, we indexed the number of children in the focal child's immediate peer group while on the playground. This idea of facility is derived from the ethologically oriented work on group centrality and dominance (Chance, 1967; Vaughn & Waters, 1981). Most dominant individuals are leaders and are sought after, central in the group, and attended to by peers. Children want to be around leaders for a number of reasons. For example, by affiliating with leaders youngsters may learn valuable social skills from and form alliances with leaders. Thus, the number of individuals surrounding an individual is an observational indicator of leadership status.

All direct observation used focal child sampling and continuous recording rules (Pellegrini, 2012). Specifically, focal children were identified daily from a randomized list of all children for whom we had informed consent. Each focal child was followed for three minutes and their behaviour was recorded continuously for that entire period. Each child was observed minimally once/month.

Game facility was also assessed in terms of peer nominations (e.g., Who's good at games?) and teacher ratings of children's facility with games (e.g., Good at games?), each conducted during the fall and spring of the school year. Children whose first language was Spanish were interviewed by a native speaker of Spanish using translated protocols.

School adjustment, too, was defined from different perspectives and aggregated into one score. Specifically, during the fall and spring of children's first grade year they were asked to rate twelve questions concerning how they felt about school (e.g., Going to school makes me happy; School is boring: yes, not sure, no). Correspondingly, teachers rated children's adjustment to school during the fall and spring of the year on an instrument derived, in part, from Ladd and Profilet's (1996) Child Behaviour Scale (e.g., Coping well with school; Has friendly and responsive relationship with teacher). The aggregate of children's and teachers' responses comprised our measure of school adjustment.

Results from this one-year longitudinal study showed that game facility predicted end-of-year school adjustment, after statistically controlling children's social competence and adjustment at the start of the school year. For boys, game facility was a more powerful predictor of adjustment than it was for girls. Boys used their facility with games as a way in which they could achieve and maintain competence with their peers and to adjust to the demands of formal schooling. This finding is consistent with the assumption that the social rules and roles that children learn in one niche (with their peers on the school playground) should predict competence in related niches, with their peers in first grade. Both niches are similar to the extent that they encourage rule-governed behaviour and cooperative interaction with peers, all in the larger context of school. These relations, however, held only for boys, not for girls. For boys, game facility was a more powerful predictor of adjustment than it was for girls. This finding is consistent with the view that male groups are hierarchic, and competence in these groups is often judged by ability to compete and lead (Blatchford et al., 2003; Maccoby, 1998; Maccoby & Jacklin, 1987; Pellegrini, 2004).

That game facility predicted boys' school adjustment is a very important finding for educational policy makers. Games probably provide opportunities to learn and practise the skills necessary for effective social interaction with peers – such as turn-taking and subordinating behaviour to socially defined rules – in an important socialization context, early schooling.

While these results do reinforce earlier research where children's peer relations in school predicted adjustment to school and school success (e.g., Ladd, Kochenderfer & Coleman, 1996), they also extend this earlier work in that the majority of the students in our work were low-income children. It is well known that children, and again boys especially, from economically disadvantaged groups have difficulty adjusting to and succeeding in school (e.g., Greenfield & Suzuki, 1998; Heath, 1983). We have demonstrated that their success in one part of the first grade school day (games at recess) can predict more general school adjustment. The mechanisms by which this happens, however, are not clearly understood and worthy of further study. In Chapter 3, we consider game facility in terms of the slightly different notion of 'game involvement' roles that children tend to engage in during games and interactions with peers in peer groups.

Recess and attention in the classroom

In this section we address what may be a more proximal effect of recess on children's cognitive performance in school by examining the experimentally manipulated effect of varying recess timing regimens on children's attention to controlled classroom tasks. Attention is a measure that is consistent with theories suggesting that breaks from concentrated schoolwork should maximize performance. Following the notion of massed vs. distributed practice (Ebbinghaus, 1885/1964; James, 1901), children should be less attentive to classroom tasks during longer, compared to shorter, seatwork periods (e.g., Stevenson & Lee, 1990). Briefly, massed vs. distributed posits that individual performance is maximized when efforts are 'distributed' across number of trials, rather than 'massed' into fewer trials. For example, a child given a total of a hundred spelling words to memorize will do better if they study the words in ten separate

10-minute sessions rather than in two 50-minute sessions. Following Stevenson and Lee's (1990) anecdotal attributions of the role of recess in Asian children's achievement, we designed a series of experiments to test the effects of recess breaks on children's classroom behaviour after recess. In the studies reported below, attention and inattention were measured in terms of children's looking/ not looking at either their seatwork or, in cases when the teacher was reading to them, at the teacher. Additionally, children's fidgeting and listlessness was also coded as a measure of inattention while children did their seatwork. While this measure of attention was less differentiated than others, such as skin conductivity or heart rate, it was practical for classroom research. Further, this measure is an important indicator of more general school achievement (Johnson, McGue & Iacano, 2005).

The effects of recess timing on children's attention to classroom work were examined, following the design used by Smith and Hagan (1980), where recess timing was defined as the amount of time before recess that children are forced to be sedentary (or are deprived of social and physical play) and attend to class work. This type of regimen typifies most primary school classrooms (Minuchin & Shapiro, 1983). The school in which this research was conducted allowed the researchers to manipulate the times that children went out for recess as well as children's seatwork before and after recess.

The children enrolled in this public elementary school were from varied social economic and ethnic backgrounds. In all of the cases, the children in each of the grades were systematically exposed to different schedules for recess timing. On counter-balanced days they went out to recess either at 10 a.m. or at 10.30 a.m. Before and after each recess period children were read an experimentally manipulated male-preferred (with male characters) or a female-preferred (with female characters) book. During this time we coded their attention/inattention to the task.

The first study, to our knowledge, to address directly this issue of outdoor recess activity and post-recess attention found that third grade children's attention before recess was lower than it was after recess, especially for boys, thus suggesting that recess facilitates attention (Pellegrini & Davis, 1993). Those findings, however, were limited to the extent that we did not control the pre- and post-recess task used to assess children's attention. Specifically, these results may have been due to the fact that attention was related to the gender role stereotypicality of the tasks on which the children worked. Specifically, in the Pellegrini and Davis study (1993) children's class work often involved listening to a story. Because the researchers did not systematically manipulate or control the stories read, it may have been the case that some of the stories read were more preferred by girls. Thus, their attention may have been related to the task, not the effect of recess. In the next series of experiments this confound was removed by systematically varying gender-preference of tasks before and after recess.

In Experiment 1 of a new series of experiments, the effects of outdoor recess timing on the classroom behaviour of boys and girls in grades K (~ 5 years old),

2 (~ 7 years old), and 4 (~9 years old) were examined (Pellegrini, Huberty & Jones, 1995). As in all experiments in this series, recess timing varied by 30 minutes. Children's attention/inattention was assessed before and after recess on male-preferred and female-preferred books.

In Experiment 1, the pre-recess results supported the suppositions of Stevenson and Lee (1990), who proposed that children are less attentive during long, compared to short, work periods. That is, children were generally more attentive after recess than before recess and older children, relative to younger children, were more attentive. For example, fourth grade children's mean attention scores were greater during the short deprivation time, relative to the long deprivation time; at each grade level the children were more inattentive before than after recess. Further, it was found that boys' and girls' attention was influenced by the gender-role stereotypicality of the story. For example, fourth grade boys in the long deprivation condition were more attentive to male-preferred stories and less attentive to female-preferred stories while the pattern was reversed for the girls. This finding is consistent with the extant literature on gender preference for stories (e.g., Monson & Sebesta, 1991).

Results from this experiment should be interpreted cautiously, primarily because of the small sample size (20 children/grade and 10 children/sex within each grade) and because there was only one classroom at each grade level. Replication is clearly needed to assure that the results are not aberrational (Lykken, 1968), especially when the results have implications for school policy.

In Experiment 2, the same outdoor recess timing and attention procedures were used as in Experiment 1; second and fourth graders (one classroom for each grade) were studied in the same school as in Experiment 1. The results from Experiment 2, similar to those from Experiment 1, revealed that children's task attention is affected by recess timing and that timing interacted with dimensions of the task as well as children's age and gender. Children generally, but especially second graders, were more attentive after recess.

In Experiment 3, students in two fourth grade classrooms were studied and the same recess timing paradigm was employed. The recess period was indoors, however. The same experiment was conducted with two separate intact classrooms. Such a design was chosen because of the relatively small samples involved in each classroom. This procedure minimizes the probability of obtaining aberrant results if similar results are obtained in both samples – thus replicating each other. The results from this experiment are similar to those from other experiments: attention was greater after the recess period than it was before the break in the second classroom. The result from the indoor recess study was similar to the outdoors results – children are generally more attentive to classroom work after recess than before. Whether recess is indoors or outdoors does not seem to matter. Again, in both cases, inattention is lower after recess.

The message from this research is clear. Breaks between periods of intense work seem to maximize children's attention to their class work. More speculatively, it is probably this increased attention that is partially responsible for the positive relations between recess and performance on achievement tests (Pellegrini, 1992b, 2005).

What we really still need to know, however, is the effect of different recess regimens on attention. A first step in this direction was already presented, as we found that indoor recess periods, like outdoor periods, seemed to be effective facilitators of children's attention to class work. This result is consistent with mass vs. distributed practice as the mechanism responsible for the effects of recess on attention. From this view, the nature of the break is somewhat less important than having a break per se. To more thoroughly examine this explanation, researchers should examine different types of breaks after periods of intense cognitive work. For example, does watching a short video or listening to music for a short period facilitate attention? Further, do these effects vary with age? Researchers should also consider the possibility that different aspects of recess regimens should have different optima for different outcome measures (Bateson, personal communication, July 2005). Findings from two randomized control trials are of relevance here. These studies suggest that what happens during lunchtime breaks affects attention and activity when children return to class afterwards. These studies of primary and secondary school children found that those that experienced an improved social and nutritional eating context showed higher levels of on-task attention generally and particularly during whole-class teaching than pupils in control groups who experienced their usual meal time experience (Golley et al., 2010; Storey et al., 2011). The meal times experienced by the control group were characterized by long queues, unpleasant surroundings and a poor nutritional standard of food provision. While a number of theories might explain these findings, including explanations focusing on nutritional quality of food, it is likely that during these times children had a heightened opportunity to socialize and enjoy the company of friends and peers (see Baines & MacIntyre, forthcoming). Of particular relevance here is the surprising finding that within the primary classrooms of the intervention group there was a higher level of socializing with peers, often off task, than evident amongst pupils in control classrooms. This finding suggests that improved socializing opportunities may have 'over-spilt' from the meal time period and led to children talking more with peers in class than was the case for children in the control group (Golley et al., 2010). This pattern was not found in the study of secondary school students, indicating that they were more able to self-regulate their behaviour or that teachers did not give them the opportunity to talk with peers in class. The main messages that result from these studies are that frequent, well-timed and enjoyable breaks may thus affect attention in class, and the social dimensions of the break time period may also be important for social competence and more general school adjustment.

Bjorklund's cognitive immaturity hypothesis provides some general guidance here (Bjorklund & Pellegrini, 2000). The theory suggests that breaks for preschool and primary school children should be 'playful' and unstructured. Providing time for children to socialize and interact with peers or materials on their own terms, that is, with minimal adult direction, should maximize attention to subsequent tasks. With older children and adults, merely providing breaks between periods of intense work might suffice to maximize attention. The research on massed vs. distributed practice with adults also supports this view.

Another crucial aspect of the recess period that needs further research is the duration of the recess period. Should it be 10 minutes, 20 minutes, 30 minutes, etc.? We simply do not know. Answers to this question have obvious implications for school policy and scheduling. We explored the issue of recess duration with a sample of preschool children (aged 4–5 years) (Holmes, Pellegrini & Schmidt, unpublished data). Procedurally, children had 'circle time' and were read a story before recess. Then they went outdoors for recess periods of 10, 20, or 30 minutes. When they returned to their classrooms they again sat in a circle and listened to a story read to them by their teachers. Attention was recorded and coded (using scan sampling and instantaneous recording procedures) for whether the child was gazing in the direction of the book or the teacher reading the book.

Consistent with earlier work with older primary school children, reported above, attention was greater following the recess period, and girls were more attentive than boys to classroom tasks in all conditions. Thus it seems reasonable to conclude that recess breaks help children attend to classroom tasks.

Regarding the differing durations of recess periods, we found that attention to classroom tasks was greatest following the 20-minute and 10-minute outdoor play periods whereas the 30-minute period resulted in higher rates of inattention. These findings are consistent with anecdotal evidence from the UK that stated that children become bored with recess after too long a period, and thus longer periods may become counter-productive (Blatchford, 1998). This work needs to be replicated as it represents only one short-term study with a relatively small sample. The duration of the recess periods is clearly important, as it is one of the persistent questions posed to us by parents and teachers. How long should the recess be? Should its duration vary with children's age? Clearly at this point we only have hints, and are not sure.

Policy implications

Theory and data presented in this chapter provide support for the positive role of recess in the school curriculum. At a basic level, providing breaks over the course of the instructional day facilitates primary school children's attention to classroom tasks. That these results were obtained using well-controlled field experiments (e.g., recess deprivation periods and classroom attention tasks were experimentally manipulated) and replicated a number of times by different groups of researchers should provide confidence in the findings.

Additionally, the studies reported above demonstrated the effects of both indoor and outdoor recess periods on attention. These effects provide insight into the role of a relatively sedentary break period on subsequent attention. From a policy perspective, educators sometimes use indoor recess as an alternative to outdoor breaks. This may be due to the fact that teachers or playground supervisors are reluctant to go outdoors during inclement weather or they may be sensitive to the possibility of law suits related to injuries on playground equipment. Our results provide support to the efficacy of indoor breaks.

Further, our results also demonstrated, in both the USA and in England, that the games that young children (i.e., in their first years in school) play in the playground at recess are related not only to school adjustment but also to dimensions of social competence, such as cooperative behaviour and peer popularity (Blatchford et al., 2003; Pellegrini et al., 2002).

Of course, the generalizability of our results is limited to our specific sample. Even with that said, we are relatively confident in the results as they are consistent with theory and were replicated across a number of studies and sites. Both of these conditions are important in minimizing Type I error. The results presented here support the anecdotal evidence from Taiwanese and Japanese schools, suggesting that in order to maintain high levels of attention, children need frequent breaks in the course of the day (Stevenson & Lee, 1990). According to Stevenson and Lee (1990) Asian schools provide frequent breaks across a relatively long school day. These breaks, they suggest, are related to children's school performance. Also as noted above, English children have frequent recess periods in their school day, but the duration of these periods, too, has been eroding (Blatchford & Baines, 2006). However, in England, as in the USA, what children do in the playground at recess has 'educational value' to the extent that children's participation in games predicts school adjustment and social competence (Blatchford et al., 2003). This evidence should inform policy and be used to guide those policy makers and politicians seeking to diminish or eliminate recess from the school curriculum.

First, and like Asian schools, American children's school days and school years should be lengthened. Such a policy would bring the total number of hours American children attend school in a year closer to other countries in the world. This increase should have the corresponding benefit of increasing achievement. Longer school days and years – with frequent breaks – should accomplish this. Additionally, a longer school day and year would ensure that children have a safe place while their parents are at work. Children would be in school, learning and interacting with their peers, rather than at home, unsupervised, or in expensive after-school care.

While recess periods alone seem to be important, it is also important to let children interact on their own terms with peers. Providing children with a physical education class as a substitute for recess, does not serve the same purpose (Pellegrini, 2005; Council on Physical Education for Children, 2001). This conclusion is supported on a number of fronts. First, and at the level of theory, both the cognitive immaturity hypothesis and massed vs. distributed practice theory suggest that after periods of intense instruction children need breaks from this instruction. A physical education class is another form of instruction and thus would not provide the sort of break needed to maximize instruction. Further, physical education classes typically do not provide the variety of rich opportunities for peer interaction that recess does. The research presented above pointed to the importance of peer interaction for both social and cognitive outcomes.

Second, the importance of physical education for classroom attention is typically predicated on the idea that children 'need to blow off steam' after periods of work, and the vigorous activity associated with physical education should serve this purpose. However, the idea of 'blowing off steam' is rooted in 'surplus energy theory' – an invalid nineteenth-century theory (Evans & Pellegrini, 1997).

Lastly, our longitudinal observations of children's games at recess during their first year of full-time schooling also reinforce the importance of relative unstructured peer interaction for development. Games with peers are both motivating and demanding, thus they maximize children's use of complex social cognitive strategies – strategies important in other dimensions of schooling, and life.

References

Baines, E. & Blatchford, P. (2011). Playground games and activities in school and their role in development. In A.D. Pellegrini (Ed.), *The Oxford Handbook of the Development of Play*. New York: Oxford University Press.

Baines, E., Blatchford, P. & Kutnick, P. (2003). Changes in grouping practice over primary and secondary school. *International Journal of Educational Research*, 39, 9–34.

Baines, E. & MacIntyre, H. (forthcoming). Children's social experiences with peers during school meal times.

Bateson, P.P.G. (1981). Discontinuities in development and changes in the organization of play in cats. In K. Immelmann, G. Barlow, L. Petrinovich & M. Main (Eds), *Behavioral Development* (pp. 281–295). New York: Cambridge University Press.

Bateson, P.P.G. (2005). Play and its role in the development of great apes and humans. In A.D. Pellegrini & P.K. Smith (Eds), *The Nature of Play: Great Apes and Humans* (pp. 13–26). New York: Guilford.

Bateson, P.P.G. & Martin, P. (1999). *Design for a Life: How Behaviour Develops*. London: Jonathan Cape.

Bjorklund, D.F. & Pellegrini, A.D. (2000). Child development and evolutionary psychology. *Child Development*, 71, 1687–1708.

Blatchford, P. (1998). *Social Life in School*. London: Falmer.

Blatchford, P. & Baines, E. (2006). *A Follow-Up National Survey of Breaktimes in Primary and Secondary Schools* (Report to Nuffield Foundation Ref: EDV/00399/G). Retrieved 10 September 2009, from www.breaktime.org.uk/NuffieldBreakTimeReport-WEBVersion.pdf.

Blatchford, P., Baines, E. & Pellegrini, A.D. (2003). The social context of school playground games: sex and ethnic differences and changes over time after entry into junior school. *British Journal of Developmental Psychology*, 21, 481–505.

Blatchford, P. & Sumpner, C. (1998). What do we know about break time? Results from a national survey of breaktime and lunch time in primary and secondary schools. *British Educational Research Journal*, 24, 79–94.

Chance, M.R.A. (1967). Attention structure as a basis for primate rank order. *Man*, 2, 503–518.

Council on Physical Education for Children (2001). *Recess in Elementary Schools: A Position Paper from the National Association for Sport and Physical Education.* Retrieved 28 September 2000 from eric.ed.uiuc.edu/naecs/position/recessplay/html.

Cronbach, L.J. (1971). Validity. In R.L. Thorndike (Ed.), *Educational Measurement* (pp. 443–507). Washington, DC: American Council on Education.

Ebbinghaus, H. (1885/1964). *Memory.* New York: Teachers College Press.

Eisenberg, N. (Ed.) (1998). *Manual of Child Psychology, Volume 3, Social, Emotional, and Personality Development.* New York: Wiley.

Eisenberg, N. (Ed.) (2006). *Handbook of Child Psychology, Volume 3, Social, Emotional, and Personality Development.* New York: Wiley.

Evans, J. (1990). The teacher role in playground supervision. *Play and Culture, 33,* 219–234.

Evans, J. & Pellegrini, A.D. (1997). Surplus energy theory: an endearing but inadequate justification for break time. *Educational Review, 49,* 229–236.

Fein, G.G. (1981). Pretend play in childhood: an integrative review. *Child Development, 52,* 1095–1118.

Garvey, C. (1990). *Play* (Second edn). Cambridge, MA: Harvard University Press.

Golley, R., Baines, E., Bassett, P., Wood, L., Pearce, J. & Nelson, M. (2010). School lunch and learning behaviour in primary schools: an intervention study. *European Journal of Clinical Nutrition, 64,* 1280–1288.

Greenfield. P.M. & Suzuki, L.K. (1998). Culture and human development: implications for parenting, education, pediatrics, and mental health. In I.E. Sigel & K.A. Renninger (Eds), *Handbook of Child Psychology, Volume 4: Child Psychology in Practice* (pp. 1059–1109). New York: Wiley.

Gump, P.V. & Sutton-Smith, B. (1955). The 'It' role in children's games. *The Group, 17,* 3–8.

Harper, L. & Sanders, K. (1975). Preschool children's use of space: sex differences in outdoor play. *Developmental Psychology, 11,* 119.

Hart, C. (1993). Children on playgrounds: applying current knowledge to future practice and inquiry. In C. Hart (Ed.), *Children on Playgrounds* (pp. 418–432). Albany, NY: SUNY Press.

Heath, S. (1983). *Ways with Words.* New York: Cambridge University Press.

Hetherington, E.M. (1983), *Handbook of Child Psychology: Vol. IV. Socialization, Personality and Social Development.* New York: Wiley.

Hughes, T. (1895). *Tom Brown's School Days.* Cambridge: Riverside Press.

James, W. (1901). *Talks to Teachers on Psychology: And to Students on Some of Life's Ideals.* New York: Holt.

Johnson, W., McGue, M. & Iacano, W.G. (2005). Disruptive behavior and school grades: genetic and environmental relations in 11-year-olds. *Journal of Educational Psychology, 97,* 391–405.

Kagan, J. (1971). *Change and Continuity in Infancy.* New York: Wiley.

Ladd, G.W., Kochenderfer, B.J. & Coleman, C.C. (1996). Friendship quality as a predictor of young children's early school adjustment. *Child Development, 67,* 1103–1118.

Ladd, G.W. & Profilet, S.M. (1996). The Child Behavior Scale: a teacher-report measure of young children's aggression, withdrawn, and prosocial behaviors. *Developmental Psychology, 32,* 1008–1024.

Lykken, D. (1968). Statistical significance in psychological research. *Psychological Bulletin, 70,* 151–159.

Maccoby, E.E. (1998). *The Two Sexes: Growing Up Apart, Coming Together.* Cambridge, MA: Harvard University Press.

Maccoby, E. & Jacklin, C. (1987). Gender segregation in childhood. In H. Reese (Ed.), *Advances in Child Development, Vol. 20* (pp. 239–287). Amsterdam: Elsevier.

Marx, K. (1867/1906). *Capital, Vol. 1.* Chicago: Charles Kerr.

Minuchin, P. & Shapiro, E. (1983). The school as a context for social development. In E.M. Hetherington (Ed.), *Manual of Child Psychology, Vol. 4* (pp. 197–274). New York: Wiley.

Monson, D. & Sebesta, S. (1991). Reading preferences. In J. Flood, J. Jensen, D. Lapp & J. Squire (Eds), *Handbook of Research on Teaching the English Language Arts* (pp. 664–673). New York: Macmillan.

National Association for the Education of Young Children (1992). *Developmentally Appropriate Practice in Early Childhood Programs Serving Infants, Toddlers, Younger Preschoolers.* Washington, DC: NAEYC.

Patte, M. (2006). What happened to recess: examining time devoted to recess in Pennsylvania's elementary schools. *Play and Folklore,* 48, 5–16.

Pellegrini, A.D. (1992a). Preference for outdoor play during early adolescence. *Journal of Adolescence,* 15, 241–254.

Pellegrini, A.D. (1992b). Kindergarten children's social cognitive status as a predictor of first grade success. *Early Childhood Research Quarterly,* 7, 565–577.

Pellegrini, A.D. (2004). Sexual segregation in childhood: a review of evidence for two hypotheses. *Animal Behaviour,* 68, 435–443.

Pellegrini, A.D. (2005). *Recess: Its Role in Development and Education.* Mahwah, NJ: Erlbaum.

Pellegrini, A.D. (2009). *The Role of Play in Human Development.* New York: Oxford University Press.

Pellegrini, A.D. (2012). *Observing Children in their Natural Worlds* (3rd edn). New York: Taylor & Francis.

Pellegrini, A. & Blatchford, P. (2002). The developmental and educational significance of breaktime in school. *The Psychologist,* 15, 2, 59–62.

Pellegrini, A.D. & Davis, P. (1993). Relations between children's playground and classroom behaviour. *British Journal of Educational Psychology,* 63, 88–95.

Pellegrini, A.D., Huberty, P.D. & Jones, I. (1995). The effects of recess timing on children's playground and classroom behaviors. *American Educational Research Journal,* 32, 845–864.

Pellegrini, A.D., Kato, K., Blatchford, P. & Baines, E. (2002). A short-term longitudinal study of children's playground games across the first year of school: implications for social competence and adjustment to school. *American Educational Research Journal,* 39, 991–1015.

Pellegrini, A.D. & Smith, P.K. (1998). Physical activity play: the nature and function of a neglected aspect of play. *Child Development,* 69, 577–598.

Piaget, J. (1965). *The Moral Judgment of the Child.* New York: Free Press.

Piaget, J. (1983). Piaget's theory. In W. Kessen (Ed.), *Handbook of Child Psychology: History, Theory, and Methods* (pp. 103–128). New York: Wiley.

Ramstetter, C., Murray, R. & Garner, A. (2010). The crucial role of recess in schools. *Journal of School Health,* 80, 517–526.

Ridgers, N., Stratton, G. & Fairclough, S. (2006). Physical activity levels of children during school playtime. *Sports Medicine,* 36, 359–371.

Roth, J.L., Brooks-Gunn, J. & Linver, M.R. (2003). What happens during the school day? Time diaries from a national sample of elementary school teachers. *Teachers College Record,* 105, 317–343.

Rubin, K.H., Fein, G. & Vandenberg, B. (1983). Play. In E.M. Hetherington (Ed.), *Handbook of Child Psychology: Volume IV, Socialization, Personality and Social Development* (pp. 693–774). New York: Wiley.

Russell, B. (1932/1972). *In Praise of Idleness and Other Essays*. New York: Simon & Schuster.

Sachs, J., Goldman, J. & Chaille, L. (1984). Planning in pretend play. In A. Pellegrini and T. Yawkey (Eds), *The Development of Oral and Written Language in Social Context* (pp. 119–128). Norwood, NJ: Ablex.

Smith, P.K. (1982). Does play matter? Functional and evolutionary aspects of animal and human play. *The Behavioral and Brain Sciences*, 5, 139–184.

Smith, P.K. & Hagan, T. (1980). Effects of deprivation on exercise play in nursery school children. *Animal Behaviour*, 28, 922–928.

Sroufe, L.A., Egelund, B. & Carlson, E.A. (1999). One social world: the integrated development of parent–child and peer relationships. In W.A. Collins & B. Laursen (Eds), *Relationships as Developmental Contexts: The Minnesota Symposia on Child Psychology*, Vol. 30 (pp. 241–261). Mahwah, NJ: Erlbaum.

Stevenson, H.W. & Lee, S.Y. (1990). Concepts of achievement. *Monographs for the Society for Research in Child Development* (Serial No. 221), 55(1/2).

Storey, C.H., Pearce, J., Ashfield-Watt, P., Wood, L., Baines, E. & Nelson, M. (2011). A randomised controlled trial of the effect of school food and dining room modifications on classroom behaviour in secondary school children. *European Journal of Clinical Nutrition*, 65(1), 32–38.

Sutton-Smith, B. (1971). A syntax for play and games. In R. Herron & B. Sutton-Smith (Eds), *Child's Play* (pp. 298–310). New York: Wiley.

Sutton-Smith, B. (1997). *The Ambiguity of Play*. Cambridge, MA: Harvard University Press.

Tawney, R.H. (1969/1926). *Religion and the Rise of Capitalism*. Harmondsworth, UK: Penguin.

Thorne, B. (1993). *Gender Play: Boys and Girls in School*. Buckingham: Open University Press.

Vaughn, B.E. & Waters, E. (1981). Attention structure, sociometric status, and dominance: interrelations, behavioral correlates, and relationships to social competence. *Developmental Psychology*, 17, 275–288.

Waters, E. & Sroufe, L.A. (1983). Social competence as developmental construct. *Developmental Review*, 3, 79–97.

6

AGGRESSION IN SCHOOL: THE SPECIFIC CASE OF BULLIES AND VICTIMS

Violence and aggression are major problems in elementary and secondary schools around the world. Problems range in severity from extreme acts of physical aggression, such as the all too frequent (especially in the USA) in-school shootouts, to acts of verbal aggression, such as teasing, shunning, and most recently 'cyber-bullying'. While aggression has an unfortunately long history in urban schools (e.g., the 'Blackboard Jungles' of 1950s American schools), the problem has crept into seemingly 'peaceful' settings like rural Scotland and repeatedly in suburban Colorado, as well as schools and youth groups in Norway and Sweden. Indeed, the prevalence and intensity of the problem of school aggression in countries such as Norway and Britain have led to national and state campaigns to remediate the problem.

Aggression in individual children can be reliably identified when they first enter preschool, where aggression is defined as acts (physical, verbal, and social/ relational) intended to harm others (Coie & Dodge, 1998). Individual levels of aggression tend to be stable across the lifespan and can become particularly acute, in terms of frequency and severity, in middle or junior high schools (Coie & Dodge, 1998; National Center for Educational Statistics, 1995).

Clearly there is a real problem, and one that shows no signs of dissipating. Unfortunately, the same scenario continues to re-play in America's schools, exacerbated by the omnipresence of guns and politicians' lack of the moral compasses necessary to enact gun-control legislation. In order to begin to remediate these problems, it is especially important to identify both aggressors and persistent targets of aggression at the most stressful periods in youngsters' lives, such as making the transition to adolescence and to a new school.

In this chapter we discuss one important dimension of the problem of school violence: bullies and victims. Bullying is defined, following Olweus (1993a), as instances of negative actions being directed at a specific youngster or group of youngsters (where there's a power imbalance) repeatedly and over time. Negative actions are broadly defined in terms of physical aggression, for example, hitting; verbal aggression, such as name calling or social exclusion; social/relational aggression (Crick, 1996; Crick & Grotpeter, 1995; Lagerspetz et al., 1988); and cyber-bullying (Smith, 2012). Bullies are the perpetrators of these actions and victims are the targets.

A brief word about definitions, generally, and about those of bullying and victimization, specifically, is warranted. First, and in the more general sense, clear definition about psychological terms is necessary for science clarity and progress. That is, the scientific enterprise depends on the dialectic relationships between inductive and deductive processes, as Bertrand Russell (1932/1972) reminded us over 80 years ago (see also Cronbach, 1957 and Smith, 2011 for interesting discussions). Induction should typify the beginning stages of the process and give rise to definitions and hypotheses. Deductive processes are employed next to test hypotheses (Popper, 1959) and are dominant in psychological research (Smith, 2011). If there is doubt regarding the pervasiveness of deduction in contemporary psychological research it is worth noting that in statistics modules in undergraduate courses there is an often stated dictum proffered by the instructor that hypotheses should be stated a priori, before statistical analyses are carried out. While this is understandable in order to reduce the risks associated with Type I error, it would be better advice if it were to be employed after induction had given rise to the hypotheses!

More specific to induction and definition, we feel it is important that psychologists should spend substantial time directly observing the phenomenon under study and, from the behavioural components of these observations, induce a category. An old, but not dated source book for this sort of enterprise is Nick Blurton Jones's (1972) *Ethological Studies of Child Behaviour.* Too often, psychologists' definitions are not based on direct observation and, consequently, lack content and construct validity. A classic case of this problem in developmental psychology is rough-and-tumble play (R&T). Psychologists (e.g., Ladd, 1983; Ladd & Profilet, 1996) often define R&T as aggressive. However, empirical studies of the definition of R&T and aggression have shown that they have different factor structures (e.g., Blurton Jones, 1972; Smith & Connolly, 1980; Pellegrini, 1989), antecedents (e.g., Humphreys & Smith, 1984), and consequences (e.g., Humphreys & Smith, 1984; Pellegrini, 1989). Thus, though the same terms may be used by different researchers, they mean very different things, resulting in confusion and ambiguity.

Regarding definitions of bullying specifically, there is very real benefit with keeping with one empirically derived definition, until it is falsified. Specifically, keeping with a specified definition is necessary for there to be unambiguous communications about the construct. For example, when comparing rates of bullying across different locales, one definition is obviously necessary. Correspondingly, one definition is necessary in comparing the efficacy of anti-bullying programs.

There are cases when different definitions are used. In these cases they should, in our view, be based on prior, careful empirical work. Then, the definitions should be explicated so that readers are aware of the ways in which they differ from other definitions. Without this, there can be little scientific or programmatic advance. An example of how not to derive a definition of bullying can be found in a recent example from a school system in the metropolitan Minneapolis area. In this case, public hearings were held to determine how the school system should define it!

Bullies, victims, and aggressive victims, and the differential use of aggression

A substantial portion of school violence involves bullies systematically targeting a group of victims (Perry et al., 1990). That is, much school violence is perpetrated by a specific group of youngsters: bullies, and the target of much of this aggression is also limited to a specific group: victims. The research of Olweus (1978, 1993b), with Scandinavian youngsters, Perry (e.g., Boldizar et al., 1989; Perry et al., 1990), with middle-class American youngsters, and Smith (Smith & Sharpe, 1994), with a diverse group of English children, has provided much information on bullies and their motives for targeting specific children. We consider possible antecedents and consequences (in terms of cost and benefits) of behaviours which lead to bullying and victimization. This process is an important first step in addressing the problem.

Bullies

Bullies are youngsters who systematically and repeatedly target another group of youngsters towards whom they are either directly and physically aggressive (e.g., hitting), or indirectly and relationally so (e.g., shunning) and via cyber-bullying (Smith, 2012). Bullies are typically bigger and stronger than their target and more frequently boys, than girls (Olweus, 1993b). Relatedly, bullies, and aggressors more generally, target same-sex peers, from preschool through adulthood (Archer, 2004; Pellegrini, 2002). They are also non-compliant and aggressive in other aspects of their life (Olweus, 1993b). Bullies represent about 7%–15% of the sampled school-age population (Olweus, 1993b; Schwartz et al., 1997; Smith & Sharpe, 1994).

Researchers have identified another form of aggression, which seems to be a particularly female form of aggression. Relational aggression (Crick, 1996; Crick & Grotpeter, 1995), or indirect aggression (Lagerspetz et al., 1988), or social aggression (Archer, 2004) involves the negative uses of peer relations, such as shunning or maligning a peer. While this line of research has not typically been framed in bully–victim terms, it should, when it occurs persistently between un-equals, be considered a form of bullying.

Most recently a new form of bullying, cyber-bullying (Smith, 2012), has emerged. Cyber-bullying is much more likely to occur outside of school, though it is still likely to be between classmates. More exactly, Peter Smith (2012) has identified seven features distinguishing cyber-bullying from the above definition of bullying: technological expertise is required; it is primarily indirect rather than direct, and thus may be anonymous and the perpetrator does not usually see the victim's reaction, at least in the short term; the variety of bystander roles in cyber-bullying is more complex than in most traditional bullying as a bystander may be with the perpetrator when an act is sent or posted, with the victim when it is received, or with neither; there is no social status display in cyber-bullying; there is a much larger potential audience in cyber-bullying; it is difficult to escape from cyber-bullying.

Socialization research suggests that the families of bullies are conflictual and often their parents use aggression and other power-assertive techniques to manage behaviour (Loeber & Dishion, 1984; Schwartz, 1993). As a result of exposure to adults using such power-assertive strategies and exposure to violence in the media, these youngsters learn that aggression can be used instrumentally, in the service of obtaining desired goals (Bandura, 1973; Dodge, 1991; Schwartz et al., 1997). For example, bullying may boost social status within a group of aggressive youngsters.

There are observational data to substantiate these claims. For example, preschool children's bullying behaviours are often reinforced by victims' responses of pain and submission (Patterson et al., 1967). Some preschool children use aggression as a way in which to secure resources in their classrooms, such as access to toys, activity centres, and peer attention (Pellegrini et al., 2007). Relatedly, older youngsters (i.e., during early adolescence) may use physically assertive behaviours as a way in which to publicly display dominance over weaker peers or rivals (Pellegrini & Long, 2002; Pellegrini & Smith, 1998). Observations of boys in early adolescence on the school playground provide support for this claim. Specifically, boys moving up in status from less to more 'tough' or 'hard' initiate physically vigorous interaction with peers of both higher and lower dominance status in an effort to gain status. On the other hand, boys declining in dominance status (that is, boys moving down in status) limit physically vigorous initiations to lower-status peers (Pellegrini, 1995a). Further, in the initial stages of group formation these physically vigorous encounters result in aggression at statistically reliable rates (Pellegrini, 1995b). By that we mean aggressive boys often turn seemingly playful but rough interaction into aggression. Targets of this rough interaction are rated by their teachers as victims (passive and aggressive victim status was not differentiated in this work).

The aggressive behaviour of bullies, especially in preschool and primary school, often results in general unpopularity and rejection with peers; that is, they tend to be more frequently disliked than liked by peers in their classrooms (Dodge, 1991; Olweus, 1993a). However, among other aggressive youngsters and during secondary school, bullies tend to be popular (Cairns et al., 1988; Pellegrini et al., 1999; Sutton, Smith & Swettenham, 1999a). Their facility in using certain forms of aggression may relate positively to their peer status within such deviant groups. More generally, and disturbingly, aggressive boys are viewed positively, e.g., nominated as dates to a hypothetical party and spending more time with girls (Pellegrini & Long, 2002, 2007). This represents a commonsensical picture of a 'gang' leader: tough and a leader of his peers.

In short, bullies are aggressive youngsters who use aggression in a systematic and calculating way against a group of weaker peers. As we will discuss, this target group is unpopular with their peers and consequently the costs associated with this type of aggression (e.g., disapproval by one's peers) are limited.

Victims

Victims are a heterogeneous group, being composed of passive victims, representing about 10% of the sampled population of school-age youngsters (Olweus, 1993b; Pellegrini et al., 1999; Schwartz et al., 1993, 1997), and aggressive victims, representing 2%–10% of the population (Olweus, 1993b; Schwartz et al., 1997). Passive victims tend to be physically slight or frail, and in middle school they tend to be average or poor students and not popular with peers (Olweus, 1993b). Behaviourally, these youngsters are not assertive; for example, in relation to non-victims, they initiate social conversation at lower rates and are less assertive (Schwartz et al., 1993). In response to peers' initiatives, they are more submissive than are comparisons (Schwartz et al., 1993). In the absence of bullies they blend into classrooms like other youngsters and they are not victimized as adults after they leave school (Olweus, 1991).

Aggressive victims, too, are systematically bullied by their peers, yet they display a hostile style of social interaction (Perry et al., 1990). Additionally, these youngsters are 'hot tempered': they use aggression reactively, not instrumentally, in response to provocation or after losing control (Schwartz et al., 1997). Descriptively, these youngsters are nominated by their peers as those who both 'start fights', 'say mean things', 'get mad easily' and 'get picked on, teased and hit or pushed' (Schwartz et al., 1997).

Aggressive victims are both similar to and different from both passive victims and bullies. Like bullies they are aggressive but their aggression is reactive, not instrumental; passive victims are not aggressive. While bullies are described by peers as starting fights and victims are described as getting picked on and teased, aggressive victims are described as both starting fights and being picked on. Unlike bullies, however, aggressive victims are not popular with any particular clique of children. Indeed, aggressive victims are the most rejected members of their peer group. Extreme rejection, in turn, puts this group at extreme risk of negative developmental outcomes, such as dropping out of school, behaviour problems (Parker & Asher, 1987) and, in extreme cases, homicide, as may be the case with some of the adolescents involved in the in-school shoot-outs mentioned at the beginning of this chapter.

The socialization histories of aggressive victims, like those of bullies, are also typified by adversarial and power-assertive interactions. However, aggressive victims describe their parents as inconsistent and are sometimes abused (Bowers et al., 1994). Further, aggressive victims perceive their families as low in warmth and parental management skills. In short, they view the world as a hostile and untrustworthy place (Bowers et al., 1994) and, based on these hostile attributions, these children often react aggressively to others' provocative social behaviour. For example, an aggressive victim would typically attribute hostile and aggressive intent to a peer accidentally bumping into him.

Aggressive victims, unlike bullies, use aggression 'reactively' (Dodge, 1991; Schwartz et al., 1997), not instrumentally. As illustrated above, they often use aggression in retaliatory circumstances, in response to what they perceive as threat. They are typically emotional responses, not calculated initiatives. Unlike bullies, these children do not systematically choose weaker children as targets of their aggression. These youngsters may use aggression as a result of losing self control. Additionally, aggressive victims may associate with bullies because they are reinforced by the bullies for doing so.

That bullies exhibit prosocial behaviour at rates similar to their non-aggressive peers (Pepler et al., 1993) suggests that they may be reinforcing victims during interaction. Relatedly, victims often imitate bullies (Dodge & Coie, 1987). It may be that bullies and aggressive victims choose to interact in similar activities, like rough games, and bullies occasionally dispense prosocial behaviour to victims as reinforcers; only occasionally are they aggressively victimized by bullies (Pellegrini et al., 1999). Aggressive victims may also imitate bullies' tactics and later use them with less dominant peers. Thus, bully–aggressive victim interaction may be mutually reinforcing.

How bullies and victims establish and maintain their relationships: the process

Social exchange theory predicts that bullies seek out targets for whom the negative consequences (or costs) of aggression are minimal in relation to the benefits. The victimization process may also begin at transitional points between schools, when children are establishing relationships with a new peer group; for example, when a child enters a school or a classroom in the middle of the school year. Bullies may initially 'sample' a wide variety of peers for potential victimization; targets become less varied as victims are identified (Perry et al., 1990). Bullies may interact with a variety of children during recess, for example. As part of this process they identify those children whom they know they can and cannot intimidate. Those children who can be intimidated become 'their' victims.

We also know that aggression (Pellegrini et al., 2007), generally, and bullying specifically (Pellegrini & Long, 2002), increases at transition points in schools. For example, when preschoolers return after their winter break, rates of aggression increase and then decrease across time (Pellegrini et al., 2007). Similarly, rates of bullying decrease across the primary school years, but when these same children move into middle school, rates of bullying increase, only to decrease later in the year (Pellegrini & Long, 2002). That is, we consider many forms of bullying as a strategy used by children and, especially, adolescents, to gain and maintain status with their peers.

The period of early adolescence is especially important for the study of bullying and victimization because during this period peers become more important in youngsters' lives and peers have been negatively and positively implicated in bullying and victimization. Specifically, bullying seems to be used as a way in which boys gain and maintain dominance status with peers. There is also concern that during this period of increased interest in heterosexual relationships aggressive boys will victimize girls, but as noted above, it is more likely to occur within the same gender. Also during this period, because of increased concern with peer status, having friends and being popular can also buffer the individual from being bullied.

More specifically and relative to earlier periods of development, aggression is viewed more positively during adolescence by peers (e.g., Bukowski et al., 2000; Graham & Juvonen, 1998; Moffitt, 1993; Pellegrini et al., 1999), possibly because aggression represents a challenge to adult roles and values (Moffitt, 1993). After all, adolescence is a time when youngsters challenge adult roles as they develop their own personality. Further, and probably exacerbating the problem, this period also witnesses a series of abrupt changes in youngsters' social lives. First, adolescence is characterized by rapid body changes. The hormonal changes associated with increased body size also relate to the onset of sexual maturity, resulting in youngsters' increased interests in heterosexual relationships (e.g., Connolly et al., 1999). Such rapid change in body size leads to the reorganization of youngsters', but especially boys', social dominance hierarchies (Pellegrini & Bartini, 2001). Bigger and stronger boys become more dominant than their smaller peers. Boys' dominance status is in turn related to their attractiveness to girls (Pellegrini & Bartini, 2001).

Secondly, that youngsters also move from typically small, personal primary schools with well-established social groups into larger, less supportive secondary schools means that they have to re-establish social relationships during a time when peer relations are particularly important (Eccles, Wigfield & Schiefele, 1998). During such transitions, aggression is often used in the service of establishing status with peers, in the form of dominance relationships (Pellegrini, 2008; Strayer, 1980). From this view, bullying is viewed as a deliberate strategy used to attain dominance as youngsters enter a new social group.

Dominance is defined as a relationship variable which orders individuals in terms of their access to resources (Dunbar, 1988). Dominance status is achieved as a result of a series of agonistic and affiliative interchanges between individuals (deWaal, 1986; Pellegrini, 2008; Strayer, 1980). The extent to which individuals use agonistic or affiliative strategies to achieve and maintain dominance depends on the 'cost' of using that strategy (e.g., sanctions by teachers or peers) and the value of the resource for which they are competing (e.g., abundant or scarce toys available) (Pellegrini, 2008). When resources are abundant and using aggression is costly (e.g., highly sanctioned by peers and adults), as is the case in most middle-class schools, individuals are more likely to use affiliative, relative to agonistic, strategies (Pellegrini, 2013; Pellegrini et al., 2007). In an empirical test of these hypotheses, we found that when resources were abundant in preschool classrooms, such that everyone received them, though the timing varied (i.e., scramble or free-for-all competition), children's affiliative strategies predicted resource control (Pellegrini et al., 2007). When resources were limited and only some children got them and others did not (i.e., contest competition), aggressive strategies predicted resource control.

As noted above, dominant individuals use both aggression and prosocial behaviour to establish and maintain status with their peers, depending on the costs and benefits associated with each, in relation to available resources. From this view, and the empirical record, aggressive strategies are often used in the initial phases of the formation of dominance relationships, such as when individuals enter a new school, especially the primary to middle school transition.

After the initial transition to middle school, more prosocial and cooperative strategies are used to consolidate status and allies and to reconcile former foes (Ljungberg et al., 1999; Pellegrini & Bartini, 2001). This description is consistent with our data as youngsters made the transition from one school (in the fifth grade) to another (in sixth and seventh grades) (Pellegrini & Long, 2002). In this multi-method, multi-informant, longitudinal study we followed youngsters from the last year of primary school (fifth grade) across the first two years of middle school (sixth and seventh grades). Children were extensively observed across the whole school day and we asked about their own as well as their peers' bullying, victimization, dominance, and heterosexual relationships. We also asked teachers about these things as well.

In this study we found that bullying increased from fifth to sixth grade, then decreased from sixth to seventh grades. Correspondingly, dominance dropped from fifth through sixth grades and increased in seventh. This result is consistent with theory to the extent that we predicted increases in aggression as youngsters are moving into a new school and thus try to establish dominance. While aggression is a high cost strategy, it is probably offset, for some youngsters, by the high value they put on social relationships and status with their new peer groups. That their dominance status decreased at the transition and then increased again is consistent with this view as well. Once dominance is established, however, aggression, in the form of bullying, decreased. Specifically, bullies no longer needed to use aggression to establish dominance as they had done so.

This theory was more formally tested in this study by examining the degree to which bullying mediated dominance from primary to middle school. Our data supported the mediation hypothesis. That is, we found that in early phases of group formation in middle school that dominance is expressed through bullying and other agonistic strategies. After groups are stabilized and the dominance hierarchy is stabilized, dominance is expressed through more prosocial and cooperative means. In short, bullying is a form of aggression used by individuals to achieve some end, in this case dominance status (Pellegrini & Bartini, 2001; Sutton, Smith & Swettenham, 1999b).

That the transition to middle school witnesses an initial increase in bullying, in the more general context of age-related decline of bullying (Smith, Madsen & Moody, 1999), is consistent with this view. Specifically, a large body of research suggests that there is a monotonic decrease in bullying, victimization, and aggression with age (see Pellegrini, 2002 for a review). By this we mean that rates of bullying and victimization generally decrease as youngsters get older. These results have been reported in a series of large-scale studies, often with nationally representative samples (see Pellegrini, 2002 for summaries). Across countries in Western Europe and North America these decreasing trends are observed.

These monotonic decreases during early adolescence, however, are evident only when youngsters do not change schools. When same-age youngsters do change schools, there is an initial increase at this transition point, followed by a decrease. More specifically, in cases where youngsters 10–14 years of age change schools there is an initial increase in reported bullying and victimization. Within a year, the down trend resumes. This decrease reflects re-established dominance relationships. Dominance hierarchies, when they are stabilized, serve the important function of reducing in-group aggression (Dunbar, 1988; Vaughn, 1999).

These trends, however, are moderated by gender differences. In keeping with extant work with younger children (e.g., Boulton & Smith, 1994), proactive aggression and bullying are more frequent among boys than girls. Indeed, boys use and endorse aggression, especially physical aggression, with other boys to establish and maintain dominance (Maccoby, 1998). Correspondingly, girls' attitudes towards bullying are more negative than those of boys (Crick & Werner, 1998; Maccoby, 1998; Pellegrini, 2002).

Gender differences reflect the fact that boys' aggression increases as they progress through middle school. It seems to be the case that boys, more than girls, view physical aggression and bullying more positively as they progress through the early phases of adolescence. This interpretation is consistent with our analyses of attitudes towards bullying. Bullying and proactive aggression are also viewed positively by peers during the period of early adolescence (e.g., Graham & Juvonen, 1998; Pellegrini et al., 1999), possibly because they represent one way in which individuals can assert their individuality and independence by exhibiting behaviour which is antithetical to adult norms (Moffett, 1993).

While girls are less likely than boys to endorse bullying, and especially physical aggression, they do engage in bullying and aggression of a different sort. Specially, girls often engage in relational (Crick & Grotpeter, 1995) or indirect aggression (Bjorkqvist, 1994). Relational aggression involves harming others' social relations, such as spreading rumours or shunning others. Relational aggression can be either direct, where perpetrators openly and directly say bad things about the victims, in their presence. Or it can be indirect aggression where, rather than confronting an opponent direct, as in a physical fight, one child (A) may say something nasty about another (B) to a third party (C). While indirect strategies seem to be proactive in the sense that they aim to get something done and they require some deliberation, they do not seem to be 'dominance' strategies, per se. Specifically, if dominance is achieved and maintained through social displays of power, indirect variants do not meet this requirement.

Ann Campbell (1999) has suggested that indirect aggression seems an especially appropriate form of aggression for females to use and frames the argument in terms of sexual selection theory. Sexual selection theory, as originally proposed by Darwin (1871) and extended by Trivers (1972), suggests that males and females use different strategies to attract mates. Males being physically bigger, stronger, and more physically active compete with each other, often using physical aggression, to gain status, as expressed in dominance hierarchies. High status relates to access to females. Females, on the other hand, are smaller and are most concerned with protecting themselves and their future offspring. Thus, they choose dominant mates and when they are aggressive against their peers, are indirect. This indirectness minimizes direct confrontation and possible harm. It has been further proposed, though not empirically validated, that girls may use relational and indirect aggression to form coalitions and alliances against rival girls so as to gain access to their goals.

The fact that youngsters', but especially boys', views of bullying became less negative with time is both interesting and troubling. This trend may be related to the fact that boys target other boys for victimization and that their empathy for boys in distress decreases during this period while boys' and girls' empathy for girls increases at this time (Olweus & Endresen, 1998).

The question of cross-sex bullying

Early adolescence witnesses the beginning of heterosexual relationships, thus study of bullying and victimization in adolescence should include examination of cross-sex victimization. Correspondingly, there has been concern voiced (Craig et al., 2001) that boys who are bullies as children will continue to be bullies in adolescence and they will target girls. This issue is exacerbated by the finding that adolescent girls find aggressive boys attractive (Bukowski et al., 2000; Pellegrini & Bartini, 2001). In this section we discuss the problem of cross-sex aggression, but especially male to female aggression.

Our research (Pellegrini & Long, 2002), as well as the results of a recent meta-analysis of same- and cross-sex aggression (Archer, 2004), suggests that cross-sex aggression is rare, relative to same-sex aggression. That is, boys are most frequently the targets of aggression initiated by other boys, and boys least frequently aim their aggression at girls. Indeed, girls were most frequently targeted by other girls. These findings are consistent with a dominance theory framework whereby males use aggression against other males, not females, to establish and maintain status in male groups (e.g., Chance, 1978; Pellegrini & Bartini, 2001). The prevalence of intra-sexual, relative to inter-sexual, aggression has also been documented in a recent meta-analysis of sex differences in aggression (Archer, 2004). Dominance status, in turn, is attractive to female adolescents (Bukowski et al., 2000; Pellegrini & Bartini, 2001).

As noted above, adolescents compete for very different resources than preschoolers. During adolescence, peer relations generally, and heterosexual relationships specifically, take on increased importance. One aspect of our work has looked at how early adolescents use aggression to access heterosexual contact in the context of monthly middle school dances.

In this work (Pellegrini & Long, 2007) we directly observed youngsters' integration and use of aggression at monthly school dances held across the first full year of middle school. From a social dominance position, we expected boys' rates of aggression to predict their frequency of interaction with girls (i.e., gender integration) over time. For males, aggression should be a stronger predictor of integration than for females.

First, and interestingly, we observed that only boys used aggression at the dances and only a few of the boys were responsible for most of the aggression. Specifically, during months 1, 3, 6, and 7 of the study, the percent of boys observed using physical aggression was, respectively, 6%, 7%, 11%, and 6%. We also found that aggression predicted heterosexual interaction. Taken together with other results (Bukowski, Sipola & Newcomb, 2000; Pellegrini & Long, 2003), these results point to the trend of youngsters using aggressive strategies to impress opposite-sex peers. Perhaps more troublesome is that girls want to affiliate with boys who use these aggressive strategies (Bukowski et al., 2000; Pellegrini & Long, 2003). With this said, and as will be discussed in the next section, dimensions of peer relations may also mitigate aggression in adolescence.

The positive role of peers: changes in peer affiliation in primary and secondary school and victimization

Another hallmark of early adolescence is the rapid and qualitative change in social affiliations. These changes are precipitated by processes associated with the onset of puberty as well as corresponding changes in social institutions – with the change from primary to secondary school being especially relevant. Correspondingly, this is also a time when the peer group is taking on increased importance for youngsters (Eccles et al., 1998; Simmons & Blyth, 1987). A longstanding critique of middle schools and junior high schools, especially in America, is that they do not support youngsters' formation of new cooperative, social groupings but instead exacerbate fractured social groups by having youngsters attend large schools which simultaneously stress individual competition over cooperation (Eccles et al., 1998).

Our research found that the number of affiliations for youngsters decreased, at least initially with the transition from primary to middle school, but it began to recover by the second year of middle school (in the seventh grade). It is probably the case that students' affiliations decreased because they were entering a new and much larger social institution, even though the schools made some effort to foster informal interaction among peers.

The middle schools we studied provided some opportunities for youngsters to affiliate with peers but they were seemingly slow to take effect. For example, the weekly free time (called 'Coke Breaks') typically occurred during the final hour of classes on Friday afternoons. Youngsters went to a central gathering place, purchased a soda, and then went back to their homerooms and interacted with their peers. More concentrated mechanisms may be needed during the first year of middle school to foster more varied and closer relationships within these larger social networks during the school day. Social and interest-specific events, such as clubs, limited to sixth graders could be organized. If the events are of adequate duration and frequency, peer relationships may be formed and increase in number. These peer affiliations, in turn, may be important buffers of subsequent victimization.

Peers as buffers against victimization

Peer affiliation is relevant to the study of victimization because, like bullying, it takes place in the context of the peer group. Further, and as we argued above, bullies often use aggression to bolster their social status. Research suggests that dimensions of peer affiliation, such as having friends and being liked by peers, buffer victimization (Hodges & Perry, 1999; Pellegrini et al., 1999; Pellegrini & Long, 2002).

Friends buffer victimization, as demonstrated by the programmatic work of Perry and Hodges (Hodges, Malone & Perry, 1997; Hodges & Perry, 1999) and others (Pellegrini et al., 1999; Slee & Rigby, 1993). Generally, youngsters who have friends, especially friends who are strong and popular, seem to inhibit bullies from picking on them. Friends may act as 'guardians' for their more vulnerable peers.

Additionally, being popular with peers also seems to buffer victimization. We (Pellegrini et al., 1999; Pellegrini & Long, 2002) found that popularity is a more robust buffer than the number of reciprocal friend nominations. Specifically, and replicating earlier analyses (Pellegrini et al., 1999), we found that the number of liked-most nominations, even when we statistically controlled the number of reciprocal friends, was a robust negative predictor of victimization across the middle school years; when we controlled like-most nomination, friendship did not predict victimization significantly (Pellegrini & Long, 2002). We argue that having a number of affiliates, relative to close friends, seems to protect against bullying because being liked by a number of peers represents the number of possible social sanctions or retaliation against bullies. In the language of cost-benefit analyses, bullying individuals who are popular is more 'costly' than doing so against less popular peers. If a child victimizes an individual who is liked by a large number of peers, he/she runs the very real risk of retaliation, public sanction, and peer disapproval. That bullies are concerned with social status among their peers would suggest that they would not target peers with allies or other social affiliations.

Contextual variation in bullying and victimization

Generally, aggression occurs in those places in the school with little adult supervision – toilets and unsupervised play yards are prime venues. When supervision is instituted, bullying declines (Olweus, 1993b). Olweus's (1993b) extensive survey work in Scandinavia is also informative for pointing out some school factors not connected to bullying. For example, he has found that there are no differences between large and small schools or between urban and rural schools in predicting bullying and victimization. What does support it is the lack of supervision and a climate which tolerates aggression (e.g., teachers being abusive to children, not punishing aggressive children, ignoring children's and parents' concerns about children being victimized). It might be tempting to feel that simply cutting out those contexts within which bullying is most likely to take place – for example, breaktime – would effectively reduce the amount of bullying. However, it is important to weigh this against the benefits of breaktime. It is not just the contexts per se that are crucial, but also the lead given by staff and the way behaviours such as bullying are dealt with (Blatchford, 1998).

Different ways of assessing aggression and bullying with preschoolers and adolescents

Collecting information on the frequency, intensity, and perpetrators and targets of aggressive acts in schools is notoriously difficult. Most basically, aggressive acts are usually committed in places and at times when there are few adult witnesses. Additionally, aggressive acts, relative to all other behaviours observed during the school day, occur at low frequencies (e.g., Humphreys & Smith, 1984; Pellegrini, 1988); therefore they are very difficult to observe directly. For these reasons researchers typically utilize some form of informant rating of students (Caspi, 1998), which include students' self-reports, peer rating/nominations, and teacher questionnaire methodologies. The extensive experience that informants have with the students being assessed usually enables them to identify aggressive youngsters with some degree of accuracy (Dodge & Coie, 1989). It is also considerably less expensive to administer questionnaires en masse to groups of youngsters and teachers than to spend months in the field observing a low frequency event.

Different data sources, however, offer complementary sources of information, and it is therefore important to recognize distinctions among data sources and the sorts of information each generates. Self-report measures tell us about an individual's perception of their experiences. A commonly used self-report measure to identify bullies and victims has been developed by Olweus (1993b) for use with children and adolescents. On the other hand, normative information, or information relative to one's peer group, on aggression and victimization can be derived from peers and teachers (Cairns et al., 1988). Peer nominations are often used to identify aggressive bullies and victims. Schwartz (Schwartz et al., 1997) and Perry (Perry, Kusel & Perry, 1988) have developed different peer nomination procedures which have been widely used with children. Both procedures reliably identify perpetrators (i.e., bullies) and victims of aggression.

A teacher rating scale, developed by Dodge and Coie (1987), has been used to identify aggressive middle school youngsters (Pellegrini & Bartini, 2000; Pellegrini, Bartini & Brooks, 1999) and preschoolers (Pellegrini et al., 2007). In our earlier work with early adolescents (Pellegrini & Bartini, 2000), we also had our research associates who spent ten weeks directly observing each child completing these teacher rating scales. We found that teachers' and researchers' ratings of youngsters' aggression were significantly, though only moderately, correlated ($r = 0.50$, $p < 0.01$); practically, this means that there was an overlap of only 25% between these ratings.

The lack of a greater overlap between these ratings may have been due to a number of factors. First, the teachers or the research associates may have been differentially deliberate in their completion of the checklists. This conclusion is not, however, supported by the similar and relatively high reliability coefficients on this measure for both teachers (Cronbach's alpha = 0.88) and research associates (Cronbach's alpha = 0.85). The second reason for the modest inter-correlation may have been teachers' being more biased than the research associates. Specifically, the teachers, while consistent in their ratings of youngsters (as indicated by the reliability coefficients), may have scored youngsters in a way that was less consistent with the ways in which the youngsters viewed themselves, relative to research associates' ratings. For example, teachers may have more readily rated youngsters in negative ways, such as rating them as aggressive. This explanation does fit our data; the teacher mean was higher, though not at a significant level, than the research associate mean on the rating scale.

Third, the modest correlation may have been due to differences in settings where each spent time with the students. Teachers observed youngsters in a limited number of settings – usually in home rooms and in one class. The research associates, on the other hand, spent sustained amounts of time observing students in many different contexts across the school year. They observed students in the halls, the cafeteria, and at free time. One specific context, the cafeteria, seemed particularly important for the research associates. This may have been due to the relatively high social density and the relatively low levels of teacher supervision, both of which support peer aggression (Smith & Connolly, 1980). Relatedly, the contexts in which each rater spent time with children may have elicited specific sets of behaviours, unique to those settings. Differences between raters (e.g., parents and teachers) of youngsters' problem behaviours are often attributed to the different demands of the situations in which each spends time with youngsters (e.g., Achenbach, 1985).

These results have important implications for school policy. If teacher rating scales are to be used in 'high stakes' assessments, e.g., to place students in special classes, we suggest that raters spend substantial and sustained periods of time observing youngsters in a variety of settings. This is a rather simple sampling issue. Reliable and valid sampling is a result of repeated observations in settings where children are relatively free to interact with each other. Additionally, these results suggest that places where large groups of youngsters congregate with minimal supervision, like the school cafeteria, can support aggressive behaviour. Vigilant supervision of such places by adults and peers does lower incidents of aggression (Olweus, 1993a).

Information from teachers, generally, correlates well with information collected from peers among older primary school and middle school children, possibly because they reflect extensive and varied experiences among the raters and nominators (Caspi, 1998). Further, teacher ratings and peer nominations should converge when they are both rating 'public' phenomena, such as public displays of aggression (Cairns et al., 1988). Aggression is public when youngsters use it as a dominance display for peers. This sort of public display is especially evident during early adolescence, a time when social status is in the state of flux, due to rapid body changes and changes in social groups. Individuals use physically coercive strategies to establish or maintain status when they are entering new peer groups, such as new schools (Pellegrini & Long, 2002).

However, using peer nominations with preschool children can present problems of reliability and validity. For example, we have known for many years (e.g., McCandless & Marshall, 1957) that preschoolers' responses are very susceptible to administration variations and these nominations of aggressive peers do not always correspond with other methods of assessment (Archer, 2004). By contrast, direct observational methods, unlike informant sources, can provide relatively unbiased accounts of focal subjects' actions and reactions in specific circumstances, regardless of comparisons with others (Cairns et al., 1988). Minimizing biases with direct observations, however, is dependent upon an extensive corpus of data. While observational measures tend not to correlate well across time (Caspi, 1998), possibly because of situational specificity and limited samples of observations (Pellegrini, 2012), these problems can be minimized by sampling behaviour in a variety of settings, across long periods of time.

Perhaps the greatest benefit of observational methods, relative to informant ratings, is their 'objectivity' (Caspi, 1998; Pellegrini, 2012). More specifically, in well designed and conducted observational studies, measures of behaviour are clearly articulated and reliably sampled and recorded by unbiased observers. Repeated training and reliability checks are necessary to maintain high reliability standards across the duration of a long-term study (Pellegrini, 2012). In our work with preschoolers (Pellegrini et al., 2007) and adolescents (Pellegrini & Long, 2002, 2003) we typically observed children in numerous school settings across the whole school day and the entire school year. Further, and importantly, reliability checks and re-training of observers occurred during alternate months across the whole school year. This level of training and checking is necessary in order to maintain high inter-rater agreement. In short, reliable and valid observational data are the 'gold standard', especially regarding preschool children, yet, like gold, they are very expensive to collect.

Direct observations cannot, however, be conducted in all settings (Pepler & Craig, 1995). For example, participants cannot be directly observed in locker rooms or lavatories, venues where bullying sometimes occurs. A class of methods, which has been labelled indirect observational, or diary, methods (Pellegrini, 2004), can be used in such settings but only with youngsters old enough to read and write. With this technique participants record their behaviours at predetermined intervals, i.e., interval-contingent responses, on standardized forms. Similar methods have been used in the child and educational psychology literature. For example, Bloch (1989) sampled children's play behaviour at home and in the community by calling their homes and asking the caregiver where and with whom children were playing. Further, Csikzentmihalyi (1990) provided participants with pagers which were programmed to 'beep' across the day, at which point participants recorded their behaviour. Diaries have also been used extensively with primary school children, who recorded relevant behaviours and participants at specified daily intervals (Pellegrini et al., 1995). The reliability and validity of indirect methods is maximized when participants are given specific sampling intervals in which to record behaviour and a specific vocabulary or categories to use to record behaviour (Pellegrini, 2012).

The indirect observations used in our work involved sampling participants' behaviour using diary methodology for one school day/month across a whole school year. Indirect methods have the advantage of sampling those areas (e.g., lavatories and locker rooms) which are typically out of bounds for direct observers but frequently afford aggression. Disadvantages of this method, however, correspond to those of self-report, such as social desirability. This sort of limitation, as well as problems associated with shared methods variance, are minimized when indirect observational data are related to other data sources, such as peer nominations.

Conclusion

The contents of this chapter, and the research on which it was based, have significant implications for policy makers, administrators, and teachers concerned with reducing the prevalence of bullying in schools. Our research indicates that levels of bullying and victimization relate to the costs of perpetrating these acts, thus maximizing costs of using aggression while simultaneously increasing the benefits of using more affiliative strategies should mitigate aggression. This can be accomplished, first, by increasing social cohesion among students.

The level of social cohesion among students is related to the frequency of aggression and bullying. When there is greater social cohesion among students the frequency of bullying decreases because students are sanctioned (a high cost) for harming a member of a cohesive group. Schools with relatively stable populations are likely to see a reduction in bullying across the school year because students are able to maintain social cohesion. With fewer new students being added to the group there are fewer disruptions to the social hierarchy and consequently fewer incidences of aggression and bullying. Therefore, teachers and administrators should pay particular attention to potential cases of bullying when new students are added to the school environment or following any event that may cause a disruption in social cohesion.

More concretely, cohesion can also be maximized by keeping cohorts of children intact as they progress across their educational experiences. When possible, children and adolescents should experience continuity in their peer groups across time. As in the case of English schools discussed above, bullying was minimized when youngsters did not change schools from primary to middle school. When they did change schools, as in American primary and middle schools, there was a spike in bullying at the transition.

In cases where it is necessary for children and adolescents to change schools, social cohesion can be maximized by keeping students in stable cohorts across an extended period of time. For example, some middle schools in Minneapolis place youngsters in a cohort of students when they enter school in the fifth grade and the youngsters stay in that cohort for their entire three-year middle school experience. In this model, group cohesion is sustained across time, and children not only form close relationships with peers, in the form of friendships, but also with teachers. These close relationships may minimize bullying by providing support and by providing an environment where children feel safe and secure in enlisting teachers' and peers' help if they are bullied. This environment is valuable because an important barrier to minimizing bullying in schools is children's reluctance to tell their teachers that they are being bullied (Eslea & Smith, 1998).

As noted in our own research, attitudes towards bullying become more positive with time across the middle school period and aggressive youngsters are popular with their peers, especially in adolescence. Because peer groups, schools, and families are major socialization agents of young adolescents, they should be made aware of these views. The negative consequences of these views for both victims and others should be presented to youngsters. Future research should also begin to search for possible origins of these views. Are there models for these sorts of behaviours in middle schools? Indeed, Olweus's (1993a) seminal work revealed that school personnel sometimes model bullying behaviour by belittling or threatening students.

Finally, we believe that future research and policy should consider the role of school-level variables in bullying, victimization, and peer affiliation. Researchers should compile descriptions of school-level variables such as school policies towards bullying, access to counsellors, adult supervision of peer interactions, and opportunities to affiliate with peers. It is important to derive these variables from the different perspectives of students, teachers, and neutral observers. This level of description could be useful in designing schools for young adolescents that support positive peer relationships and reduce victimization.

References

Achenbach, T.M. (1985). *Assessment and Taxonomy of Child and Adolescent Psychopathology.* Thousand Oaks, CA: Sage.

Archer, J. (2004). Sex differences in aggression in real-word settings: a meta-analytic review. *Review of General Psychology,* 8, 191–198.

Bandura, A. (1973). *Aggression: A Social Learning Analysis.* Englewood Cliffs, NJ: Prentice-Hall.

Bjorkqvist, K. (1994). Sex differences in physical, verbal, and indirect aggression: a review of recent research. *Sex Roles,* 30, 177–188.

Blatchford, P. (1998). *Social Life in School: Pupils' Experience of Breaktime and Recess from 7 to 16 Years.* London: Falmer.

Bloch, M. (1989). Young boys' and young girls' play at home and in the community. In M. Bloch & A.D. Pellegrini (Eds), *The Ecological Context of Children's Play* (pp. 20–154). Norwood, NJ: Ablex.

Blurton-Jones, N. (Ed.) (1972). *Ethological Studies of Child Behavior.* London: Cambridge University Press.

Boldizar, J., Perry, D. & Perry, L. (1989). Outcome values and aggression. *Child Development,* 60, 571–579.

Boulton, M.J. & Smith, P.K. (1994). Bully/victim problems in middle school children: stability, self-perceived competence, peer perceptions, and peer acceptance. *British Journal of Developmental Psychology,* 12, 315–329.

Bowers, L., Smith, P.K. & Binney, V. (1994). Perceived family relationships of bullies, victims and bully/victims in middle childhood. *Journal of Social and Personal Relationships,* 11, 215–232.

Bukowski, W.M., Sippola, L.A. & Newcomb, A.F. (2000). Variations in patterns of attraction to same- and other-sex peers during early adolescence. *Developmental Psychology,* 36, 147–154.

Cairns, R.B., Cairns, B.D., Neckerman, H.J., Gest, S.D. & Gariépy, J.L. (1988). Social networks and aggressive behavior: peer support or peer rejection? *Developmental Psychology,* 24(6), 815.

Campbell, A. (1999). Staying alive: evolution, culture, and women's intrasexual aggression. *Behavioral and Brain Sciences,* 22, 203–252.

Caspi, A. (1998). Personality development across the life course. In W. Damon & N. Eisenberg (Eds), *Handbook of Child Psychology: Vol. 3 Social, Emotional, and Personality Development* (pp. 311–388). New York: Wiley.

Chance, M.R.A. (1978). Sex differences in attention structures. In Tiger, L. & Fowler, H.T. (Eds), *Female Hierarchies* (pp. 135–162). Chicago: Beresford.

Coie, J.D. & Dodge, K.A. (1998). Aggression and antisocial behavior. In N. Eisenberg (Ed.), *Handbook of Child Psychology* (pp. 779–786). New York: Wiley.

Connolly, J., Goldberg, A., Pepler, D. & Craig, W.M. (1999). Development and significance of cross-sex activities in early adolescence. *Journal of Youth and Adolescence,* 24, 123–130.

Craig, W.M., Pepler, D., Connolly, J. & Henderson, K. (2001). Developmental context of peer harassment in early adolescence: the role of puberty and the peer group. In

J. Juvonen and S. Graham (Eds), *Peer Harassment in School: The Plight of the Vulnerable and Victimized* (pp. 242–262). New York: Guilford.

Crick, N.R. (1996). The role of relational aggression, overt aggression, and prosocial behavior in the prediction of children's future social adjustment. *Child Development,* 67, 2317–2327.

Crick, N.R. & Grotpeter, J.K. (1995). Relational aggression, gender, and social-psychological adjustment. *Child Development,* 66, 710–722.

Crick, N.R. & Werner, N.E. (1998). Response decision processes in relational and overt aggression. *Child Development,* 69, 1630–1639.

Cronbach, L.J. (1957). The two disciplines of scientific psychology. *American Psychologist,* 12, 671–684.

Csikszentmihalyi, M. (1990). *Flow: The Psychology of Optimal Experience.* New York: HarperCollins.

Darwin, C. (1871). *The Descent of Man, and Selection in Relation to Sex.* London: John Murray.

DeWaal, F.B.M. (1986). The integration of dominance and social bonding in primates. *Journal of Theoretical Biology,* 61, 459–479.

Dodge, K. (1991). The function and structure of reactive and proactive aggression. In Pepler, D. and Rubin, K.H. (Eds) *The Development and Treatment of Childhood Aggression.* Hillsdale, NJ: Erlbaum.

Dodge, K.A. & Coie, J.D. (1987). Social information processing factors in reactive and proactive aggression in children's peer groups. *Journal of Personality and Social Psychology,* 53, 1146–1158.

Dodge, K. & Coie, J. (1989). Bully–victim relationships in boys' play groups. Paper presented at the biennial meetings of the Society for Research in Child Development, Kansas City.

Dunbar, R.I.M. (1988). *Primate Social Systems.* Ithaca, NY: Cornell University Press.

Eccles, J.S., Wigfield, A. & Schiefele, U. (1998). Motivation to succeed. In N. Eisenberg (Ed.), *Handbook of Child Psychology* (pp. 1017–1096). New York: Wiley.

Eslea, M. & Smith, P.K. (1998). The long-term effectiveness of anti-bullying work in primary schools. *Educational Research,* 40(2), 203–218.

Graham, S. & Juvonen, J. (1998). A social cognitive perspective on peer aggression and victimization. In R. Vasta (Ed.), *Annals of Child Development* (pp. 23–70). London: Jessica Kingsley.

Hodges, E.V., Malone, M.J. & Perry, D.G. (1997). Individual risk and social risk as interacting determinants of victimization in the peer group. *Developmental Psychology,* 33, 1032–1039.

Hodges, E.V. & Perry, D.G. (1999). Personal and interpersonal antecedents and consequences of victimization by peers. *Journal of Personality and Social Psychology,* 76, 677–685.

Humphreys, A. & Smith, P.K. (1984). Rough-and-tumble in preschool on a playground. In Smith, P.K. (Ed.) *Play in Animals and Humans* (pp. 291–370). London: Blackwell.

Ladd, G.W. (1983). Social networks of popular, average, and rejected children in school settings. *Merrill-Palmer Quarterly,* 29, 283–307.

Ladd, G.W. & Profilet, S.M. (1996). The Child Behavior Scale: a teacher-report measure of young children's aggressive, withdrawn, and prosocial behaviors. *Developmental Psychology,* 32(6), 1008.

Lagerspetz, K.M., Bjorkquist, K. & Peltonen, T. (1988). Is indirect aggression more typical of females? *Aggressive Behavior,* 14, 403–414.

Ljungberg, T., Westlund, K., Forsberg, A.J.L. (1999). Conflict resolution in 5-year-old boys. *Animal Behaviour,* 58, 1007–1016.

Loeber, R. & Dishion, T.J. (1984). Boys who fight at home and school: family conditions influencing cross-setting consistency. *Journal of Consulting and Clinical Psychology*, 52, 759–768.

Maccoby, E.E. (1998). *The Two Sexes: Growing Up Apart, Coming Together*. London: Harvard University Press.

McCandless, B.R. & Marshall, H.R. (1957). A picture sociometric technique for preschool children and its relation to teacher judgments of friendship. *Child Development*, 28, 139–147.

Moffitt, T.E. (1993). Adolescent-limited and life-course-persistent anti-social behavior: a developmental taxonomy. *Psychological Review*, 100, 674–701.

National Center for Educational Statistics (1995). *Student Victimization in Schools*. Washington, DC: US Department of Education.

Olweus, D. (1978). *Aggression in Schools*. Washington, DC: Hemisphere.

Olweus, D. (1991). Bully–victim problems among school children: basic facts and effects of a school based intervention program. In K. Rubin and D. Pepler (Eds) *The Development and Treatment of Childhood Aggression*. Hillsdale, NJ: Erlbaum.

Olweus, D. (1993a). *Bullying at School*. Cambridge, MA: Blackwell.

Olweus, D. (1993b). Victimization by peers. In K.H. Rubin and J. Asendorf (Eds), *Social Withdrawal, Inhibition, and Shyness in Childhood* (pp. 315–341). Hillsdale, NJ: Erlbaum.

Olweus, D. & Endresen, I.M. (1998). The importance of sex-of-stimulus object: age trends and sex differences in empathetic responses. *Social Development*, 7, 370–388.

Parker, J.G. & Asher, S.R. (1987). Peer relations and later personal adjustment: are low-accepted children at risk? *Psychological Bulletin*, 102(3), 357–389.

Patterson, G., Littman, R. & Bricker, W. (1967). *Assertive Behavior in Children: A Step Toward a Theory of Aggression*. Monographs of the Society for Research in Child Development, 35, 5, Serial No. 113.

Pellegrini, A.D. (1988). Elementary school children's rough-and-tumble play and social competence. *Developmental Psychology*, 24, 802–806.

Pellegrini, A. (1989). Elementary school children's rough-and-tumble play. *Early Childhood Research Quarterly*, 4, 245–260.

Pellegrini, A. (1995a). A longitudinal study of adolescent boys' rough-and-tumble play and dominance during early adolescence. *Journal of Applied Developmental Psychology*, 16, 77–93.

Pellegrini, A. (1995b). *School Recess and Playground Behaviour: Educational and Developmental Roles*. Albany, NY: State University of New York Press.

Pellegrini, A.D. (2002). Bullying, victimization, and sexual harassment during the transition to middle school. *Educational Psychologist*, 37, 151–163.

Pellegrini, A.D. (2004). Sexual segregation in childhood: a review of evidence for two hypotheses. *Animal Behaviour*, 68, 435–443.

Pellegrini, A.D. (2008). The roles of aggression and affiliation in resource control: a behavioral ecological perspective. *Developmental Review*, 28, 461–487.

Pellegrini, A.D. (2012). *Observing Children in the Natural Worlds: A Methodological Primer*. New York: Taylor & Francis.

Pellegrini, A.D. (2013). Object use in childhood: development and possible functions. *Behaviour*, 150, 813–843.

Pellegrini, A.D. & Bartini, M. (2000). A longitudinal study of bullying, victimization, and peer affiliation during the transition from primary school to middle school. *American Educational Research Journal*, 37(3), 699–725.

Pellegrini, A.D. & Bartini, M. (2001). Dominance in early adolescent boys: affiliative and aggressive dimensions and possible functions. *Merrill-Palmer Quarterly*, 47, 142–163.

Pellegrini, A.D., Bartini, M. & Brooks, F. (1999). School bullies, victims, and aggressive victims: factors relating to group affiliation and victimization. *Journal of Education Psychology,* 91, 216–227.

Pellegrini, A.D., Galda, L., Shockley, B. & Stahl, S. (1995). The nexus of social and literacy experiences at home and school: implications for primary school oral language and literacy. *British Journal of Educational Psychology,* 65(3), 273–285.

Pellegrini, A.D. & Long, J. (2002). A longitudinal study of bullying, dominance, and victimization during the transition from primary to secondary school. *British Journal of Developmental Psychology,* 20, 259–280.

Pellegrini, A.D. & Long, J.D. (2003). A sexual selection theory longitudinal analysis of sexual segregation and integration in early adolescence. *Journal of Experimental Child Psychology,* 85(3), 257–278.

Pellegrini, A.D. & Long, J.D. (2007). An observational study of early heterosexual interaction at middle school dances. *Journal of Research in Adolescence* 17, 613–638.

Pellegrini, A.D., Roseth, C., Mliner, S., Bohn, C., Van Ryzin, M., Vance, N., Cheatham, C.L. & Tarullo, A. (2007). Social dominance in preschool classrooms. *Journal of Comparative Psychology,* 121, 54–64.

Pellegrini, A.D. & Smith, P.K. (1998). Physical activity play: the nature and function of a neglected aspect of play. *Child Development,* 69, 577–598.

Pepler, D.J. & Craig, W.M. (1995). A peek behind the fence: naturalistic observations of aggressive children with remote audiovisual recording. *Developmental Psychology,* 31(4), 548.

Pepler, D.J., Craig, W. & Roberts, W. (1993). Aggression on the playground: a normative behavior. Paper presented at the biennial meetings of the Society for Research in Child Development, New Orleans.

Perry, D.G., Kusel, S.J. & Perry, L.C. (1988). Victims of peer aggression. *Developmental Psychology,* 24(6), 807.

Perry, D.G., Willard, J. & Perry, L. (1990). Peers' perceptions of consequences that victimized children provide aggressors. *Child Development,* 61, 1289–1309.

Popper, K.R. (1959/1972). *The Logic of Scientific Discovery.* New York: Basic Books.

Russell, B. (1972). *In Praise of Idleness.* New York: Simon & Schuster. (Original work published 1932).

Schwartz, D. (1993). Antecedents of aggression and peer victimization: a prospective study. Paper presented at the biennial meetings of the Society for Research in Child Development, New Orleans.

Schwartz, D., Dodge, K.A. & Coie, J.D. (1993). The emergence of chronic peer victimization in boys' play groups. *Child Development,* 64, 1755–1772.

Schwartz, D., Dodge, K.A., Petit, G.S. & Bates, J.E. (1997). The early socialization and adjustment of aggressive victims of bullying. *Child Development,* 68, 1755–1772.

Simmons, R.G. & Blyth, D.A. (1987). *Moving into Adolescence: The Impact of Pubertal Change and School Context.* Hawthorn, NY: Aldine de Gruyter.

Slee, P.T. & Rigby, K. (1993). Australian school children's self-appraisal of interpersonal relations: the bullying experience. *Child Psychiatry and Human Development,* 23, 273–287.

Smith, P.K. (2011). Observational methods in studying play. In A.D. Pellegrini (Ed.), *The Oxford Handbook of the Development of Play* (pp. 138–152). New York: Oxford University Press.

Smith, P.K. (2012). Cyberbullying and cyber aggression. In S.R. Jimerson, A.B. Nickerson, M.J. Mayer, and M.J. Furlong (Eds), *Handbook of School Violence and School Safety: International Research and Practice* (pp. 93–103). New York: Routledge.

Smith, P.K. & Connolly, K. (1980). *The Ecology of Preschool Behavior.* Cambridge: Cambridge University Press.

Smith, P.K., Madsen, K.C. & Moody, J.C. (1999). What causes the age decline in reports of being bullied at school? Toward a developmental analysis of risks of being bullied. *Educational Research,* 41, 267–285.

Smith, P.K. & Sharp, S. (1994). The problem of school bullying. In P.K. Smith and S. Sharp (Eds), *School Bullying* (pp. 1–19). London: Routledge.

Strayer, F. (1980). Social ecology of the preschool peer group. In W.A. Collins (Ed.), *The Minnesota Symposia on Child Psychology: Development of Cognition, Affect, and Social Relations* (pp. 165–196). Hillsdale, NJ: Erlbaum.

Sutton, J., Smith, P.K. & Swettenham, J. (1999a). Bullying and 'theory of mind': a critique of the 'social skills deficit' view of anti-social behaviour. *Social Development,* 8(1), 117–127.

Sutton, J., Smith, P.K. & Swettenham, J. (1999b). Socially undesirable need not be incompetent: a response to Crick and Dodge. *Social Development,* 8, 132–134.

Trivers, R. (1972). Parental investment and sexual selection. In B. Campbell (Ed.), *Sexual Selection and the Descent of Man* (pp. 136–179). Chicago: Aldine.

Vaughn, B.E. (1999). Power is knowledge (and vice versa): a commentary on winning some and losing some: a social relations approach to social dominance in toddlers. *Merrill-Palmer Quarterly,* 45, 215–225.

7

PEER RELATIONS AND
SCHOOL LEARNING

Within the school classroom there is often little scope for peer interactions and socialization with friends (Epstein 1983). Teaching and learning approaches in classrooms are dominated by whole-class teaching and independent work (Baines, Blatchford & Kutnick, 2003; Galton, Simon & Croll, 1980; Galton et al., 1999; Kutnick, Blatchford & Baines, 2005). In this chapter we argue that despite this neglect, peer relations affect classroom experiences and classroom learning in ways that are often underestimated by teachers and underexplored by researchers. We also argue that there is now strong evidence that learning in peer contexts, e.g., through collaborative group work, is an important factor that can lead to successful learning outcomes and productive learning interactions and orientations.

There are a number of reviews of research on peer relations (Blatchford & Baines, 2010; Bukowski, Newcomb & Hartup, 1996; Dunn, 1993, 2004; Gifford-Smith & Brownell, 2003; Howe, 2010; Howe & Mercer, 2007; Ladd, 2005; Rubin, Bukowski & Parker, 2006; Rubin et al., 2005) that provide a comprehensive coverage of current knowledge. Much of the research on peer relations has been concerned with difficulties in terms of, for example, peer rejection, bullying, victimization and withdrawal. But there is also a well-established position that peer relations have particular value for social and even cognitive development. As we saw in Chapter 3, Youniss (1980) adapted the theories of Piaget (1932) and Sullivan (1953) to show how child–peer relations differed from child–adult relations by showing equality, cooperation, reciprocity and mutuality – all of which make a contribution to social development. This positive view was given an added dimension with a more recent (though contested, see Howe, 2010) theory of socialization which downplays the role of parents and other adults in favour of the important role of the group and particularly the peer group in development (Harris, 1995).

Important as these theories are in showing the positive role of peer relations in development, they are not sufficient to support an understanding of the connections between peer relations and learning specifically in school contexts. In this chapter we explore some ways in which this connection operates.

As every teacher knows, pupils in classrooms vary a good deal in how well they work together. Some pupils are helpful and constructive, others are over-dominating, some are passive and left out, some serious and some full of fun, and still others are destructive and unhelpful. These differences are important because they can mean the difference between a class that is easy to teach and academically productive and a class that is not. Teachers know – albeit informally – that peer relations affect the quality of classroom processes and learning and they can cause difficulties that must then be resolved, yet we know surprisingly little about how these features of informal peer relations actually affect classroom dynamics and functioning. Peer relations researchers have tended to focus almost exclusively on the connection between peer relations and social adjustment and competence and less on their relationship with school academic outcomes.

One powerful description of the link between peer relations and performance in school has been provided by Schmuck and Schmuck (2001). They give the example of their own 7-year-old son to show how the emotional dynamics of the informal peer group can go hand-in-hand with academic learning. He was struggling to make new friends, particularly those interested in team sports, and at the same time was having a frustrating time learning to read. In consequence he became for a short time out of control at home, and withdrew into excessive, sullen TV viewing. More success in his relations with others meant that school learning benefited. Schmuck and Schmuck argue that the formal school curriculum and classroom learning and instruction cannot be separated from the powerful informal relationships within the peer group. Peer relationships will affect academic learning and vice versa. Exploration of the connections between informal peer relations and school learning is therefore a main theme of this chapter. This is a relatively new area but one which we believe is very important to understanding social and academic development.

There is also a developmental perspective here. Wentzel (2009) argues that the role of peers in school learning is likely to change with age and development. Although peers are important throughout development, they may be especially critical during the middle and high school years when children seem particularly involved in and dependent on their peers (Youniss & Smollar, 1989, in Wentzel, 2009). Also with age, different and larger peer groups (e.g., peer cliques, networks and crowds) emerge during the middle school years, though interestingly the peer group may diminish in importance by the end of school (Brown, 1989, in Wentzel, 2009). So the attempt to understand the relationships between peer relationships and academic learning must be sensitive to the types of relationships peers have with each other at different points in their school careers.

Peer relations in classrooms

In Chapter 8 there is a classroom map which shows that the classroom is in large measure a community of peers, albeit led by a teacher, and classroom life is largely a group-based affair. In the UK, children of primary school age often sit in groups (though in other countries classrooms can be more orientated to the whole class (Alexander, 2001)).

In Chapter 8 we describe some of the characteristics of these within-class group settings and their influence on learning. We also introduced a central paradox of classroom learning: although children are seated in groups, the 'cooperative mode' (where children cooperate with each other in service of learning), which might be expected to follow from this arrangement, is rare and despite the seating arrangements a 'performance mode' (where children adopt particular roles, as respondent or audience, in relation to the largely teacher-led talk exchanges that take place in the classroom) is far more common (see Howe, 2010).

In this chapter we are not so much concerned with the characteristics and effects of grouping arrangements as with the relationships between peers and the effect this has on their learning. In this chapter we consider:

1. Peer relationships and school outcomes in terms of:
    (a) peer relations and school attainment and academic adjustment;
    (b) social networks and school outcomes;
    (c) friendships and learning interactions.
2. Effects of school factors on peer relations.
3. The formal role of peer relations in classroom learning – specifically, research on collaborative and cooperative group work.

Peer relationships and school outcomes

Peer relations and school attainment and academic adjustment

One way in which peer relations have been examined in relation to school learning is in terms of the status in the peer group, e.g., in terms of rejection and popularity (see Chapter 3 for more on these terms). A substantial body of work indicates that pupils who have difficulties in their relations with peers, and tend to be rejected by them, experience academic difficulties (Wentzel, 2009). Children who are low in peer acceptance or characterized as rejected are more likely to show poor social skills and higher levels of aggression and non-compliance (Coie, Dodge & Kupersmidt, 1990, in Wentzel & Asher, 1995) but are also likely to show disengagement, anti-school attitudes, and low achievement, academic motivation and readiness to learn (Buhs, Ladd & Herald, 2006; DeRosier, Kupersmidt & Patterson, 1994; Ladd, Kochenderfer & Coleman, 1996; Vandell & Hembree, 1994; Wentzel, 1991; Wentzel & Asher, 1995). Studies of sociometric status and friendship have consistently reported concurrent and longitudinal connections with school attainment and adjustment outcomes. Such research typically shows that popular/accepted students tend to do well academically, are more prosocial and have higher self-regulatory skills (Coie *et al.,* 1990, in Wentzel & Asher, 1995; Rubin, LeMare & Lollis, 1990; Wentzel, 1991; Wentzel & Asher, 1995; Wentzel & Caldwell, 1997). Neglected pupils achieve higher than average academic levels, are more motivated and compliant and are often liked by teachers. Controversial children achieve at lower than average levels, are more aggressive and less compliant (Wentzel, 1991; Wentzel & Asher, 1995).

Studies examining the long-term consequences of peer difficulties (in terms of peer acceptance, aggressiveness, and shyness/withdrawal) suggest that aggression and lack of acceptance in particular are related to increased levels of depression, anxiety, lower academic achievement and drop out of school (Ladd & Troop-Gordon, 2003; Parker & Asher, 1987).

Researchers have examined variables that potentially mediate longitudinal connections between acceptance profiles and school adjustment variables. Wentzel (2003) examined the possible mediating effects of perceived support from classmates and social and academic motivation. While negative associations were found between controversial status and learning effort, rejected status and prosocial goals, and neglected status and perceived support from peers, these variables were not found to mediate the connection between sociometric status and school adjustment. In another longitudinal study of children from kindergarten through to fifth grade, Buhs et al. (2006) found that classroom engagement mediated connections between peer rejection and learning for rejected-excluded children but not rejected-victimized children. The latter group tended to drop out of school – but attendance did not mediate reductions in achievement.

Wentzel (2003) identified different profiles to those identified by previous research, for popular, neglected and controversial children. Girls who were controversial and neglected achieved higher than average, whereas for boys with these profiles the opposite was the case. Popular children only achieved at average levels and were more inclined to display irresponsible behaviour.

Reasons why peer relations and academic functioning are related

The evidence on the association between peer relations and academic functioning seems well established but what is less clear is why this might be the case. One reason for this is that many studies are essentially correlational in nature (despite sometimes involving sophisticated regression analyses) and so causal direction (i.e., from peer relations to outcomes) cannot be exactly inferred.

Wentzel (2009) has put forward several possible explanations for the link. One explanation is that peers, like parents and teachers, communicate to each other academic values and expectations for performance, and this then affects academic performance. This though will presumably only apply in cases where students do have positive academic orientations, and Wentzel also acknowledges that this effect might decline as students advance through middle and high school years. Another explanation offered stems from research on the strong connection between academic self-perceptions and performance (e.g., Schunk & Pajares, 2005, in Wentzel, 2009). So pupils use peers for comparative purposes to monitor and evaluate their own abilities, which in turn will affect their actual school performance.

Perhaps the strongest explanation offered by Wentzel is the direct way that peers can influence students' academic competence by the help they give them. So a supportive relationship with peers is likely to give them greater access to information and resources that will help them in academic tasks. Although teachers are obviously important sources of advice and information, students also report that peers are as or more important sources of instrumental aid than their teachers (Lempers & Clark-Lempers, 1992, in Wentzel, 2009). This reliance on peers for information is likely to become magnified when students move to secondary schools and they experience multiple different teachers. Supporting evidence for the role of peers in giving help to each other has been provided by Webb and Mastergeorge (2003).

Another possible explanation of the relationship between peer relations and academic functioning relates more to the way that the peer group can provide emotional support, so that children who feel that their friends and other peers support and care for them will tend to be interested and engaged in positive aspects of classroom life (see Chapter 3 for ways in which friendship relations can act as emotional support in other ways). The converse situation is that pupils who are excluded from supportive peer relationships might be more at risk of emotional distress, loneliness and depression (Wentzel & Caldwell, 1997), which might in turn be expected to be connected in a negative way to academic progress. A lack of supportive relationships might also be part of an allied tendency for victimization and bullying which is also known to relate negatively to academic outcomes (also see Chapter 6).

Yet another explanation for the link is the way that peer acceptance and having friends might be related to prosocial, socially responsible and sensitive behaviour, which might in turn be related to academic performance. This connection might be explained by helping, cooperation and sharing, which form part of prosocial behaviour, mediating relations between peer relations and academic outcomes. This is similar to the way that having friends and academic outcomes might be explained by prosocial forms of behaviour that facilitate cooperation and task performance. An obvious question here concerns the direction of causality. Wentzel argues that 'An unanswered question concerns the degree to which peer relationships at school also promote these positive forms of social behaviour' (2009, p. 539). It is highly likely that the direction of causality in fact works both ways. As argued elsewhere in this book, we feel there is likely to be a large degree of overlap between the kinds of social skills and competencies exhibited in everyday informal peer relations and those that underpin high quality collaborative group work. It may be that these vital social competencies are in turn basic requirements for pupils to benefit from school and teaching.

One limitation of much research on peer relations and academic functioning is that studies tend to treat sociometric status as a trait-like characteristic of individual pupils. Yet, there are indications that sociometric status may vary by school peer group (Cairns et al., 1988; Hargreaves, 1967; Wentzel, 2003). There are reports of marked changes in sociometric status after transfer to a new school. For example, Sluckin reported the case of Neil who had been popular at primary school and then went on to become rejected after transfer to a secondary school (Sluckin, 1981). The suggestion is that particular values and forms of behaviour linked with popularity in one context may or may not be associated with acceptance in another. Peer groups in different schools can have different sets of values, and a child's sociometric status may be determined partly by these values. For example, different correlates of sociometric status might be expected in an affluent and perhaps selective high attaining school, where academic learning and responsible behaviours may be viewed positively, and in a school in a more deprived area, where attitudes to formal education may be more negative. Sociometric status may also vary according to other social factors such as socioeconomic, cultural and ethnic background of students in the peer group. There may, however, be particular correlates that are consistently related to particular profiles regardless of the school, such as pro-sociability, internalizing/externalizing behaviours, anxiety, aggression, and so on. The research reviewed above suggests that there is a fairly distinct profile associated with peer rejection, but that other peer acceptance status profiles may vary across circumstances.

There has also been little attention paid to the possibility that individuals may have some control over their social status. While this may not be the case for those children who are rejected, students may be able to raise or lower their salience within the peer group. For example, within a context where academic success is seen as 'uncool' by the peer group, some academically capable students may reduce their explicit effort and involvement in school to avoid detection and possible rejection (e.g., see Robinson, 2013). Such strategies when combined with others (e.g., engagement in disruptive behaviour) may inflate social acceptance. In a similar fashion, researchers interested in bullying roles have noted that 'outsiders', those children that do not get involved in bullying episodes, appear to be able to avoid being bullied or victimized. Such avoidance behaviour may also help students go unnoticed by evading others' attention, but equally this behaviour may lead to an 'average' or 'neglected' sociometric status. Such possibilities deserve more attention from researchers.

Social networks and school outcomes

While most research on peer relations has focused on an individual pupil's status within the peer group, research over the last decade or so has become increasingly interested in the role a child's immediate social network plays in development

(Blatchford & Baines, 2010). Here we examine research on the connection between social networks and school outcomes.

Social network researchers have paid attention to selection and socialization processes. Selection processes reflect the common finding that social networks are often homogeneous on a number of dimensions, that is, people with similar views and values are attracted to each other to form or become members of a group (Cairns, Xie & Leung, 1998). Socialization processes refer to the tendency for group members to become increasingly similar over time. These processes are harder to identify because it is difficult to eliminate explanations that draw on external factors that may have had a role in selection. The majority of research on social influence processes tends to focus on adolescence because it is generally believed that at this time social networks become more important than position in the overall peer group (Gifford-Smith & Brownell, 2003).

Farmer et al. (2003) studied the connection between seventh graders' levels of aggression, teacher-rated popularity and social network membership relative to future school drop-out (up to the end of high school). Findings show that being a member of an aggressive group (defined in terms of proportion of aggressive members) was linked to higher levels of drop-out for aggressive students (but not non-aggressive students). Being part of a popular group or a group with no popular members was also linked to dropping out. Groups that were mixed in terms of aggression were protective for aggressive students. Both popular and non-popular students who associated with aggressive peers were more likely to drop out.

These findings have a bearing on models used to explain connections between peer rejection and long-term adjustment problems and drop out of school reported earlier (Parker & Asher, 1987). Models either give a primary role to peer relations, or see peer relations as a reflection of other underlying characteristics, but both are primarily concerned with characteristics of the individual child and pay scant attention to the role of peers or social context in mediating these negative outcomes. The findings from Farmer and colleagues suggest a third model in which peer networks play an influential role in facilitating delinquency, school adjustment and drop-out. When aggressive and/or rejected children get together to form a deviant group, then individual school drop-out and other adjustment difficulties may occur. Socializing in groups of similar minded peers may therefore serve to facilitate children with high levels of aggression or at risk of rejection into negative adjustment outcomes, whereas socializing with sympathetic but different minded peers may function to discourage negative outcomes. Other studies offer insights into these socialization processes. Dishion et al. (1996) discuss the notion of 'deviancy training' whereby members of deviant groups reinforce and elevate the status of deviant behaviour and activities through laughter and approval. Other studies have identified social network and friendship socialization effects on deviant activities such as drug use, cigarette smoking and alcohol use (Dishion et al., 1995; Mounts & Steinberg, 1995; Pilgrim, Luo & Urberg 1999; Urberg, Degirmencioglu & Pilgrim 1997).

These studies, apart from Farmer et al. (2003), do not examine school-related outcomes, but similar deviant patterns may be expected in the case of anti-school attitudes and other academic outcomes. There is an increasing literature on socializing effects and academic achievement and engagement (Berndt & Keefe, 1995; Sage & Kinderman, 1999). Kindermann (2007) found small levels of peer network influence on students' classroom engagement (as reported by teachers) after taking selection and teacher and parental involvement into account. While homogeneity in peer network engagement levels existed over the year, there was a marked instability in network composition over time, suggesting that when networks split students sought out new groups/members with similar engagement profiles. Although these effects seem small, Kindermann argues that they should not be viewed as such since these findings were evident within the context of high levels of stability in engagement profiles over the year and above and beyond the possibility of selection effects.

Ryan (2001) found evidence of peer friendship network socializing effects on academic achievement (averaged across grades in English, maths, science and social studies) in measures of school liking, but not on the perceived value of school or beliefs about future school success. These latter two findings are important because they question the general view that peers are responsible for negative attitudes about the value of learning and education. These findings also reinforce the view of Brown, Dolcini and Leventhal (1997) that peer influence is selective, influencing certain aspects of behaviour and beliefs but not others. Many school-related values may be more affected by family and teacher attitudes, given that students may have most discussions about school with these people. There are also suggestions that other types of peer relations, such as best friends (Hallinan & Williams, 1990), may be more influential in particular aspects of the socialization. For instance, Urberg et al. (1997) found that while a peer group was responsible for the socialization of levels of alcohol intoxication, it was the best friend that had influenced individuals to drink alcohol in the first place. Similarly, Kindermann and Skinner (2012) report that both friendships and peer group members explained peer influence effects on classroom engagement but also that these different aspects may function in a cumulative and synergistic manner such that friendships affect emotional engagement with school while the peer group may be of a greater influence on the behavioural aspects of engagement. Other aspects of peer relationships may also be important – for example, it may be the case that general cultural attitudes across the peer group as a whole affect the extent to which school is valued. A host of other factors may also play a role, such as socioeconomic background, neighbourhood, and school factors.

It is likely that students will self-select into peer groups that have similar attitudes to schools, and that the distinctive academic orientations within these groups will become stronger and more similar over time (Kindermann, 1993). Wentzel (2009) describes research on how adolescent peer groups differ in the degree to which they pressure members to become involved in academic activities. Clasen and Brown (1985, in Wentzel, 2009), for example, found that 'Jocks' and Popular' groups, more than other groups, had significantly more pressure on academic involvement than other peer groups. In the UK, Pollard (1985) provided an insightful sociological analysis of the way pupils in primary schools form peer groups, which have distinctly different attitudes to the importance of school learning. This area of research seems particularly amenable to ethnographic research because of the way it can access the dynamics and longer-term formation of peer group norms. In Chapter 11 we look at Moss's ethnographic research on gender differences in peer relations and ways in which self-perceptions affect school progress in literacy.

The literature on social networks therefore suggests that peer group influence can affect individual children's academic orientations in both negative and positive ways. Efforts are thus needed to try to maximize and take advantage of the beneficial effects of peer influence to enhance school adjustment and engagement outcomes. Research on peer influence on school outcomes is at a relatively early stage and further developments in methodological and statistical approaches are required to press this work forward.

Friendships and learning interactions

As we saw in Chapter 3, one important facet of peer relations is friendships. In the classroom context there are often strongly held professional views, e.g., about whether friends should be seated together. Some teachers believe that children will work less effectively when with a friend because they will distract each other. Some support for this comes from Hamm and Faircloth (2005) who found that students report that friends often distract them from engaging in class. On the other hand, it might be expected that when working together friends will work better, because they know each other well and their collaboration would be more effective.

So what does the evidence show? In an influential review of research on friends as co-workers, Zajac and Hartup (1997) showed that working with friends can be beneficial for learning; friends are better at cooperating, collaborating and discussing than non-friends; and friends show more disagreement, more elaboration of their own and partners' ideas and more frequent checking of progress. An important finding is that when disagreements arise between friends these encourage more deductive reasoning rather than leading to petty disputes as can be the case with non-friends. There is also evidence that the nature of the task might be important; friends appear to work better together on more challenging tasks, but can be more distracted on easier, repetitive tasks. Friends may perform better on written narratives, specifically creative writing, which might be seen as a kind of complex problem-solving task.

In a meta-analysis of the differences between friends and non-friends on cognitive tasks, Newcomb and Bagwell (1995) reviewed 82 studies in which 524 variables were examined in relation to friendship status and learning.

There were four main advantages in favour of friends. First, there was more positive engagement between friends (talking, smiling and cooperation); second, better conflict management (resolving conflicts constructively); third, more task activity (staying on task, communicating about performance); and fourth, relationship properties were better (concern with equality and loyalty, less dominance and submission). This suggests teachers might be advised to put friends together to work on tasks, though, as we have just seen, there is evidence that friends work better together on difficult rather than easy tasks.

There are several reasons for the superior performance of friends on some tasks. In essence: friends know each other better, they have more commitment, are more likely to help each other, they are more secure with each other so they are more likely to speak up and disagree with each other, and finally they are better disposed to resolving conflicts. Research in the UK (Miell & MacDonald, 2000) suggests that friends work more effectively on creative work in music because of the higher-level, 'transactive' quality of their collaborations, within which friends extend and elaborate ideas that have already been discussed. However in a peer tutoring task, where an expert must teach a novice, friends may not perform as well as non-friends because this requires a dominance relationship that conflicts with the mutual nature of friendships (Foot & Barron, 1990). As classroom learning experiences are often adult-led, involve independent work and can be uninspiring (Baines et al., 2003; Galton et al., 1999; Phelan, Yu & Davidson, 1994), it is little wonder that friends draw each other off task (Hamm & Faircloth, 2005; Kutnick & Kington, 2005). Indeed, Hamm and Fairlcloth (2005) report that reduced opportunities to interact with friends in classrooms led to reports of boredom and disengage-ment, and Kutnick and Kington (2005) found that boys in particular were most likely to be off task when working with a friend. These findings again suggest advantages in grouping friends together at least for certain types of academic tasks, rather than separating them, as is commonly done in many classrooms (Baines et al., 2003).

Studies of learning interactions between friends are limited by the artificiality of the situation in which they are conducted (Zajac & Hartup 1997). These studies often involve testing of friends in small groups away from the classroom and usually on novel activities. The extent to which such findings may extend to real classroom settings is questionable. Another shortcoming is that research has not considered differences in the quality of friendships relative to learning interactions.

School effects on peer relations

So far we have looked at whether peer relations are related to academic outcomes. However, there is another body of literature (albeit much smaller) that looks at the connections in the reverse order, that is, at the impact of school organization and school life on peer relationships.

As we will see in Chapter 8, in many schools children are often grouped in classrooms primarily on the basis of age and then within classes often according to ability. Pupils spend a lot of time in these groupings and classes and it is therefore reasonable to suggest that they may have a marked impact on friendships, peer groups and social status. Indeed many investigators examine friendship in school or use the class as a bounded unit or context from which to make judgements about sociometric status. The experiences of students within these class and group contexts and the way the teacher approaches classroom life and learning within these contexts may have a marked effect on the nature of peer relations (see Schmuck & Schmuck, 2001, for a review). However, only very limited research has examined these effects. Specifically, there appears to be very little knowledge about how the social organization of schools and the dynamics of classrooms affect friendship formation and collaboration between friends (Zajac & Hartup, 1997). It might be thought, for example, that in more individualistic, and more competitive classrooms, friendship relations may be affected and collaboration between friends in class may not be so effective, but there has been little research to test this.

Maureen Hallinan (1976) compared schools where classes were arranged on traditional lines (e.g., based on same age and grouped homogeneously by ability within schools) with classes of a more 'open' arrangement where classes were more mixed in terms of age and where groupings for instruction were more strategic (e.g., where pupils could work alone, in pairs or other forms of groupings). Hallinan found that the friendship structures in open schools were more diffuse or spread out, while in traditional schools they were more focused with a few very popular children and a few isolates. She suggested that these social structures arose from the increased opportunities for communication with a range of peers in open-arrangement schools (Hallinan, 1976; Hallinan & Tuma, 1978). Homogeneous ability grouping within classes leads to friendships between students of similar ability rather than across ability levels (Hallinan & Sorenson, 1985).

Similarly, Epstein (1983) examined how the nature of the physical structure and classroom layout, the nature of grouping practices and levels of encouragement and tolerance within schools affected the nature and structure of friendships. So-called 'high participatory' schools encouraged friendship patterns that were more varied in terms of sex and ethnic mixing and fewer isolates and highly popular children. Ramsey (1991) reports results from Bossert (1979) who compared social patterns in classrooms structured around ability grouping and academic competence, and those in which children worked in interest groups and on several tasks at once. In the former, friendships tended to be between children of similar ability, while in the latter, friendships developed out of shared interest. Interestingly, friendship patterns changed when children changed settings, so that when, in the following year, children in the multi-task setting changed to a competitive one, they abandoned previous friends and interacted with same-ability peers. The reverse pattern occurred in the case of children moving from a competitive to a multi-task classroom.

Barton and Cohen (2004) showed how change in classroom composition could have a marked impact on peer relations. They examined children's peer relations following the transition from mixed-sex fourth grade classrooms to same-sex fifth and then sixth grade classrooms. The change to same-sex classrooms was associated with more mutual friendship nominations among boys in both fifth and sixth grades. Nominations of physical and relational aggression, victimization, rejection, and passive/withdrawn increased for girls in fifth grade, but decreased in sixth grade.

A number of studies indicate that teachers have a key role to play in encouraging and changing relationships in the classroom. Schmuck (1966) found that in classes where there was a more centrally structured peer group with a narrow focus of rejection and acceptance nominations, teachers were less likely to involve students that were on the fringes of the peer group. By contrast, emotionally supportive peer groups tended to have teachers that encouraged prosocial and helpful behaviours. Research by Flanders and Havumaki (1960) indicates that teacher praise and positive behaviour can have an impact on the way students are perceived by peers. This work also showed how a combination of positive reinforcement and effort to get popular and unpopular children to work together paid off in relation to the less popular students.

Wentzel (2009) points out that school-level reforms designed to instil a sense of community and opportunities for social and moral development have resulted in schools within which students engage in positive prosocial interactions with peers, perceive strong levels of emotional support and caring, and hold positive orientations to both social and academic outcomes (Solomon et al., 1988). It is also possible that the effect can be a negative one. One could see this happening in situations where a school does not provide a strong moral lead for positive peer relations and support and which therefore leads to possible negative inter-group relations, bullying and dominance of aggressive culture. Schools can play a central role in interventions that lead to more positive peer relations (Olweus, 1993).

But Wentzel (2009) also points out that negative school influences on peer relations can occur through deliberate teaching and school management policies – for example, when schools establish competitive academic standards and norm-referenced evaluations of achievement that heighten social comparisons between pupils. This is a troubling suggestion, given that this is exactly the kind of school culture being encouraged by political leaders in the UK and other countries. This is worrying, given that such practices can lead to a focus on performance rather than mastery orientations (i.e., a concern with how one performs on a task rather than how to get better at it) and that this can have particularly negative implications for low-attaining pupils who may in turn react by adopting even lower levels of academic efficacy and aspirations (Butler, 2005, in Wentzel, 2009). Chapter 10 on teacher expectations gives more insights into the negative effects of these kinds of processes and how some pupils can adjust in a negative way to what, for them, is an untenable situation.

This leads to a wider consideration of how the quality of teacher–pupil relations can affect the quality of relations between pupils – for example, through the creation of social norms that affect peer relationships in class, negatively or positively. Hamre and Pianta (2001, in Wentzel 2009) show that the affective quality of teacher–student relationships predicts peer-related and behavioural competence up to eight years later. So although, as we have seen, the direction of causality between teacher–pupil and pupil–pupil relations is not always clear, it seems reasonable to conclude that the development of positive relations between peers can be affected by positive adult–child relations in school settings.

The formal role of peer relations in classroom learning

As we have seen, although much of the educational experience of pupils in class-rooms is directed by the teacher, pupils will spend the majority of classroom time in the presence of peers (whether simply sitting next to or actually working with other children). Moreover, as will be evident in Chapter 9, observation studies have shown that each pupil will have a very limited amount of time to interact with their teacher and we need therefore to consider the role of within-class grouping and, in particular, collaborative group work in relation to the pupil's learning and the quality of classroom interactions with peers as well as teachers.

Despite the potential of collaborative group work to enhance cognitive development and school attainment (Damon & Phelps, 1989; Johnson & Johnson, 2003; Webb & Palincsar, 1996), research in the UK has shown that children, as well as their teachers, often do not like working in groups (Cowie & Rudduck, 1988). Galton (1990) found that children often feel insecure and threatened when told to work in groups – and pupils respond to this threat by withdrawal from participation or looking to the teacher to give legitimacy to their responses within groups. Teachers have expressed particular concern about: loss of classroom control, increased disruption and off-task behaviour (Gillies & Boyle, 2010); children not being able to learn from one another (Lewis & Cowie, 1993); group work being overly time-consuming; assessing children when working in interactive groups is problematic (Plummer & Dudley, 1993); and only the more academically able profit from group work. Teachers have also expressed the view that pupils, particularly boys, will misbehave during group work and that discussion within group work may cause conflict between pupils (Cowie, 1995). Kutnick and Blatchford (2013) describe the 'resistances' that can be shown by teachers and pupils to collaborative group work.

A number of studies show that we cannot just put children into groups and expect them to work well together; group-work skills have to be developed (Webb & Mastergeorge, 2003). It is well known (see Gillies, 2003; Mercer, Wegerif & Dawes, 1999) that pupils need to have the skills to communicate effectively through listening, explaining and sharing ideas. But effective group work involves more than this; pupils have to learn to trust and respect each other (Galton, 1990). They also need skills in how to plan and organize their group work, make considered group decisions, reach a compromise and avoid petty disputes (Baines, Blatchford & Chowne, 2007). The overall problem seems to be that there is little coordination between the size of pupil groupings, their composition, pedagogic purpose of learning task and interactions among group members. Blatchford et al. (2003) and Kutnick and Blatchford (2013) argue that there is little awareness of 'social pedagogical' relationships inherent in the classroom, and they make a number of suggestions for developing successful peer learning in classrooms. Further discussion of the links between collaborative group work and cognitive development can be found in a recent review by Howe and Mercer (2007) and more on the background to peer-based learning in Kutnick and Blatchford (2013).

How to make peer learning more effective: research on collaborative and cooperative group work

Some studies in an experimental tradition of cooperative learning (Johnson & Johnson, 2003; Slavin, 1995) stem from social psychological theories of Deutsch (1949) and Lippett and White (1943) and stress the advantages of interdependence within heterogeneous groups. Findings show consistent enhanced relational and pro-school attitudes among pupils, and moderate learning gains (Gillies, 2003; Johnson & Johnson, 2003; Slavin, Hurley & Chamberlain, 2003). These experimental studies are insightful but necessarily focus on singular aspects of behaviour within classrooms (e.g., communication) and take place over a limited duration of time. They tend not to consider the whole classroom context within which group work takes place.

There are a number of studies that have explored ways in which group work and group-work processes can be more effective. One set of studies explores group processes connected to cognitive and attainment progress (see Webb & Farivar, 1994; Webb & Mastergeorge, 2003). Webb (2009) has argued that effective group working is dependent on effective communication among group members (including pupil–pupil explanations, pupil ability to help others in need and ability to ask for help from others). Researchers in England and Mexico, especially Mercer (2000) and Rojas-Drummond and colleagues (e.g., Wegerif et al., 2005), have developed programmes to enhance 'exploratory' talk (a concept similar to explanatory or elaborative discussion – see Chapter 9). Pupils who undertake focused questioning, exploration of alternative answers and explanation for these answers are more likely to solve cognitive-based problems.

During the course of the 1990s, Howe and Tolmie conducted laboratory-based research on group work in science at all levels of the curriculum, with the object of trying to define the basic processes which led to productive outcomes for learning. This research established that tasks which uncover differences between group members' personal ideas about the topic in hand and lead to an exchange of views are central to growth in understanding (Howe, Rodgers & Tolmie, 1990; Howe, Tolmie & Anderson, 1991; Howe et al., 1992; Tolmie et al., 1993). This research also indicated that discussion of this kind can have two effects – post-activity reflection and individual change, or on-task synthesis of different perspectives (Howe, Tolmie & Rodgers, 1992; Howe et al., 1995; Tolmie & Howe, 1993; Williams & Tolmie, 2000). Subsequent work focused on the design and support of group activities to promote the gathering, exchange and coordination of views. This research found it is most productive to direct support at initial procedures for gathering information and achieving a consensus about which elements are important, and then leave group members to debate its wider meaning among themselves (Howe & Tolmie, 1998, 2003; Howe et al., 2000). Recently, tests of applicability of these basic findings to non-laboratory settings have confirmed the central influence on learning in classroom group work is the exchange of differing views, and also the importance of initial teacher resourcing and support of debate between pupils (Howe et al., 2007).

Programmes which are strongly grounded in the development of group dynamics (Kingsley-Mills, McNamara & Woodward, 1992; Stanford, 1990; Thacker, Stoate & Feest, 1992) clearly specify particular attitudes and skills to be addressed and developed in preparation for the productive work which should follow. A range of materials emerging from group work research also identifies skills to be taught quite explicitly and suggests that they should be clearly specified as goals, and practised and reflected upon within group-work activities (Aronson & Patnoe, 1997; Farivar & Webb, 1991; Johnson & Johnson, 2003). Farivar & Webb give a particular order in which different attitudes and skills should be addressed: first 'class-building' activities, then group-work skills, then communication and cooperative skills and finally helping skills.

The SPRinG project

The SPRinG (Social Pedagogic Research into Group work) project, co-directed by Blatchford, Kutnick and Galton (Blatchford et al., 2005; Galton et al., 2009; Kutnick & Blatchford, 2013), was one of the few approaches to collaborative group work based on a large-scale quasi-experimental study. It was set up to address the wide gap between the potential of group work and its limited use in UK schools. To do this successfully suggested that a new approach to conceptualizing group work in classrooms was needed – an approach that would ground itself in the reality of everyday school life and the concerns of teachers and pupils, and integrate group work into the fabric of the school day.

The SPRinG project is therefore distinctive in being a general programme that applies group work across the curriculum and over the school year. The research team worked with teachers to develop a programme of group work which took on board the concerns and difficulties teachers can have with group work. The programme built on and extended previous research by stressing four key principles:

- First, it stresses the development of supportive relationships between pupils through a 'relational' approach. Activities were designed to help pupils communicate effectively through listening, explaining and sharing ideas, but also to help them trust and respect each other, and plan, organize and evaluate their group work.

- Second, for group work to be successful, the classroom and groups need to be organized and managed in supportive ways. There was guidance on classroom seating arrangements, and characteristics of groups such as their size, composition and stability over time.
- Third, the programme provides guidance on the key role of the teacher in adapting grouping practices for different purposes and learning tasks to legitimize group work.
- Fourth, the supportive and facilitative involvement of teachers and other adults in the classroom in working with and guiding groups engaged in group work. The key aim is to encourage pupil independence rather than directly teaching pupils.

The project was extensively evaluated (see Baines et al., 2007; Baines, Rubie-Davies & Blatchford, 2009; Blatchford et al., 2006; Blatchford et al., 2005; Kutnick & Blatchford, 2013). Its effectiveness was tested by comparing pupils trained with the SPRinG programme with pupils who were not, but who were engaged in parallel educational research. The main research question was whether the group-work programme led to increases in learning and attainment, more 'favourable' behavioural and dialogue patterns supportive of learning and motivational patterns and attitudes to learning. The study involved an intervention over a longer time frame than many such studies, taking a full school year, rather than being performed just before and after the usual brief intervention period.

The research found that, far from impeding learning, group work led to raised levels of achievement. At KS2 (age 7–11), for example, the programme concentrated on science activities and led to significantly higher attainment and higher conceptual understanding and inferential thinking (effect sizes 0.21–0.58). At KS1 (5–7) in reading/literacy, children in the experimental condition improved more than those in the control group (effect size 0.23). In mathematics, children in the experimental group improved more than the control children (effect size 0.71). Despite some teachers' worries that group work might be disruptive, systematic classroom observations showed it actually improved pupils' behaviour in class. SPRinG group work raised pupil levels of engagement in learning, encouraged them to become more actively engaged in the learning process and facilitated more higher-level, thoughtful learning processes. Group work seemed to be most effective when adopted by the whole school, rather than the individual teacher (Baines, 2013), so that there could be integration of principles of group learning between classes and across the school experience. Teachers working in areas of deprivation or in difficult circumstances found that group work could be used successfully and could aid classroom relationships and integration.

Conclusions

This chapter has addressed some selected ways in which peer relationships and school learning are connected. It examined relations between peer relations and school attainment and academic adjustment; social networks and school outcomes; friendships and learning interactions; the effects of school factors on peer relations; and finally the formal role of peer relations in classroom learning – specifically, research on collaborative group work. We have tried to capture the advances in understanding peer relations, classroom groupings and peer collaborative group work.

We argue that there are no simple answers to ways in which schools should deal with questions about peer relations and friendships in classrooms. In the case of friendships, for example, decisions about seating friends together in classrooms will need to be informed by a number of factors; as we have seen, friends may be good for some tasks and learning situations but not others. Teachers need to take account of these and use friendship groups accordingly. Friends tend to be similar to each other and there may therefore be problems when friends are antisocial – they may be more aggressive and less stable. It may not therefore be advisable to put such children together, or they would need to be monitored closely by the teacher.

It is likely that the possible negative influences of friendships are more salient to teachers and affect their decisions about classroom organization. Teachers may assume that more troublesome students will adversely affect their friends if seated together, but this may inform a more general strategy concerning the seating of friends in classrooms. This strategy may avoid unnecessary trouble but is largely reactive and may weaken existing friendships and will not help children make new friends. Berndt and Keefe (1992) suggest this may lead to further deterioration in friendship relations and hence a less positive view of school.

In the SPRinG project it was found that the potentially important role of peer learning in classrooms was hindered by the common resistances that teachers had to innovations they feel threaten statutory coverage of the curriculum. There were also resistances from teachers and pupils to new practices that threatened to disrupt the common rules of engagement, which often involve whole-class teaching and compliant and passive student learning. It was found that these resistances, once overcome, can mean a more productive learning experience which coincidentally helped to improve attainment in the main curriculum subjects, but also led to productive and engaged forms of classroom interaction. Teachers working in areas of deprivation or in difficult circumstances found that group work could be used successfully and could aid classroom relationships and integration. But we have also found that group work is most effective when adopted by the whole school, rather than individual teachers in isolation, so that there could be integration of principles of group learning between classes and across the school experience (see Kutnick & Blatchford, 2013, for a fuller treatment of these issues).

Importance of informal peer relations to learning

Yet we also argue that there is still much more work to be done on the connection between peer relations and classroom learning, both theoretically and empirically. One important area which needs more attention concerns the connections between informal peer relations and peer learning in classrooms. The success of peer relations and group work in classrooms will depend ultimately on the separate informal network of relationships between peers in the school. We feel it is vital for researchers to seek better understanding of the linkages between informal and school-based peer relations, because of its contribution to the wider study of peer relations but also because of its relevance to school learning and the ways schools deal with peer relations. These connections would do much to strengthen understanding of the antecedents and contexts for what Howe (2010) has called the 'cooperative' mode of learning in schools.

Consideration of peer relations may help to bring out the potential of more informal contexts for learning. For example, Vygotskian thought on learning contexts has tended to stress the one-to-one tutorial relationship – usually adult to child, or at least expert to novice – and relations between intellectual equals (and relationships around informal, playful activities) are not therefore central. However, peer relations can be an inherently motivating context for action and learning. In contrast to adult–child relations, they are more horizontally organized and power is more likely to be evenly shared. In comparison to adult–child tutoring relations, peers would tend to be seen as less effective, but we need to recognize and value the distinctively different nature of peer relations to adult–child relations. This may require more recognition of the qualities that make them different to adult–child relations (see Damon & Phelps, 1989). Given the difficulties adults can have in adjusting to the child's way of looking at things, it may be that peers are better able to understand each other directly, and therefore, to use Vygotskian terms, be better agents of 'intersubjectivity'. Peer relations may, to use yet other Vygotskian terms, be a good inter-psychological context to further intra-psychological functioning. There is something paradoxical in the view that cognitive development depends on adults having to be very skilful in accommodating children into joint actions, and in a sense pretending to be at a level they are not, while children (e.g., during play with each other) typically and naturally have no such difficulty with each other – just watch any school playground (Pellegrini & Blatchford, 2002) or friends in the home. We too easily ignore the inherently informal and motivating nature of peer and friendship relations (see Blatchford et al., 2003, for a longer treatment of these points).

We do of course have to be cautious about the direct transfer of informal peer relations into the classroom. While we argue that there are strong benefits in the social aspects of peer-based learning, we must also be aware that some informal playground actions can promote social attitudes that would run counter to those required to support high quality group work, e.g., stereotypically gendered and status-exclusive behaviours. One of the important processes promoted in the

SPRinG programme is that children should develop their group working skills with all of their classmates – not just with preferred friends. We need then to be aware that the interaction of the informal and formal peer-learning process is, minimally, a two-way interaction; classroom developments may be transferred to the playground and playground preferences may be transferred to the classroom. In either case, teachers and pupils must be aware of this interaction and the resulting effects.

A 'relational approach': bridging informal and class-based peer relations

Recently researchers have begun to emphasize the importance of a relational approach to training in group work skills. Such an approach aims to develop and build social relationships in the classroom, and the result is to provide a firm foundation on which communication, group planning and problem-solving skills can be added (e.g., Baines, Blatchford & Kutnick 2008; Baines et al., 2009). The approach aims to take advantage of the processes developed in everyday friendship relations to underpin suggestions concerning successful group working. The SPRinG programme, for example, seeks to develop these in the classroom.

We therefore propose that relational skills shown in informal peer relations can overlap with relational skills that can benefit peer co-learning in classrooms. They are likely to involve similar social processes, e.g., perspective taking, mutuality, conflict resolution, problem solving and trust. So rather than see informal and class-based peer relations as separate, we could do more to examine linkages between, and the common processes underpinning, informal and formal expressions of peer relations. A focus on helping productive classroom relationships needs awareness of peer relations in different contexts – and there may be a feedback loop to better understanding and facilitating informal peer relations, e.g., at breaktime. To use a different term, informal peer relations can, under the right circumstances, provide conditions for 'psychological safety' (Chang & Lee, 2001), i.e., when students feel comfortable speaking up in front of others because they know that their contributions and views will be listened to, valued and respected.

References

Alexander, R. (2001). *Culture and Pedagogy: International Comparisons in Primary Education.* Oxford: Blackwell.

Aronson, E. & Patnoe, S. (1997). *The Jigsaw Classroom: Building Cooperation in the Classroom.* Harlow: Longman.

Baines, E. (2013). Teachers' experiences of implementing the SPRinG Programme in schools. In P. Kutnick & P. Blatchford (Eds), *Effective Group Work in Primary School Classrooms: The Spring Approach.* London: Springer.

Baines, E., Blatchford, P. & Chowne, A. (2007). Improving the effectiveness of collaborative group work in primary schools: effects on science attainment. *British Educational Research Journal, 33,* 663–680.

Baines, E., Blatchford, P. & Kutnick, P. (2003). Changes in grouping practice over primary and secondary school. *International Journal of Educational Research*, 39, 9–34.

Baines, E., Blatchford, P. & Kutnick, P. (2008). Pupil grouping for learning: developing a social pedagogy of the classroom. In R. Gillies, A. Ashman & J. Terwel (Eds) *The Teacher's Role in Implementing Cooperative Learning in the Classroom*. New York: Springer-Verlag.

Baines, E., Rubie-Davies, C. & Blatchford, P. (2009). Improving pupil group work interaction and dialogue in primary classrooms: results from a year-long intervention study. *Cambridge Journal of Education*, 39(1), 95–117.

Barton, B.K. & Cohen, R. (2004). Classroom gender composition and children's peer relationships. *Child Study Journal*, 34, 29–45.

Berndt, T.J. & Keefe, K. (1992) Friends' influence on adolescents' perceptions of themselves at school. In D. Schunk & J. Meece (Eds) *Student Perceptions in the Classroom*. Hillsdale, NJ: Lawrence Erlbaum.

Berndt, T. & Keefe, K. (1995). Friends' influence on adolescents' adjustment to school. *Child Development*, 66, 1312–1329.

Blatchford. P. & Baines, E. (2010). Peer relations in school. In K. Littleton, C. Wood & J. Kleine-Staarman (Eds), *International Handbook of Psychology in Education*. Bingley, UK: Emerald.

Blatchford, P., Baines, E., Rubie-Davies, C., Bassett, P. & Chowne, A. (2006). The effect of a new approach to group-work on pupil–pupil and teacher–pupil interaction. *Journal of Educational Psychology*, 98, 750–765.

Blatchford, P., Galton, M., Kutnick, P. & Baines, E. (2005). *Improving the Effectiveness of Pupils Groups in Classrooms* (ESRC/TLRP Final Report). London: ESRC.

Blatchford, P., Kutnick, P., Baines, E. & Galton, M. (2003). Toward a social pedagogy of classroom group work. *International Journal of Educational Research*, 39, 153–172.

Bossert, S.T. (1979). *Tasks and Social Relationships in Classrooms*. New York: Cambridge University Press.

Brown, B.B., Dolcini, M.M. & Leventhal, A. (1997). Transformations in peer relationships at adolescence: implications for health-related behaviour. In J. Schulenberg, J.L. Maggs & K. Hurrelmann (Eds) *Health Risks and Developmental Transitions During Adolescence*. New York: Cambridge University Press.

Buhs, E.S., Ladd, G.W. & Herald, S.L. (2006). Peer exclusion and victimization: processes that mediate the relation between peer group rejection and children's classroom engagement and achievement? *Journal of Educational Psychology*, 98, 1–13.

Bukowski, W.M., Newcomb, A.F. and Hartup, W.W. (1996) *The Company They Keep: Friendship in Childhood and Adolescence*. New York: Cambridge University Press.

Cairns, R.B., Cairns, B.D., Neckerman, H.J., Gest, S.D. & Gariepy, J.L. (1988). Social networks and aggressive behavior: peer support or peer rejection. *Developmental Psychology*, 24, 815–823.

Cairns, R.B., Xie, H. & Leung, M-C. (1998). The popularity of friendship and the neglect of social networks: toward a new balance. In W. Bukowski & A. Cillessen (Eds) *Sociometry Then and Now* (New Directions for Child Development, no. 80). San Francisco: Jossey-Bass.

Chang, H-T. & Lee, A.T. (2001) The relationship between psychological safety, organization context support and team learning behaviour in Taiwan. *Global Journal of Engineering Education*, 5: 185–192.

Cowie, H. (1995). Co-operative group work: a perspective from the UK. *International Journal of Educational Research*, 23, 227–238.

Cowie, H. & Rudduck, J. (1988). Learning together – working together. In Vol. 1: *Cooperative Group Work – An Overview* and Vol. 2: *School and Classroom Studies*. London: BP Educational Service.

Damon, W. & Phelps, E. (1989). Critical distinctions among three approaches to peer education. *International Journal of Educational Research*, 13, 9–19.

DeRosier, M.E., Kupersmidt, J.B. & Patterson, C.J. (1994). Children's academic and behavioural adjustment as a function of the chronicity and proximity of peer rejection. *Child Development*, 65, 1799–1813.

Deutsch, M. (1949). A theory of cooperation and competition. *Human Relations*, 2, 129–152.

Dishion, T., Capaldi, D., Spracklen, K. & Li, F. (1995). Peer ecology of male adolescent drug use. *Development and Psychopathology*, 7, 803–824.

Dishion, T., Spracklen, K., Andrews, D. & Patterson, G. (1996). Deviancy training in male adolescent friendships. *Behavior Therapy*, 27, 373–390.

Dunn, J. (1993). *Young Children's Close Relationships: Beyond Attachment*. Newbury Park, CA: Sage.

Dunn, J. (2004). *Children's Friendships: The Beginnings of Intimacy*. Malden, MA: Blackwell.

Epstein, J.L. (1983). The influence of friends on achievement and affective outcomes. In Epstein, J.L. & Karweit, N. (Eds) *Friends in School: Patterns of Selection and Influence in Secondary Schools*. New York: Academic Press.

Farivar, S. & Webb, N. (1991). *Helping Behavior Activities Handbook: Cooperative Small Group Problem Solving in Middle School Mathematics*. Los Angeles: UCLA.

Farmer, T.W., Estell, D.B., Leung, M., Trott, H., Bishop J. & Cairns, B. (2003). Individual characteristics, early adolescent peer affiliations, and school dropout: an examination of aggressive and popular group types. *Journal of School Psychology*, 41, 217–232.

Flanders, N.A. & Havumaki, S. (1960). The effect of teacher-pupil contacts involving praise on the sociometric choices of students. *Journal of Educational Psychology*, 57, 65–68.

Foot, H. & Barron, A.M. (1990). Friendship and task management in children's peer-tutoring. *Educational Studies*, 16, 237–250.

Galton, M. (1990). Grouping and group work. In Rogers, C. & Kutnick, P. (Eds) *The Social Psychology of the Primary School*. London: Routledge.

Galton, M.J., Hargreaves, L., Comber, C., Wall, D. & Pell, A. (1999). *Inside the Primary Classroom: 20 Years On*. London: Routledge.

Galton, M., Simon, B. & Croll, P. (1980). *Inside the Primary Classroom*. London: Routledge & Kegan Paul.

Galton, M.J., Steward, S., Hargreaves, L., Page, C. & Pell, A. (2009). *Motivating Your Secondary Class*. London: Sage.

Gifford-Smith, M. & Brownell, C. (2003). Childhood peer relationships: social acceptance, friendships, and peer networks, *Journal of School Psychology*, 41, 235–284.

Gillies, R. (2003). Structuring cooperative group work in classrooms. *International Journal of Educational Research*, 39, 35–49.

Gillies, R.M. & Boyle, M. (2010). Teachers' reflections on cooperative learning: issues of implementation. *Teaching and Teacher Education*, 26, 938–940.

Hallinan, M.T. (1976). Friendship patterns in open and traditional classrooms. *Sociology of Education*, 49, 254–265.

Hallinan, M.T. & Sorenson, A.B. (1985). Ability grouping and student friendships. *American Educational Research Journal*, 22, 485–499.

Hallinan, M.T. & Tuma, N.B. (1978). Classroom effects on change in children's friendships. *Sociology of Education*, 51, 270–282.

Hallinan, M.T. & Williams, R.A. (1990). Students' characteristics and the peer-influence process. *Sociology of Education,* 63, 122–132.

Hamm, J.V. & Faircloth, B.S. (2005). *The Role of Friendship in Adolescents' Sense of School Belonging* (New Directions for Child and Adolescent Development, no. 107). San Francisco: Jossey-Bass.

Hargreaves, D.H. (1967). *Social Relations in a Secondary School.* London: Routledge & Kegan Paul.

Harris, J.R. (1995). Where is the child's environment? A group socialization theory of development. *Psychological Review,* 102, 458–489.

Howe, C. (2010). *Peer Groups and Children's Development.* Oxford: Wiley-Blackwell.

Howe, C. & Mercer, N. (2007). *Children's Social Development, Peer Interaction and Classroom Learning* (Primary Review Research Survey 2/1b). Cambridge: University of Cambridge Faculty of Education.

Howe, C.J., Rodgers, C. & Tolmie, A. (1990). Physics in the primary school: peer interaction and the understanding of floating and sinking. *European Journal of Psychology of Education,* 4, 459–475.

Howe, C.J. & Tolmie, A. (1998). Productive interaction in the context of computer-supported collaborative learning in science. In K. Littleton and P. Light (Eds) *Learning with Computers: Analysing Productive Interaction.* London: Routledge.

Howe, C.J. & Tolmie, A. (2003). Group work in primary school science: discussion, consensus and guidance from experts. *International Journal of Educational Research,* 39, 51–72.

Howe, C.J., Tolmie, A. & Anderson, A. (1991). Information technology and group work in physics. *Journal of Computer Assisted Learning,* 7, 133–143.

Howe, C.J., Tolmie, A., Anderson, A. & Mackenzie, M. (1992). Conceptual knowledge in physics: the role of group interaction in computer-supported teaching. *Learning and Instruction,* 2, 161–183.

Howe, C.J., Tolmie, A., Duchak-Tanner, V. & Rattray, C. (2000). Hypothesis testing in science: group consensus and the acquisition of conceptual and procedural knowledge. *Learning and Instruction,* 10, 361–391.

Howe, C.J., Tolmie, A., Greer, K. & Mackenzie, M. (1995). Peer collaboration and conceptual growth in physics: task influences on children's understanding of heating and cooling. *Cognition and Instruction,* 13, 483–503.

Howe, C.J., Tolmie, A. & Rodgers, C. (1992). The acquisition of conceptual knowledge in science by primary school children: group interaction and the understanding of motion down an incline. *British Journal of Developmental Psychology,* 10, 113–130.

Howe, C., Tolmie, A., Thurston, A., Topping, K., Christie, D., Livingston, K., Jessiman, E. & Donaldson, C. (2007). Group work in elementary science: towards organizational principles for supporting pupil learning. *Learning and Instruction,* 17, 549–563.

Johnson, D.W. & Johnson, F. (2003). *Joining Together: Group Theory and Research.* Boston: Allyn & Bacon.

Kindermann, T.A. (1993). Natural peer groups as contexts for individual development: the case of children's motivation in school. *Developmental Psychology,* 29, 970–977.

Kindermann, T.A. (2007). Effects of naturally existing peer groups on changes in academic engagement in a cohort of sixth graders. *Child Development,* 78, 1186–1203.

Kindermann, T.A. & Skinner, E.A. (2012). Will the real peer group please stand up? A 'tensegrity' approach to examining the synergistic influences of peer groups and friendship networks on academic development. In A.M. Ryan & G.W. Ladd (Eds), *Peer Relationships and Adjustment at School* (pp. 51–78). Charlotte, NC: Information Age Publishing.

Kingsley-Mills, C., McNamara, S. & Woodward, L. (1992) *Out From Behind the Desk: A Practical Guide to Group Work Skills and Processes.* Leicester: Leicestershire County Council.

Kutnick, P. & Blatchford, P. (2013). *Effective Group Work in Primary School Classrooms: The SPRinG Approach.* Dordrecht: Springer.

Kutnick, P., Blatchford, P. & Baines, E. (2005). Grouping of pupils in secondary school classrooms: possible links between pedagogy and learning. *Social Psychology of Education,* 8(4), 349–374.

Kutnick, P. & Kington, A. (2005). Children's friendships and learning in school: cognitive enhancement through social interaction? *British Journal of Educational Psychology,* 75, 521–538.

Ladd, G.W. (2005). *Children's Peer Relations and Social Competence: A Century of Progress.* New Haven, CT: Yale University Press.

Ladd, G.W., Kochenderfer, B.J. & Coleman, C.C. (1996). Friendship quality as a predictor of young children's early school adjustment. *Child Development,* 67, 1103–1118.

Ladd, G.W. & Troop-Gordon, W. (2003). The role of chronic peer difficulties in the development of children's psychological adjustment problems. *Child Development,* 74, 1344–1367.

Lewis, J. & Cowie, H. (1993). Cooperative group work, promises and limitations: a study of teachers' values. *Education Section Review,* 17(2), 77–84.

Lippitt, R. & White, R.R. (1943). The social climate of children's groups. In R.G. Barker, J.S. Kounin and H.F. Wright (Eds) *Child Behaviour and Development.* New York: McGraw-Hill.

Mercer, N. (2000). *Words and Minds: How We Use Language to Think Together.* London: Routledge.

Mercer, N., Wegerif, R. & Dawes, L. (1999). Children's talk and the development of reasoning in the classroom. *British Educational Research Journal,* 25(1), 95–113.

Miell, D. & MacDonald, R. (2000). Children's creative collaborations: the importance of friendship when working together on a music composition. *Social Development,* 9, 348–369.

Mounts, N.S. & Steinberg, L. (1995). An ecological analysis of peer influence on adolescent grade point average and drug use. *Developmental Psychology,* 31, 915–922.

Newcomb, A.F. & Bagwell, C.L. (1995). Children's friendship relations: a meta-analytic review. *Psychological Bulletin,* 117, 306–347.

Olweus, D. (1993). *Bullying at School.* Cambridge, MA: Blackwell.

Parker, J.G. & Asher, S.R. (1987). Peer relations and later personal adjustment: are low-accepted children at risk? *Psychological Bulletin,* 10(3), 357–389.

Pellegrini, A. & Blatchford, P. (2002). The developmental and educational significance of break time in school. *The Psychologist,* 15, 59–62.

Phelan, P., Yu, H.C. & Davidson, A. (1994). Navigating the psychosocial pressures of adolescence: the voices and experiences of high school youth. *American Educational Research Journal,* 31, 415–447.

Piaget, J. (1932). *The Moral Judgment of the Child.* London: Kegan Paul.

Pilgrim, C., Luo, Q. & Urberg, K. (1999). Influence of peers, parents and individual characteristics on adolescent drug use in two cultures. *Merrill-Palmer Quarterly,* 45, 85–107.

Plummer, G. & Dudley P. (1993). *Assessing Children Learning Collaboratively*. Chelmsford: Essex Development Advisory Service.

Pollard, A. (1985). *The Social World of the Primary School*. London: Holt, Rinehart & Winston.

Ramsey, P.G. (1991). *Making Friends in School: Promoting Peer Relationships in Early Childhood Education*. New York: Teachers College Press.

Robinson, T. (2013). Exploring the narratives of African Caribbean high attaining boys: perceived peer influences in education. Unpublished Doctoral (DEdPsy) thesis, Institute of Education, University of London.

Rubin, K.H., Bukowski, W. and Parker, J.G. (2006) Peer interactions, relationships, and groups. In W. Damon, R.M. Lerner, and N. Eisenberg (Eds), *Handbook of Child Psychology: Vol. 3, Social, Emotional, and Personality Development* (Sixth edn). New York: Wiley.

Rubin, K.H., Coplan, R.J., Chen, X., Buskirk, A. & Wojslawowicz, J. (2005). Peer relationships in childhood. In M. Bornstein and M. Lamb (Eds), *Developmental Science: An Advanced Textbook* (Fifth edn). Hillsdale, NJ: Erlbaum.

Rubin, K.H., LeMare, L.J. & Lollis, S. (1990). Social withdrawal in childhood: developmental pathways to peer rejection. In S.R. Asher and J.D. Coie (Eds), *Peer Rejection in Childhood*. New York: Cambridge University Press.

Ryan, A. (2001). The peer group as a context for the development of young adolescent motivation and achievement. *Child Development,* 72: 1135–1150.

Sage, N.A. & Kindermann, T. (1999). Peer networks, behavior contingencies, and children's engagement in the classroom. *Merrill-Palmer Quarterly*, 45, 143–171.

Schmuck, R. (1966). Some aspects of classroom social climate. *Psychology in the Schools,* 3, 59–65.

Schmuck, R. & Schmuck, P. (2001). *Group Processes in the Classroom*. Boston: McGraw-Hill.

Slavin, R. (1995). *Cooperative Learning* (Second edn). Boston: Allyn & Bacon.

Slavin, R., Hurley, E.A. & Chamberlain, A. (2003). Cooperative learning and achievement: theory and research. In W.M. Reynolds and G.E. Miller (Eds) *Handbook of Psychology: Educational Psychology* (vol. 7). New York: Wiley.

Sluckin, A. (1981). *Growing Up in the Playground: The Social Development of Children*. London: Routledge & Kegan Paul.

Solomon, D., Watson, M., Delucchi, K., Schaps, E. & Battistich, V. (1988). Enhancing children's prosocial behavior in the classroom. *American Educational Research Journal,* 25, 527–554.

Stanford, G. (1990). *Developing Effective Classroom Groups*. Bristol: Acora Books.

Sullivan, H. (1953). *The Interpersonal Theory of Psychiatry*. New York: Norton.

Thacker, J., Stoate, P. & Feest, G. (1992). *Using Group Work in the Primary Classroom*. Crediton, UK: Southgate.

Tolmie, A. & Howe, C.J. (1993). Gender and dialogue in secondary school physics. *Gender and Education*, 5, 191–209.

Tolmie, A., Howe, C.J., Mackenzie, M. & Greer, K. (1993). Task design as an influence on dialogue and learning: primary school group work with object flotation. *Social Development*, 2, 183–201.

Urberg, K.A., Degirmencioglu, S.D. & Pilgrim, C. (1997). Close friend and group influence on adolescent cigarette smoking and alcohol use. *Developmental Psychology*, 33, 834–844.

Vandell, D. & Hembree, S. (1994). Social status and friendship: independent contributors to children's social and academic adjustment. *Merrill-Palmer Quarterly*, 40, 461–477.

Webb, N. (2009). The teacher's role in promoting collaborative dialogue in the classroom. *British Journal of Educational Psychology*, 79, 1–28.

Webb, N. & Farivar, S. (1994). Promoting helping behavior in cooperative small groups in middle school mathematics. *American Educational Research Journal*, 31, 369–395.

Webb, N. & Mastergeorge, A. (2003). Promoting effective helping behaviour in peer directed groups. *International Journal of Educational Research*, 39, 73–97.

Webb, N. & Palincsar, A.S. (1996). Group processes in the classroom. In D.C. Berliner and R.C. Calfee (Eds) *Handbook of Educational Psychology*. New York: Macmillan.

Wegerif, R., Linares, J., Rojas-Drummond, S., Mercer, N. & Velez, M. (2005). Thinking together in the UK and Mexico: transfer of an educational innovation. *Journal of Classroom Interaction*, 40, 40–48.

Wentzel, K. (1991). Relations between social competence and academic achievement in early adolescence. *Child Development*, 62, 1066–1078.

Wentzel, K. (2003). Sociometric status and adjustment in middle school: a longitudinal study. *Journal of Early Adolescence*, 23, 5–28.

Wentzel, K. (2009). Peers and academic functioning at school. In K.H. Rubin, W.M. Bukowski & B. Laursen (Eds), *Handbook of Peer Interactions, Relationships and Groups* (pp. 531–547). New York: Guilford Press.

Wentzel, K. & Asher, S. (1995). The academic lives of neglected, rejected, popular and controversial children. *Child Development*, 66, 754–763.

Wentzel, K. & Caldwell, K. (1997). Friendships, peer acceptance and group membership: relations to academic achievement in middle school. *Child Development*, 68(6), 1198–1209.

Williams, J.M. & Tolmie, A. (2000). Conceptual change in biology: group interaction and the understanding of inheritance. *British Journal of Developmental Psychology*, 18, 625–649.

Youniss, J. (1980). *Parents and Peers in Social Development: A Sullivan-Piaget Perspective*. Chicago: University of Chicago Press.

Zajac, R.J. & Hartup, W.W. (1997). Friends as coworkers: research review and classroom implications. *The Elementary School Journal*, 98, 3–13.

8

CLASSROOM ENVIRONMENTS

The physical classroom environment will vary between countries, in terms of size, furniture, whether laid out in tables or rows, etc. In some countries classrooms are made up of desks facing the teacher, but in many Western primary school classrooms, a fairly typical 'map' of a classroom (see Figure 8.1) shows a complex layout of furniture. Marked on the map are different types of learning activities taking place, the location of pupils, the gender of pupils and the location of the teacher and her desk. In the UK and in other countries an additional feature of many classrooms today is the presence of an additional adult – a Teaching Assistant or equivalent – who often works with low-attaining pupils or those with special educational needs (see Chapter 9).

One distinct characteristic of primary school classrooms therefore is the seating arrangements for pupils. Until the 1960s/1970s in the UK, seating of pupils had been traditionally based at the individual desk, often set out in rows that faced the front of the room. One of the authors (PB) was vividly reminded of this during a recent visit on the occasion of the centenary of the East London primary school he attended as a young boy in the 1950s. While the classroom today was brightly coloured and laid out in tables, it was not difficult to call to mind the way the same space in the 1950s was occupied by over fifty small desks set out in tightly packed but very neat rows, all facing the teacher's desk at the front. This arrangement has been understandably associated with whole-class teaching approaches (Hastings & Chantry, 2002). But the traditional desk arrangement gave way to the large-scale adoption of small tables of various designs around which four, five or six children sit (Hastings & Chantry, 2002). On the Figure 8.1 map, various 'groupings' of children have been identified, along with the particular tasks they are engaged in, and whether there is an adult present or not.

There are other features of the whole classroom which can be gauged from the map, such as the physical classroom size and the number of pupils in the

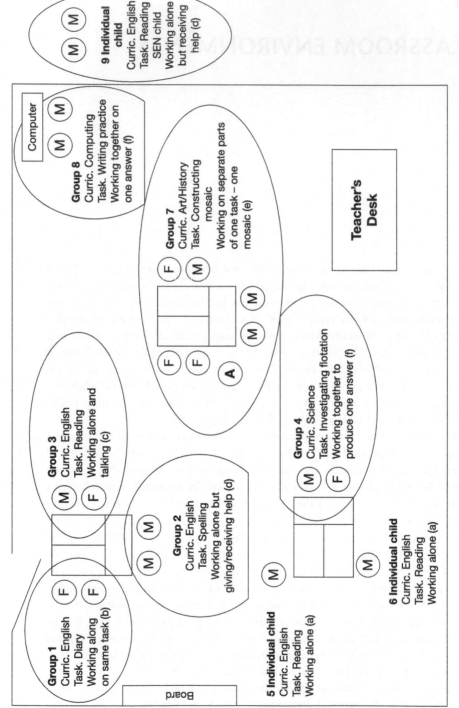

FIGURE 8.1 A typical primary school classroom 'map'

Source: Kutnick, Blatchford & Baines, Pupil groupings in primary school classrooms: sites for learning and social pedagogy? *British Educational Research*

class. There are other features not revealed in this map, but which could be – for example, the composition of the class and the groups in terms of pupil attainment, friendship relations, etc., as well as physical features such as the lighting, noise levels and air quality.

In this and following chapters we will address a number of features of the classroom environment shown in this map. We will see that the classroom is a distinct and complex setting for teaching and learning, especially so when one considers the interconnections between these discrete features. This does not mean that school-level environments and policies are unimportant. It is clear from research on school effectiveness that there can be important differences between schools in their effects on pupils' educational progress, and some of the constituent factors in successful schools are well understood (Mortimore et al., 1988). However, as Doyle (1986) has argued, there are boundaries separating the classroom from the school. This reflects the way school-level processes are somewhat distal from pupils and it is the closer 'proximal' classroom processes that are more important, but it is also because the two environments have tended to be studied separately. The classroom is the main academic context in primary school pupils' lives.

One orientating point, basic to social psychology, is that behaviour is affected by both individual personality and situation. This idea goes back to Kurt Lewin in the 1930s, and the idea that the environment and its interaction with personal characteristics of individuals were important determinants of actual behaviour. This was expressed in the basic formula $B = f(P,E)$, that is, behaviour is a function of both person and environment. Ross and Nesbett (1991) show how easy it is to underestimate the effect of the situation on behaviour – this is the 'basic attribution error'. When applied to classrooms, the idea is that different classroom activities and structures have forces, different to other contexts, which pull events and participants along with them.

There has been a tendency in educational psychology and educational research to consider the effects of teaching and teacher–pupil interactions independently of the environment in which these interactions occur. As we shall see in the next chapter, research on teaching has understandably focused on classroom processes in terms of teachers' actions towards pupils and pupils' learning or attainments, rather than in terms of wider, contextual dimensions affecting pupils and teachers together. But teachers do not meet pupils individually out of context – the classroom environment, in its many guises, also shapes the nature of the tasks and the interactions between teachers and pupils, and defines the kinds of interactive skills or competencies that pupils and teachers need. In terms of influences of effects, this turns on its head the usual way of conceiving classroom effects; that is, in terms of teaching (in research terms the independent variable) affecting pupil learning or attainment (the dependent or outcome variable). In this chapter we consider interactions and behaviour as dependent variables, with the context or environment of the focus of attention as the independent variable. Another way to view this is to say that the teacher is not viewed just in terms of attempts to teach or socialize children, but as someone who necessarily adapts to the demands of the classroom environment (Weinstein, 1991). Simultaneously, this reversal of 'independent' and 'dependent' variables makes an important point: people and contexts affect each other in a variety of ways. It is not simply a matter of X affecting Y.

There are a number of models which have conceptualized contextual influences on pupils in schools. An early, influential conception of the immediate environment as a factor in everyday behaviour was the ecological psychology of Barker and Wright and their colleagues (Barker, 1968). They showed ways in which different contexts – classroom, home, street, as well as smaller, within-school class contexts such as different activities, could be seen as niches or settings with predictable and systematic consequences in terms of teachers' and pupils' behaviour. As we shall see below, it was Paul Gump (1967) who did most to show how the stream of behaviours that make up a day in the classroom can be segmented into behavioural settings.

One of the earliest and most widely cited models is that in Dunkin and Biddle (1974), which supported research in the 'process-product' tradition of teaching effectiveness. There were four stages: presage, context, process and product. Though helpful, one of the limitations of models like these, strongly suggested by the research reported in this chapter, is that contextual features are seen as background, necessarily 'distal' factors affecting teachers and pupils, and are therefore consigned to a relatively minor role. In this chapter we work towards a more dynamic and nuanced approach to classroom contexts.

Another early and still very influential conception of the ecological context of behaviour is that of Bronfenbrenner (1979). He is often credited with assisting the recognition that psychology needs to concern itself with naturally occurring behaviour and the effects of contexts within which behaviour takes place. He was one of the first to offer a nested or multilevel hierarchical model that is now commonplace in statistical modelling of influences on behaviour, for example, as seen in school effectiveness research (Goldstein, 1995). He identified an immediate context (microsystem), for example, the family or the school; a mesosystem, which involved links between microsystems, for example, those between home and school; an exosystem, which would include parents' conditions of employment; and a macrosystem, which could include government policy on employment and working conditions. Like many seminal ideas, the basic structure of Bronfenbrenner's model has been influential, even if the vocabulary has changed. For example, a later thorough review of factors influencing school progress made a distinction between 'distal' and 'proximal' variables (which in Bronfenbrenner's terms roughly translates as macro- and micro-systems), arguing that the former – for example, centralized curriculum reforms – were much less important than the latter – such as teaching and learning processes in classrooms (Wang et al., 1993).

Even this system needs to be extended. The school can be seen as one type of microsystem, but within this level there will be units, such as the classroom and the playground, which are parallel to each other and which, as we see throughout this book, are very different contexts with qualitatively different sets of relationships, rules and dynamics. In addition, some contexts are nested within these sub-microsystems; for example, within a class of children there are often separate groupings of children within which children work. As we shall see, these groupings can differ in terms of the types of relationship, tasks and adult role.

In this chapter we will review some of the ways in which classroom contexts have been conceived and researched. The literature overall is vast and we can only provide a selective review. We will do this in two main sections. First we look at class-level contexts, in terms of the physical features of classrooms, the number of pupils in a class, the allocation of pupils to classes on the basis of ability, the interactive and social characteristics of classrooms, and the classroom psychological environment. We then look at units within the class, such as segments, activities and tasks, and within-class groupings. We will highlight research on class-size differences and within-class grouping practices that took place at the Institute of Education, UK.

In the conclusions to this chapter we return to ways of thinking about the influence of the classroom context on teacher and pupils, and offer a new way of conceiving of the influences involved.

Class level

Physical environment of the classroom

Perhaps the most obvious way of looking at the effects of the classroom environment is in terms of its physical nature (see reviews by Arends, 1994; Doyle, 1986; Higgins et al., 2005). An influential early study of UK secondary schools by Rutter et al. (1979) found that the pupils' perception of the quality of working conditions in the school was positively related to their exam scores. One of the authors (PB) visited a recently built single-storey South London primary school. Despite the excellent work going on in the school, and the bright and pleasant classrooms, it was difficult to avoid the conclusion that the L-shaped classrooms presented unnecessary problems for the teacher, who often did not have full sight of all the pupils in the classroom. Not for the first time, it seemed that architects had not talked to teachers!

One way the physical environment might be influential is that the layout of the classroom seating – for example, in terms of circles, U-shape or traditional rows – affects behaviour within it. Similarly, the organization of the classroom environment in terms of, for example, divisions created with bookcases to produce separate areas, can affect things like the density of students and interaction patterns. Ecological psychologists used the term 'synomorphy' to refer to the compatibility between the design of a setting and the activities and actions in that setting. A number of authors have recommended a 'horseshoe' shaped arrangement of tables so that students can see each other and the teacher, though one worry is that this then becomes rather teacher-dominated (Higgins et al., 2005).

Early observation research by Adams and Biddle (1970) was one of the first to make use of videotapes for research purposes. They found that when arranged in traditional rows there was an 'action zone' comprising of pupils in the front and centre of the classroom. There has been debate over whether this is best described as a 'T' shape or as a triangle, but it seems to be evident even after students are randomly allocated to seats (Higgins et al., 2005).

Walberg (in Weinstein, 1987) found that students who preferred to sit at the front generally expressed positive views, whilst those sitting at the back expressed negative views, about school, studying and their capacity for success. It also seems that some pupils actively seek out locations in the classroom which enable them to participate more. Weinstein (1987) concluded that characteristics of seating and the individual pupil both contribute to student participation, but that pupil attitudes are predicted by seating (being nearer the teacher enhances affective outcomes).

Several studies have compared pupils' work and behaviour in traditional rows as opposed to other configurations. Axelrod et al. (1979) found more disruptive and less on-task behaviour in groups. Wheldall et al. (1981) in Britain observed two Year 6 classes for two weeks each in groups, then rows and then groups again. The results showed an increase in on-task behaviour when children were in rows. Bennett and Blundell (1983) found a marked improvement in the quantity of work when seated in rows. The quality of work was the same when in rows as opposed to groups, and there was a less marked decline in quantity when re-seated in groups. Teachers in this study thought classroom behaviour improved in rows, followed by an increase in talking when re-seated in groups. Pupils' reactions were more mixed in that some liked the quieter atmosphere in rows, but others did not like restrictions on space available. However, other studies report opposing results with more off-task and less on-task behaviour in rows as well as more student withdrawal (Rosenfield et al., 1985; Weinstein, 1987).

Research concerning the physical dimensions of schools has examined differences between traditional classrooms and open-plan designed schools (see reviews in Bennett, 1987; Doyle, 1986; Weinstein, 1979). Research on open offices has found that employees find them less satisfactory (Brennan et al., 2003, in Higgins et al., 2005). Gump (1974) researched primary (first and second) and intermediate (fifth and sixth) grades in two open-plan and two traditional school buildings. This research tradition clearly conceptualizes the environment as having a 'main effect' on behaviour. In Barker's terms, environments are 'coercive'. Differences were clearer at the primary stage, though the small sample makes such findings tenuous. At primary level, students in open-plan settings occupied a greater variety of sites than students in traditional classrooms, and also more time in settings in which they worked together. More time in open settings was spent in transitions, waiting and organizing.

Bennett (1987) reviewed research in this area in the UK and also reports more time wasting in open-plan settings. Overall, he concludes that physical differences in teaching areas do not differentiate teaching practices. There is much agreement that no architectural solution can work without considering what use teachers make of it. There is not a simple relationship between design and teaching. Teachers have been found to adapt open spaces to form discrete areas and reclaim their own space, and one reason for this might be that workloads and preparation appear to increase in open-plan settings. Bennett also reports that studies suggest that conventional school designs result in pupils with higher achievements. There seems to be an interaction between physical design and social class of pupils, with pupils with low attainment or low socioeconomic status doing worse in more open settings, and better in more structured settings.

Higgins et al. (2005) show that a number of additional, often taken-for-granted features of the physical classroom environment can be important. They review research which shows that temperature and air quality and noise levels can adversely affect pupil attainment, engagement and wellbeing. Higgins et al. (2005) also point out that although many authors propose a link between the classroom environment and student attitudes we should beware of a simple architectural determinism; it is the interactions between, and combined effects of, these separate features that are as important as the individual aspects.

Number of children in the class

We can see in Figure 8.1 that one of the main features of the classroom environment is the number of pupils – at the time when the map was constructed there were 19 pupils, relatively few by UK standards.

Class size has been the subject of a huge amount of intense and at times aggressive debate. There are two opposed views. The first view, supported by teacher surveys, is that small classes allow a better quality of teaching, more individual attention to pupils' individual characteristics, and a higher level of performance. Some educationalists have argued that small classes are so important that they should be a main plank of education policy (Achilles, 1999). Inspired by this idea, and despite already having high average levels of school performance, there have been recent class-size reduction programmes in countries and regions in East Asia (e.g., in mainland China, Hong Kong, Singapore, South Korea and Japan), as well as in the USA, the Netherlands and Canada. In the UK, the Labour Government under Tony Blair was sufficiently persuaded about the effect of class sizes to introduce a cap of 30 in a class for English children aged up to 7 years of age. The Scottish Government went even further and introduced a cap of 25 pupils in the class.

But there are powerful voices against smaller classes. In the 1980s in the UK, in response to lobbying by teacher associations and local authorities to reduce class sizes, Conservative education ministers were keen to say there was no proven link between class size and pupil achievement and a number of commentators influenced by economists such as Eric Hanushek (2011) argue that reducing class sizes is not a cost-effective use of public funds and that money would be better spent in other forms of investment, in particular improving teaching quality.

In this section, we shall look at two main types of research: first, research on the effects of class size on pupils' academic performance and, second, research that investigates effects on classroom processes such as teaching and pupil attention. Given our space limits, this chapter is inevitably selective and will concentrate on pedagogical and educational implications of class-size effects. For more on class-size research, see Blatchford (2003a, 2003b, 2011) and Ehrenberg et al. (2001).

Does the number of pupils in a class affect pupils' educational attainment and progress?

This is perhaps the most commonly asked question about class size in schools. It is a deceptively simple question, and it is frustrating to many people that the clear answer likely to be given by teachers and others is not matched by research findings. There are several reasons why research findings are unclear. Earlier British research, which looked at naturally occurring associations between size of class or pupil-teacher ratios and pupils' performance, tended to find little or no relationship between class size and outcomes in terms of attainment or found that pupils in larger classes did somewhat better than pupils in smaller classes (Blatchford, 2003b). But the now well-understood problem with this kind of research is that we often do not know whether the results can be explained by another factor, for example, that poor attainers tend to be allocated to smaller classes, or more experienced teachers are given larger classes. In other words there may be reasons which could explain the results other than the unlikely conclusion that large classes are better for pupils.

Another approach to evidence on the effects of class size on pupil outcomes has been through reviews of the research literature. Glass et al.'s meta-analysis (Glass et al., 1982) was influential at the time it was published in the 1970s. It involved taking the results from 77 studies and calculating overall effects using a common metric for each study. Results showed that effects on attainment increased as class size decreased, with the largest effects for classes smaller than 20. However, results are difficult to interpret because conclusions will inevitably depend on the quality of the studies included, and some of these are rather suspect (Slavin, 1989).

Another way of approaching associations between class size and pupil performance is to compare the educational performances of countries with different class sizes. In recent international comparisons, countries with the largest class sizes like Japan and South Korea have amongst the highest levels of performance while countries with the smallest class sizes like Italy have lower levels of educational performance (DfE, 2011). Unfortunately global international comparisons of this sort are fraught with many methodological caveats (e.g., not controlling for other potentially influential factors in pupil achievement levels or private tutoring), and results might be attributable to a host of cultural, educational and economic differences.

Yet another frequently used method of evaluating the effects of class size and class-size reduction (CSR) is to compare them with other initiatives in terms of their effects on pupils' attainments. A number of authors (including the influential meta-analysis of Hattie, 2005) conclude that class size reductions are less effective than other and less costly alternative reforms. However, this kind of comparison is questionable in the sense that educational initiatives, with which CSR is often compared – such as one-to-one tutoring, peer tutoring and computer-assisted learning – are distinctive *methods* of teaching, while CSR merely sets limits on the numbers of pupils in a class involved. To be a fair test we would need to also take into account what teaching and instruction would be appropriate in classes of different sizes, and we return to this point at the end of this section.

Experimental studies

To overcome the problem that simple correlational designs do not control for potentially important extraneous variables like pupil prior attainment, it is often argued that experimental designs should be used, in which pupils and teachers are randomly assigned to classes of different sizes. If this allocation is done properly, then any relationships between class size and later differences in pupils' academic performance in classes of a different size must be attributable to class size and not to any other factor. Studies of this sort are rare in educational research and this is one reason for the high profile achieved by the STAR research, based in Tennessee, which involved the random allocation of pupils and teachers to three types of classes in the same school: 'small' classes (13–17), 'regular' classes (22–25), and 'regular' with full-time teacher aide. The project involved over 7,000 pupils in 79 schools and students who were followed from kindergarten (aged 5) to third grade (aged 8). Pupils in small classes performed significantly better than pupils in regular classes and gains were still evident after Grade 4, when pupils returned to normal class sizes (Finn & Achilles, 1999; Finn et al., 2005).

The STAR project results have provided the basis for a number of educational initiatives and policies in the USA and other countries. There have been criticisms, e.g., student attrition from the study, the lack of pupil baseline data, and the possible effect of the allocation to experimental conditions on the validity of conclusions, but later re-analyses tend to support the main findings. There have also been several other experimental research projects in the USA (the main ones are SAGE, Primetime, California – see Ehrenberg et al., 2001), and in Hong Kong (see Galton & Pell, 2010), but, overall, the research designs were not strong, and results from these studies are not conclusive (Blatchford, 2011).

Longitudinal correlational studies

Despite the common view that they provide the gold standard of evidence in the social sciences, experimental designs can have some often overlooked limitations (e.g., not covering the full range of class sizes, and unintended effects of assignment to small or larger classes on the attitudes and behaviour of participants). An alternative, and possibly more valid, approach is to examine relationships between class size and pupil academic outcomes, as they occur in the real world, and to make adjustments, statistically, for potentially confounding factors such as pupils' prior attainment, teacher characteristics, and so on. This was the approach adopted by a large-scale study in the UK (the Class Size and Pupil Adult Ratio (CSPAR) project). This study used a longitudinal, naturalistic design and studied the effect of class size on pupils' academic attainment, and also classroom processes such as teaching and pupil attention (Blatchford, 2003a; Blatchford et al., 2003). It tracked over 10,000 pupils in over 300 schools from school entry (at 4 or 5 years) to the end of the primary school stage (11 years).

There was a clear effect of class size on children's academic attainment over the first year of school (4 or 5 years), in both literacy and mathematics, even after adjusting for other possible confounding factors. The effect sizes were comparable to that reported by the STAR project. There was a statistically significant increase in attainment for all high-, middle- and low-attaining groups, though the effect was larger for pupils with lower baseline attainment. Effects were still evident on literacy progress at the end of the second year of school (Year 1), though by the end of the third year the effects were not clear. There were no clear longer-term effects of class-size differences on mathematics achievement. In other results it was also found that moving to a class of a different size, especially a larger class, had a negative 'disruption' effect on students' academic progress.

Who benefits most?

Perhaps the strongest conclusion from research on the connection between class size and pupil attainment is that there appears to be an important connection between the age of child and class-size reductions. The experimental STAR project and the longitudinal CSPAR study (probably the best designed studies in this field) both show that the effects of class size on academic outcomes are clearest with the youngest students. There is no evidence we know that class-size reductions on their own positively impact on the academic attainment of older children. This is one reason why it is likely that class-size reductions are effective as a policy of prevention, not remediation (Blatchford, 2003).

Are processes within classrooms affected by class-size differences?

Information on classroom processes affected by class-size differences is important because without it there are difficulties in explaining effects on pupils' academic performance, and it is also difficult to offer practical guidance on how to maximize the opportunities provided. Knowledge about mediating classroom processes is still relatively limited and this lack of clear research evidence is not helped by methodological weaknesses in much research in this area (Finn et al., 2003).

The evidence suggests that there are two main classroom processes affected by class-size differences: effects on teachers and effects on pupils (Finn et al., 2003). Perhaps the most consistently identified classroom process affected by reduced class size is individual attention by teachers. Glass and Smith concluded that smaller classes resulted in greater teacher knowledge of pupils and frequency of one-to-one contacts between teachers and pupils. Other studies also report more individual teaching and attention in smaller classes, more feedback, better relationships with and knowledge of pupils, and more differentiation (see Blatchford, 2011).

Systematic observation techniques allow a reliable method of measuring teacher attention to pupils. In an early Canadian study (Shapson et al., 1980), one of the few observation measures on which there were differences was the proportion of pupils addressed as individuals. This proportion increased in a linear way as class sizes decreased from 37, 30, 23 to 16. In the CSPAR, large-scale systematic observation studies conducted when pupils were 4 or 5 years (Blatchford, 2003b) and 10 or 11 years (Blatchford, Bassett & Brown, 2005) showed that at both ages pupils in small classes were more likely to experience one-to-one teaching and were more often the focus of a teacher's attention. In a further UK observation study, this finding was replicated, and, moreover, it was found to continue into secondary schools (Blatchford, Bassett & Brown, 2011). The connection between class size and individualization therefore seems a robust finding. There is also an indication from research, though less strong, that small classes have benefits in terms of easier classroom control and management, lower teacher stress and higher morale.

Research on classroom processes related to pupil achievement, dating back to the 1970s, has often pointed to pupil attentiveness, reflected, for example, in the notion of 'time on task' (see Shulman, 1986), having a key role in models set up to explain factors influencing pupils' educational progress (e.g., Creemers, 1994; Dunkin & Biddle, 1974). It is therefore significant that studies of class-size effects show that pupils in smaller classes attend and participate more and spend more time on task (Cahen, in Cooper, 1989; Carter, 1984 in Cooper, 1989). In explaining why small classes might be linked to attentiveness, Cahen et al. (1983 in Cooper, 1989) argue that pupil attention is greater because pupils are not lost in the crowd and have more opportunities for participating.

Not all research has found a connection: Shapson et al. (1980), in a systematic observation study, did not find that pupils in smaller classes participated more in assigned tasks. But Finn and Achilles (1999) and Finn et al. (2003) claim that student classroom engagement is the key process that explains why smaller classes lead to better attainment and conclude that class size affects student engagement more than teaching.

More recent research in the UK (Blatchford, Bassett & Brown, 2011) examined class size and pupil attentiveness across both primary and secondary years and found a statistical interaction between class size and pupil attainment group (i.e., whether the pupil is from high-, medium- or low-attainment groups) and pupil behaviour; low-attaining pupils were far more likely to be off task in larger classes, and, conversely, more likely to benefit from smaller classes, in comparison to middle- and high-attaining pupils.

Overall then the research literature suggests that class size affects individual attention and pupil engagement.

Effective teaching in small classes

There is evidence that teachers do not always change their style of teaching in small classes, and do not make the most of opportunities that small classes provide, which might explain the relatively modest effects on pupil performance found in some research. Research has found, for example, less collaborative group work in smaller classes, probably because teachers feel the need to maximize their teaching with individual pupils (Blatchford et al., 2001). This is unfortunate because, as we saw in Chapter 7, research evidence supports the use of collaborative group work as part of an everyday pedagogical approach and it is likely to be most effectively introduced with fewer pupils in a class (though this suggestion requires more research).

Benefits of class-size reduction or small classes are therefore not likely to be maximized without attention to effective teaching in small classes. From a different point of view, teachers in many schools now face increasing challenges, e.g., in terms of the number of pupils with behavioural difficulties or with special educational needs. Recent research (Webster & Blatchford, 2013) suggests that in such circumstances smaller classes would greatly help teachers in terms of classroom management, pedagogy and inclusion, but, again, this will not happen automatically, i.e., by just reducing the number of pupils in a class. Work on this aspect has begun in East Asian countries (see Blatchford, 2011) but is lacking in Western countries. Given the enormous financial and staffing stakes involved in decisions about class size, it is important to move towards an evidence base that can help.

Allocation to classes on the basis of ability

Along with the debate over class sizes in schools, another contentious issue relating to the classroom environment is over the organization of pupils in relation to their ability. The rationale for 'ability' grouping is that it seems to make practical sense because we can then appropriately target resources, teaching expertise, learning support, and so on. Some form of ability grouping is regularly advocated by politicians and those on the political right. It is important to note that 'ability' is hard to assess and is unlikely to be the basis for the allocation of pupils. A better term is 'attainment' because pupils are usually assigned on the basis of performance on a test or a teacher judgement of attainment.

Types of ability grouping

Grouping by attainment is a form of selection that can be implemented at different organizational levels within the school system. Allocation of pupils to secondary schools on the basis of attainment was once the common system in England when pupils were selected for grammar, technical or secondary modern schools on the basis of their scores on an IQ test at 11 years. Selection is still a feature of some schools, and some selective grammar schools still exist. But in this section we are concerned with ability grouping within schools at the class level and this normally takes three main forms in the UK: 'setting', 'within-class ability grouping', and to a lesser extent 'streaming'.

'Streaming' (or 'tracking' as it is called in the USA) involves allocating students to classes for most or all curriculum subjects based on general assessments or combined attainment results. In the USA, tracking may involve students undertaking a markedly different curriculum to those in other tracks. In the UK, students usually undertake approximately the same curriculum, but high-ability classes are taken through it at a faster pace and/or greater depth (see Baines, 2012).

'Setting', in contrast to streaming, is a form of ability grouping that is very common in the UK (sometimes referred to as 'regrouping' in the USA), and involves children being allocated to classes on the basis of similar attainment levels for a particular curriculum area. Setting allows students to be in different ability groups for different subject domains but also means that they can be taught in mixed-ability classes in other parts of the curriculum.

'Within-class ability grouping' involves the formation of ability groups within classes, and students may receive instruction, work and learning tasks that are appropriate for their particular level of perceived ability. We look at this later in this chapter.

Ability grouping and pupil academic performance

So what does the research evidence tell us about the impact of ability grouping in general on academic achievement and progress? The well-known Programme for International Student Assessment (PISA) studies, which take place every three years and involve assessments in reading or mathematics or science of 15-year-olds across a large number of OECD and non-OECD countries, have repeatedly found that the more schools group by ability, the lower the pupil performance overall (OECD, 2010). In contrast to the view of many politicians, therefore, ability grouping in schools seems to depress academic performance. It seems that ability grouping can exacerbate inequalities already in the system, e.g., in terms of socio-economic status.

Streaming

In a synthesis of 29 studies of ability grouping in secondary schools, Slavin concluded that there were no consistent effects of homogeneous ability grouping, as opposed to mixed-ability classes, on achievement in any curriculum area and actually slightly negative effects in social studies (Slavin, 1990). Similarly when data were separated by ability group, no one ability level was found to benefit more than any other.

A widely cited earlier meta-analysis of 51 studies by Kulik and Kulik (1982) also found little consistent effect of streaming on academic performance. There were positive effects for specific programmes of study for gifted students but these seemed attributable to the enriched curriculum experiences these students encountered, rather than anything to do with the composition of the class. Consistent with this interpretation were the results of a later meta-analysis of a range of different forms of ability grouping in which Kulik and Kulik (1992) reported little effect of ability grouping (streaming and setting) on achievement but only when there was little variation in instructional experience. When the instructional experience varied by ability group, the effects were more marked in favour of ability grouping, particularly for high-ability students.

Since these meta-analyses were undertaken, there have been a number of naturalistic studies which have examined tracking where the curriculum is likely to be matched to the students' ability. Under these circumstances, students in high-ability classes benefit from ability grouping but low-ability students do much worse and actually fare better in mixed-ability classrooms (Hallinan & Kubitscek, 1999; Callahan, 2005). These results are similar to those found by the PISA studies. The effects of ability grouping then seem to be largely attributable to differential access to an enriched or accelerated curriculum.

Setting

Relatively few studies have examined the effect of setting or regrouping on pupils' academic performance. One potential advantage of setting is that it offers the advantage of greater accuracy in group placement and a better match with the appropriate level of instruction offered, as well as potentially more flexibility in re-assignment to a more appropriate set.

In his 'best evidence' synthesis, Slavin reported inconclusive findings relative to the use of setting at primary level, largely because of the absence of studies that met the strict methodological requirements of the review (Slavin, 1990). However, of the seven studies he examined, five showed positive effects in favour of ability grouping in reading and/or mathematics and one study found in favour of mixed-ability classes. Slavin concluded that regrouping can be successful when instruction is substantially adjusted to match the ability level but has little impact when this procedure is not undertaken.

Despite its prevalence in the UK, there are only a few studies of setting at secondary level. In a substantial longitudinal study of setting in 45 comprehensive schools in England involving some 6,000 students, Judy Ireson and Susan Hallam compared pupils who experienced mixed-ability classes with those who experienced different levels of setting (from setting in a few subjects to setting for most subjects). The authors found few effects of setting on student performance in national tests of mathematics, English and science at 13–14 years and later at 15–16 years (Ireson & Hallam, 2001; Ireson, Hallam & Hurley, 2005). However, low-ability students made slightly less progress in mathematics by the end of Key Stage 3 (13–14 years) when put in ability groups compared with students in mixed-ability classes, and high-ability students made slightly more progress when they were in sets. Similarly, Wiliam and Bartholomew (2004) in a study of six secondary schools reported a similar divergence between students in high- and low-ability maths sets. Those in the high-ability sets made greater progress whilst those in the low-ability sets dropped further and further behind.

One problem with setting is that it can be progressively harder for students to move between sets as they have so much to catch up. Another worrying issue is that schools may tend to allocate the most knowledgeable and experienced teachers to the high-ability groups and the less knowledgeable or experienced teachers to the low-ability and difficult classes (Boaler, Wiliam & Brown, 2000; Oakes, 2005).

It is also likely that allocation to sets affects school and teacher expectations (Boaler et al., 2000). As we see in Chapter 10, lower teacher expectations, perhaps influenced by the level of set to which pupils have been allocated, may lead to less engaging approaches to teaching and learning. Importantly, students placed in sets above their assessed level of achievement make more progress than students of equivalent ability who are in ability groups at approximately the 'right' level (Ireson, Hallam & Hurley, 2005). Tellingly, placing students in groups below their level of ability tends to reduce their progress, irrespective of their attainment level. Similarly, schools can implicitly convey greater value to students in the higher sets or streams and it is little wonder that students in these higher-ability groups are more engaged in school and potentially feel a greater sense of belonging.

One of the strongest arguments against ability grouping has been provided by Jeannie Oakes (2005) who points to the variable opportunities to access the curriculum, learning resources and educator expertise; concerns about the stigma associated with being in a low-ability group (and in some cases being in a high-ability group); and most importantly the likelihood that ability grouping also tends to inadvertently organize students by social class, race and gender.

Social and psychological dimensions of classrooms

The areas looked at so far – the physical nature of the classroom, the number of pupils and ability grouping – represent only part of the way that classrooms may have effects. There are a number of other ways that classrooms may be looked at. A sometimes bewildering set of concepts and vocabulary has evolved, stemming from quite diverse disciplines – not just educational and social psychology (including ecological psychology) but microethnography and sociolinguistics – making summary very difficult.

Perhaps because we have all spent many years in classrooms, it is very easy to take characteristics of classroom environments for granted and not look objectively at their distinctive nature. Weinstein (1991) describes classrooms as 'crowded, competitive, coercive'. Doyle (e.g., 1986) has been very influential in showing there are important elements in place over and above the characteristics of particular teachers and pupils. He identifies six distinctive elements of classroom environments:

1. Multidimensionality: The classroom is often a crowded place, and there are a large quantity of events and tasks in the classroom. Events have to be planned to meet individual requirements and changing demands. There are many management functions, records to be kept, resources to be ordered and planned for.
2. Simultaneity: Many things happen at once in classrooms, perhaps especially in primary schools with the tradition of helping individuals and groups working at different paces and tasks. But even in a whole-class setting an eye has to be kept on whether students are following, whilst watching for misbehaviour, whilst answering pupil questions, whilst trying to keep the logic of the presentation going, and so on.
3. Immediacy: There is a rapid pace in classroom events. Gump and Jackson have separately estimated that a primary school teacher has 500 exchanges with individual students each day. There is little time to reflect on practice!
4. Unpredictability: Classroom events often take unexpected turns. Interruptions are frequent, and it is not easy to anticipate how an activity will go on a particular day with a particular group of students.
5. Publicness: Classrooms are public places, and events are often witnessed by most of the pupils. If a teacher fails to notice a pupil's behaviour, this is likely to be noticed and acted on by other pupils.
6. History: Classes accumulate a common set of experiences and norms which provide the foundation for future actions. Classes are affected by new arrivals and the departure of students.

Doyle argues that these six dimensions create pressures that shape the task of teaching. Their effect varies no doubt but the pressures operate in all classrooms regardless of how teachers organize activities.

Classroom psychological environment

Another way of conceiving of effects at the classroom level, which has received a good deal of attention going back many decades, is the 'classroom psychological environment'. The theoretical roots of the concept come from Kurt Lewin. The concept is rather abstract but refers to the climate or atmosphere of the class as a social group, which can influence what students learn. Paradoxically, given its abstract nature, it is usually measured in very concrete, psychometric terms by asking students and teachers to rate psychological characteristics of their class on questionnaire items. This approach has tended to focus rather more on emotional and organizational aspects of classrooms rather than instruction or pedagogy.

Dimensions include cohesiveness, satisfaction, goal direction, difficulty, competitiveness and friction. There are overlaps with the term 'classroom climate', though this tends to be drawn from observational measures and is more linked to process product research (see Chapter 9). From the late 1960s on, researchers have sought to link classroom environment to learning outcomes. Key early research programmes were conducted by Marjoribanks, Walberg, Moos and Frazer. Moos developed the highly influential 'Classroom Environment Scale' comprising three areas: interpersonal relationships within the classroom; individual personal development; and system maintenance and change, including classroom control. In the 1990s, Fraser and his colleagues, as part of an influential programme of work, developed the 'What is Happening in Class' (WIHIC) scale which focused on student perceptions of a wide range of dimensions including cohesiveness, teacher support, task orientation, cooperation and equity (Fraser, 1998).

Reviews by MacAulay (1990) and others conclude that many studies have shown that classroom environments have important influences on student achievements and self-concept. Such work also points to the person-environment 'fit', that is, students achieve better when there is a higher similarity between the actual class environment and that preferred by students. This also suggests that different types of pupils, for example, in terms of temperament, will perform in different ways, and react differently, in different classes.

A more contemporary approach to the classroom psychological environment has been provided by Pianta and his colleagues. As we see in Chapter 9, the CLASS (Classroom Assessment Scoring System) is a theoretically derived approach that examines classrooms in terms of three overarching dimensions: (1) emotional supports, (2) classroom organization, and (3) general instructional supports (see Hamre & Pianta, 2010). Within each dimension, specific behaviour and indicators are rated in terms of being high or low. There is some coverage of dimensions relating to teacher–pupil interaction but much operates at the overall classroom level.

Classroom task and reward structures

Another direction of research on classrooms has conceived of the class in terms of task or goal structures. One version of this can be found in the work of the Johnsons (Johnson & Johnson, 1987) who were interested in the way students related to each other in terms of the degree of interdependence they sought while working towards instructional goals. Goal structures could be cooperative, competitive, or individualistic (see review in Arends, 1994). A connected notion concerns the extent to which reward structures are cooperative, competitive or individualistic. The way teachers organize goal and reward structures determines which types of goals are accomplished.

An allied area of research, but stemming more from theory and research in the area of motivation, has made much progress in linking classrooms to the kinds of goals students pursue. Again this is a huge area of research and its coverage and theoretical underpinnings can only be hinted at here. One central theme has been the extent to which classrooms encourage 'mastery' or 'performance' orientation. This basic notion from motivational research is applied to whole-classroom environments and concerns the extent to which students are encouraged to be independent and in control of their learning. In a statement of immense relevance to current trends in education in England and Wales, Eccles and her colleagues have concluded: 'In general, environmental settings which emphasize evaluation, social comparison, and competition appear to increase self-focus or an ego-involved orientation' (Eccles et al., 1984, p. 307). Eccles and others argue that schools typically are not well matched to students' needs as learners. Eccles's work is grounded in Atkinson's expectancy value model (see Pintrich & Schunk, 1996). Other research stems from a goal theory approach to motivation. Again the distinction between task mastery/intrinsic interest vs. ability/self-focus is key. Ames (1992) has shown that if there is a stress on ability relative to others' grades and performance, then students will adopt ability-focused goals, while emphasis on mastery, effort and improvement is likely to lead to task-focused goals. There is an overlap here with Doyle's (1979, in Arends, 1994) view that the primary features of classroom life are rules concerning how students 'exchange (their) performance for grades' (in Arends, 1994, p. 108).

Contexts within classrooms

Some of the most interesting early research on classrooms was an attempt to locate and study meaningful units below or rather within the level of the class. Different contexts within classrooms may place different interactional demands on participants, and the educational effects may need to be examined in terms of these units or contexts. Classrooms are composed of numerous sub-settings that vary in rules that are appropriate and in the behaviour they elicit from teachers and pupils. Hargreaves et al. (1986) showed that classroom rules had to be understood as operating within contexts, or phases of lessons. Five phases were identified: entry, settling down or preparation, the lesson itself, clearing up and exit. Students were typically allowed to speak quietly amongst themselves during entry and preparation, but after the signal that the lesson proper had begun they were expected to attend to the teacher and not talk to each other. Recommendations for the 'literacy hour' in England and Wales stated that it should be divided into discrete phases – whole-class teaching, work in ability groups, followed by a class plenary – and it seems likely that different rules and expectations operate for each.

A review of research relevant to this section is again made difficult by the variety of different approaches, often from quite different academic disciplines and literatures. One approach again has its roots in the ecological psychology of Barker and Wright. Segments of classroom life are identified on the basis of painstakingly collected narrative records of the classroom 'behavioural stream'. In analysis, the continuous temporal record is divided into segments that are natural units of action, and these segments are identified on the basis of, for example, changes in participants (small group to whole class), resources used in the lesson, roles of participants (e.g., verbal answering to writing) and rules governing behaviours (talking allowed vs. silence during individual work). A change in one of these can mean a change in the nature of the segment (see Doyle, 1986; and Gump, 1967). Once the segments have been identified the kinds of behaviours, participants, etc. that occur within them can be examined.

Segments, as used in ecological psychology, are units resulting from the cutting up of the temporal stream of behaviour, but other analyses of settings within classrooms refer to settings that operate at particular moments in time. Doyle (1986) and Weinstein (1991) have summarized research on different activity types. Berliner's (1983, in Doyle, 1986) list is typical of US research: reading circle, seatwork, one-way presentation, mediated presentation (for example, involving audio recordings), silent reading, construction, games, play, transitions and housekeeping. Weinstein (1991) organizes her review around the following activities: recitation, teacher-directed small groups, seatwork, and student-directed small groups. In US research a few activity types seem to dominate, with 'seatwork' taking up the bulk of time, followed by whole-class presentation and then transitions and other housekeeping events (Gump, 1967).

The point of relevance to this chapter is that different activities or segments can demand different kinds of behaviours from both teacher and pupils. Mehan (1979) showed how competent participation in classrooms requires an understanding of what context one is in and when contexts change, as well as what behaviour is appropriate in different classroom contexts. Gump (1967, in Doyle, 1986) found that teachers engaged in more acts in whole-class than reading groups, and dealing with difficulties in pupils' behaviour may be more common in some segments than others. Bossert (1979) found that teachers were more inclined to seek control in larger groups and so were more concerned with controlling misbehaviour. Understandably, teachers provide more individual help during seatwork, though interestingly Galton et al. (1980) showed that the cognitive level of language use can be higher in whole-class settings. Research on the nature of teacher language in classes with overlapping activities (Bossert, 1979) indicates that the frequency of reprimands is less in multi-task classrooms than whole-class settings, though this may just mean there are fewer interactions overall. Blumenfeld et al. (1983) found teacher talk in 'open activity structures' (that is, where students work on different activities at the same time) was less negative, more about academic performance, and was less about procedure, than teacher talk in single-task classrooms. The extent of multiple tasks is likely to vary between countries. There has been a tradition in some English primary schools of parallel and different activities in small groups. Recent educational reforms in the UK, under successive governments, may mean that multi-task classrooms are less common.

Student behaviour can also vary by activity type. Gump (1967) found that pupil involvement was highest in teacher-led small groups, then whole-class recitations and teacher presentations, and was lowest for individual study and pupil presentations. Also, behaviours seen as problematic can be affected by activity type. Silverstein (1979 in Doyle, 1986) in a study of fourth grade classes found such behaviours (from daydreaming to disruption) more common during seatwork and less common in small group and whole-class settings. Gump (1967) examined behaviour during the opening part of segments – the first four minutes – and found involvement significantly lower than during the remainder of the segment. So here there is variation by phase of segment. Students did most of their work near the end of a segment, if a product or end product was required.

Blatchford et al. (1982), on the basis of an observational study of two nursery classes attached to London primary schools, examined behaviour of newcomers in two main types of activity: free play and so-called 'directed' sessions. Interest was in how such young children, new to school settings, would behave in the more formal, directed settings. Five such sessions were examined: register, milk, story, rhymes and music. For the most part children behaved 'appropriately' in all five sessions, though there was rather less attention in register, probably because their attention wandered after their name had been called. In one class this session was much more concerned with individuals rather than the whole group and this would explain the increase in 'move away' and 'lost' behaviour in this session. More inappropriate and disruptive behaviour occurred in rhymes and singing sessions, most probably because children had difficulties with the words and actions, and in one of the nursery classes this appeared to go on too long. Some directed sessions were therefore less prone than others to hold children's attention. These kinds of results are useful if it is agreed that newcomers to school will become more easily assimilated if there is a continuity and focus to events.

There may also be systematic associations between sequencing of activities and pupil involvement. Gump (1967) found that involvement in the beginning phase of seatwork was especially low after recess/breaktime (see also Chapter 5). Krantz and Risley (1977, in Doyle, 1986) found off-task behaviour was high when story time occurred after recess – which may be one reason why staff can find afternoon play disruptive and why it is being eliminated in some English schools (Blatchford & Baines, 2010).

Tasks

There has been interest in ways in which subject matter content is enacted in classrooms. One approach to this has been to see the classroom 'task' as the unit of analysis – that is, short blocks of classroom time during which students are arranged in a particular way for a particular activity. Doyle (Doyle, 1986; Doyle & Carter, 1984; see also Bennett et al., 1984 for the UK) has used the notion of the 'academic task' to account for how the curriculum becomes a programme of action in classrooms. So subject matter appears, or is manifested, in classrooms as work. Researchers have calculated the number of activities typical during the school day to be more than 30 in an average elementary school class (Ross, 1984 in Doyle, 1986). Activities can also overlap with each other. Doyle, following Gump (1967), states that this is rarely more than two at one time but in some primary school classes in the UK, as seen in the map in Figure 8.1, it has been common for four or five task activities to run parallel to each other at one time.

Key dimensions of tasks include 'accountability' (e.g., evaluated strictly by the teacher) which will affect the seriousness with which such tasks are taken by pupils. Another dimension involves ambiguity and risk, so that higher cognitive tasks requiring understanding, reasoning, and problem formulation are high in ambiguity and risk for students, because the correct answers cannot be so obviously predicted and so failure is a possibility. This will affect pupils' attitudes to work, so that pupils may be more positive towards tasks which are low on challenge but also low on risk. Doyle and Carter (1984), in a study of three junior high English classes, found tasks involving descriptive or expository writing were difficult for the teacher to manage. They could extend over several days, involved frequent student questions, and clarification and assistance, while, in contrast, more predictable and less ambiguous tasks involving recall or predictable algorithms, e.g., as found in vocabulary or grammar assignments, proceeded smoothly and efficiently. This situation will presumably be affected by the way ambiguity is dealt with by teachers, and also by individual differences between pupils. There are surely tasks that may be challenging but also carry more reward. As Doyle says, safe can be boring.

Within-class groupings

One of the main features of a typical British classroom as seen in the classroom map in Figure 8.1 is the way it is organized into small groups. On the map, various 'groupings' of children have been identified. It can be seen that there are a variety of group sizes and compositions, and different curriculum areas are being worked on simultaneously (English, science, history). Learning tasks being undertaken by the children may be approached individually (groups 1, 2, 3, 5 and 6) or on an interactive basis (groups 4 and 8). Adults are present with some groups (groups 7 and 9) while a number of groups are working without a teacher or other adult present.

In other mappings, taken at different points in time, there may be a different constellation of groupings, activities and curriculum areas, e.g., the whole class may be found working within a single curriculum area at the same time or each child can be found undertaking an individualized assignment. When a number of different maps are collated it is possible, as in the research soon to be described, to build up a general picture of the social contexts and conditions for learning in classrooms.

There is an important distinction to be made between being seated in a group and actually working as a group; being seated around tables does not mean that pupils will or can work as a small group. Galton and Williamson (1992) showed that teachers do not always coordinate learning task and type of groupings. Kutnick and Blatchford (2013) review a wealth of research which shows that there are a number of 'resistances' to the learning potential of small groups, e.g., in terms of collaborative group work (see Chapter 7).

Yet grouping of pupils is connected in a more positive way to current theories of learning and development – for example, the benefits of peer interactive groupings (Doise & Mugny, 1984; Howe et al., 1992; Rogoff, 1990; Vygotsky, 1978; Webb & Palincsar, 1996). Experimental research on cooperative group work also paints a more positive picture (Slavin, 1990; Johnson & Johnson, 1987). Although widely cited, such studies are difficult to interpret in the sense that they may not reflect the everyday conditions in classrooms, and can demand a good deal of preparation for teachers (Kutnick & Blatchford, 2013). Doyle (1986) argued that there is little information on the problems classroom teachers have in managing multiple groups at one time.

We therefore need more information on the everyday way in which within-class groupings operate. If teachers are to be effective in their classrooms they must be aware of the potential for learning in classroom units, including small groupings. At the time of the first edition of this book surprisingly little was known about the nature of groupings used in an everyday way in classrooms, but since 2000 we have a much better understanding of within-class groupings, their multifaceted nature and the way they can inhibit or facilitate learning (Kutnick & Blatchford, 2013).

In this section we review research which has described the nature of within-class groupings, drawing in particular on a programme of research on groupings in British schools (Baines, Blatchford & Kutnick, 2003; Blatchford et al., 2001; Kutnick & Blatchford, 2013; Kutnick, Blatchford & Baines, 2005 for fuller analyses). The research is based on analysis of 4924 groupings from 672 Reception, Year 2 and Year 5 classes in 331 primary schools, and 248 Year 7 and Year 10 classes in 47 secondary schools. The data came from a 'classroom mapping' methodology which produced maps similar to that in Figure 8.1. These were completed by teachers at a particular point in the school day and when collated provided a representative description of the nature and use of groupings in terms of the number and size of groupings, the composition of the group in terms of attainment, gender, etc., the type of working interaction between pupils, the presence of adults, and the type of task that groupings were engaged in.

The findings reveal interesting ways in which classroom organization and grouping practices change over primary and secondary schooling, and allow us to see how multiple actions in the classroom take place at the same time, as suggested by Doyle (1986).

In all classrooms, individuated work (where children work independently but on the same tasks as others in the class) was the predominant working arrangement for groupings. Primary-age pupils rarely worked together, though small-group seating was the most frequent furniture arrangement, but rather engaged in individuated work.

Results showed that there were changes in grouping practices with pupil age. As pupils got older they were increasingly likely to experience whole-class ability-based sets (ability grouping) for core curriculum subjects and more formal row/pair seating arrangements. Group size decreased as pupils got older. Primary-age children were most likely to work on individual work, either alone or with the support of an adult. Primary school teachers most often used small groups, but from Year 5 they allocated work to dyads increasingly. Primary teachers decreasingly used large groups of 7–10 pupils and secondary school teachers made greater use of very large groupings of 11+ pupils.

As children got older, classroom tasks were more likely to involve the application of existing knowledge and less likely to involve practising skills. At secondary school level, there were indications that teachers coordinated grouping size, working interaction type and learning task. Changing grouping practices are aimed at maintaining control and on-task attention and maximizing individual and teacher-directed learning but also, in secondary classrooms only, offering pupils opportunities for peer interaction.

Of the various features of within-class groupings, perhaps most attention has been paid to the composition of groups (Webb & Palincsar, 1996; Kutnick & Blatchford, 2013). Teachers necessarily have to make decisions concerning who should be in groups, taking into consideration various factors including ability, sex distribution and friendships between pupils.

Research has concentrated almost exclusively on the ability mix of groups (Webb et al., 1997). As we saw above, some politicians and commentators are convinced that some form of ability grouping is a necessary way of organizing pupils for learning, and this applies to within-class grouping as well as class-level groupings like streaming or setting. Many on the political right claim that mixed-ability teaching reflects outdated and ineffectual progressive methods of teaching.

In fact the evidence in favour of mixed vs. same-ability within-class groupings is mixed (see Baines, 2012). A number of meta-analyses of effects at primary school level have been conducted and tend to indicate that ability grouping within classes has moderate effects on attainment when compared to no grouping or mixed-ability grouping. This is especially the case when used with an enhanced curriculum (e.g. for use with gifted students). Slavin reported that within-class ability grouping in primary school mathematics was related to higher performance in all eight studies considered with an effect size of +0.34, as well as in other subject areas. However the number of studies considered overall was small. In another analysis, Lou and colleagues reported that students in mathematics and science benefited equally from homogeneous and heterogeneous within-class ability grouping but found moderately in favour of ability grouping for reading instruction (Lou et al., 1996).

An important point to emerge from the literature (Baines, 2012) is that low-attaining students appear to benefit more from mixed-ability grouping than homogeneous ability grouping, whilst high-ability students benefit equally from both approaches. High-ability groups can benefit from the enriched or accelerated curriculum found in high-attaining groups while lower-attainment students can be negatively affected by a lower level curriculum. This is similar to the findings for ability grouping at the class level discussed earlier in this chapter.

Mixed-ability groups can help promote the use of elaboration, explanation and collaborative discussion between peers – all essential ingredients for developing high level understanding and high level thinking skills (Baines et al., 2007). Homogeneous ability groups are less likely to facilitate these forms of talk, possibly because all participants have similar understandings or assume that others already have these understandings.

Within-class grouping can also be used for peer co-learning (including peer tutoring, cooperative and collaborative learning). These infrequently used strategies involve pupils tutoring, helping and supporting each other or working collaboratively as part of a team and independently of adults. Under these circumstances, mixed-ability groups are preferred for academic and social reasons, though even here, there are suggestions that some effort to reduce the variability in attainment within the group can be helpful. Noreen Webb suggests that mixing low- and middle-ability students and middle- and high-ability students can help overcome some of the problems associated with using strict ability grouping or very wide mixed-ability grouping for cooperative or collaborative learning activities (Boaler, Wiliam & Brown, 2000). Such an approach can mean that the more able students do not get frustrated by having to work with very low ability peers and that the context is less intimidating for the less able. But, most importantly, this approach can ensure that a range of perspectives and conceptual understandings remain present within the group.

Size of group

Another main way of examining within-class groups is in terms of their size. As seen in Figure 8.1, group sizes may vary from children working as individuals (with or without the presence of other children, as in groups 5 and 6, but also groups 1, 2 and 3), working in pairs (groups 4 and 8), and in larger groups (group 7, with this group size ranging between four and ten children at times).

In the classroom mapping studies, described above, small groups usually consisted of four, five or six children seated around a table, and this was the predominant seating arrangement found in the middle and later years of the primary school (Years 2 and 5) as well as the early years of secondary school. Small groups accounted for approximately 60% of the observations made in these classes. Most of these small groups would have to work without a teacher present because with a larger number of small groups in a class, the teacher would necessarily only be able to work with one group at a time. These older children may therefore have more opportunity for peer-interactive learning (see Kutnick & Blatchford, 2013).

Other features of group composition are also important, including gender mix (Bennett & Dunne, 1992; Howe, 1997) and friendship mix (see Chapter 3). It can be seen in Figure 8.1 that in this classroom, at this particular time, groups tended to be made up of either boys or girls. We do not know the nature of the friendship mix, though we know that this issue can be a concern for teachers, and some try to avoid putting friends together for fear they may get distracted from work (see Chapters 3 and 7). Another feature of groups, rarely discussed or researched, is their stability in terms of members over time (see Kutnick & Blatchford, 2013).

Grouping practices within classes and class size

The class and the group can be thought of as two types of environmental contexts within a classroom, with the group level usually nested within the level of the whole class (except when the children are all working together – with whole-class interactive teaching there is only one grouping!). It is likely that the two levels are connected. It might be expected, for example, that in a large class the teacher would be forced to organize the children into more and/or larger groups. One aspect that may be important, therefore, is the connection between the size of class and grouping practices within the class. However, as far as we know, this possibility has not been looked at systematically before or since. It has been possible to study this in a systematic way in the Institute of Education class-size study, and the parallel project on grouping practices, also described above. Connections between class size and grouping practices in terms of number and size of groups, group composition, presence of adults, and the nature of the curriculum, task and activity type were explored at Reception, Year 2 and Year 5 age levels. As might be expected, results showed that class size increased with age of child; the youngest children in school (in Reception classes) were in smaller classes. Class size was found to constrain within-class groupings in several fundamental ways. Surprisingly, given the expectation that in larger classes teachers would be forced to use more whole-class teaching, it was found that there was a greater use of whole-class interactive teaching in small classes. Contrary to expectation, the number of very large groups, including whole-class teaching, decreased with size of class. What increased with size of class was the increased use of large groups of seven to ten pupils (Blatchford et al., 2001). Teachers therefore appear to prefer to organize learning in terms of groups, but because of the number of children, they are forced to teach to larger groups than they would like (Blatchford et al., 2001).

Conclusions

This chapter has necessarily had to cover a wealth of research, often from very different conceptual and empirical research traditions. One overarching conclusion to be drawn from the research reviewed here is the point that classroom contexts can be influential in affecting teachers and pupils, the interactions between them and the potential for learning in the classroom. The chapter was structured in two parts: first, in terms of ways of conceiving contexts at the class level, in terms of the physical layout of classrooms, the number of pupils, allocation to classes on the basis of pupil ability, the psychological environment, classroom task, reward structures and participation structures; and, second, in terms of within-class contexts, such as behavioural segments, tasks, activities and within-class groupings. Finally, we looked at just one way that the different contexts can be linked through the connections between class size and the size and number of within-class groupings.

The aspects of the classroom environment reviewed in this chapter have profound implications for theory, policy and practice. Research on class size, for example, shows the need for research on effective teaching approaches in classes of different sizes, and the way that this is important conceptually but also in terms of informing school policies on class-size reduction.

Research on organizing pupils for learning on the basis of attainment/ability, both at the whole-class and within-class grouping level, indicates that current policy in the UK and other countries, in favour of ability grouping, is almost certainly misguided. A main problem seems to be the way that ability grouping fails to provide the opportunity to conquer, and arguably exacerbates, societal divisions because it also unintentionally groups students by social class, ethnicity and gender. It is important to understand and address why low-attaining students struggle to make progress under an ability-grouped system (Baines, 2012) but a general point supported by research is that ability grouping can create an educational rut which it is difficult for pupils to get out of. It is important to remember that some of the most educationally successful countries in the world (such as Finland and Japan) avoid grouping students by ability until around 14 years of age. These countries go to great lengths to encourage students to work to the best of their abilities and discourage the view that there is such a thing as inherent and fixed ability (see Chapter 10) but also go to great lengths to help students keep up with their more able peers. It is notable that many of these countries also experience greater levels of equality within their societies.

Another controversial aspect of ability grouping, which links with other chapters in this book, is that it can affect who children make friends with. One theory, suggested over forty years ago, proposes that ability grouping can provoke a polarization in peer cultural attitudes to school amongst consistently high- and low-ability students (Kelly & Covay, 2008). Ability grouping at the class level, and especially streaming, makes this polarization even more likely. Polarization is particularly problematic for the lower-ability classes since it can result in a counter-productive, anti-learning peer culture which can exacerbate poor behaviour and eventual alienation from school.

One theme to emerge from the work described in this chapter and further developed in Blatchford et al. (2010) is that implications for practice are evident at both whole-class and within-class levels but perhaps clearer for the second compared to the first level. One avenue for future research is on identification of other links between class-level and within-class level contexts. Staying with class size, this could include links between class size and the nature and effectiveness of learning tasks in different groups. It may be that, given a class of a given size (a large class of 32, say), certain consequences may then follow in terms of the size and number of groups, and these in turn may affect the educational experiences of pupils in those groups.

In many countries across the world educational systems are being adapted to be more inclusive, e.g., for pupils with special educational needs. As many have found, there are enormous challenges that have to be addressed by practitioners, policy makers and researchers (see Florian, 2006). Once again, though, it is possible that the classroom environment has been underestimated. One problem, often taken for granted, is the way that teachers will inevitably face huge pedagogical and classroom management problems when seeking to integrate pupils with SEN in a class of say 25–30 other pupils. Rather than consider the appropriate classroom environment (for example, much smaller classes, or particular approaches to within-class grouping), a common solution to this problem in the UK has been the parallel introduction of many para-professionals (TAs) to work with these children; as we will see in Chapter 9, rather than solving the problem this use of TAs has made it worse.

Social pedagogy: the multidimensional nature of classrooms

We end this chapter with a look at conceptions of the classroom as a context for learning. We have seen earlier in this chapter that one expression of a concern with contextual factors is the well-known ecological model of Bronfenbrenner (1979) and the ecological psychology approach of Kounin and Gump (1974). The basic idea, as we have seen, is that within the school there will be smaller contexts, such as the classroom and the playground, which have qualitatively distinct sets of relationships, rules and dynamics, which influence both teachers and pupils. This is a more sophisticated view of contextual influences compared to that in the Dunkin and Biddle model, described earlier, where the model is more static and feeds in a linear way into influences on teaching and pupils. The ecological approach is better able to account for the influence of contextual factors on both teacher and pupils.

At the same time, the ecological approach is overly deterministic in the sense that it assumes the behaviour of teachers and pupils are both directed by contextual factors. One important extra feature not usually included in consideration of an ecological approach is the adaptability needed by teachers when faced with a range of contextual factors, like the number and attainment range of children in a classroom or the number and size of pupil groups. There are other ways in which the ecological model is limited. Teachers and pupils will also face two important other factors in classrooms – the curriculum and pedagogy. Further, their classrooms will have to be organized to meet the demands of school policy and national curricular policy.

As we have seen in this chapter, an important facet of classrooms is their multifaceted and interconnected nature. This chapter has attempted to show that we need to recognize the multidimensional nature of grouping in classrooms in terms of group composition (in turn in relation to ability, sex and friendship mix), the size and number of groups in the class, but also the interconnections with classroom-level factors like class size, and classroom layout. All of these need to be considered in relation to the curriculum, task and activity type, as well the role of adults and support of groups. A full appreciation of the classroom environment, and its influence, therefore requires study not just of the separate dimensions on their own, but the interconnections between them.

Kutnick and Blatchford (2013) extend this discussion and show that each dimension of grouping will have different pedagogic 'potential', and that consideration of the interconnections also has pedagogical implications. Given that most children, no matter what their age, can be observed to be seated or working in pairs, or in small or larger groups, it is worrying that the social pedagogic potential for learning in classroom groups is not often considered by teachers. There is often little relationship, for example, between the size of groups and the learning tasks or types of interaction assigned to them by the teacher.

Models are needed in which all these factors, i.e., group size and composition, teaching roles, learning tasks, and perceptions of different curriculum and pedagogy come together in a dynamic relationship. It is important to adapt teaching to 'fixed' classroom-level factors but also to include classroom size, seating arrangements, characteristics of children and the curriculum as well as larger contexts such as the school and society. It is also important to recognize that the less 'fixed' classroom factors, such as the groupings, activity contexts and the nature of interaction encouraged to take place and within which children experience their learning, are *constructed* by teachers as part of the process of teaching (Baines et al., 2003). Blatchford et al., (2003) introduced and used the term 'social pedagogy' to help show how classrooms are not so much the undefined context within which teachers simply exert an influence on students, and this was further developed by Kutnick and Blatchford (2013). Classrooms involve distinct physical and social settings within which decisions are taken about how to best coordinate and manage the various factors involved. These components exist in dynamic relationship with each other, and effective teaching requires an understanding of their separate and interconnecting influences.

References

Achilles, C.A. (1999). *Let's Put Kids First, Finally: Getting Class Size Right.* Thousand Oaks, CA: Corwin Press

Adams, R.S. & Biddle, B.J. (1970). *The Realities of Teaching: Exploration with Videotape.* New York: Holt, Rinehart & Winston.

Ames, C. (1992). Classrooms: goals, structures and student motivation. *Journal of Educational Psychology*, 84, 261–271.

Arends, R.I. (1994). *Learning to Teach* (Third edn). New York: McGraw-Hill.

Axelrod, S., Hall, V. & Tams, A. (1979). Comparison of two common classroom seating arrangements. *Academic Therapy*, 15(1), 29–36.

Baines, E. (2012). Grouping pupils by ability in school: class size: is small better? In Adey, P. and Dillon, J. (Eds), *Bad Education: Debunking Myths in Education* (pp. 37–55). Maidenhead, UK: Open University Press.

Baines, E., Blatchford, P. & Chowne, A. (2007). Improving the effectiveness of collaborative group work in primary schools: effects on science attainment. *British Educational Research Journal*, 33(5), 663–680.

Baines, E., Blatchford, P. & Kutnick, P. (2003). Changes in grouping practices over primary and secondary school. *International Journal of Educational Research*, 39, 9–34.

Barker, R. (1968). *Ecological Psychology.* Stanford, CA: Stanford University Press.

Bennett, S.N. (1987). Architecture. In Dunkin, M. (Ed.) *International Encyclopaedia of Teaching and Teacher Education.* Oxford: Pergamon.

Bennett, N. & Blundel, D. (1983). Quantity and quality of work in rows and classroom groups. *Educational Psychology*, 3, 93–105.

Bennett, N. & Dunne, E. (1992). *Managing Groups.* Hemel Hempstead: Simon & Schuster.

Bennett, N., Desforges, C., Cockburn, A. & Wilkinson, B. (1984). *The Quality of Pupil Learning Experiences.* London: Erlbaum.

Blatchford, P. (2003a). *The Class Size Debate: Is Small Better?* Maidenhead, UK: Open University Press.

Blatchford, P. (2003b). A systematic observational study of teachers' and pupils' behaviour in large and small classes. *Learning and Instruction,* 13(6), 569–595.

Blatchford, P. (2011). Three generations of research on class size effects. In K.R. Harris, S. Graham & T. Urdan (Eds), *The American Psychological Association Educational Psychology Handbook: Vol. 2 Individual Differences and Cultural and Contextual Factors* (pp. 529–554). Washington, DC: American Psychological Association.

Blatchford. P. & Baines, E. (2010). Peer relations in school. In K. Littleton, C. Wood and J. Kleine Staarman (Eds), *Elsevier Handbook of Educational Psychology: New Perspectives on Learning and Teaching.* Bingley, UK: Emerald.

Blatchford, P., Baines, E., Kutnick, P. & Martin, C. (2001). Classroom contexts: connections between class size and within-class grouping. *British Journal of Educational Psychology,* 71, 283–302.

Blatchford, P., Bassett, P. & Brown, P. (2005). Teachers' and pupils' behaviour in large and small classes: a systematic observation study of pupils aged 10/11 years. *Journal of Educational Psychology,* 97(3), 454–467.

Blatchford, P., Bassett, P. & Brown, P. (2011). Examining the effect of class size on classroom engagement and teacher–pupil interaction: differences in relation to prior pupil attainment and primary vs. secondary schools. *Learning and Instruction,* 21, 715–730.

Blatchford, P., Bassett, P., Goldstein, H. & Martin. C. (2003). Are class size differences related to pupils' educational progress and classroom processes? Findings from the

Institute of Education Class Size Study of children aged 5–7 years. *British Educational Research Journal*, 29(5), 709–730.

Blatchford, P., Battle, S. & Mays, J. (1982). *The First Transition: Home to Pre-school*. Windsor, UK: NFER-Nelson.

Blatchford, P., Hallam, S., Ireson, J. & Kutnick, P. with Creech, A. (2010). Classes, groups and transitions: structures for learning and teaching. In R. Alexander (Ed.) *The Cambridge Primary Review Research Surveys*. London: Routledge.

Blatchford, P., Kutnick, P., Baines, E. & Galton, M. (2003). Toward a social pedagogy of classroom group work. In P. Blatchford & P. Kutnick (Eds), special edition of *International Journal of Educational Research*, 39, 153–172.

Blatchford, P. & Martin, C. (1998). The effects of class size on classroom processes: 'It's a bit like a treadmill – working hard and getting nowhere fast!' *British Journal of Educational Studies*, 46, 2, 118–137.

Blumenfield, P.C., Hamilton, V.L., Bossert, S.T., Wessels, K. & Meece, J. (1983). Teacher talk and student thought: socialization into the student role. In Levine, J. and Wang, M. (Eds), *Teacher and Student Perceptions: Implications for Learning*. Hillsdale, NJ: Erlbaum Associates.

Boaler, J., Wiliam, D. & Brown, M. (2000). Students' experiences of ability grouping: disaffection, polarization and the construction of failure. *British Educational Research Journal*, 26, 631–648.

Bossert, S. (1979). *Tasks and Social Relationships in Classrooms*. New York: Cambridge University Press.

Bronfenbrenner, U. (1979). *The Ecology of Human Development*. Cambridge, MA: Harvard University Press.

Callahan, A.M. (2005). Tracking and high school English learners: limiting opportunity to learn. *American Educational Research Journal*, 42, 305–328.

Cooper, H.M. (1989). Does reducing student-to-instructor ratios affect achievement? *Educational Psychologist*, 24(1), 79–98.

Creemers, B. (1994). *The Effective Classroom*. London: Cassell.

Department for Education (DfE) (2011). Class size and education in England evidence report (Research Report DFE-RR169). London: DfE.

Doise, W. & Mugny, G. (1984). *The Social Development of the Intellect*. Oxford: Pergamon.

Doyle, W. (1986). Classroom organization and management. In Wittrock, M.C. (Ed.) *Handbook of Research on Teaching* (Third edn). New York: Macmillan.

Doyle, W. & Carter, K. (1984). Academic tasks in the classroom. *Curriculum Inquiry*, 14(2), 129–149.

Dunkin, M.J. & Biddle, B.J. (1974). *The Study of Teaching*. Lanham, MD: Holt, Rinehart & Winston.

Eccles, J., Midgley, C. & Adler, T.F. (1984). Grade-related changes in the school environment: effects on achievement motivation. *Advances in Motivation and Achievement*, 3, 283–331.

Ehrenberg, R.G., Brewer, D.J., Gamoran, A. & Willms, J.D. (2001). Class size and student achievement. *Psychological Science in the Public Interest*, 2(1), 1–30.

Finn, J.D. & Achilles, C.M. (1999). Tennessee's class size study: findings, implications, misconceptions. *Educational Evaluation and Policy Analysis*, 21(2), 97–109.

Finn, J.D. Gerber, S.B. & Boyd-Zaharias, J. (2005). Small classes in the early grades, academic achievement, and graduating from High School. *Journal of Educational Psychology*, 97, 214–223.

Finn, J.D., Pannozzo, G.M. & Achilles, C.M. (2003). The 'why's' of class size: student behaviour in small classes. *Review of Educational Research*, 73, 321–368.

Florian, L. (Ed.) (2006). *The SAGE Handbook of Special Education*. London: Sage.

Fraser, B.J. (1998). Classroom environment instruments: development, validity and applications. *Learning Environments Research,* 1, 7–33.

Galton, M. & Pell, T. (2010). *Study on Class Teaching in Primary Schools in Hong Kong: Final Report*. Cambridge: University of Cambridge.

Galton, M., Simon, B. & Croll, B. (1980). *Inside the Primary Classroom*. London: Routledge & Kegan Paul.

Galton, M. & Williamson, J. (1992). *Group Work in the Primary School*. London: Routledge.

Glass, G.V., Cahen, L., Smith, M.L. & Filby, N. (1982). *School Class Size*. Beverly Hills, CA: Sage.

Goldstein, H. (1995). *Multilevel Statistical Models*. London: Edward Arnold.

Gump, P. (1967). *The Classroom Behavior Setting: Its Nature and Relation to Student Behavior* (Final Report). Washington DC: US Office of Education, Bureau of Research (ERIC Document Reproduction Service No. ED 015 515).

Gump, P. (1974). Operating environments in schools of open and traditional design. *School Review,* 82(4), 575–593.

Hallinan, M.T. & Kubitschek, W.N. (1999). Curriculum differentiation and high school achievement. *Social Psychology of Education,* 2, 1–22.

Hamre, B.K. & Pianta, R.C. (2010) Classroom environments and developmental processes: conceptualization and measurement. In Meece, J.L. & Eccles, J.S. (Eds), *Handbook of Research on Schools, Schooling and Human Development*. New York and London: Routledge.

Hanushek, E. (2011). The economic value of higher teacher quality. *Economics of Education Review,* 30, 466–479.

Hargreaves, D.H., Hestor, S.K. and Mellor, F.J. (1986). A theory of typing. In Hammersley, M. (Ed.) *Case Studies in Classroom Research* (pp. 180–209). Milton Keynes: Open University.

Hastings, N. & Chantry, K. (2002). *Reorganising Primary Classroom Learning*. Buckingham: Open University Press.

Hattie, J. (2005). The paradox of reducing class size and improving learning outcomes. *International Journal of Educational Research,* 43, 387–425.

Higgins, S., Hall, E., Wall, K., Woolner, P. & McCaughey, C. (2005). *The Impact of School Environments: A Literature Review*. Newcastle: Centre for Learning and Teaching, School of Education, Communication and Language Science, University of Newcastle.

Howe, C.J. (1997) *Gender and Classroom Interaction: A Research Review*. Edinburgh: Scottish Council for Research in Education.

Howe, C.J., Tolmie, A. & Rodgers, C. (1992). The acquisition of conceptual knowledge in science by primary school children: group interaction and the understanding of motion down an inclined plane. *British Journal of Developmental Psychology,* 10, 113–130.

Ireson, J. & Hallam, S. (2001). *Ability Grouping in Education*. London: Chapman.

Ireson, J., Hallam, S. & Hurley, C. (2005). What are the effects of ability grouping on GCSE attainment? *British Educational Research Journal,* 31, 443–458.

Johnson, D. & Johnson, R. (1987). *Learning Together and Alone*. Englewood Cliffs, NJ: Prentice-Hall.

Kelly, S. & Covay, E. (2008). *Curriculum Tracking: Reviewing the Evidence on a Controversial but Resilient Educational Policy*. In T. Good (Ed.) *21st Century Education: A Reference Handbook*. Thousand Oaks, CA: Sage.

Kounin, J.S. & Gump, P.V. (1974). Signal systems of lesson settings and the task-related behaviour of pre-school children. *Journal of Educational Psychology,* 6(4), 554–562.

Kulik, C.-L. & Kulik, J. (1982). Effects of ability grouping on secondary school students: a meta-analysis of evaluation findings. *American Educational Research Journal*, 19, 415–428.

Kulik, J. & Kulik, C.-L. (1992). Meta-analytic findings on grouping programs. *Gifted Child Quarterly*, 36, 73–77.

Kutnick, P. & Blatchford, P. (2013). *Effective Group Work in Primary School Classrooms: The SPRinG Approach*. Dordrecht: Springer.

Kutnick, P., Blatchford, P. & Baines, E. (2005). Grouping of pupils in secondary school classrooms: possible links between pedagogy and learning. *Social Psychology of Education*, 8(4), 349–374.

Lou, Y., Abrami, P., Spence, J., Chambers, B., Poulsen, C. & d'Apollonia, S. (1996). Within-class grouping: a meta-analysis. *Review of Educational Research*, 66, 423–458.

MacAulay, D.J. (1990). Classroom environment: a literature review. *Educational Psychology*, 10(3), 239–253.

Mehan, H. (1979). *Learning Lessons*. Cambridge, MA: Harvard University Press.

Mortimore, P., Sammons, P., Stoll, L. & Ecob, R. (1988). *School Matters: The Junior Years*. Wells, UK: Open Books.

Oakes, J. (2005). *Keeping Track: How Schools Structure Inequality* (Second edn). New Haven, CT: Yale University Press.

OECD (2010). PISA 2009 Results: What Makes a School Successful? Resources, Policies and Practices (Vol. IV) http://dx.doi.org/10.1787/9789264091559-en (accessed 1 December 2012).

Pintrich, P.R. & Schunk, D.H. (1996). *Motivation in Education: Theory, Research and Applications*. Englewood Cliffs, NJ: Prentice-Hall.

Rogoff, B. (1990). *Apprenticeship in Thinking: Cognitive Development in Social Context*. New York: Oxford University Press.

Rosenfield, P., Lambert, N. & Black, A. (1985). Desk arrangement effects on pupil classroom behaviour. *Journal of Educational Psychology*, 77, 101–108.

Ross, L. & Nesbett, R.E. (1991). *The Person and the Situation: Perspectives of Social Psychology*. New York: McGraw-Hill.

Rutter, M., Maughan, B., Mortimore, P., Ouston, J. & Smith, A. (1979). *Fifteen Thousand Hours: Secondary Schools and their Effects on Children*. London: Open Books.

Shapson, S.M., Wright, E.N., Eason, G. & Fitzgerald, J. (1980). An experimental study of the effects of class size. *American Educational Research Journal*, 17, 144–152.

Shulman, L.S. (1986). Paradigms and research programs in the study of teaching. In Wittrock, M.C. (Ed.) *Handbook of Research on Teaching* (Third edn). New York: Macmillan.

Slavin, R. (1989). Class size and student achievement: small effects of small classes. *Educational Psychologist*, 24(1), 99–110.

Slavin, R. (1990). Ability grouping in secondary schools: a best-evidence synthesis. *Review of Educational Research*, 60, 471–499.

Vygotsky, L. (1978). *Mind in Society: The Development of Higher Mental Processes*. Cambridge, MA: Harvard University Press.

Wang, M.C., Haertel, G.D. and Walberg, H.J. (1993). Toward a knowledge base for school learning. *Review of Educational Research*, 63(3), 249–294.

Webb, N. & Palincsar, A.S. (1996). Group processes in the classroom. In D.C. Berliner & R.C. Calfee (Eds) *Handbook of Educational Psychology*. New York: Macmillan.

Webster, R. & Blatchford, P. (2013). The educational experiences of pupils with a Statement for special educational needs in mainstream primary schools: results from a systematic observation study. *European Journal of Special Needs Education*, 28(4), 463–479.

Weinstein, C. (1979). The physical environment of the school: a review of the research. *Review of Educational Research,* 49(4), 557–610.

Weinstein, C. (1987). Seating patterns. In Dunkin, M. (Ed.) *International Encyclopaedia of Teaching and Teacher Education.* Oxford: Pergamon.

Weinstein, R. (1991). The classroom as a social context for learning. *Annual Review of Psychology,* 42, 493–525.

Wheldall, K., Morris, M., Vaughan, P. & Ng, Y.Y. (1981). Rows versus tables: an example of the use of behavioural ecology in two classes of eleven-year-old children. *Educational Psychology,* 1, 171–184.

Wiliam, D. & Bartholomew, H. (2004). It's not which school but which set you're in that matters: the influence of ability grouping practices on student progress in mathematics. *British Educational Research Journal,* 30, 279–295.

9

ADULT–PUPIL INTERACTIONS IN THE CLASSROOM

The actual problem to be solved is not what to teach, but how to teach.
Charles William Eliot, 1869 Inaugural Address, Harvard College (in Gage, 1985)

This chapter is perhaps the most difficult one to write. One reason for this is that the study of talk and interactions in classrooms is a huge area, that has extended over many decades and been studied from a number of different academic disciplines – linguistics, sociolinguistics, ethnomethodology, ethnography, educational psychology, for example – all of which bring to the study a different set of paradigms, foci and methodologies. For good measure there is also a lot of strident debate between at least some of these disciplines, with arguments about the appropriate level of content to be studied, quantification of findings, and arguments about measurement and validity.

In a general sense, the terms 'teaching' and 'pedagogy' cover a number of features: tasks and activities, interactions and judgements, framed and supported by classroom organization, pupil organization, time and the curriculum, and classroom routines, rules and rituals. In this chapter we are particularly interested in teacher–pupil interactions. Although this narrows the scope of the chapter, it is justified because it then has a similar remit to other chapters in this book, i.e., the focus on interactions, but also because what unites many different traditions of work is the central role of classroom talk and interaction.

Arends (1994) provides another way of introducing the focus of this chapter. He has argued that teachers, regardless of the age of their pupils, their subject areas, or the types of schools in which they teach, are asked to perform three important functions: first, executive (providing leadership to students); second, interactive (face-to-face instruction with students); and third, organizational (working with colleagues, parents and others). In this chapter, and in line with the focus of this book, we are concerned with the second of these, that is, with the interactive function of teaching. Though there are a range of new developments in education – for example, those involving computers, interactive white boards and distance learning – face-to-face interactions are still a main feature of most classrooms and still lie at the heart of the learning process, and this is likely to be true across all types of schools, subject areas and ages. Gage's conclusion in the mid-1980s still stands: 'Teaching is the central process of education' (Gage, 1985). And in line with Gage's 1985 monograph, in this chapter we consider classroom teaching in terms of such things as: 'lecturing and tutoring but all other types of interactions such as teacher–pupil questioning, pupil responding and initiations, as well as pupil work at tables and desks, and the managerial activities that maintain the whole process'.

The fundamental role of language in education has perhaps its most developed theoretical underpinnings in sociocultural approaches, which take their lead from the influential ideas of Vygotsky (see Wertsch, 1985). Vygotsky was interested in cognitive processes of thinking and reasoning ('higher mental functions') and argued that the origins of these are in social interaction. As children develop ways of understanding through language these become internalized and this transforms thinking. The language of the educator is therefore absolutely crucial in the child's development because it has a primary role in the development, content and structure of thinking and understanding. We will come back to this kind of approach later in the chapter.

The title of this chapter is deliberately changed from the first edition in order to broaden its scope to include interactions not only between teachers and pupils but also the growing number of other adults and paraprofessionals with a teaching role in classrooms. We consider the research evidence on the nature and impact of talk between Teaching Assistants and pupils later in this chapter.

Some time ago it was recognized that there was a gap between research on teaching and research on learning (e.g., Bennett et al., 1984). In line with this, Biggs and Moore (1993) identified ways in which conceptualizations of teaching and conceptualizations of learning are linked. While recognizing that there are important connections between teaching and learning, this chapter will focus more narrowly on interactions between teachers (and other adults) and pupils rather than on the psychological and learning processes in the child.

The chapter has two main sections: first, descriptive research on the nature of interactions in classrooms and, second, the effects of these interactions on pupil learning and achievement. The chapter ends by looking more generally at issues involved in research on teaching.

Descriptive research on teaching

Howe and Abedin (2013) conclude on the basis of an exhaustive review of studies of teacher–pupil dialogue that the main aim of research in the field has been a descriptive one – that is, to describe the nature of teacher–pupil interactions rather than their effects on pupils. And indeed some of the seminal studies in the literature have provided new ways of looking at teaching and classroom interactions. To select but a few works, books by Adams and Biddle (1970), Alexander (2001), Barnes et al. (1969), Cazden (1972, 2001), Dunkin and Biddle (1974), Edwards and Westgate (1994), Edwards and Mercer (1987), Flanders (1970), Galton, Simon and Croll (1980), Jackson (1968), Kounin (1970), Sinclair and Coulthard (1975) and Stubbs (1983) have all contributed in very different ways. Broadly speaking, these descriptive studies of teaching can be divided into those that adopt quantitative methods and those that use qualitative methods.

Quantitative studies of teaching

One main trend in research had its roots in quantitative social sciences and the use of direct systematic observation methods. One reason for this was the realization in the 1960s that earlier approaches to the study of teaching were not insightful enough because they focused more on teachers' personalities than what they actually did in classrooms. One early pioneering approach to classroom interaction was that by Flanders (1970) based on the use of an observation system they developed called Flanders Interaction Analysis Categories (FIAC). This was a simple ten-category system (seven for the teacher, two for the pupil and a 'dustbin' category), and it is the most widely used (and criticized) systematic observation approach. Flanders' results led to the one well-known result – the two-thirds rule. This has been neatly summarized by Alexander (2001):

> for about two-thirds of the duration of most school lessons someone is talking ... about two-thirds of this talking is done by the teacher; and ... two-thirds of the teacher's talk consists of direct instruction in the form of questions, instructions and exposition.

In the UK an early example of the use of systematic observation in service of a description of teaching in primary schools was the so-called ORACLE study, based at Leicester University (e.g., Galton et al., 1980; Galton & Simon, 1980). The aim of the study was to describe teacher and pupil classroom interactions and activities in a sample of junior school classrooms and then relate these to pupils' progress in school. The study was conducted in the context of a backlash against the Plowden Report in the late 1960s and the supposed dominance of child-centred, progressive education in schools. A couple of primary schools had collapsed and this led to a clamour of right-wing recriminations about the state of public education. This movement led to the then Prime Minister James Callaghan's Ruskin Lecture, the right-wing 'Black Papers', and to the widely held view that progressive ideas had led to an over-concern with pupil freedoms, out-of-control children and ineffectual teaching, with little work on the basic subjects of literacy and mathematics.

The first ORACLE book (Galton et al., 1980) showed that the premises of this view were almost entirely wrong. The researchers found that around three-quarters of classroom time was spent on curriculum-related activities, lessons were dominated by basic skills of number and language, and there were very low levels of disruption. The value of the study is that the observations were so extensive and carefully collected that it was a damning verdict on the extreme portrayal of schools by some on the political right.

In one of the interesting findings, the 'asymmetry' of teacher–pupil contact was highlighted. That is, from the teacher's point of view she interacts with children a lot, and often with individuals, but from an individual pupil's point of view, they often work alone, interacting with the teacher in only one-sixth of the lesson time, and even then most often as one pupil in the whole class. In general, there was a good deal of individual work, but little individual attention or instruction, and little cooperative group work.

The publication of the ORACLE studies was particularly significant for one of us (PB) because in 1980 he joined a research team led by Barbara Tizard at the Thomas Coram Research Unit (TCRU, part of the Institute of Education in London) and had a main responsibility for the construction of an observation system to be used to study younger, infant school aged children (5 to 7 years).

The TCRU study was a longitudinal study of children's progress in London schools from school entry (Blatchford et al., 1987; Tizard et al., 1988). An observation system was devised which covered individual children's behaviour in interaction with their teacher, with other children, and when not interacting. Within each of these last three 'social modes', there were categories denoting whether behaviour was on-task, procedural, social or 'task avoidance'. Each child was observed for six 5-minute periods each day, divided into consecutive 10-second time intervals. This kind of observation work, like the ORACLE study, is extremely time-consuming to conduct and process. Some measure of this comes from the total number of 10-second interval observation points – nearly 200,000!

In summary, this exhaustive observation study showed that for the bulk of their time children, even at this tender age, were busy and involved mostly in individual work in the basics of language and mathematics. Interactions with their teachers were predominantly business-like and concerned with the basic areas of reading, writing and maths (see Blatchford et al., 1987 for a full description).

The ORACLE and TCRU studies are rather dated now. Since then there have been several large-scale systematic observation studies in the UK – e.g., the PACE study (Pollard et al., 2000) and also a follow-up ORACLE study conducted twenty years later by Galton and his colleagues (Galton et al., 1999). Since his time at TCRU, Peter Blatchford has also directed several large-scale studies which involved extensive systematic observation components. For the purposes of this book we thought it would be helpful to integrate main results from this research by drawing on work done by Rob Webster, in which he collated results from selected UK observation studies of junior schools (KS2, 7–11 years) over the past forty years (Blatchford & Webster, in press; Webster, 2015). There are clearly enormous problems in comparing different studies over time and for this reason it was necessary to select studies that had a similar design, deployed similar sampling and data-collection methods, studied pupils of a similar age, and collected data on similar categories of behaviour. Even so, it would be unwise to draw any exact conclusions from these comparisons between different studies. Data were also included from studies that collected data on pupils identified as having special educational needs, as well as on 'average' control pupils,[1] and data on interactions between pupils and Teaching Assistants (discussed later in this chapter).

Details of the sample sizes of each study, and the sources from which data were drawn, are shown in Table 9.1.

Whilst each study captured data on different aspects of pupils' interactions and activities, and contextual information about the classroom and/or lesson, all of them collected data on three 'social modes':

- pupil interaction with adults (teachers and TAs) and the contexts in which interaction with adults occurred (i.e., as part of the class, group, or one-to-one);
- interactions with classmates;
- when no interaction took place.

TABLE 9.1 Systematic observation studies included in the analysis

Name of study and data source	Period conducted	Schools (n)	Year group	Classes (n)	Pupils (n)	Pupils with SEN (%)
ORACLE, Galton et al. (1980)	1976/77	19	3–6	58	489	—
One in Five, Croll & Moses (1990)	1981/82	20	4	32	280	19%
PACE, Pollard et al. (2000)	1993–96	9	3–6	18	54	—
ORACLE 2, Galton et al. (1999)	1995/96	14	4–6	28	600	0%
DISS, Blatchford et al. (2009)	2005/06	22	3	22	164	35%★
MAST, Webster & Blatchford (2013)	2011/12	45	5	48	199	24%★★

Notes: ORACLE = Observational Research and Classroom Learning Environment; PACE = Primary Assessment, Curriculum and Experience; DISS = Deployment and Impact of Support Staff; MAST = Making a Statement.
★ 20% School Action; 12% School Action Plus; 4% Statement of SEN.
★★ 100% Statement of SEN.

These variables were used as the basis for a comparison of pupils' experiences over time (see Table 9.2).

The results show an interesting trend: time spent interacting with the teacher has more than doubled over the last 35 years, and this seems attributable to an increase in interactions with the teacher as part of the whole class. This seems to have led to a much more passive role for the pupil, with much of their increased time with the teacher spent listening to them teach.

What might account for this change? The ORACLE and PACE study researchers were clear on the indirect effect of the National Curriculum (introduced in England and Wales in 1988) on classroom pedagogy. Pollard et al. (2000) reported that teachers had 'with reluctance' adopted a different approach to pedagogy 'because of the amount of subject content and standards of attainment that were now required'. And after the second ORACLE study, Maurice Galton and his colleagues concluded that fitting the new statutory requirements into the school day placed 'too heavy an imperative on teachers to cut down the amount of pupil participation in order to "get through" the curriculum content' (Galton et al., 1999). An additional influence, as found in the ORACLE and PACE studies, as well as others, is that the intense focus on national testing and examination results in core subjects has led teachers in upper Key Stage 2 to devote more time to direct instruction and direct test preparation (Galton et al., 2002; Harlen, 2007; Pollard et al., 2000; Tymms & Merrell, 2007).

The most recent data from the DISS and MAST projects indicate that if anything this trend towards more teacher–pupil interaction has increased still further and that teachers now spend much of this time addressing the class, and about a quarter of the time working with individuals and small groups (Blatchford et al., 2012; Webster & Blatchford, 2013).

The results in Table 9.2 also suggest pupils overall now spend much less time on individual work. This general trend towards less time spent working independently might suggest that the primary classroom has become a more interactive, dialogue-rich environment, until we remember that much of the increase in interaction as we have seen is passively listening to teachers talking. We will come back to this trend a little later in the chapter.

Qualitative descriptions of classroom interaction

In contrast to quantitative approaches to teacher–pupil interactions described so far, another important tradition in research on teaching stems from more qualitative traditions of research. This includes work from sociology, anthropology and ethnomethodology (which Shulman, 1986, collects together under the label 'classroom ecology'), and it is at times difficult to be precise about the theoretical bases. There are also overlaps with linguistic analysis of classroom talk (e.g., Sinclair & Coulthard, 1975 and Cazden's book on classroom discourse, 2001). Mercer (2010) in a review of methods in research on classroom talk categorizes

TABLE 9.2 Comparison of the classroom experiences of pupils with and without SEN

		Pupils without SEN						Pupils with SEN		
		ORACLE 1976/77	One in Five 1981/82	PACE 1993–96	ORACLE 2 1995/96	DISS 2005/06	MAST 2011/12	One in Five* 1981/82	DISS 2005/06	MAST 2011/12
Pupil and teacher	Class	12%	23%	24%	21%	44%	35%	21%	36%	30%
	Group	2%	3%	2%	4%	3%	2%	2%	3%	2%
	One-to-one	2%	2%	4%	3%	4%	3%	3%	7%	4%
	Teacher total	16%	28%	30%	28%	51%	40%	26%	46%	36%
Pupil and TA	Class	—	—	<1%	—	0%	1%	—	<1%	3%
	Group	—	—	<1%	—	2%	1%	—	5%	5%
	One-to-one	—	—	<1%	—	2%	1%	—	9%	13%
	TA total	—	—	<1%	—	4%	2%	—	15%	20%
	Peer interaction	19%	19%	22%	27%	20%	32%	18%	16%	18%
	No interaction	66%	53%	46%	45%	25%	26%	56%	23%	26%
	Total interaction	100%	100%	100%	100%	100%	100%	100%	100%	100%

* Croll and Moses (1990) present data for pupils with learning difficulties and behavioural difficulties separately. Here, these results are summed and the mean value given.

Please note data in this table have been rounded up and therefore totals may not add up.

qualitative methods in terms of ethnographic analysis, sociolinguistic discourse analysis, conversation analysis and sociocultural discourse analysis.

The general picture that emerges from this tradition, at least in regard to classroom interactions in the UK and USA, is very consistent with results from systematic observation studies in showing that there is a lot of talk in classrooms but a large majority of it is by the teacher to pupils, and pupil contributions tend to be brief and limited. There is also much agreement with the 'asymmetry' of classroom talk. What also comes across from the many detailed descriptions of classroom talk is its highly stylized nature and the rather odd way in which it differs from talk in other contexts. Much of this literature is critical of typical forms of classroom talk.

Teacher questioning

A lot of attention has been given to teachers' questioning, widely recognized as one of the main forms of teacher-to-pupil talk. Myhill et al. (2007) refer to four broad types of questioning originally identified by Douglas Barnes: first, closed, factual questions with a simple right answer; second, reasoning questions, which draw on logical or sequential thought; third, open questions to which there is no anticipated right answer; and fourth, social questions which invite children to share their experiences. Myhill et al., along with many other studies, found that closed questions are the most common form, and open questions are rare. The ORACLE study came to a similar conclusion. Though Edwards and Mercer (1987) caution us that open questions do not always mean a higher cognitive demand on pupils – and that much will depend on the context and prior interactive history behind specific questions – this is in general all part of what Goodwin (2001, in Myhill et al., 2007) describes as a 'recitation script'. This is a very commonly described feature of classroom talk in which the teacher dominates, the teacher selects speakers, elaboration by pupils is not encouraged, and pupils for the most part seek to find the 'right' answer, already determined by the teacher.

The early and much quoted linguistic work of Sinclair and Coulthard (1975) identified, on the basis of very careful analysis of classroom-talk transcripts, three kinds of classroom discourse: 'informative' (telling or expounding); 'elicitation' (asking questions); and 'directives' (commanding); and they identified five levels of analysis – lesson, transaction, exchange, move and act. They showed that the main feature of classroom teaching is the IRF sequence, i.e., the teacher initiates (I), pupils respond (R) and then the teacher gives feedback (F) on the answer. Many studies have confirmed this common pattern of classroom talk. It is logically consistent with Flanders' two-thirds rule, described earlier, because the teacher is responsible for two of the three acts in the move.

Howe and Abedin (2013) in their systematic review of 225 studies of classroom dialogue provide good evidence of the ubiquity of the IRF sequence. Moreover, many recent studies in the review were conducted in communities where

English was not the primary language, suggesting that the IRF pattern is universal across cultures.

Alexander (2004) and many others have criticized this common form of classroom talk. At its worst it is a non-productive game in which pupils have to guess the answer the teacher has in mind. As Cazden (2001) puts it, the questions asked in this kind of sequence are often 'inauthentic', and many educational researchers argue that questioning would be more effective if it was more 'authentic'. The underlying problem is that closed questioning often demands simple factual right or wrong answers and this is unlikely to develop pupils' knowledge or understanding. Alexander (2000) found this strategy of questioning was common across five countries with very different traditions and that the potential for questioning as an effective instructional tool was not often exploited.

Myhill et al. (2007) show that one reason for the ubiquitous place of this style of questioning is the close connection with teacher control, especially important given the size of many classes and the curriculum and assessment imperatives within which teachers have to operate. 'Where the relationship between control and questioning is close, the effect on interaction can be to produce passive, compliant or non-participative children' (Myhill et al. 2007, p. 19).

Alexander (2004, p. 24) suggests there are three predominant patterns of teacher talk:

1. 'rote' which involves 'the drilling of facts, ideas and routines through constant repetition';
2. 'recitation' 'which involves strong cueing of answers and the accumulation of knowledge and understanding through questions designed to test or stimulate recall of what has been encountered previously';
3. 'instruction/exposition' which is more directive, involving 'telling pupils what to do, and/or imparting information, and/or explaining facts, principles or procedures'.

Less frequently, two other forms can be found:

4. 'discussion' which is the exchange of ideas with a view to sharing information and solving problems;
5. 'dialogue' which aims to achieve common understanding through structured questioning and discussion which guides, prompts, and helps in the handover of concepts and principles.

One common observation is that there is a dearth of talk in the last two categories – talk which really challenges pupils to think. Alexander summarizes the problem thus:

> Among the features on the debit side which seem particularly resistant to change are the relative scarcity of talk which really challenges children

to think for themselves, and especially the low level of cognitive demand in many classroom questions; the continuing prevalence of questions which remain closed despite claims to be interested in fostering more open forms of enquiry; the habitual and perhaps unthinking use of bland, all-purpose praise rather than feedback of a kind which diagnoses and informs.

(Alexander, 2004, p. 9)

A feature of many classroom studies in the qualitative tradition has been a concern with making explicit what are unwritten, implicit but powerful rules about classroom discourse. Edwards (in Alexander, 2001) shows that in order to function in classrooms pupils acquire a sophisticated 'communicative competence' that includes understanding that they need to: listen to the teacher, often for long periods; bid properly for the right to speak; and realize that the teacher is not interested in knowing something but whether you know something (p. 434). Edwards and Westgate (1994) argue that the crucial unwritten rule of classroom discourse involves pupils learning that they have 'unequal communication rights'. Wragg (in Alexander, 2001) identified another basic rule of classroom interaction – putting your hand up when you want to speak; it is often pointed out that following this rule in everyday conversation would be seen as very strange! These kinds of rules have no doubt evolved as a management device when faced with a classroom environment in which there are a relatively large number of pupils to one teacher.

Robin Alexander (2001) has provided fascinating insights into how the study of classroom talk needs to be supplemented by an understanding of the cultural, intellectual, school and classroom forces in different countries. His results are complex and cover a number of different facets of pedagogy (beyond classroom discourse) but show interesting differences between Russia, India, France, England and the USA. Alexander points to a distinction between central European traditions, with a stress on structured and public talk to the class as a whole, and Anglo-American traditions which stress seatwork, reading, writing and relatively unstructured, informal and semi-private talk with individuals and groups. In Russia there was the most consistent instructional focus in classroom talk while in Michigan and England there was the least consistent instructional focus, with far more pupil distraction, interactions about discipline and routine matters and waiting for the teacher. A main reason for this, Alexander argues, is the stronger historical emphasis in the Anglo-American countries on the values of individualization (and one-to-one monitoring), collaboration and negotiation (themselves connected democratic traditions) along with classrooms organized in complex ways with a focus on individual and group activities. In Russia, by contrast, teaching was conducted as a whole class. It did not really matter that only a few children were chosen to talk in the class context because the often sustained and investigative style of teacher questioning was publicly available to all the other children as well.

Research on the effects of teaching

So far we have concentrated on the nature of interactions between teachers and pupils. However, much research has sought to go beyond this in order to examine the effects of such interactions on pupils' learning and educational achievement. This is an important developmental topic, and one of the most obvious and basic questions asked in educational research. That is, to what extent do differences between teachers, in their interactions with their pupils, affect differences in their pupils' educational progress? Here teaching is considered as an independent variable, with pupil educational attainment or progress the outcome or dependent variable.

We will see in this section that the task of identifying effective teaching practices has been a preoccupation of quantitative approaches in particular, and more recently this has been driven in many countries by a concern with improving positions in international league tables of academic success, and identifying effective teaching methods that might bring this about. It is little surprise that quantitative methods are used because they allow an obvious set of metrics of use when relating teaching to pupil outcomes and also allow summarizing data across studies, as in the hugely influential meta-analyses of John Hattie (2009). In contrast, qualitative traditions of research on classroom talk are not concerned in such a clear way with addressing the impact or effectiveness of talk. The more interpretive approaches – of Edwards and Mercer (1987), for example – lead to a more implicit idea of what counts as effective in teaching, though this is not to say, of course, that this is any less valuable or full of insights.

Quantitative research on the effects of teaching

Dichotomies and styles

Margaret Brown (2012) has pointed out that there is a perennial complaint in Anglo-Saxon countries, promulgated by politicians and reinforced by the predominantly right-wing printed media, that educational standards are falling and too low relative to other countries, and that this has much to do with the educational 'establishment' and its preference for progressive educational methods. The answer usually given is to return to what is often seen as a golden age of education in which there was a traditional no-nonsense approach, with an emphasis on the transmission of facts and procedures and the basics of literacy, numeracy and traditional subject areas. This is contrasted with 'progressive' education, characterized as favouring the development of the whole person, problem solving, creative thinking and team work. Margaret Brown (2012) has recently evaluated the evidence on traditional and progressive approaches, and finds that there is little to show that either one is superior in terms of general test scores (which are often used in international comparisons). There may, however, be different effects on different pupil 'outcomes', e.g., routine memory tasks vs. creative problem solving, and this would need to be factored into any assessment of their effectiveness (a point also made by Kyriacou, 2009). There may also be unintended and unwanted consequences on other factors like pupil motivation and confidence. Brown concludes that the evidence 'if anything ... suggests that another dimension entirely, concerned with fostering a complex network of conceptually connected knowledge and skills, is what makes the real difference' (2012, p. 107).

The problem with describing teaching in terms of dichotomies is that it reduces analysis to stereotypes, and has little to do with what actually goes on in schools. A more nuanced approach is to seek to identify the effectiveness of different 'styles' of teaching. This was the aim of a famous study by Bennett (1976) which used the then novel statistical technique of cluster analysis to systematically sort respondents to a teacher completed questionnaire on the basis of their similarity into a number of groups, but then collapsed these groups into a rather crude comparison of traditional and progressive approaches. Although the study found initial support for the superiority of traditional approaches, later more sophisticated statistical analysis found this effect disappeared.

The ORACLE study also developed a typology of teaching styles, this time on the basis of a cluster analysis of observation data on teachers. A strength of this approach is that teachers are allocated to groups on the basis of their similarity across day-to-day classroom interactions. This resulted in six teaching styles: individual monitors, class enquirers, group instructors, infrequent changers, rotating changers and habitual changers; and associations were then examined with progress in mathematics, language and study skills (Galton & Simon, 1980). The authors claim that results do not show any one style is better than others, though they do report that 'class enquirers', who carried out above average amounts of whole-class teaching, were most likely to use challenging questions and reduce intermittent working in pupils, and had pupils who made more academic progress. 'Individual monitors' who engaged in most conversations with pupils had pupils who did better in reading tests. The least successful style was that of 'rotating changers'. We shall see that whole-class teaching approaches tend to be cited in many studies in the process product research tradition.

Process product research

Perhaps the most prevalent type of quantitative research on teaching has been so-called 'process product' approaches. To understand this approach it is helpful to be aware of what were seen as weaknesses in earlier research. As we have seen, around the beginning of the 1970s there was a general recognition that research needed to shift from an interest in teachers' personal traits, and effectiveness in terms of global ratings, to teachers' actual behaviour in classrooms (e.g., Brophy, 1986). By the time of the third edition of *The Handbook of Research on Teaching* (Wittrock, 1986), review chapters were immersed in observational studies of teaching (e.g., Brophy & Good, 1986).

In the language of an influential review by Dunkin and Biddle (1974) the task was to examine the 'process' of classroom interaction in relation to pupil outcomes or 'product'. The obvious methodology for studying and measuring interactive processes was seen to be naturalistic direct observation. This model provided a vocabulary that has been widely used in subsequent research. According to Shulman (1986), the characteristics of process product research have been: a concern with teaching effectiveness; teaching measured on the basis of observation of behaviour in naturalistic classroom settings; the use of 'low inference' categories of behaviour; the use of relatively large samples over periods of time; and numerical analysis of data in terms of correlations between measures of the frequency of teaching behaviours (e.g., question types, lecturing, praise) and measures of outcomes in terms of pupil achievement test scores. So effectiveness in teaching is assessed in terms of correlations with indicators of achievement, relatively independent of particular classrooms and contexts such as particular school subjects. The implicit aim was the search for laws to describe generalizable relationships between teaching and pupil outcomes. Although researchers like Brophy (1986) warned against simplistic prescriptions the implications for practice seemed relatively straightforward, in the sense that correlations between teacher behaviours and attainment could be easily translated into action.

A main feature of this approach is therefore the use of direct systematic observation, and this led to the development of sophisticated observation systems and a concern with methods (Croll, 1986; Galton, 1978; Medley & Mitzel, 1963; Simon & Boyer, 1970). In this regard there were similarities with developmental psychology (e.g., Bakeman & Gottman, 1986; Blurton Jones, 1972; Hutt & Hutt, 1970; Pellegrini, 1996), and research on mother–child interaction (see e.g., Clarke-Stewart, 1973). In both, there has been much concern with reliability of observation systems. Early on, it was realized that high inference categories, such as enthusiasm, warmth and clarity of presentation, are problematic, as they are difficult to code reliably and require interpretation on the part of observers. Low inference categories are often favoured because they require less interpretation and are therefore more reliable. There were sophisticated treatments of this topic as far back as Medley and Mitzel (1963). Some critics argue that reliability is often achieved at the expense of validity, that is, high reliability may mean that observers agree on how to code a set of categories, but these categories may be relatively superficial and miss important aspects of teaching.

As said above, it is not intended or possible to review all findings from this research. The single most comprehensive overview of research in this tradition is probably provided by Brophy and Good (1986). As well as maximizing 'time on task', successful teachers spend much time actively instructing their students, so there are more interactive lessons, featuring teacher–student interaction and less time on independent 'seatwork'. Reviews (e.g., Brophy, 1986) supported the notion of 'active teaching', that is, there should be a good deal of teacher talk, which is academic rather than managerial or procedural, and which involves much asking of questions and giving of feedback rather than extended lecturing (Brophy, 1986). A similar notion is what Rosenshine (1987, in Creemers, 1994) called 'direct instruction'. Creemers considers this a form of explicit stepwise instruction, emphasizing student learning and cognitive achievement. It is summed up succinctly by Rosenshine: 'If you want students to learn something, teach it to them directly' (Rosenshine, 1987, in Creemers, 1994, p. 258).

Creemers (1994) reminds us that direct instruction, stemming as it does from the behaviourist roots of the process product research tradition, is most applicable to small steps and basic skills. These are obviously very important, especially in the early years of school, but teaching also needs to be directed at promoting higher cognitive processes such as learning strategies, problem solving and meta-cognitive strategies, which will require more strategic teaching methods. Creemers feels that direct instruction which was used only to achieve specific objectives is now best seen in the context of, and used to serve, more complex and overarching teaching strategies which are concerned with basic skills but also provide scaffolds (such as how to proceed, modelling, thinking aloud and social support from peers) to support meta-cognitive knowledge and skills.

Recent quantitative research involving classrooms has tended to shift more towards studies of school and teacher effectiveness, and this work also finds that direct instruction, in which the teacher actively engages pupils by bringing the content to the whole class, has strong benefits for pupil academic outcomes (see Ko & Sammons, 2013; Kyriacou, 2009; Muijs & Reynolds, 2011). Ko and Sammons (2013) and Rubie-Davies et al. (2010) suggest that several aspects of instruction are effective: clarity of instructional goals; making links to prior learning; communicating expectations; introducing concepts by providing high levels of instructional talk and checking/ensuring pupil understanding; frequent feedback to students about their learning; encouraging student participation; clear articulation of concepts and ideas; and expert use of existing instructional materials, allowing more time to be devoted to practices that enrich and clarify the content.

Muijs and Reynolds (2011) conclude that direct instruction, in which the teacher actively engages pupils by bringing the content to the whole class, has been shown to have strong benefits for pupil academic outcomes. They therefore connect direct instruction with the context in which it takes place (i.e. whole-class teaching), not the least because they argue it is a more efficient way of reaching more pupils and because individual pupil misunderstandings can be shared with and benefit the whole class. They contrast direct instruction with 'interactive teaching', the evidence for which they feel is more mixed. These kinds of findings and interpretations have supported policies of UK governments, and in particular the stress on whole-class interactive teaching in the Labour Government's literacy and numeracy strategies. One unfortunate consequence of successive government policies on the curriculum and assessment, however, as we have seen, has been the growing trend for pupils in British primary schools to be more and more passive in class, predominantly listening to the teacher. Interestingly, in East Asian provinces like Shanghai and Hong Kong, often championed by politicians as examples of effective educational systems, there is a developing recognition of the problems with passive learning and the desire to develop methods of teaching that more actively involve pupils in their own learning.

Recent scholarly articles from a psychological perspective which bear on teaching approaches, e.g., in the recent *APA Educational Psychology Handbook* (2012), have included generic chapters that cover 'Effective classrooms' (Patrick, Mantzicopoulos & Sears, 2012) and 'Effective teachers and teaching' (Roehig et al., 2012) which appear to have a similar aim and coverage. Roehig et al. summarize the recent US literature and their descriptive model extends beyond interactions to include classroom atmosphere, classroom management and pupil self-regulation. In terms of effective teaching, they identify four key dimensions: developing caring classroom communities; enhancing students' motivation to learn; planning and delivering engaging, assessment-driven instruction; and supporting student's deep processing and self-regulation (p. 516). Patrick et al. list a number of characteristics of effective classrooms, though it is not clear how the material was selected.

The *APA Educational Psychology Handbook* also reveals another trend in research on teaching: the chapters deal with teaching in a more fragmented way, with separate chapters on: instruction in relation to thinking and reasoning in science (Sinatra & Chinn, 2012); instruction for the development of strategies (MacArthur, 2012); and problem-based learning (Loyens, Kirshner & Paas, 2012). So research on teaching seems to have become more compartmentalized and specialized. Within one field – reading instruction – Kamil (2012) points out that it is very difficult to keep up with all the new developments in the literature, such is the volume of work.

However, one recent trend in research on teaching has reinvigorated a more generic approach to teaching in classrooms. Increased interest in classrooms by psychologists has led to the development of approaches in which developmental and educational research are more integrated (Hamre & Pianta, 2010). A recent significant contribution to the quantitative psychological literature on teaching is by Pianta and his colleagues with their CLASS (Classroom Assessment Scoring System) which is more conceptually and theoretically grounded than earlier classroom research. The CLASS approach has been used by a lot of researchers in schools around the world (Hamre & Pianta, 2010). It is based on a developmentally informed analysis of features of classrooms likely to produce developmental change, and has three broad domains: (1) emotional supports; (2) classroom organization; and (3) general instructional supports.

Perhaps the main distinguishing feature that separates this approach from earlier observational approaches is that CLASS is designed to capture a latent or underlying structure that developmental theory would predict is important for academic and social outcomes, whereas the earlier approaches made use of more straightforward and visible incidences of behavioural categories (like types of questions). Another difference is that within each dimension, indicators are judged in terms of qualitative ratings rather than frequencies of occurrence (though in some cases the two approaches are merged). Hamre and Pianta refer to confirmatory factor analysis that confirmed that there was a fit between the three latent domain organizations and actual observations in large numbers of classrooms.

Qualitative approaches to effective teaching

Sociocultural approaches

In contrast to quantitative approaches to teacher–pupil interactions described so far another important tradition in research on teaching stems from sociocultural theories. As we have seen, sociocultural approaches in general build on interpretations of Vygotskian theory in which the use of language is seen to have a privileged role in transforming children's thinking. One key idea is that it is through joint interaction that new understanding develops. Cazden (2001) gives a quote from Douglas Barnes which nicely encapsulates insights from this approach: 'Speech unites the cognitive and the social' (see Staarman & Mercer, 2010, and Mercer & Howe, 2012, for helpful discussions of sociocultural approaches).

Early pioneers in the UK were Douglas Barnes and in the USA Courtney Cazden, and a number of studies in this tradition have provided the source of general guidance on effective teaching approaches (see review by Mercer & Howe, 2012). They make the point, following Mortimer and Scott (2003), that effective teaching needs to balance what they call 'authoritative' talk, common in classrooms, which emphasizes the transmission of information and instruction and checking understanding, with 'dialogue', which is a more open-ended form of discourse within which teachers prompt students to explore their thinking and reasoning.

Exploratory talk

Barnes and Todd (1981) were early exponents of the value of negotiation in talk and also the influential idea of 'exploratory talk' which to Mercer and Howe (2012) 'represents a joint, co-ordinated form of co-reasoning in language, with speakers sharing knowledge, challenging ideas, evaluating evidence and consolidating options in a reasoned and equitable way'. Howe and Abedin (2013) see the origins of exploratory talk in the work of Piaget (1932) who first identified the important cognitive processes stemming from the expression of competing points of view and the resolution of disagreements through the evaluation of justifications. They argue that this was the basis of Barnes and Todd's first coining the term 'exploratory talk', which was then further developed by Mercer and colleagues and more recent work. Howe and Abedin (2013) point to problems teachers find in developing exploratory talk in the classroom, including the tension between the need for classroom control and the value of providing students with the opportunity for exploring views, and getting the balance right between whole-class interactions and splitting the class into small groups where exploratory talk can be maximized. Mercer and Howe (2012) point out that there is very limited true dialogue in classroom talk.

Other sociocultural perspectives, like that of Myhill et al. (2007), involve a general view of what counts as effectiveness in classroom talk. Effective teaching (and learning) is seen in terms of the importance of relating current teaching to pupils' prior knowledge. From a sociocultural perspective, teaching, to be effective, has to engage with and help develop pupils' deep-rooted schemas about the world or risk the danger of scratching the surface, not affecting what is held in long-term memory and not leading to fundamental shifts in understanding. In this sense teaching that follows sociocultural approaches is more likely to lead to significant steps in learning than traditional transmission approaches.

Scaffolding

The idea of 'scaffolding' is a key (if overworked) concept deriving from Vygotskian ideas, though the term itself is usually attributed to the paper by Wood, Bruner and Ross (1976). The basic idea is that the adult sensitively and strategically adjusts their verbal and non-verbal support so that the child is stretched just enough for there to be meaningful learning. Too little and there is minimum learning, too much and there is confusion. A more modern version is Rogoff's 'apprenticeship in thinking' (Myhill et al., 2007). A common way of conceiving of this idea is in terms of Vygotsky's 'zone of proximal development' which is the distance between a child's current level and what is possible under adult (or expert peer) supervision and guidance. Alexander (2004) points out that 'proximal' is perhaps too spatial a term and that it might more appropriately be seen as 'potential'. Myhill et al. (2007) also discuss the over-loose way the term 'scaffolding' has been used and that it is in danger of becoming a catch-all description of any form of general teaching support for pupils.

There is a developmental dimension here because the scaffold will need to be adjusted continuously as the pupil develops. Cazden (2001) describes scaffolding assistance in relation to different stages and contexts. A good example of scaffolding is the often exaggerated steps mothers will take to achieve a 'conversation' with their young infants, at first filling in for their babies, interpreting burps and yawns as part of their babies' turns, but later at about 7 months of age only accepting speech-like sounds. As Cazden, quoting Catherine Snow, puts it: 'As the mother raises the ante, the child's development proceeds' (Cazden, 2001, p. 61).

Cazden used examples from videotapes of Reading Recovery tutorial lessons to describe scaffolding of individual pupils in schools, e.g., the way a teacher constructs various types of scaffolding assistance to ask questions, model actions and direct the child's practice specifically through calling attention to the sounds in spoken words, prompting visual memory of previous experience with specific written words, drawing boxes to correspond to the sounds in the word, asking the child to develop and use their visual memory for words, praising strategies even if the result is only partially correct, and introducing new information.

Cazden also describes a refinement of the scaffolding approach where it is used for small groups. The best known example of this is 'reciprocal teaching' (RT) developed by Brown and Palincsar. Like Reading Recovery it was designed to be of particular help for pupils struggling with literacy and also offers strategies, based on those used by expert readers, for providing interactional assistance that helps learning. RT typically involves a teacher and four or five students who each take turns leading a discussion of a passage of writing. The teacher guides the group using four comprehension strategies: questioning, clarifying, summarizing and predicting, in order to help students enhance their self-monitoring of text comprehension. Later versions of RT were broadened to take on the whole classroom in a 'community of learners'.

Howe and Abedin (2013) argue that it is important to be clear about the strengths and differences between exploratory talk and scaffolding, e.g., that the latter more explicitly has its intellectual roots in Vygotsky. Howe and Abedin define scaffolding as 'calibrated guidance towards target understanding', i.e., allowing students to reshape their understanding gradually in response to questions and suggestions from more expert partners. They argue that the research literature shows that inadequate use of scaffolding is widespread, with one particular challenge being understanding student ideas in sufficient depth to allow appropriate feedback. They point to Weltse (2006, in Hamre & Pianta, 2010) who highlights the difficulties teachers have in deciding on the appropriate balance of scaffolding and exploratory talk and how the two forms of classroom talk can be brought together. A lot of professional advice to date fudges this important issue.

Dialogic teaching

'Dialogic teaching' is a more recent development stemming from sociocultural theory which has particularly taken off in the UK. One main exponent of this approach is Robin Alexander who has been very influential in developing and spreading the idea in UK schools. Alexander (2004) developed the concept of 'dialogic teaching' to stress the way he feels classroom pedagogy should maximize the amount of substantial contributions from teachers and pupils with the aim of exploring ideas, testing evidence and moving pupils' thinking on.

Research on interactions between teaching assistants and pupils

In the past twenty years there has been a revolution in UK classrooms which has changed the landscape of schools and classroom interaction. Over this period there has been a huge and unprecedented increase in teaching assistants/aides (TAs). This rise in TAs can be seen as part of a general increase in education paraprofessionals with similar roles worldwide. Schools in Australia, Italy, Sweden, Canada, Finland, Germany, Hong Kong, Iceland, Ireland, Malta, South Africa, as well as the USA, have experienced similar increases in paraprofessionals (Giangreco & Doyle, 2007). TAs now comprise a quarter of the workforce in English and Welsh mainstream schools, where they are also known as 'learning support assistants' and 'classroom assistants'. In the USA the titles 'teacher aides' and 'paraeducators' are commonplace. In this chapter, we will refer to all those with equivalent classroom-based support roles collectively as TAs.

The reasons for this increase are to provide extra clerical assistance for teachers, help raise pupil standards, and help with policies of inclusion of pupils with special educational needs (see Blatchford et al., 2012). The largest study of TAs' deployment and impact worldwide (the Deployment and Impact of Support Staff (DISS) project) found two key things: first, TAs spent much of their time in classrooms in a direct instructional role with pupils and much of this time was spent with low-attaining pupils and those with special educational needs. For such pupils, TAs had often become the primary educator. The second main finding was the amount of support from a TA (based on teacher estimates and measures from systematic observation) had a negative relationship with pupils' academic progress in English, mathematics and science. Two cohorts of over 8000 pupils in seven age groups in mainstream schools were tracked over one year each. Those pupils receiving the most support from TAs made less progress than similar pupils who received little or no support from TAs. It is extremely unlikely that these results are explained by existing characteristics of pupils who received TA support, because the analysis controlled for pre-existing pupil characteristics that typically affect progress and the reason why pupils are allocated TA support, in particular SEN status and prior attainment. There was evidence from the DISS study that the negative effect of TA support on learning outcomes is most marked for pupils with the highest levels of need (Blatchford et al., 2012; Blatchford et al., 2011; Webster et al., 2010).

The researchers on the multi-method DISS project developed the Wider Pedagogical Role model to integrate different forms of data from systematic observations, teacher, TA and headteacher interactions and questionnaires, case studies of schools and TAs, time-logs of activities and verbatim transcripts of classroom interaction during the school day to help explain these troubling results (see Blatchford et al., 2012). There are three core components – preparedness, deployment and practice – and from the point of view of this chapter, the most relevant findings concern the 'practice' of TAs, i.e., the nature of face-to-face interactions between TAs and pupils and teachers and pupils. Systematic observations showed that the interactions of teachers and TAs with pupils were both quantitatively and qualitatively different in several areas. In terms of talk more obviously directed at pupil learning, teachers spent more time explaining concepts than TAs, and TAs' explanations were sometimes inaccurate or confusing. Teachers used prompts and questions to encourage thinking and check understanding, while TAs more frequently supplied pupils with answers. Teachers tended to use feedback to encourage learning, while TAs were more often concerned with task completion (see Rubie-Davies et al., 2010). A more detailed 'conversation analysis' (CA) showed that teachers used at least some strategies that fostered pupil independence and encouraged pupils to think for themselves. By contrast, TAs *'closed down'* pupils in several ways, which resulted in pupils having less active involvement in learning talk. TAs emphasized task completion and, in relation to repair, when pupils made errors or failed to find the answer, TAs readily supplied it or corrected immediately. There was an absence of scaffolding strategies, such as prompts, hints and withholding the answer, which meant that pupils had fewer opportunities to think for themselves (see Radford et al., 2011).

Overall, it seemed clear that help was required to ensure that TAs can use strategies that foster active pupil participation in learning. Radford et al. (2014) have built on the CA analysis above to develop forms of classroom discourse that can be used productively by TAs to supplement teachers' input. If a key problem is ensuring effective classroom discourse, when TAs often lack subject and pedagogical knowledge, then one approach has been to develop a type of scaffolding (called 'heuristic' scaffolding) through which TAs can facilitate pupils' independence as learners, even though TAs may not have the same level of subject knowledge as teachers.

Some issues in research on teaching

One of the main tasks in this field is to get a bearing on the quality of teaching and its effects on pupil learning and as we have seen it is understandable if researchers have approached this from the point of view of quantitative methods because they offer the hope of accessing important aspects of teaching that can then be related numerically to aspects of pupil learning. In this section we concentrate on some methodological issues involved in such approaches to teaching. The review by Dunkin and Biddle (1974), as well as the paper by Medley and Mitzel (1963), still repay careful reading concerning issues related to observation methods.

Quantitative approaches, as we have seen, have been criticized for focusing on readily measurable teacher characteristics even though harder-to-measure (and more high inference – see below) dimensions may be just as vital. An allied problem concerns the unit of analysis when researching teaching. There has been criticism of the way some quantitative approaches have tended to operationalize teaching in terms of small discrete aspects of teaching behaviour, and some have therefore sought, as we have seen, to operationalize teaching in terms of higher level units. One underlying issue, then, relates to the tension in research on teaching between measurement in terms of smaller more 'atomic' units, as in much process product research, and more general 'molecular' categories, such as 'formal' vs. 'informal'. We have seen that we also need to be careful about over-simple general characterizations of teaching, even though they do unfortunately tend to match everyday conceptions of learning and teaching (see also Watkins and Mortimore, 1999).

Given the difficulties with both types of measurement, it is understandable that the ORACLE study sought a compromise by constructing more molecular constructs (i.e., styles) out of atomic units of behaviour, measured on the basis of systematic observation. However, there are costs, in that it can, as in the ORACLE study, become difficult to know which of a cluster of behaviours contributed to any associations found and which, if any, behaviours interact with each other. The psychological reality or validity of the clusters is also unclear. There are again parallels to observational research in developmental psychology, e.g., research on mother–child interaction (Bakeman & Gottman, 1986).

The CLASS approach, developed by Pianta and colleagues, deliberately addressed this limitation of much research on teaching by identifying that a latent structure of effective teaching and classrooms drawn from developmental theory (e.g., on home environments) is used to structure a set of theoretically informed and validated ratings instead of counts of discrete behaviours. There is no question about the rigour with which this work has been addressed and used, nor the advance in terms of the application of theory and validation through sophisticated statistical analysis, but it is difficult to avoid the conclusion that something is lost when multiple behavioural events are summarized in a rating (although the CLASS authors offer support from observation studies for their structure). In particular, detailed moment-by-moment observations can provide a rich and real-time account that cannot be adequately captured by other methods of data collection.

One of the characteristics of early quantitative approaches to teaching, and one of their limitations, according to Shulman (1986), has been their 'unabashedly empirical and non-theoretical' nature (Shulman, 1986, p. 13) – an emphasis on what worked rather than why it worked. Quantitative research on teaching has also typically measured teaching in terms of frequencies of occurrence. Findings therefore say more about the amount of teaching behaviours than the quality of instruction, for example, what form it takes and how well it is implemented (Brophy, 1989). One consideration, to which all can no doubt testify, is that even infrequent teaching behaviours may be influential. It is possible, for example, that just one praise or comment, concerning a child's work, can have a lasting impression on that child.

Connected to the collection of data on frequencies of occurrence is the point that problems can arise when teaching is conceptualized or at least measured in terms of a continuous variable; for example, it may not be easy to get at differences between teachers who are outstanding and those who are merely adequate. In other words, there are problems in searching for linear associations between frequencies of occurrence and other variables like pupil outcomes.

Other ways of treating distributions may need to be considered. Also, prescriptions should remain within a certain range (though this may be difficult to establish); because a particular behaviour is related to achievement does not mean a huge increase in it will produce similar gains – indeed it is easy to think of examples that may be counter-productive (e.g., too much homework, too much praise or criticism). It is worth reminding ourselves (Brophy, 1986) that findings from research are only strictly generalizable to other similar classes and may not therefore generalize to other different classrooms, e.g., from mainstream to special education.

It is not just qualitative researchers who feel that effective teaching may be revealed in more complex ways than frequencies of behaviours. As Dunkin and Biddle (1974) realized early on, it is important to examine sequences of behaviours as well as individual occurrences, but this is difficult to do in terms of observation techniques and statistical analysis of data once collected, and has proved to be problematic in research on teaching and other social relations, e.g., mother–child interaction. Despite some early exceptions (e.g., in Flanders' work) this approach to research on teaching has not taken off in a rigorous way in quantitative educational research (though it has had more success in developmental psychology (see Bakeman & Gottman, 1986; Yodder & Symons, 2010).

Even sequences of behaviours may miss important aspects of teaching, e.g., the overarching strategic nature of teaching, for example, in terms of the enactment of lesson plans or instructional intentions. There is also a broader cultural and temporal context within which teaching takes place, which needs to be taken into account to explain the impact of teaching. Mercer has recently argued that we have neglected for too long the longer-term influence of teacher–pupil interactions, with most studies taking place in a relatively narrow timeframe, of a school year at most:

> there is now a widespread appreciation of how important the cumulative history of teacher-student talk – how it proceeds through time – is for understanding the successes and failures of teaching and learning . . . shared experience amongst teachers and students, developed and consolidated through talk, can support the learning of pupils.
>
> *(Mercer, 2014, p. 17)*

Pupil outcomes

A final issue, related to quantitative studies of teaching, concerns the appropriate ways of addressing the effects on pupils – in other words, what are the appropriate ways of measuring or describing pupil 'outcomes'. Much research over the years has made use of test scores in the basic areas of literacy, mathematics and science, not the least because such scores are relatively easily collected and often collected anyway as part of public examination and testing regimes. Although such measures have wide currency in education, they only tell part of the story.

There is clearly more to teaching and learning than measured academic performance. We just mention here one other important aspect. A good deal of research and theory shows the importance of developing within children resources and motivational processes that equip them to be independent learners. One commonly used distinction is between 'mastery' and 'performance' orientations, that is, between the confidence to seek mastery and understanding of a task, as opposed to simply striving for good grades. There is much consensus that, in the long run, performance orientation is dysfunctional, and that teaching should aim to encourage a 'mastery' orientation (see Pintrich & Schunk, 1996 for a review). An attention to pupil learning and attainment must not be at the expense of the development of attitudes that are at the heart of independent learning and functional forms of motivation.

Reconciling quantitative and qualitative approaches

Over the years there has been a sometimes acrimonious debate between quantitative and qualitative research approaches, and there have been a number of attempts to find a way of reconciling the two. Perhaps the most coherent and even-handed attempt at reconciling differences between the two approaches is by Gage (1985). He characterizes what he calls the ethnographic-sociolinguistic paradigm as seeing teaching as an instance of symbolic interaction, that is, the process by which people (teachers and pupils) develop meaning in terms of situations (mainly classrooms) and their own actions. The concern of research in this tradition is with meanings that participants have about their situations. Such research, in contrast with process product research, seeks 'thick' and critical descriptions, on the basis of qualitative and interpretative methods. Research in this tradition has dealt with a variety of aspects of classroom discourse, participation structures, and so on, as we have seen. Ethnographic-sociolinguistic research is 'ideographic' in seeking to understand particular cases.

In seeking to identify the scientific basis for what he quite readily sees as the 'art' of teaching, Gage employs 'ideographic' knowledge, which, as we have just seen, applies to the understanding of a particular event or individual, with 'nomothetic' knowledge, which is general across individuals and is identified with the scientific method, usually producing knowledge about relationships between variables. Gage is fully aware that in the case of research on teaching we are often applying nomothetic knowledge to the ideographic, that is, to a particular situation or teacher; indeed, Gage argues this is just what engineers, physicians and other scientists do all the time – they just differ in the amount of nomothetic knowledge available to them. All of us, including teachers, must compensate for the inadequacies in our nomothetic knowledge, which in the case of knowledge on teaching is relatively large, by the use of artistry and craftsmanship. The distinction (nomothetic/ideographic) is useful in helping to place usually opposing perspectives (quantitative/positivist vs. qualitative/ideographic) into one framework, and emphasizes their complementarity.

Mixing methods

One recent development which has a bearing on reconciling quantitative and qualitative approaches has been efforts to mix different forms of classroom observation. Lefstein and Snell (2014), for example, collected video observations on small samples of teachers in order – through the use of systematic observations – to address their similarities and differences in using dialogic teaching methods, but also in the context of broader linguistic and ethnographic methods.

Another possible way of approaching the analysis of teaching is to build a multilevel system of analysis with embedded methods of observation at different levels of specificity and detail. In this chapter we have seen a number of approaches, and each type of approach has different strengths and weaknesses. One obvious way ahead is to work towards a hybrid system that combines elements of the various approaches, and maximizes the strengths of each. One level might involve ratings of classroom practice, as in the CLASS system, but this might be supplemented by ongoing codings of categories of teacher–pupil interaction and talk, and a more detailed 'micro' analysis of a strategic selection of teacher–pupil interaction sequences. This integration of coding methods promises to provide a richer and more valid analysis of key aspects of effective teaching.

Conclusions

One of the key points to emerge from the review undertaken in preparation for this chapter is a tension between, on the one hand, teachers' desire to maintain control through classroom talk – in order to enhance classroom management, coverage of the curriculum and lesson plans, and the demands of accountability – and, on the other hand, developing classroom talk that is relevant to pupils and their prior knowledge, encourages a higher cognitive content, challenges them to think and advance conceptually, and which in the long run is likely to have a positive influence on their learning and understanding.

It is interesting that despite the tensions and differences between quantitative and qualitative approaches to research on teaching, a common theme to emerge is agreement about the primary importance of teaching interactions and in particular a more interactive form of teacher to pupil talk. As Mercer has recently concluded:

> Forty years on from the first explorations, we know significantly more about the nature and functions of teacher-student talk in classroom education. With increased confidence, researchers can encourage teachers to develop critical awareness of how they use talk as a main tool of their trade, and point to the kinds of talk strategies habitually used by very effective teachers.
>
> *(Mercer, 2014, p. 17)*

It has been argued that the most important driver of an effective education system is the quality of teaching (Wiliam, 2013). It is therefore vital that we seek to better understand effective modes of classroom interaction. Yet this is not straightforward. It is interesting how in the UK and USA when it comes to classroom teaching there is a much less developed view of, and engagement with, a body of knowledge and theory on pedagogy, in comparison to other countries in central and eastern Europe, and this is reflected in the extent to which it does not figure very highly in teacher training, professional development or even everyday lesson planning in schools. Rather alarmingly, Staarman and Mercer (2010) conclude that research on classroom talk has had very little influence on initial teacher education. This is likely to get worse as the training of teachers is either ignored altogether (there are growing numbers of unqualified teachers in England) or the preparation of new teachers is handed more and more over to schools, with progressively less input from higher education.

In contrast to current approaches which develop lists of effective teaching approaches, we believe that teachers need to have a sound understanding of research and theory relating to teaching and pedagogy. It does not help to know that a particular approach has a large 'effect size' if there is little understanding on how this approach is to be developed in everyday classrooms. Interestingly, the limitation of some current approaches to effective teaching becomes very evident in the case of perhaps the most obviously quantitative approach of all – econometric analysis of teaching – which is often referenced by politicians and their advisors. While Hanushek and others in this tradition insist that teachers are the most important school influences on learning, they also concede that 'it has not been possible to identify any specific characteristics of teachers that are reliably related to student outcomes' (Hanushek, 2011, p. 467). That is to say, these researchers – although often quoted in connection with policy on teaching – have nothing to say about what constitutes a good teacher or good teaching, and there is little therefore to help guide the training of good teachers.

We also need to be mindful of the important point made by Lefstein and Snell (2014) that it is simplistic to think that teaching can be made more effective, and standards in schools raised, just by getting teachers to follow examples of good practice. The main reason for this is because teaching is a complex, multifaceted activity that has to respond to types of pupils and contextual factors, and teaching requires a lot more than just implementing practices found by research to be related to pupil outcomes. All teachers can benefit from seeing examples of what works well, but the development of effective teaching is more likely to come from professional development connected to close attention to, and reflection on, one's own teaching interactions.

But there is still more to be done and it is here that we believe there is a real opportunity for research to influence politicians and policy makers in ways not previously seen. This is connected to the point made by Howe and Abedin (2013), mentioned above, that the predominant aim of many studies has been descriptive and a major limitation is that there has been little attention paid to whether different methods of teaching and dialogue have different implications for pupil learning. Quantitative studies have been more concerned with effects on outcomes, but very few studies have, for example, systematically evaluated the consequences of teacher–pupil dialogue on pupil learning, e.g., whether scaffolding approaches are better than dialogic approaches.

Howe and Abedin (2013) attribute this limitation in classroom interaction research partly to continuing arguments between qualitative and quantitative research, and widespread unease about the use of quantitative methods in studying classroom dialogue. They argue that although qualitative approaches are responsive to subtleties of dialogue they are not well able to rise to what they see as an important challenge for research now – helping to make judgements about whether certain approaches to dialogue are more or less effective than other approaches. They argue that quantitative approaches, despite their limitations in capturing nuances of interactions, are well set up to answer these kinds of questions. Furthermore, despite reservations by qualitative researchers, it is now appropriate to take the risk and use quantitative methods, not the least because there are few obvious alternatives (see also Mercer, 2010).

Note

1 The 'control' pupil sample constructed for the analysis in this paper is composed of pupils who, by and large, had not been identified as having SEN. The control samples from the One in Five, ORACLE 2, DISS and MAST projects did not include pupils with SEN. The first ORACLE study did not distinguish between pupils with and without SEN, but collected data from a representative sample of pupils in each class. The sample for the PACE project was selected at random from each class list. SEN designation was not recorded, although teacher ratings classified pupils according to attainment: 7% low; 16% below average; 32% average; 29% above average; and 15% high. Attainment is not a perfect proxy for SEN, but on this basis, PACE does appear to lean towards an attainment profile slightly above average.

References

Adams, R.S. & Biddle, B.J. (1970). *The Realities of Teaching: Exploration with Videotape.* New York: Holt, Rinehart & Winston.

Alexander, R. (2001). *Culture and Pedagogy: International Comparisons in Primary Education.* Oxford: Blackwell.

Alexander, R. (2004). *Towards Dialogic Teaching: Rethinking Classroom Talk* (Second edn). London: Dialogis UK.

Arends, R.I. (1994). *Learning to Teach* (Third edn). New York: McGraw-Hill.

Bakeman, R. & Gottman, J.M. (1986). *Observing Interaction: An Introduction to Sequential Analysis.* Cambridge: Cambridge University Press.

Barnes, D., Britton, J. & Rosen, H. (1969). *Language, the Learner and the School.* Harmondsworth: Penguin Books.

Barnes, D. & Todd, F. (1981). Talk in small learning groups: analysis of strategies. In Adelman, C. (Ed.) *Uttering and Muttering.* London: Grant McIntyre.

Bennett, N. (1976). *Teaching Styles and Pupil Progress*. London: Open Books.

Bennett, N., Desforges, C., Cockburn, A.M. & Wilkinson, B. (1984). *The Quality of Pupil Learning Experience*. London: Erlbaum.

Biggs, J.B. & Moore, P.J. (1993) *The Process of Learning* (Third edn). Englewood Cliffs, NJ: Prentice-Hall.

Blatchford, P., Bassett, P., Brown, P., Martin, C., Russell, A. & Webster, P. (2011). The impact of support staff on pupils' 'positive approaches to learning' and their academic progress. *British Educational Research Journal*, 37(3), 443–464.

Blatchford, P., Burke, J., Farquhar, C., Plewis, I. & Tizard, B. (1987). A systematic observation study of children's behaviour at infant school. *Research Papers in Education*, 2(1), 47–62.

Blatchford, P., Russell, A. & Webster, R. (2012) *Reassessing the Impact of Teaching Assistants: How Research Challenges Practice and Policy*. Abingdon, UK: Routledge.

Blatchford, P. & Webster, R. (in press) ORACLE to MAST: 40 years of observation studies in UK junior school classrooms. In Maclean, R. & Myhill, M. (Eds) *International Handbook on Life in Schools and Classrooms: Past, Present and Future Visions*. Nottingham: DfES.

Blurton-Jones, N. (1972). Characteristics of ethological studies of human behavior. In Blurton Jones, N. (Ed.) *Ethological Studies of Child Behaviour* (pp. 3–33). London: Cambridge University Press.

Brophy, J. (1986). Teacher influences on student behaviour. *American Psychologist*, 41, 1069–1077.

Brophy, J. (1989). Research on teacher effects: uses and abuses. *The Elementary School Journal*, 9, 3–21.

Brophy, J. & Good, T. (1986). Teacher behavior and student achievement. In Wittrock, M. (Ed.) *Handbook of Research on Teaching*. New York: Macmillan.

Brown, M. (2012). Traditional versus progressive education. In Adey, P and Dillon, J. (Eds) *Bad Education: Debunking Myths in Education* (pp. 95–109). Maidenhead, UK: Open University Press.

Cazden, C. (Ed.) (1972). *The Functions of Language in the Classroom*. New York: Teachers College Press.

Cazden, C.B. (2001). *Classroom Discourse: The Language of Teaching and Learning* (Second edn). Portsmouth, NH: Heinemann.

Clarke-Stewart, A. (1973) Interactions between mothers and their young children: characteristics and consequences. *Monographs of the Society for Research in Child Development* (Serial No. 153), 38(6/7).

Creemers, B. (1994). *The Effective Classroom*. London: Cassell.

Croll, P. (1986). *Systematic Classroom Observation*. Basingstoke: Falmer.

Croll, P. & Moses, D. (1990). Sex roles in the primary classroom. In Rogers, C. and Kutnick, P. (Eds) *Social Psychology of the Primary School*. London: Routledge.

Dunkin, M.J. & Biddle, B.J. (1974). *The Study of Teaching*. Lanham, MD: Holt, Rinehart & Winston.

Edwards, D. & Mercer, N. (1987). *Common Knowledge: The Development of Understanding in the Classroom*. London: Methuen.

Edwards, A.D. & Westgate, D. (1994). *Investigating Classroom Talk* (Second edn). London: Falmer.

Flanders, N. (1970). *Analysing Teacher Behaviour*. Reading, MA: Addison-Wesley.

Gage, N.L. (1985). *Hard Gains in the Soft Sciences: The Case of Pedagogy: A CEDR Monograph for Phi Delta Kappan*. Bloomington, IN: CEDR.

Galton, M. (Ed.) (1978). *British Mirrors: A Collection of Classroom Observation Instruments*. Leicester: Leicester University, School of Education.

Galton, M., Hargreaves, L., Comber, C., Wall, D. & Pell, T. (1999). Changes in patterns of teacher interaction in primary classrooms 1976–1996. *British Educational Research Journal*, 25(1), 23–37.

Galton, M. & Simon, B. (1980). *Progress and Performance in the Primary School*. London: Routledge & Kegan Paul.

Galton, M., Simon, B. & Croll, B. (1980). *Inside the Primary Classroom*. London: Routledge & Kegan Paul.

Giangreco, M.F. & Doyle, M.B. (2007). Teacher assistants in inclusive schools. In L. Florian (Ed.) *The SAGE Handbook of Special Education* (pp. 429–439). London: Sage.

Hamre, B.K. & Pianta, R.C. (2010) Classroom environments and developmental processes: conceptualization and measurement. In Meece, J.L. & Eccles, J.S. (Eds) *Handbook of Research on Schools, Schooling and Human Development*. New York and London: Routledge.

Hanushek, E. (2011). The economic value of higher teacher quality. *Economics of Education Review*, 30, 466–479.

Harlen, W. (2007). *The Quality of Learning: Assessment Alternatives for Primary Education* (Primary Review Research Survey 3/4). Cambridge: University of Cambridge.

Hattie, J. (2009). *Visible Learning: A Synthesis of Over 800 Meta-Analyses Relating to Achievement*. Abingdon, UK: Routledge.

Howe, C. & Abedin, M. (2013) Classroom dialogue: a systematic review across four decades of research. *Cambridge Journal of Education*, 43, 325–356.

Hutt, S.J. & Hutt, C. (1970). *Direct Observation and Measurement of Behaviour*. Springfield, IL: Charles C. Thomas.

Jackson, P. (1968). *Life in classrooms*. New York: Holt, Rinehart & Winston.

Kamil, M.L. (2012). Current and historical perspectives on reading research and instruction. In Harris, K.R., Graham, S. & Urdan, T. (Eds) *APA Educational Psychology Handbook, Vol. 3* (pp. 161–188). Washington, DC: American Psychological Association.

Ko, J. & Sammons, P. (2013). Effective teaching: a review of research and evidence. Reading, UK: CfBT Education Trust.

Kounin, J. (1970) *Discipline and Group Management in Classrooms*. New York: Holt, Rinehart & Winston.

Kyriacou, C. (2009). *Effective Teaching in Schools: Theory and Practice*. Cheltenham, UK: Nelson Thornes.

Lefstein, A. & Snell, J. (2014). *Better Than Best Practice: Developing Teaching and Learning through Dialogue*. Abingdon, UK: Routledge.

Loyens, S.M.M., Kirschner, P.A. & Paas, F. (2012). Problem-based learning. In Harris, K.R., Graham, S. & Urdan, T. (Eds) *APA Educational Psychology Handbook, Vol. 3*. Washington, DC: American Psychological Association.

MacArthur, C.A. (2012). Strategies instruction. In Harris, K.R., Graham, S. & Urdan, T. (Eds) *APA Educational Psychology Handbook, Vol. 3* (pp. 379–401). Washington, DC: American Psychological Association.

Medley, D. & Mitzel, H. (1963). The scientific study of teacher behaviour. In Bellack, A. (Ed.) *Theory and Research in Teaching*. New York: Teachers College Press.

Mercer, N. (2010). The analysis of classroom talk: methods and methodologies. *British Journal of Educational Psychology*, 80, 1–14.

Mercer, N. (2014). 40 years on: research into teacher–student talk. *Research Intelligence*, 123, 16–17.

Mercer, N. & Howe, C. (2012). Explaining the dialogic processes of teaching and learning: the value and potential of sociocultural theory. *Learning Culture and Interaction*, 1(1), 12–21.

Mortimer, E.F. & Scott, P.H. (2003). *Meaning Making in Science Classrooms*. Milton Keynes, UK: Open University Press.

Muijs, D. & Reynolds, D. (2011). *Effective Teaching: Evidence and Practice* (Third edn). London: Sage.

Myhill, D., Jones, S. & Hopper, R. (2007). *Talking, Listening, Learning: Effective Talk in the Primary Classroom*. Maidenhead, UK: Open University Press.

Patrick, H., Mantzicopoulos, P. & Sears, D. (2012). Effective classrooms. In Harris, K.R., Graham, S. & Urdan, T. (Eds) *APA Educational Psychology Handbook, Vol. 2* (pp. 443–469). Washington, DC: American Psychological Association.

Pellegrini, A. (1996) *Observing Children in their Natural Worlds: A Methodological Primer*. Mahwah, NJ: Erlbaum.

Piaget, J. (1932). *The Moral Judgement of the Child*. London: Routledge & Kegan Paul.

Pintrich, P.R. & Schunk, D.H. (1996). *Motivation in Education: Theory, Research and Applications*. Englewood Cliffs, NJ: Prentice-Hall.

Pollard, A. & Triggs, P., with Broadfoot, P., McNess, E. & Osborn, M. (2000). *What Pupils Say: Changing Policy and Practice in Primary Education: Findings from the PACE Project*. London: Continuum.

Radford, J., Blatchford, P. & Webster, R. (2011). Opening up and closing down: how teachers and TAs manage turn-taking, topic and repair in mathematics lessons. *Learning and Instruction*, 21, 625–635.

Radford, J., Bosanquet, P., Webster, R., Blatchford, P. & Rubie-Davies, C. (2014). Fostering learner independence through heuristic scaffolding: a valuable role for teaching assistants. *International Journal of Educational Research*, 63, 116–126.

Roehig, A.D., Turner, J.E., Arrastia, M.C., Christesen, E., McElhaney, S. & Jakiel, L.M. (2012). Effective teachers and teaching: characteristics and practices related to positive student outcomes. In Harris, K.R., Graham, S. & Urdan, T. (Eds) *APA Educational Psychology Handbook, Vol. 2* (pp. 501–527). Washington, DC: American Psychological Association.

Rubie-Davies, C., Blatchford, P., Webster, R., Koutsoubou, M. & Bassett, P. (2010). Enhancing learning? A comparison of teacher and teaching assistant interactions with pupils. *School Effectiveness and School Improvement*, 21(4), 429–449.

Shulman, L.S. (1986). Paradigms and research programs in the study of teaching. In Wittrock, M.C. (Ed.) *Handbook of Research on Teaching* (Third edn). New York: Macmillan.

Simon, A. & Boyer, E.G. (Eds) (1970). Mirrors for behaviour II: an anthology of observational instruments. *Classroom Interaction Newsletter* (special edition).

Sinatra, G.M. & Chinn, C.A. (2012). Thinking and reasoning in science: promoting epistemic conceptual change. In Harris, K.R., Graham, S. & Urdan, T. (Eds) *APA Educational Psychology Handbook, Vol. 1* (pp. 257–282). Washington, DC: American Psychological Association.

Sinclair, J. & Coulthard, M. (1975). *Towards an Analysis of Discourse: The English Used by Teachers and Pupils*. London: Oxford University Press.

Staarman, J.K. & Mercer, N. (2010). The guided construction of knowledge: talk between teachers and students. In K. Littleton, C. Wood & J. Staarman (Eds), *International Handbook of Psychology in Education*. Bingley, UK: Emerald.

Stubbs, M. (1983). *Language, Schools and Classrooms*. London: Methuen.

Tizard, B., Blatchford, P., Burke, J., Farquhar, C. & Plewis, I. (1988). *Young Children at School in the Inner City*. Hove, UK: Lawrence Erlbaum Associates.

Tymms, P. & Merrell, C. (2007). *Standards and Quality in English Primary Schools over Time: The National Evidence* (Primary Review Research Survey 4/1). Cambridge: University of Cambridge.

Watkins, C. & Mortimore, P. (1999). Pedagogy: what do we know? In Mortimore, P. (Ed.) *Understanding Pedagogy and its Impact on Learning*. London: Paul Chapman.

Webster, R. (2015). The classroom experiences of pupils with special educational needs in mainstream primary schools – 1976 to 2012. What do data from systematic observation studies reveal about pupils' educational experiences over time? *British Educational Research Journal*, published online 10 March.

Webster, R. & Blatchford, P. (2013). The educational experiences of pupils with a Statement for special educational needs in mainstream primary schools: results from a systematic observation study. *European Journal of Special Education*, 28, 463–479.

Webster, R., Blatchford, P., Bassett, P., Brown, P., Martin, C. & Russell, A. (2010). Double standards and first principles: framing teaching assistant support for pupils with special educational needs. *European Journal of Special Educational Needs*, 25(4), 319–336.

Wertsch, J.V. (1985). *Vygotsky and the Social Formation of Mind*. Cambridge, MA: Harvard University Press.

Wiliam, D. (2013). The importance of teaching. In J. Clifton (Ed.), *Excellence and Equity: Tackling Educational Disadvantage in England's Secondary Schools*. London: Institute for Public Policy Research.

Wittrock, M. (Ed.) (1986). *Handbook of Research on Teaching*. New York: Macmillan.

Wood, D.J., Bruner, J.S. & Ross, G. (1976). The role of tutoring in problems solving. *Journal of Psychology and Psychiatry*, 17(2), 89–100.

Yodder, P. & Symons, F. (2010). *Observational Measurement of Behaviour*. New York: Springer.

10

TEACHER EXPECTATIONS

As we saw in Chapter 9, there has been an enormous amount of research on classroom interaction and teacher–pupil interactions in particular. In the next two chapters we concentrate on two specific topics, involving teacher–pupil interactions, that have been the subject of much debate and research. In this chapter we look at teachers' expectations and then, in the next chapter, differences between boys and girls in their interactions with their teachers. We have chosen these two areas because they are educationally important, involve lively debate and controversy, are informed by psychological perspectives and are centrally connected to classroom interactions.

Teacher expectancies

Historically, one main aspect of research on teaching has been that on teachers' 'expectations' and in particular the possible effects they have on pupils' educational progress. It is seen as synonymous with the idea of the 'self-fulfilling prophecy', which was defined by the sociologist Merton in 1948 as 'a false definition of the situation, evoking a new behaviour which makes the original false conception come true' (quoted in Weinstein, 2002). But Weinstein shows that it has a far longer history in human ideas, and credits Francis Bacon in 1620 with one of the earliest definitions: 'when any proposition has been laid down, the human understanding forces everything else to add fresh support and confirmation'. The expectancy idea arrived as an important idea in the education world with the publication of the *Pygmalion in the Classroom* book (Rosenthal & Jacobson, 1968). We look more closely at this study below, but here we just summarize the basic argument: when teachers expect children to do well academically, even when this is not based on accurate information on their abilities, there is a tendency for such children to do well. As noted by Weinstein (2002) and McKown et al.

(2010) there has been less academic research on the topic over the past two decades which they – and we – believe is unfortunate because the topic continues to be a very important one and teacher expectations are a powerful and important driver of educational success and failure. As Braun (1987) concludes:

> The consequences for the individual learner of how the [teacher expectation] cycle is perpetuated … are staggering: the implications for the educator are sobering.

There are several reasons for the importance of examining teacher expectations. First, teacher expectations have been assigned a leading role in explanations of educational failure. It is commonplace to hear pupils' educational under-achievement attributed to low teacher expectations. This has been a feature of political rhetoric in the UK from all political parties over many years. Wineburg shows how in the USA the self-fulfilling prophecy has been seen as a main mechanism through which social inequalities and poverty are perpetuated: 'Behind the failure of minority children lurked the bigotry of teachers' (1987, p. 32). Weinstein (1998) has pointed to the wide disparities in expectations (beyond those predicted by actual achievements and motivation towards school) and argues that these can be expected to increase with rising levels of poverty and diversity between students. In the UK, a main claim of the Swann Report (1985) was that low expectations were a main factor in the relatively poor educational progress of ethnic minority children.

Conversely, and secondly, teacher expectations also have a main role in conceptualizations of school effectiveness and improvement, except the emphasis in this work is on high expectations. As Rogers (1998) points out, many models of school effectiveness (e.g., Mortimore et al., 1988) have high expectations as a leading attribute of successful schools. It is common for politicians in the UK to refer to 'raising expectations' as part of the regular drive to raise educational standards.

A third main reason for the importance of teacher expectations is that it is an example of an educational process to which social psychological theory has been systematically applied, and which, in contrast to much other research on teacher–pupil relations, has been insightful and to a degree successful in explaining links with student outcomes. Much research on teaching has been criticized for being atheoretical and heavily descriptive (Shulman, 1986). In contrast, research on teacher expectations and their effects has been much more informed by psychological concepts, research and theory on topics such as motivation, attributions, self-concept, prejudice, stereotypes, labelling, impression formation and person perception (e.g. Dusek, 1985). Babad (2009) and Rogers (1982) have used the expectancy process as the central notion in books that sought to offer a wider social psychology of schooling.

An allied and fourth point to make is that research on teacher expectations serves to highlight some important issues and dilemmas in any attempt to understand relationships between teaching and student outcomes. Important questions are raised about the certainty with which claims for causality can be made, the extent to which mediating variables can be identified and the limitations and appropriateness of alternative research approaches.

Expectations can be considered developmentally. There is evidence that they are most influential in the early years of schooling – the Pygmalion study in fact only found effects in the first two grades of school. As we shall see below, the study by Rist (1970) has been influential in the implicit acceptance of a developmental conception of expectations – that is, the teacher's expectation of children at the point of entry to school can set in train powerful processes that profoundly shape children's subsequent school careers. McKown et al. (2010) review research which shows that between the ages of 6 and 10 years children's ability to infer other's expectations and awareness of stereotypes becomes more accurate and detailed. The indications are that underlying changes in social cognitive development can affect pupils' susceptibility to expectancy effects. Interestingly, though, the effect of expectations later in children's school careers may not be so profound. This is especially likely once children have left primary school, and experience many different teachers for different subjects. Moreover, with age, children are not so dependent on adults for their self-view – as we see elsewhere in this book, friendship and peer groups can be alternative frames of reference and influence.

In this chapter we look critically at the literature on teachers' expectations in four ways. First, what is the nature of expectations, and how can they be defined? Second, do expectations affect student academic outcomes? Third, what classroom processes mediate the effect of expectations on outcomes? Fourth, what factors influence expectations? The chapter will highlight what we feel are main issues, review some main research studies and refer to research (involving one of the authors – PB) at the Institute of Education.

What are expectations?

Although the term 'teacher expectations' is widely used and its effects often cited, its exact meaning is often implicit and there is surprisingly little attention paid to its actual nature and definition. What exactly are 'expectations'? In an everyday sense they might refer to expectations about a student's current academic performance, expectations about the future – say, by the end of the school year – or expectations about behaviour or effort in class. Prescriptions about the need for high expectations are less convincing if the actual reference is not clear. Despite the political rhetoric about raising expectations, it is difficult for teachers to know how to do this is if the nature of expectations is vague.

Rogers (1982, 1998) has drawn a useful distinction between probabilistic and prescriptive expectations. Probabilistic expectations are what teachers feel is likely to happen, while prescriptive expectations refer to levels a student ought to attain. It is the second of these two types of expectations which are, albeit implicitly, central to notions of effectiveness. Expectations will be connected to assumptions teachers have about factors influencing students' success at school, their ability and their motivation, as well as beliefs about their own ability to change students' progress. A similar distinction is between expectations as descriptive and expectations as the basis for action. If teachers have low expectations, and little belief that they can change things, the prognosis for students is gloomy. However if they have low expectations (which may be realistic, perhaps on the basis of past performance), but a strong belief in their ability to change things, then the improvements in students' achievements may be high.

Cooper (1985) sought to clarify the different definitions of expectations that have been used. He categorized these into four groups: first, ability or achievement measures (which usually involve a rating of a student's current ability or achievement and, although used extensively in the expectation literature, are really not expectation measures at all); second, expected improvement (how much progress is expected over a given time period – the most obvious measure of what is usually understood as 'expectation'); third, manipulated expectations (as in the Rosenthal and Jacobson study, expectations are created by false information); and, fourth, natural discrepancy measures (how much a teacher overestimates or underestimates a student's performance, usually calculated on the basis of the degree of mismatch between teacher estimates of a child's ability or achievement and test scores or some other objective measure).

At an even more general level, there are two ways of looking at expectations. On the one hand there is the view that expectations are relatively broad-brush. Some researchers have seen teachers' conceptions of their pupils in terms of relatively general, static categories, sometimes applied to whole classes, so that they are perceived and dealt with in terms of stereotypes (Keddie, 1971). In a sociological study, Sharp and Green (1975) categorized teacher perceptions of their pupils into those where pupils were known to the teachers ('consociates') and those where pupils were not known so well ('contemporary'). This general classification appeared to have implications for teacher–pupil relations. The suggestion is that if a child has a 'contemporary' relationship with the teacher, and initial impressions lead a teacher to think a child is difficult, then the expectancy effect can begin and is then difficult to change. This and other work is consistent with the view that negative impressions are more salient and long-lasting than positive impressions. McKown et al. (2010) have argued for more recognition of the salience of general stereotypes of academic ability, based on criteria such as ethnicity, and for greater integration of research on teacher expectations and stereotypes about academic ability.

The first view is then relatively comfortable with a conceptualization of teachers' expectations in terms of broad, relatively static categories. An alternative view, expressed by, for example, Hargreaves, Hestor and Mellor (1986), is that expectations are more complex, dynamic and open to change. Drawing on labelling theory, they document the development of expectations over time in terms of 'typifications'. This process, whereby individual pupils gradually become known to teachers, is seen to go through several stages, that is, an initial stage of 'speculation' (little confidence), to 'evaluation' (ideal matching, still tentative and relatively simple), 'elaboration', and, finally, 'stabilization' (by which time knowledge of pupils is more complex). Hargreaves et al. argue that the processes involved can be generalized to apply to social perception more generally:

> there is also in our theory an implicit general theory about how any person comes to type any other person. What teachers are doing with respect to children is not a phenomenon confined to schools; it is a phenomenon common to all people in all places at all times.
>
> *(Hargreaves et al., 1986, p. 182)*

The notion of elaboration over time in expectations is also seen in Jussim's (1986) distinction between 'flexible' and 'rigid' expectations. Expectations, if anything, are a psychological phenomenon. Schmuck and Schmuck (1983) have shown how integral expectations are to everyday life: 'Expectations are such a natural part of interpersonal relations that for our own security and cognitive clarity, we normally make subconscious predictions about how an interpersonal interchange will transpire' (p. 70). As Schmuck and Schmuck argue, expectations as interpersonal predictions are communicated in a multitude of direct and indirect ways. Research has not been concerned with expectations in terms of hopes or aspirations, but more in terms of working predictions that are used in relating to others in the classroom (Schmuck & Schmuck, 1983). As Jussim (1986) has shown, a good deal of research in social and cognitive psychology has addressed the nature and accuracy of intuitive prediction processes, of which expectations are presumably one. There have been a number of attempts to describe the nature of expectations using psychological theory (e.g., Babad, 2009; Braun, 1987; Jussim, 1986; Peterson & Barger, 1985).

Expectations can be seen as one aspect of person perception, and inaccuracies have been examined in terms of stereotyping and prejudice. More particularly, attribution theory has been used to explain teacher expectations; for example, Peterson and Barger (1985) draw on Weiner's theory to show how teachers use information about a student's past performance to make attributions for the causes of their present performance, for instance by forming attributions that maintain a 'consistent' picture of the causes of performance. So, in the case of a high-ability student, an expected outcome such as success in school work is attributed to a stable factor like the student's ability, while an unexpected outcome, such as success on the same task by a low-ability student, is likely to be attributed to an 'unstable' factor such as luck or the nature of the task. An early and more common-sense version of this idea was advanced by Finn (1972, in Schmuck & Schmuck, 1983) who defined expectations as evaluations that one person forms of another which lead the evaluator to treat the person being evaluated as though the assessment were valid. The evaluator then tends to predict that the other person will act in a manner consistent with the assessment.

Attribution theorists have also distinguished attributions of actors or participants in a situation from those of onlookers uninvolved in the social interaction.
The basic notion here is that the participants – in this case teachers – have a vested
interest, and so engage in self-serving (sometimes called 'ego-enhancing') attributions, the most widely cited being that they will accept responsibility for student
success but blame the student if they fail. This is similar to Snyder's (in Rogers,
1998) notion that expectations have an ego-defence function. For example, a
failing student may reflect badly on a teacher, so holding low expectations of the
student will serve to reduce the possibility of perceived lack of success on the
teacher's part. However, one of the problems with attribution theory has been
the plausibility of quite opposing trends. Peterson and Barger (1985) review
studies that show teachers blame themselves for student failure and credit students
for their own successes. The adaptability, but also the imprecision, of attribution
theory is reflected in yet another term from this literature – teachers' 'humility
bias' has been used to describe the reluctance of teachers to attribute pupils' performance to their own influence. The literature is therefore complex – Jussim's
(1986) review remains one of the most thorough accounts.

Rogers (1998) has helpfully integrated the connections between motivational
theories and expectations in terms of three different models. The first (following
Atkinson) sees motivation as a function of personality, the second (following
Weiner – see above) sees motivation as a function of information processing,
and the third (following Dweck (1986) and many others) sees motivation as a
function of learning goals (especially ego or performance vs. learning or mastery
goals). As Rogers points out, these three models could be seen to represent the
chronological development of motivational theory more generally, as it has
moved from stable personality characteristics through to less stable and changeable
features like learning goals. It is the more recent theories, such as those concerning
learning goals, which give most room to teacher influences, in that learning goals
may be affected by what the teacher does in class in terms of feedback, face-to-
face teaching, etc.

Do expectations causally affect pupils' achievements?

The concern about teachers' expectations has been that if they are not accurate
and not open to corrective feedback – if they are based perhaps on stereotypes,
children's social status, or personal appearance – they may then serve to affect
adversely the learning opportunities and attainments of pupils. To what extent
has research supported this concern? At the outset it is important to distinguish
between two main types of effects. Although a number of different and sometimes
confusing terms have been used, the essential distinction is between, first,
judgements of pupils that are accurate and, second, those which are biased and
causally and adversely affect pupils. To take an example: one way to look at the
association between expectations and pupil achievement would be to collect
expectations at the beginning of the school year, by, say, getting teachers to rank

the children in terms of their academic potential, and to then correlate this with pupils' achievement, measured at the end of the school year. Research has shown this correlation to be high (Blatchford et al., 1989). But this finding is not remarkable – it just means that teachers are generally good judges of how well children in their class will do. What is of concern is the possibility that the judgement of teachers actually brings about a change in children's performance rather than just reflecting it. Rogers (1982) used the notion of the tipster and the racehorse to help explain this distinction. The success of the tipster might be measured in terms of the accuracy of their predictions about runners in a race, but we would be seriously worried if it was felt the tipster actually caused the success or not of a horse.

Brophy (1983) uses the terms 'expectancy' and 'bias' to describe these two types of effects, and claims there is much evidence for an expectancy, but less for a bias, effect. Cooper (1985) uses the terms 'maintaining' and 'enhancing' to describe the same distinction. There is nothing remarkable about maintaining differential treatment of students, if this relates to real differences between children – indeed taking account of pupil differences is an essential part of teaching – but there is little evidence for teachers 'enhancing' these differences.

How can we discover whether expectations have an effect? What kind of research design would help settle the issue? A review of different approaches to this is informative about more general difficulties facing educational and psychological research when addressing issues of causality.

Experimental designs

The traditional way of establishing causality is by use of an experimental design – that is, a design in which the variable of interest, in this case teacher expectations, is manipulated or controlled in such a way that any change in outcomes can be reliably attributed to it. The study by Rosenthal and Jacobson is the most famous example of an experimental approach to the expectancy effect (and probably educational research more generally). The basic components of the research were the testing of children at the beginning of the school year, the feeding to teachers of information on the 20 per cent expected to 'bloom' (though in fact these children were chosen at random) and the examination of whether these high-expectation children fared any better by the end of the school year. The logic of the experiment was that, because of random selection, any differences between high-expectation and other children must be attributable to the inculcation of high (though false) expectations, and not because of any other factor such as the characteristics of the children.

There has been enormous controversy over the validity of the results, which cannot be described in full here (see Babad, 2009; Rogers, 1982). Criticisms have included worries about the validity and reliability of the tests used, and the fact that results were in the expected direction for only some of the age groups studied. There has also been a noticeable lack of replications of the study

(Brophy, 1985; Rogers, 1982), though this might not necessarily mean the effect was not real – it could even be, for example, that the publicity generated by the original experiment served to alter the behaviour of participants in future experiments. In a more recent forum on the expectancy effect, Wineburg (1987) criticizes the experiment and the way the expectancy idea, supported by the study, has, in his view, quite unfairly taken on a degree of certainty in the USA, even to the point of being used as evidence in court cases.

But over and above these arguments about the credibility of this one study, there is a general difficulty with the research approach used. Even if in the Pygmalion experiment the independent variable really did causally affect the outcome, and thus in this sense the expectancy effect was proven, the problem remains that expectations generated by the feeding of information (whether fictitious or not) are not the same as expectations and judgements of children built up naturally over the early days after entry to a class. There is, in other words, a question about the validity of findings from experimental research.

Naturalistic quantitative studies

This point reflects a central problem with evidence in educational research that we feel deserves more attention. The usual position adopted is to assume that experiments are the 'gold standard' in any test of causality. This is the position often adopted by politicians and policy makers who assume education, like medicine, needs the kind of certainty afforded by randomized controlled trials, and other research designs are seen as a kind of second best. But if, as discussed above, there are problems with the validity of findings of experimental research in education, how, without experiments, can one establish causality? There is indeed an alternative point of view that experiments in education have a number of difficulties of interpretation that render them less able to answer questions about causality, and that more naturalistic designs are actually more valid. This argument is developed with regard to research on class-size differences by Goldstein and Blatchford (1998).

One such alternative approach has been used in research on teacher expectations, and we review this here in order to examine its strengths and limitations. As we have said, simply finding a correlation between start-of-year teacher expectations and end-of-year pupil attainments is not evidence of an expectation effect, because it may simply reflect the accurate judgements made by teachers of a child's abilities and attainments. One way to overcome this problem, at least partially, is to conduct longitudinal studies, and then control for, or partial out, the child's start-of-year attainments when calculating the association between start-of-year expectations and end-of-year attainments. The logic of this is that the aspect of expectations which overlaps with initial attainment – that is, which reflects accurate matching to attainment – is thereby controlled, and any remaining effect reflects an independent expectation effect. This method can begin to approach the strength of experimental research

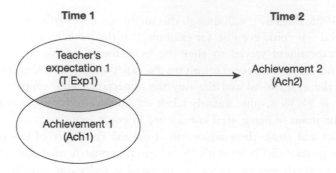

FIGURE 10.1 Relationships between teachers' expectations and children's achievement

without the attendant validity problems. It should allow us to distinguish between expectancy and bias effects.

The logic of this approach is shown in Figure 10.1. There may well be a correlation between T Exp1 and Ach2, and there is likely to be a correlation between Ach1 and Ach2, but some of the correlation between T Exp1 and Ach2 may be explained by that between Ach1 and Ach2 (teachers will hold expectations in line with pupils' initial achievements). If we control for the overlap between T Exp1 and Ach1 (the shaded area in Figure 10.1) and there is still an association between T Exp1 and Ach2 then this should be evidence for an independent effect of T Exp1 on Ach2.

Brophy (1985), in a comprehensive review, found that the size of effect found in studies of this sort was not great, but statistically and educationally significant. He suggests 5%–10% of the variance on average. Smith (in Brophy, 1985) found on the basis of meta-analysis an effect size of 0.38 standard deviations for expectations on student achievement. This means that on a standardized reading test, teachers' expectations are likely to make a difference of about 5 points either way to a child's progress. This is about the same effect size as that commonly reported for sex and ethnic differences (Tizard et al., 1988).

As far as we know this non-experimental longitudinal approach has only been used systematically in one UK study. In the Institute of Education longitudinal study (Blatchford et al., 1989) over 300 children in 33 inner London infant schools were followed from entry over the first three years of school. Teacher expectations were assessed by asking teachers three weeks (on average) after the beginning of each school year to judge the academic potential of each child in terms of whether they were above average, average or below average. In the first year (the reception year) teachers were asked about academic work in general, and in the second and third year they were asked the questions separately for maths and reading. The pupils' attainments in maths and reading were assessed at the beginning and at the end of each school year. It was therefore possible to, first, find out whether expectations were associated with end-of-year attainments

TABLE 10.1 Associations between teacher expectations and attainment

	Range of effects (SD units)[1]	P
RECEPTION (4/5 years) (N = 238)		
Mathematics	0.9	<0.001
Reading and writing[2]	1.5	<0.01
MIDDLE (5/6 years) (N = 420)[3]		
Mathematics	1.4	<0.001
Reading	1.5	<0.001
TOP (6/7 years) (N = 353)[3]		
Mathematics	1.7	<0.001
Reading	1.9	<0.001

Source: Adapted from Blatchford et al., 1989
Notes:
1. i.e., from above average to below average on the teacher expectation scale.
2. Reading and writing were combined for the reception year because of their conceptual and actual association. Writing was not assessed at the end of middle infants so progress measures for both middle and top infants were restricted to reading.
3. Numbers of children had increased by middle infants because the sample now included all children who had entered in September, 1982, and not just those from the nursery class. By top infants some children were lost, because, for example, they had moved or gone into the junior school.

(see Table 10.1). Results showed they were. But the question of most interest, as we have just seen, is whether this association still holds when start-of-year attainments were controlled for. Table 10.2 shows that they were. The size of effects – 0.4 to 0.8 of a standard deviation – is substantial, especially when compared to effects noted in Brophy's review. In fact this association still held when a range of other factors were examined in relation to pupils' progress (see Tizard et al., 1988). Teacher expectations were one of two main school variables related to progress (the other was curriculum coverage, which we come to below).

Have we therefore shown that teacher expectations causally affect attainment? Probably. But the problem, as is often said, is that correlation does not prove causality. Longitudinal research and multiple regression, if used properly, can go a long way in controlling for possibly connected variables but can still not entirely rule out the possibility that another variable may be causing the association. For example, it may be that teachers, even after the short time they have children before giving the expectation rating, draw on a wider range of information about a child than that provided by an initial assessment of their attainments. They may, for instance, have formed an impression of the child's rate of learning and it may be this which relates to expectations at 'Time 1' and which overlaps with expectation judgements. In this sense the association between teacher expectations and later attainment may still reflect accurate

TABLE 10.2 Associations between teacher expectations and progress

	Range of effects (SD units)[1]	P
RECEPTION (4/5 years) (N = 238)		
Mathematics	0.4	<0.01
Reading and writing[2]	0.6	<0.001
MIDDLE (5/6 years) (N = 407)[3]		
Mathematics	0.7	<0.001
Reading	0.4	<0.01
TOP (6/7 years) (N = 326)[3]		
Mathematics	0.5	<0.001
Reading	0.8	<0.001

Source: Adapted from Blatchford et al., 1989
Notes:
1. i.e., from above average to below average on the teacher expectation scale.
2. See Note 2 to Table 10.1.
3. See Note 3 to Table 10.1. Numbers of children are slightly lower than in Table 10.1 because analyses on progress were only possible on those children for whom there were test data at both the beginning and end of each school year.

judgements of the child by the teacher. The association, in other words, could still be child-driven rather than teacher-driven.

Case studies

A very different approach to research has provided perhaps the most compelling but controversial evidence for the negative effects of an expectation effect. Once again it is important to evaluate critically the claims made, particularly with regard to the validity of the evidence and interpretation of results.

Perhaps the most widely cited study in this tradition is that by Ray Rist (1970). This is an account of how one kindergarten teacher in an all black school grouped her children after only eight days, ostensibly on academic criteria, but, according to Rist, actually on the basis of physical appearance, cleanliness and the newness of clothes, whether they spoke Standard American, their parents' income, education and the size of the family – all of which were known to the teacher beforehand. Rist argues that the teacher had an ideal type of pupil in mind – middle-class and well-educated – and it was this rather than the pupils' ability that was the basis for her initial grouping. The consequence of this early grouping was profound. The teacher concentrated on the first table and more often penalized and ignored the children at the second and third tables. The children at the first table identified with the teacher and ridiculed the other children. The second and third tables were forced to discuss amongst themselves what they should be doing (secondary learning), and came to insult each other.

In a depressing finding, Rist argues that the children at the third table could not even see the blackboard properly, as if they were not disadvantaged enough! Rist's argument has a convincing logic to it:

1. teacher has an ideal type – that is, characteristics necessary for success – and this is related to social class;
2. students on entry are subjectively evaluated in terms of the presence of these characteristics and put into groups expected to succeed (fast learners) or fail (slow learners);
3. the groups are differentially treated by the teacher – the fast learners receiving most teacher time. Slow learners are taught infrequently, receive more control and receive little support from the teacher;
4. interactional patterns become rigid and caste like with the completion of academic material widening over the year;
5. the process continues into later years but is now no longer based on subjective judgements but on objective performance information (which the judgements originally served to cause).

This is a coherent argument and a vivid description of how the self-fulfilling prophecy might work. However, there is in this case an inverse relationship between the clarity of the conclusions and the strength of the data on which the conclusions are based. There are a number of difficulties of interpretation. It could be for example that the teacher did base her judgements on academic criteria and that Rist was actually wrong. In this case it may be that later differences were more the result of teacher responses to initial child differences. Perhaps most importantly, even if Rist's description is valid, it relates only to one teacher. It may be that Rist chanced upon a truly awful teacher – a teacher who behaved in a professionally and ethically unacceptable way.

Teacher susceptibility to expectancy effects

As Brophy (1985) has argued, what may underlie an average teacher expectation effect is the possibility that it may be found in only a minority of teachers, and not at all in the majority. In other words, most teachers base their teaching and curriculum on appropriate and accurate judgements about the children in their care, but some are biased in their expectations and allow this to affect their classroom interactions and ultimately the pupils' educational achievements. Babad (2009) reviewed evidence from studies by himself and colleagues and found that about a quarter of teachers are highly biased (e.g., attributing higher scores to higher-status individuals) and also found that expectancy effects (e.g., negative treatment of low-expectancy students) were far more likely with such teachers. Babad and Inbar (1981) found that biased teachers had defined personality characteristics. They were more conventional, conformist to social rules, concerned with authority and dogmatic.

What processes mediate the connection between expectations and achievement?

Even if an expectation effect on pupils' educational attainments is found, this still leaves open questions about just how it works. There must be some mechanism or process by which the expectation works, that is, which mediates the expectation effect. Unfortunately the Rosenthal and Jacobson study had little to offer in terms of explaining why there was an expectation effect.

There are likely to be many varied and subtle ways that expectations are conveyed and received by students. Expectations may be reflected in the opportunities afforded a student in class, in terms of the tone and nature of interactions and feedback, but also the work they are set, written comments on work, facial and non-verbal expressions, allocation to groups and classes, and registration for examinations. Expectations may be detected by pupils in terms of everyday encounters but also through one critical interchange or behaviour. One of the authors remembers well a brief encounter with an older technical drawing teacher who, in a kindly and interested voice (not common in that school), showed his expectation for a future career not previously considered by the pupil. Just a few sentences opened up a different possible future, and perhaps laid the seed of a wish to succeed.

There have been many models that attempt to describe the processes that might operate (Braun, 1987; Cooper, 1979, 1985; Darley & Fazio, 1980; Jussim, 1986). Harris (Harris & Rosenthal, 1985, cited in Dusek, 1985) suggested four social psychological mechanisms by which expectations are communicated: climate (e.g. teacher's warmth towards high-expectation children); input (teaching of increasingly difficult material to children of whom they have high expectations); verbal output (teacher's persistence in and frequency of academic interactions; greater opportunities for high-expectation children to respond); and feedback (increasingly differentiated and positive information to children of whom they have high expectations). Weinstein (1998) used children's reports, rather than observers', and drew up a model of expectancy communication in the classroom, which elaborates Rosenthal's four-factor model. Elements are:

1. ways in which students are grouped for instruction (if grouped by ability, ability comparisons are heightened);
2. the tasks through which the curriculum is enacted (a differential curriculum lessens opportunities for low-expectation children);
3. the motivational strategies that teachers use to engage learning (competitive reward systems heighten ability comparisons, decrease intrinsic motivation);
4. the role that students are asked to play in directing their own learning (differential opportunities for responsibility – limited pupil agency diminishes pupil motivation);
5. evaluation (teacher ability beliefs affect provision of performance opportunities for evaluation);

6.   differential allocation of warmth, trust, humour and concern;
7.   different parent–class relations for high and lows.

There is not space to fully review all the possible mediating processes. Here we discuss four main possibilities – teacher–pupil interactions, pupil self-perceptions, curriculum coverage, and organizational decisions on grouping and differentiating pupils for learning.

Teacher–pupil interaction

Common sense might suggest that a teacher's expectations would be mediated, or realized, through the nature of the interactions a teacher has with pupils. This would be consistent with what Rogers has called 'interactional behavioural effects'. This was seen in Rist's descriptions of the teacher concentrating her teaching on the high-expectancy group, reflected in more and qualitatively different interactions. But we need to look at other systematic studies, involving more classrooms, to examine the connection between expectations and interactions. Perhaps the most widely cited is the study by Brophy and Good (1986). Structured observations were conducted during the spring term in four first grade classes. There were three boys and three girls classified on the basis of teacher rankings as 'highs' and three boys and three girls classified as 'lows'. Brophy and Good were surprised to find that the highs received more praise by teachers and more work-related contacts. There was none of the expected teacher 'compensation' for lows, who might have been expected to receive more attention and feedback in order to help them catch up.

Brophy and Good recognized that these differences between expectation groups might be due to differences between the children themselves, in the sense that teachers were merely responding to differences between children. The effect may therefore be child-driven. To deal with this they calculated further measures that took account of absolute differences in frequencies of behaviour, and to thus allow comparisons of teachers' behaviour to groups in equivalent situations. So these measures were not the number of correct child answers (which would represent child differences) or the amount of teacher praise, but, for example, the percentage of correct answers followed by praise. Using this method they found that highs received a higher percentage of correct answers followed by praise, more repetition/rephrasing following wrong answers, and more giving of clues following reading problems. Lows received more criticisms following wrong answers, and more answers not followed by any feedback from teachers. In short, teachers appeared to favour highs by 'demanding and reinforcing quality performance'.

The calculation of these ratio variables is a useful addition to the more common use of basic frequencies of occurrence of individual categories. The clarity of the study, and perhaps the way results were consistent with a negative expectation effect, may help to explain its frequent citation. But once again, what at first appear to be convincing results, on closer inspection and testing prove less so. One problem is the small number of classes and teachers. The timing of the collection of 'expectation' ratings makes claims that this is a study of expectations problematic. Had teachers' interactions already changed by the spring? Perhaps at the beginning of the year there were no differences? Brophy and Good, to their credit, sought to replicate their findings in a follow-up study of nine first grade classes, and with expectation ratings given at the beginning of the school year. This time they found that, overall, teachers were not treating lows differently, though three of the nine teachers did, suggesting again that only some teachers show a bias affect.

The link between teacher expectations and classroom interactions is by no means clear-cut (Hall & Merkel, 1985). Weinstein (1976), in a study of teacher–pupil interaction in three first grade classes, did not find consistent differences between high-, medium- and low-expectancy groups. In the Institute of Education study (Blatchford et al., 1989) the connection between teachers' expectations and teacher–pupil interactions and child behaviours in class was examined. In line with Brophy and Good and other studies, it was hypothesized that children rated above average would have higher mean frequencies of teacher praise, teacher instruction, teacher feedback on work and initiations to the teacher, and lower mean frequencies of criticism from teachers and 'task avoidance' behaviour. Whilst mean frequencies for the expectation groups were sometimes in the expected direction for some of the three years, there were no strong or consistent relationships over the three years.

It may be that the manifestation of expectancy effects is very subtly expressed in teacher behaviours and not easily captured by systematic observation protocols. McKown et al. (2010) suggest that expectations are reflected in styles of interactions, e.g., low-expectation pupils get fewer opportunities for inferential thinking, less teacher probing and more low-level, memory questions. It seems, though, that pupils are often aware of behaviours that communicate expectations, e.g., pupils perceive that high achievers have less negative comments, fewer rules and more privileges. It also seems that the more teachers treat high and low achievers differently, the closer the link between teacher expectations and pupil achievement and self-concept (McKown et al., 2010; Weinstein, 2002).

One possible way that expectations may be linked to interactions in classrooms is that teachers are more concerned about the control of low-expectation pupils, so interactions with them are not so much concerned with performance as with controlling behaviour (Cooper, 1979, 1985). Accordingly, they receive less praise for performance, and they decrease performance initiations, and this in turn increases the teacher's attempted control. Eccles and Wigfield (1985) support this idea and suggest that this may make low-expectancy students less likely to seek out the teacher. The explanation here is therefore in terms of the ways the teacher controls opportunities for interaction (which Eccles and Wigfield prefer to an attribution explanation).

Pupil self-perceptions

A second possible mediating process, involved in the expectancy process, is through pupil self-perceptions. Teachers may differ in their behaviour towards expectation groups and this may affect the educational experience of pupils, but, presumably, pupils have also to take on in some way a teacher's expectation for it to have an effect. There has been an enormous body of work on pupils' self-perceptions in educational settings which are relevant to the expectation effect, which can only be touched on here. Relevant areas of interest include motivation, self-concept and ability perceptions, attributions for success and failure, self-efficacy (see Anderman & Maehr, 1994; Eccles & Wigfield, 1985; Jussim, 1986; Pintrich & Schunk, 1996; Rogers, 1982; Weinstein, 2002). A difficulty with this literature is the plethora of convincing possibilities, often overlapping and difficult to review or synthesize effectively. Here we look at just a few of the more closely examined processes.

Jussim (1986) points out that one of the most important links between expectations and pupil perceptions concerns effort-outcome covariation. If it is the case that high-expectation pupils differ in terms of teacher feedback – an example would be getting more praise for strong efforts – then highs, but not lows, will come to feel their efforts will lead to success. Once again attribution analysis has been used. In general terms, an attribution account would see pupils' explanations of their own success or failure at school tasks affecting their future efforts. One attribution version of processes connected to success and failure at school work runs something like this: if pupils do not do well or fail and they see this as attributable to internal and uncontrollable factors such as their ability, this will undermine their confidence and they may be more likely to give up. If, on the other hand, failure is seen as surmountable and due to something changeable like lack of effort or knowledge then the student will be less likely to give up and will believe that increased effort will improve future results (see, e.g., Jussim, 1986). This shows that both teachers *and* pupils can be mistaken – i.e., both can have an attributional bias.

The effect teachers have on these processes is more speculative but, conceptually, if teachers' low expectations are expressed through explanations of pupils' poor performance in terms of low ability, then pupils' own explanations will be reinforced. On the other hand, if teachers do not have a fixed view of the child, and see performance as changeable and uncontrollable, then the pupil may come to see their own attainments as changeable. Much hinges on the degree to which teachers' interpretations of a child's performance and behaviour are fixed. More specifically, if teachers provide non-contingent and less favourable feedback to low-expectation children they may lead such children to believe performance is not contingent on effort. Consequently such children will try less hard, and ultimately their attainments will suffer. A child's belief that their own actions do not affect outcomes is central to the attribution approach to 'learned helplessness'. In a well-known extension of this account, Dweck (e.g., Dweck et al., 1978, in Eccles & Wigfield, 1985) suggests that differences in teacher feedback patterns might predispose boys and girls to develop different attribution patterns for themselves.

Logical though this account may appear, Eccles and Wigfield (1985) question the findings related to sex differences. In contrast to Dweck (see next chapter) they found that teachers gave more work-related criticism to boys, there were no differences in criticism about non-intellectual aspects of their work, and there were no sex differences in pupil attributions – almost all attributions were to lack of effort (a finding replicated by Blatchford, 1996). Furthermore, they argue that children's everyday experiences of teacher affective feedback and teacher attributions are not powerful determinants of their classroom motivation. This is partly because these are not common in the course of classroom life. Eccles and Wigfield argue that:

> teachers' influences on student motivation are mediated by teachers' confidence to teach all students (teachers' sense of personal efficacy) and by teachers' knowledge of effective teaching practices for children of different ability levels. Low teacher expectancies have a debilitating effect on children's motivation when the teacher believes that low expectancy children can't improve their performance and when the teacher doesn't know effective teaching practices for low skill-level children – that is, when teachers believe that they cannot succeed at teaching low skill-level children.
>
> *(Eccles & Wigfield, 1985, p. 188)*

Pupils' perceptions of their own ability may also be affected by expectations. There is an enormous body of research which has examined the links between ability self-perceptions and achievement in school (e.g. Eccles & Wigfield, 1985; Pintrich & Schunk, 1996).

More recent research has investigated the effects of teacher expectations on pupil self-perceptions at the classroom rather than the individual pupil level. In New Zealand, Rubie-Davies (2006) found that in classrooms in elementary schools where teachers held generally lower expectations, pupils' reading and mathematics self-concept declined and when teachers held generally higher expectations, reading and mathematics self-concepts increased.

Curriculum coverage

In Chapter 9 we looked at research that showed that, as a proportion of a pupil's time in school, interactions between teachers and pupils occurred relatively infrequently and often when the child was a part of a larger group or the whole class. Most time was spent on individual work. As we saw, recent curriculum and other reforms in the UK seem to have increased the amount of interaction between teachers and pupils, but individual children will still rarely be the focus of a teacher's attention. If it is the case that expectation effects are not obviously mediated through interactions between teachers and pupils, this raises the possibility that expectations may be reflected in the level and difficulty of the work they are set.

In an early experimental study (Beez, 1968), sixty graduate students were taught the meaning of a series of pictorial signs. Each of these 'teachers' then worked with one 5- or 6-year-old. The teachers were provided with a faked psychological report on the child and the extent to which they were expected to benefit from education (the children were involved in the US Head Start programme). The children were categorized as either of normal intelligence or of low average intelligence and school adjustment was expected to be difficult, though in reality the reports were allocated at random. It was found that the teachers of 'higher ability' children attempted to teach nearly twice as many signs as teachers of 'low ability' pupils. Also, 'higher ability' children learned more signs – 77% of them learned five or more signs, compared to only 13% of 'low ability' pupils. They also received higher ratings in terms of, for example, intelligence. The study seems to show that the curriculum provided to pupils, and in turn their attainments, are affected by the expectations held by teachers. Once again, though, there is a problem with the validity of an experimental study. These were not real teachers, the 'curriculum' was artificial, and there is no guarantee that results would be replicated in the real world of the classroom and in the way teachers actually form expectations and judgements of children.

In the Institute of Education longitudinal study (Blatchford et al., 1989) it was possible to examine, using a naturalistic longitudinal design, the possibility that teachers' expectations were mediated through curriculum experiences. In order to provide a measure of the range and depth of children's curriculum experiences, teachers completed checklists of activities in mathematics and written language to which children had been introduced. We have already seen that in this study expectations were related to attainment and to progress. It was also found that teachers' expectations were related to curriculum coverage in the second and third years (the analysis could not be done for the first year). Teachers' expectations and curriculum coverage were still related to each other, even after controlling for initial attainment, indicating that the association was more than just accurate matching of curriculum to entry skills. Further regression analyses also showed that when teacher expectations, curriculum coverage and entry skills were regressed on end-of-year school attainments, teacher expectations and curriculum coverage were independently related to end-of-year attainments. This indicates that, although there was overlap between expectations and curriculum coverage, this did not fully account for the effect of expectations on progress.

If it is possible, therefore, that we overrate the influence of interaction factors on pupils' progress and, as a mediator of expectation effects, it may be that we underestimate the way in which the curriculum presented to children is informed by teachers' expectations. The curriculum may affect pupils' academic progress by setting limits on children's academic experiences. This is not to suggest that curriculum experiences will need to be the same for every child, but these results indicate that differences will need to be well founded. As Braun (1987, p. 604) has said, the teacher expectation cycle is 'maintained more than anything by the intellectual and affective constraints characteristic of the curriculum of the failing child ... Curricular constraints frequently restrict the failing child to sterile, irrelevant, artificially contrived learning experiences'.

Organizational decisions on grouping and differentiating pupils for learning

A fourth likely mediating factor for expectancy effects concerns the organizational decisions made about grouping and differentiating pupils for learning. As we have seen, research indicates that in classrooms where children perceive high differential treatment, children's own academic expectations more closely matched the teachers' expectations than was the case in classrooms with more equal treatment of students. Other studies using observer (rather than student) information supports this link between highly differentiated classrooms and greater stratification of pupil-ability perceptions. By fifth grade, children in classes where teachers held low expectations reported more negative-ability perceptions, whether in high or low differentiated classrooms (cf. Weinstein, 1998). Weinstein makes the point that children's expectations about their ability come from differential access to learning but also their awareness of differential treatment by teachers.

In Chapter 8 we looked at the connections between allocation to attainment-defined groupings and classes and pupils' academic performance. A key connected classroom process is likely to be the way that allocation to attainment grouping becomes interconnected with teacher expectations. It is easy to see how teachers will need to make a number of pedagogical decisions in relation to the expected level of pupils in each group or set. However, as we saw in Chapter 8, there is a worry that once pupils are placed in differentiated learning groups they experience large differences in curriculum and teaching which then sets limits on their academic achievements – which then in turn reinforces decisions originally made about their placement. Rather in the way illustrated by Rist's study reviewed earlier, the danger is that once so allocated, whether or not this is an accurate reflection of a child's attainment or capabilities, the pupil and the teacher may adjust their own perceptions to that set by the organizational judgement within which they find themselves. In short, the placement becomes the key driver for a self-fulfilling process, and it can become difficult to move from this group. There are many powerful examples of how this process works in Rhona Weinstein's troubling book (2002). This has particular resonance in the case of children classified as having special educational needs in mainstream educational settings, and who can experience a teaching regime quite separate from the rest of the class (Blatchford et al., 2012; Webster & Blatchford, 2013).

What factors affect expectations?

Finally, in order to complete this account of teacher expectations, we turn to factors that might influence expectations – what Braun (1987) calls 'input factors'. One of the main concerns about teachers' expectations is that they may be based on a feature such as the child's ethnic group or gender, they may be inaccurate and stereotypical with respect to pupils' academic potential, and this may in turn have a deleterious effect on the child's educational progress. A meta-analysis of North American research suggests that teacher expectations are to some extent influenced by social class and race, but less often by gender (Dusek & Joseph, 1985).

It was possible in the Institute of Education longitudinal study to test the extent to which expectations were affected by gender and ethnic origin (see Tizard et al., 1988). In order to research these connections it is important to control for children's abilities and school achievements. Three sources of knowledge were collected: first, information on child characteristics including gender and ethnic origin; second, children's academic achievement; and, third, teachers' expectations. As part of the study, a novel method was used to assess the match or mismatch between expectation and children's attainment. Each child was given an expectation rating by the teacher in terms of above average, average and below average (as described above). Children were then ranked from high to low on the basis of their test scores and put into three groups – above average, average, and below average – the same size as the three expectation groups. A mismatch or misclassification was said to have occurred when the teacher expectation rating was not the same as the test rating. Results were calculated separately for maths and reading and for the four groups in the study – black boys and girls and white boys and girls.

For reading there was no evidence of mismatch or misclassification in relation to gender or ethnic group but there was in the case of maths. As can be seen in Table 10.3, teachers' expectations for black boys during Year 2 (top infants) were high relative to their test scores, that is, more were put in the top group by their teachers, and fewer in the bottom group, than would have been expected from their test results. On the other hand, expectations for white girls were low, in the sense that more were put into the average group when on the basis of their test results we would have expected them to be in the top group. The black boys were therefore overestimated and the white girls underestimated.

These are complex results that require careful and cautious interpretation. Overall the white girls in comparison to the other three ethnic/gender groups appeared to be more 'invisible' to teachers (Tizard et al., 1988). As a group, they received less disapproval and criticism from the teachers than did the other children, but also less praise. They were less often said to have behaviour problems. They were less likely to say they found school interesting (see Tizard et al., 1988). All this may indicate that the teachers' perception of white (mostly working class) girls is less well developed than that of other groups and, accordingly, their expectations, at least in maths, are less accurate.

TABLE 10.3 Mismatch between teacher expectations and test results for maths, by ethnic group and sex (top infants)

Teacher expectations	White boys (n = 95)		White girls (n = 82)		Black boys (n = 50)		Black girls (n = 49)	
	Expect. %	Test %	Expect. %	Test %	Expect. %	Test %	Expect. %	Test %
Above average	38	39	24	38	46	26	39	33
Average	39	42	56	39	30	44	43	51
Below average	23	19	20	23	23	30	18	16

The results concerning white girls are worrying when set alongside other results from the same study concerning the girls' self-assessments of academic attainment. The white girls were the least likely of the four groups at 11 years to consider themselves better than others at reading, and at 7 and 11 years were more likely to underestimate themselves in both reading and mathematics. At 16 years the white girls still underestimated themselves in English (Blatchford, 1997). Other self-report data at 11 years also showed that white girls were more likely to say they did not like maths because it was not interesting to them, and were more likely to say they were not pleased with their work because of their ability (Blatchford, 1997). Whilst the causal connections involved are difficult to disentangle, it is interesting that long-term underestimation by this group of children appears to be preceded in the early school years by lower teacher expectations. It might also be worth noting that the long-term attainments of these girls at 16 years were poor in terms of GCSEs. There has been much comment on the tendency of girls to have less confidence in schoolwork than boys (Meece & Courtney, 1992). Here this trend seems true of just the white girls, not the black girls. These results on London children indicate that gender and ethnic origin need to be considered together.

Teachers' expectations may be based on factors other than ethnic group and sex. There is some evidence that teachers tend to have lower expectations of children with non-standard English and lower verbal skills (Brophy & Good, 1986; Rist, 1970). It has also been found that expectations can be affected by children's social-class background (e.g. Baron et al., 1985; Dusek & Joseph, 1985). There is some indication from early research that placement of children into ability groups in school is affected by socio-economic status (Barker Lunn, 1970). Brophy (1983) and Cooper (1979) conclude that teachers are more likely to have lower expectations of children with problem behaviour, particularly when it threatens control of the class. There are also a number of suggestions that teachers tend to have higher expectations of children who are more physically attractive. Studies have found that attractive children are seen as possessing a higher IQ, greater educational potential and more interested parents than less attractive children (Clifford & Worstyer, 1973, in Braun, 1987). Crano and

Mellon (1978) found that teachers had higher expectations of children who they thought were a pleasure to have in the class.

Once again it is important to assess the influence of these 'input' characteristics on teacher expectations, while controlling for student achievement. In the longitudinal study, just described, the mismatch between teacher expectations and tested performance was examined in relation to four factors:

1. children's verbal skills, as measured by the Wechsler Pre-school and Primary Scale of Intelligence Vocabulary sub-test scores, assessed at the point of school entry;
2. parental income (a measure of home circumstances);
3. whether children were seen by teachers as having a behaviour problem that interfered with their learning;
4. whether children were seen as a pleasure to teach.

Of these four, two were found to be connected: first, children who had higher verbal skills were misclassified upwards (that is, expectations were higher than would be expected from test scores) and, second, children who had worse verbal skills and were not seen as a pleasure to teach were misclassified downwards (that is, expectations were too low relative to tested attainment). These results suggest that the personal relationships between teacher and child, as well as attributes of the child, can affect judgements about a child's academic potential and that this can be over and above the child's actual attainment.

Conclusions

So how strong is the evidence of a teacher expectancy effect? Evidence from experimental, naturalistic quantitative studies and case studies indicates that there is an average expectation effect over and above what might have been expected when considering the judgements based on pupils' existing achievements. However, research indicates that the effect is likely to be found in some teachers more than others (Babad, 2009; Brophy, 1985).

This chapter has been concerned with ways in which expectations are formed and what effects they have. As Rogers (1998) has pointed out, the literature has been less clear on why these things happen. Some insights come from psychological theory, as we saw above, for example, with regard to explanations such as ego defence (teachers have low expectations of pupils in order to protect themselves from the possibility of being seen as failing). Perhaps the key message to emerge from the more recent work of Weinstein (2000) and McKown et al. (2010) is this: expectancy effects work for some teachers, for some subgroups, in some settings, under some conditions. The main task therefore for future research is to clarify the conditions under which expectancies are heightened or minimized. We need to address the qualities of teachers, schools and students that predict susceptibility to expectancy effects.

The main implications for education policy would be that we need to rethink the common belief systems of teachers about pupil capabilities. In line with what has been said above, we need to encourage 'incremental' over 'entity' views of children's abilities, encourage the development of effort-based learning and encourage teachers to feel that lower attaining pupils can learn. This is not just about teachers; as important, we need to encourage students to develop similar effort-based beliefs about intelligence and their own abilities, and we need to shift to school cultures that emphasize perception of potential not ability.

But this raises important questions about the broader context of expectations in schools. If we are to take an active as well as an analytical view of expectations we need to be concerned with how expectations work in the context of schools today and how psychological theories and explanations can be used to help students.

Weinstein locates the expectancy effect in commonplace features of teaching that can go unchallenged. She argues that the education system in the USA is largely built on beliefs and practices that emphasize negative aspects of pupil development and stress differences in, and limits to, individual children's abilities. She argues that expectations of ability are 'too low, too narrowly construed, too bound in time and speed and too differentiated (high for some, low for others) by social status factors that are irrelevant to the potential to learn' (Weinstein, 2000, p. 1). As a consequence of responding to individual differences between children we lower expectations, provide inferior educational opportunities and underestimate the capacity of all children to grow intellectually. Given the growing diversity of children attending schools, Weinstein argues very forcibly that we need to support a different pedagogical vision that sets out to maximize the educational achievement of all children.

Weinstein criticizes much psychological research on teacher expectations because it has prioritized short-term consequences and evidence in terms of individual teachers and specific interactive behaviours in classrooms and neglected the way that expectations are reinforced by classroom cultures and institutional arrangements in classrooms, schools, families and wider society. Psychological research has therefore concentrated too much on intra- and inter-personal perspectives rather than social and institutional factors involved in self-fulfilling prophecies.

From this point of view much research has only scratched the surface of the powerful but subtle contextual ways in which the expectancy effect works. Much research has also been short-term when the processes connected to expectation effects are cumulative over school careers. We therefore need more attention to these longer-term school-wide influences, e.g., in school culture, grouping practices, and differentiation for learning.

References

Anderman, E.M. & Maehr, M.L. (1994). Motivation and schooling in the middle grades. *Review of Educational Research,* 64(2), 287–309.

Babad, E. (2009). *The Social Psychology of the Classroom.* Abingdon, UK: Routledge.

Babad, W. & Inbar, J. (1981). Performance and personality correlates of teachers' susceptibility to biasing information. *Journal of Personality and Social Psychology,* 40, 553–561.

Barker Lunn, J.C. (1970). *Streaming in the Primary School.* Windsor: NFER.

Baron, R.M., Tom, D.Y.H. & Cooper, H.M. (1985). Social class, race and teacher expectations. In Dusek, J.B. (Ed.), *Teacher Expectancies.* London: Erlbaum.

Beez, W.V. (1968). Influence of biased psychological reports on teacher behaviour and pupil performance. *Proceedings of the 76th Annual Convention of the American Psychological Association,* 3, 605–606.

Blatchford, P. (1996). Pupils' views on school and school work from 7 to 16 years. *Research Papers in Education,* 11(3), 263–288.

Blatchford, P. (1997). Pupils' perceived academic attainment at 7, 11 and 16 years: effects of sex and ethnic group. *British Journal of Educational Psychology,* 67, 169–184.

Blatchford, P., Burke, J., Farquar, C., Plewis, I. & Tizard, B. (1989). Teachers' expectations in infant school: associations with attainment and progress, curriculum coverage and classroom interaction. *British Journal of Educational Psychology,* 59, 19–30.

Braun, C. (1987). Teachers' expectations. In Dunkin, M. (Ed.), *International Encyclopaedia of Teaching and Teacher Education* (pp. 598–605). Oxford: Pergamon.

Brophy, J. (1983). Research on the self-fulfilling prophecy and teacher expectations. *Journal of Educational Psychology,* 75, 631–661.

Brophy, J. (1985). Teacher–student interaction. In Dusak, J.B. (Ed.), *Teacher Expectancies.* London: Erlbaum.

Brophy, J. & Good, T. (1986b). Naturalistic studies of teacher expectation effects. In Hammersley, M. (Ed.), *Case Studies in Classroom Research.* Milton Keynes: Open University.

Cooper, H.M. (1979). Pygmalion grows up: a model for teacher expectation communication and performance influence. *Review of Educational Research,* 49, 389–410.

Cooper, H.M. (1985). Models of teacher expectation communication. In Dusek, J.B. (Ed.), *Teacher Expectancies.* London: Erlbaum.

Crano, W.D. & Mellon, D.M. (1978). Causal influence of teachers' expectations on children's academic performance: a crossed lagged panel analysis. *Journal of Educational Psychology,* 70, 39–49.

Darley, J.M. & Fazio, R.H. (1980). Expectancy confirmation processes arising in the social interaction sequence. *American Psychologist,* 35, 867–881.

Dusek, J.B. (Ed.) (1985). *Teacher Expectancies.* London: Erlbaum.

Dusek, J.B. & Joseph, G. (1985). The bases of teacher expectancies. In Dusek, J.B (Ed.), *Teacher Expectancies* (pp. 229–250). London: Erlbaum.

Dweck, C. (1986). Motivational processes affecting learning. *American Psychologist,* 41, 1040–1048.

Dweck, C.S., Davidson, W., Nelson, S. & Enna, B. (1978). Sex differences in learned helplessness II: the contingencies of evaluative feedback in the classroom: an experimental analysis. *Developmental Psychology,* 24, 268–276.

Eccles, J. & Wigfield, A. (1985). Teacher expectations and student motivation. In Dusek, J.B. (Ed.), *Teacher Expectancies* (pp. 185–226). London: Erlbaum.

Goldstein, H. & Blatchford, P. (1998). Class size and educational achievement: a review of methodology with particular reference to study design. *British Educational Research Journal,* 24, 3.

Hall, V.C. & Merkel, S.P. (1985). Teacher expectancy effects and educational psychology. In Dusek, J.B. (Ed.), *Teacher Expectancies*. London: Erlbaum.

Hargreaves, D.H., Hestor, S.K. & Mellor, F.J. (1986). A theory of typing. In Hammersley, M. (Ed.), *Case Studies in Classroom Research* (pp. 180–209). Milton Keynes: Open University.

Jussim, L. (1986). Self-fulfilling prophecies: a theoretical and integrative review. *Psychological Review*, 93(4), 429–445.

Keddie, N. (1971). Classroom knowledge. In Young, M.F.D. (Ed.), *Knowledge and Control*. London: Collier Macmillan.

McKown, C., Gregory, A. & Weinstein, R.S. (2010). Expectations, stereotypes, and self-fulfilling prophecies in classroom and school life. In Meece, J.L and Eccles, J.S. (Eds), *Handbook of Research on Schools, Schooling and Human Development*. New York: Routledge.

Meece, J.L. & Courtney, D.P. (1992). Gender differences in students' perceptions: consequences for achievement-related choices. In Schunk, D.H. & Meece, J.L. (Eds) *Student Perceptions in the Classroom*. Hillsdale, NJ: Lawrence Erlbaum.

Mortimore, P., Sammons, P., Stoll, L. & Ecob, R. (1988). *School Matters: The Junior Years*. Wells, UK: Open Books.

Peterson, P.L. & Barger, S.A. (1985). Attribution theory and teacher expectancy. In Dusek, J.B. (Ed.), *Teacher Expectancies* (pp. 159–184). London: Erlbaum.

Pintrich, P.R. & Schunk, D.H. (1996). *Motivation in Education: Theory, Research and Applications*. Englewood Cliffs, NJ: Prentice-Hall.

Rist, R. (1970). Student social class and teacher expectations: the self-fulfilling prophecy in ghetto education. *Harvard Education Review*, 40, 411–451.

Rogers, C. (1982). *A Social Psychology of Schooling: The Expectancy Process*. London: Routledge & Kegan Paul.

Rogers, C. (1998). Teacher expectations: implications for school improvement. In Shorricks-Taylor, D. (Ed.), *Directions in Educational Psychology*. London: Whurr.

Rosenthal, R. & Jacobson, L. (1968). *Pygmalion in the Classroom: Teacher Expectation and Pupils' Intellectual Development*. New York: Holt, Rinehart & Winston.

Rubie-Davies, C. (2006). Teacher expectations and student self-perceptions: exploring relationships. *Psychology in the Schools*, 45(5), 537–552.

Schmuck, R.A. & Schmuck, P.A. (1983). *Group Processes in the Classroom* (Fourth edn). Dubuque, IA: William. C. Brown.

Sharp, R. & Green, A. (1975). *Education and Social Control: A Study in Progressive Primary Education*. London: Routledge & Kegan Paul.

Shulman, L.S. (1986). Paradigms and research programs in the study of teaching. In Wittrock, M.C. (Ed.), *Handbook of Research on Teaching* (Third edn). New York: Macmillan.

Swann Report (1985). *Education for All: Final Report of the Committee of Inquiry in Education of Children from Ethnic Minority Groups*. London: HMSO.

Tizard, B., Blatchford, P., Burke, J., Farquhar, C. & Plewis, I. (1988). *Young Children at School in the Inner City*. Hove, UK: Erlbaum.

Webster, R. & Blatchford, P. (2013). The educational experiences of pupils with a Statement for special educational needs in mainstream primary schools: results from a systematic observation study. *European Journal of Special Needs Education*, 28(4), 463–479.

Weinstein, R. (1976). Reading group membership in first grade: teacher behaviours and pupil experience over time. *Journal of Educational Psychology*, 68, 103–116.

Weinstein, R. (1998). Promoting positive expectations in schooling. In Lambert, N.M. & McCombs, B.L. (Eds), *How Students Learn: Reforming Schools Through Learner-Centred Education.* Washington, DC: American Psychological Association.

Weinstein, R.S. (2002). *Reaching Higher: The Power of Expectations in Schooling.* Cambridge, MA: Harvard University Press.

Wineburg, S. (1987). The self-fulfillment of the self-fulfilling prophecy. *Educational Researcher,* December.

11
DIFFERENCES IN CLASSROOM INTERACTION IN RELATION TO GENDER

In September 2013 the General Secretary of the UK Teachers and Lecturers Union, Mary Bousted, wrote an article in the *Times Educational Supplement* in which she said that boys were being allowed to dominate the classroom with little intervention from adults. She wrote:

> You might say, 'well maybe, but not in my classroom'. If that is your reaction, please do one thing. Make an audio recording of your lesson (better than filming because it is less intrusive) and replay it, counting up the number of times that boys and girls have spoken. I did, and the results shocked me. As a good feminist, I thought that my classroom was a haven of equal opportunities. It was not. It was a place where five boys dominated speaking time, spoke for longer when they answered a question, and disrupted the answers of girls and quiet boys.

She added that it could be 'dangerous for girls to be assertive, speak confidently, take up class talk time or defend their opinions' because they could become targets of abuse. There is an almost innate sense of how the sexes should behave, reinforced by peer pressure, and girls who defy this expectation can be vilified by boys and girls. She argued that schools could do more to tackle this inequality but that this ingrained inequality between the sexes far outweighs exhortations to equality by schools and society.

In this chapter we address evidence that in many regards supports the comments made by Mary Bousted. We will explore sex differences in classroom interactions between children and their teachers, and connections with academic performance.

One of the most important and topical debates at present in education concerns the relatively recent advance of girls over boys in academic performance, at least in the UK. From the point of view of classroom interaction, there is something of a central puzzle, which serves as a theme running through this chapter. We shall see below that boys get more attention from teachers and engage in more interactions with them, in comparison to girls, and yet over the last decade or so they seem overall to be doing less well academically. The debate about sex differences in classroom interaction has shifted from a concern with the possible disadvantages suffered by female students to a concern with, and something of a mystery about, the failing male student.

Gender differences are not the only way in which groups of pupils differ from each other. There are also differences in relation to attainment, ethnicity and social class, and whether or not children have special educational needs or not. We could have extended this chapter to include these other group differences but this would have required too large a coverage. It is also worth noting that Howe and Abedin (2013), in a systematic review of all the possible pupil characteristics that have been examined in relation to classroom dialogue, found that gender was by far the most common characteristic examined in research. Nevertheless we also need to recognize that gender differences can interconnect with other group differences like ethnicity and we briefly consider this at the end of the chapter.

Better understanding of influences on the relative performance of boys and girls is a main challenge for educational research, with important theoretical and practical implications. Exploration of the links between sex differences, classroom interaction and academic achievement is also important because it is one way of assessing the extent to which interactions in educational settings impact on learning and educational progress.

In this chapter we are concerned with two main questions:

1. Are there differences between girls and boys in their academic interactions with teachers?
2. What is the role of such interactions in the educational achievement and progress of boys and girls?

In line with the overall concern of this book with interactions in school, this chapter will focus on the role of teaching and classroom interactions, but we also look at ways in which other factors such as self-perceptions, self-concept and motivational processes and peer pressure help inform gender differences in interaction and achievement.

The educational attainments of girls and boys

In order to provide a background to the discussion of classroom interactions we need, first, to briefly review information on the relative performance of boys and girls during the school years. Given that much of the literature on classroom interaction that we will be reviewing stems from the UK, here we concentrate on school achievements in the UK, and more specifically England. There have been for a number of years a National Curriculum and accompanying assessment arrangements, which means that students have been faced with assessments at the end of each of the first three 'Key Stages', that is, at 7, 11 and 14 years (though testing has been dropped recently at 14 years and further changes are due to be made), and at the end of Key Stage 4, at 16 years, pupils take GCSE exams. At 18 years they take 'A level' exams. All of these assessments are nationally implemented and results broken down by gender, and so we have a very clear idea about the school attainments of boys and girls, probably more so than any other country.

Results in this section are largely drawn from a helpful and comprehensive government report on gender and education (DfES, 2007). In English, girls far outperform boys, and the gap grows with each Key Stage; the percentage gender gap in achieving the expected level at each Key Stage in reading is 9% at Key Stage 1, 11% at Key Stage 2 and 15% at Key Stage 3, in favour of girls. Although there is some evidence for a narrowing of the gender gap between 1997 and 2006, the difference between girls and boys in English is still very marked indeed. In maths, boys have traditionally performed better than girls, but over the last decade or so girls have performed slightly better than boys at Key Stages 1 and 3. Results for science show very little difference between boys and girls and this has been stable over time.

Results at 16 years have national importance as a landmark measure of pupil and school performance, and in England a key threshold of success is taken to be the percentage of pupils in a school who gained five or more GCSEs or equivalent. Exploration of trends over time from 1962 to 2006 (DfES, 2007) shows that between 1968 and 1986 there was little difference between the sexes, but that since 1988 a significant gap in favour of girls has opened up, with the percentage of girls receiving five GCSEs in 2006 being 63.4% and boys 53.8%. Moreover, girls do better than boys in the majority of GCSE subjects, with the exceptions being chemistry (no difference) and physics and biological sciences (boys very slightly better). A similar situation exists at the time of writing (2014).

Exam results at 18 years are interesting. Girls are now more likely to be entered for A levels – a contrast with the 1950s and 1960s when only a third of A level entries were by girls. Gender differences in subject choices are more marked at 18 than earlier years, with girls particularly likely to choose English and unlikely to choose physics. In terms of pass rates, these are narrower than at 16 years, with an inconsistent pattern over time.

As for data from other countries, Leaper (2013), in a comprehensive review of gender development during childhood, draws on US Government statistics to show that females tend to attain higher levels of education from elementary school through to college. In addition more women than men attain undergraduate and MA degrees. Although males tended to outperform females in mathematics and life sciences this difference has narrowed over the years. Stromquist (2007) provides an international perspective on sex differences in attainment in reading, maths and science. Perhaps in contrast to the UK, in many countries girls have historically lagged behind boys, but the main trend across many countries was for a gradual convergence of boys and girls. The British Government report referred to above (DfES, 2007) also reports international evidence from the OECD-run Programme for International Student Assessment (PISA). In general these results show that girls have significantly better reading scores than boys across almost all countries in the OECD; in maths boys were ahead of girls in half the countries but there were no differences in the other half; and in science there were no gender differences.

Younger et al. (2005) and the DCSF (2009a) argue that despite the legitimate concern regarding the average academic performance of boys, it is crucial when seeking for explanations to hold in mind three points about the data on pupil performance:

1. Achievement test scores through school have been rising over time, but girls' performance has taken off in a more pronounced fashion.
2. There is diversity within the broad gender groups so that many boys in fact achieve to a high level, and conversely there are some girls who achieve poorly and who risk being missed in the face of overriding concern with boys' underachievement.
3. The achievement gaps for gender are often not as wide as those for ethnicity and social class. Strand (2008) calculated that the percentage gap in 5+ A*–C including English and maths was 7% for gender, 28% for ethnic group and 57% for socio-economic class.

Nevertheless, the overall findings on average attainment levels for boys and girls have led to worldwide concern about the performance of boys, with many commentators and the media regularly worrying about the underachievement of boys. Younger et al. (2005) point out that similar concerns are expressed in Australia, the USA, Belgium, Sweden and Germany. Despite the caveats about overstressing the gender gap, and despite important caveats when seeking to understand the evidence on gender differences in academic performance, there is a persistent and strong finding of differences between boys and girls and considerable evidence of relative underachievement on the part of at least some boys. It is also interesting that this gap seems to have become more pronounced over recent years, certainly in the UK. There is therefore something important that needs to be accounted for.

There have been a number of explanations for the gender gap, including changes in assessment regimes; the introduction of coursework; neurological differences between boys and girls; the predominance of female teachers, especially at primary level; and mixed-sex classes, though these do not appear to explain the historical shift in favour of girls (see DfES, 2007; DCSF 2009a). One explanation for the developing gender gap commonly expressed is the way the curriculum has become more friendly to girls, and this has led to the possible strategy of a more boy-friendly curriculum. But this explanation, as Moss (2007) has pointed out, is probably wrong and the suggested strategy that follows from it is accordingly misguided.

Gender differences in classroom interaction

In this section we look at the evidence for gender differences in classroom interaction. Are girls and boys treated differently? Do they have different educational experiences? If so, what implications do these have for later development and educational achievements?

There has been a strong tradition of sociological work on the construction of masculinities, peer cultures and the use of language, which have been influential in understanding gender differences in schools, along with many other social and cultural influences in the creation of gender identities (see Moss, 2007; Arnot et al., 1998). But in this chapter, consistent with the theme of the book, we will for the most part concentrate on observation studies of the interactions between teachers and pupils in school contexts, because they provide perhaps the clearest evidence on whether teachers' interactions with girls and boy students do in fact differ. An effort has been made to update the earlier literature review in the first edition (in 2000), but despite the widespread recognition of the importance of gender differences in academic attainment in schools, this has not been matched by many recent studies of classroom interaction. Stromquist (2007) has provided a valuable international review. She found that most studies have been conducted in English-speaking countries (UK, USA, Australia and Canada), and there are few studies from the developing world and no cross-national comparisons.

Much of the early interest in gender differences in teacher–pupil interactions was generated by a concern with the supposed underachievement of girls and an attempt to show ways in which they are disadvantaged at school through the quality and quantity of interactions with their teachers. A number of writers argued that the education system is in various ways implicated in the disadvantages that females suffer later in life. As Croll and Moses (1990) showed, the view has been that schools not only reflect the different sex roles in society but also emphasize traditional female roles and discriminate further against girls. Spender has often been quoted in this regard. She argued that boys receive much more attention from teachers than girls, and that gender imbalances are routine and so deeply ingrained that they occur even when teachers try to equalize attention (see Croll & Moses, 1990). However compelling this argument, we need to question whether it is supported by convincing evidence.

One early study in this tradition of research and argumentation, by Stanworth (1981), was interested in the extent to which gender was a salient factor in teachers' perceptions of their pupils. This study was based on interviews with teachers about their attitudes to particular pupils. One technique she used was to present to teachers of sixth form pupils (aged 16–18 years) a number of sets of cards bearing the names of two boys and one girl or two girls and one boy and then to ask teachers to choose children who were alike in some educationally important way. The number of times teachers paired pupils of the same sex was then calculated. It was found that male teachers were more likely to select same-sex pairs, and this is explained in terms of male teachers being much more likely to view the sexes as discrete groups. Stanworth also found that teachers were more attached to, and concerned for, boys and were more likely to reject girls. This applied to teachers of both sexes, but was more pronounced for male teachers.

One of the teacher interview transcripts used to illustrate this argument is as follows:

> Question: What were your first impressions of Emma?
> (Male) teacher. Nothing ically. I can only remember first impressions of a few who stood out right away: Adrian, of course; and Phillip; and David Levick; and Marion, too, because among the girls she was the earliest to say something in class. In fact, it was quite some time before I could tell some of the girls apart.
> Question: Who was that?
> (Male) teacher: Well, Angie, and her friends Leonore and Helen. They seemed rather silent at first, and they were friends, I think, and there was no way — that's how it seemed at the time — of telling one from the other. In fact, they are very different in appearance, I can see that now. One's fair and one's dark, for a start. But in the beginning they were just three quiet girls.
>
> (Stanworth, 1981, p. 27)

Stanworth argues that girls are more invisible than boys, particularly if they are quiet. She also documents differences in teachers' views about the future careers of boys and girls. Teachers were not so confident that girls would complete their A levels, and had stereotypical job expectations for girls – for example, that they would become a nurse, secretary or teacher. These careers did not match the girls' own aspirations. Marriage was often mentioned in the case of girls but never boys. Stanworth, like others, argued that it is only when a girl contradicts this pattern of behaviour that she is looked at differently by teachers, and noticed.

This early work is interesting – but much has changed in the world of work and education and teacher attitudes. It is also unclear whether teachers' perceptions and attitudes are reflected in actual classroom interactions. In this regard a possible imbalance between teacher perceptions and their classroom practice can also work in a different way. Although teachers may believe they treat girls and boys equally and may hold a very deliberate non-sexist view, with an accompanying philosophy of empowering girls, their classroom interaction may, as Mary Bousted at the beginning of this chapter found, still follow traditional lines, with boys dominating.

French and French (1984) used a more systematic methodology based on direct observation of primary-aged children. They obtained verbatim descriptions of a fourth year junior class (10–11 years) lesson. There were 16 boys and 13 girls and a male teacher. Observations were of a class discussion on 'What I do on Mondays and what I would like to do on Mondays'. French and French found that boys had more turns than girls (50 vs. 16), but report that the gender difference was due to a small group of four boys who tended to dominate classroom interactions with the teacher. French and French felt this dominance is not due to a bias on the teacher's part so much as due to interactional methods used by these pupils to get attention, and to the newsworthiness of their comments. These behaviours can be largely invisible to teachers who may be powerless to stop the dominance of classroom talk by some boys. Gender differences in classroom participation are therefore related to classroom management and control.

This suggests that teachers find it hard to avoid giving boys more attention. A kind of 'collaboration' between teachers and boys is also seen in the work of Swann and Graddol (1988), who show how teachers, in monitoring boys' behaviour for signs of potential trouble, and in the strategic positioning of children in places where they can be seen, can look at boys more (more 'gaze attention') and so bring about their greater involvement. The reason, therefore, that boys get more attention is because the teacher finds it difficult not to respond to certain children in the class, despite efforts to distribute attention evenly. The differences become apparent when interaction is analysed in fine detail, and teachers are probably not aware of any preference for boys.

One problem with the research so far considered is that sample sizes can be small (in the case of French and French, only one lesson), and the reliability of data is not often examined. It is possible that unusual cases, for example, where there is very much more attention paid to either boys or girls, can be seen as typical. For this reason it is important to also look at studies of sex differences which have used systematic observation methods, with larger and more carefully chosen samples, predetermined categories, systematic sampling of behaviour, and numerical analysis. This is not to say that such methods do not have limitations (see McIntyre & MacLeod, 1986), but they are well suited to provide quite precise estimates of the frequencies of main types of teacher interaction with boys and girls.

Given limitations of space, it is helpful to provide an overview of these studies, and Kelly (1988) has provided one of the best early reviews. She conducted a meta-analysis of 81 studies, mostly American, which had employed systematic observation techniques and where quantitative results were available. The main results have been adapted and are presented in Table 11.1.

This shows that, on average, girls received 44% of all interactions with their teachers, while boys received 56%. Boys in fact received more of almost all main categories of behaviour. They received more praise, more criticism overall and criticism for behaviour, more total questions and abstract or process questions, and more opportunities to respond. Much of this may be because boys also initiated more to teachers (though teachers also initiated more contacts to boys)

TABLE 11.1 Average percentage amount of teacher interaction with boys and girls

	Girls %	Boys %
Total teacher–pupil interaction	44	56
Total teacher initiated	44	56
Total pupil initiated	46	54
Total praise	48	52
Total criticism	35	65
Pupil volunteering, hands up	52	48
Pupil call outs	41	59
Process of abstract questions	43	57
Total response opportunities	44	56
Total questions	44	56
Criticism for behaviour	32	68

Source: Adapted from Kelly, 1988
Notes: Ratio variables

% correct answers praised
% wrong answers criticized
% response not followed by feedback } no difference
% praise for academic work
% wrong answers followed by second chance g > b
% criticism for behaviour b > g

and called out more. Interestingly, the one category where girls exceeded boys was volunteering and hands up – indicating that girls were actually keen to be involved. Kelly found that these differences applied to different countries, to different social class and ethnic groups, across different curriculum subjects and with both male and female teachers (though more so with male teachers).

With regard to age differences, she found a marked concentration of studies of younger children, particularly in US studies, over half of which involved children under 9 years of age. She detected some noticeable patterns with age. Girls at nursery school received only 41% of the teacher's attention, while slightly older girls of infant school age received almost their fair share of praise and also criticism. Infant boys, however, were taught more than girls. Girls in the 6–9 year age group received almost as much instruction as boys, but thereafter the amount of instruction declined markedly (Kelly, 1988).

Another helpful review of studies using systematic observation methods was conducted by Croll and Moses (1990). In contrast to Kelly, they reviewed UK studies – choosing five studies, only one of which was included in the Kelly meta-analysis. In three of these studies – the ORACLE research (Galton et al., 1980), One in Five (Croll & Moses, 1990), and the ILEA junior school study (Mortimore et al., 1988) – differences very similar to those reported in the Kelly meta-analysis were found. The percentage of individual teacher attention received by boys was 54% in the ORACLE study, 54% in the One in Five study, and 54% and 58% in the ILEA study (for the second and third-year juniors respectively). However, it is worth stating that in the ORACLE study, when all interactions were added (including whole-class contacts that dominate), boys and girls received very much the same amount of attention (51% and 49%).

There is some suggestion from Kelly's meta-analysis that sex differences in classroom interaction are more pronounced in the case of male than female teachers. This was deliberately tested by Merritt and Wheldall (1992) who also compared primary and secondary schools. In the primary sample there were 22 women teachers and 10 men, and in the secondary sample there were 21 men and 17 women. In contrast to other research their results indicate that there were no differences at primary level. However, at secondary level boys received more total positive, total negative and more total teacher responses overall than girls. Interesting differences were found for male and female teachers at secondary level. Male teachers were more likely to respond positively to boys' academic behaviour, while female teachers were more likely to respond negatively to boys' social behaviour. The authors interpret these results in terms of female teachers experiencing, and reacting more to, disruptive behaviours from boys, and that boys work harder for male teachers. However there appeared to be no differences overall in on-task behaviour.

More recent studies suggest a similar picture. A meta-analysis of 11 quantitative studies of classroom interaction in the USA corroborates Kelly's conclusions: teachers direct more negative behaviours (reprimands, criticism and behaviour warnings) to boys than girls (Jones & Dindia, 2004). Stromquist (2007) found extensive evidence that boys tended to monopolize teachers. She refers to earlier studies in the 1980s which found that boys tend to be more assertive, aggressive, competitive and outspoken, and because they command more attention teachers tend to give them more praise, criticism and feedback than they do girls. She finds that more recent studies report similar patterns, again reflecting what appears to be a robust finding over time. While girls tend to work together, boys tend to be more disruptive and dominate the classroom environment. Moreover, boys in general receive more attention than girls even in countries with very different social and political contexts. Another study by Klein also reports that teacher favouritism towards boys over girls, in terms of, for example, giving more attention, continues to be found (Klein et al., 2007, in Stromquist, 2007).

Younger et al. (1999) in a study of eight British secondary schools found that although teachers believed they gave equal treatment to boys and girls in support of their learning, boys still dominated, though the types of difference revealed a more nuanced picture. Boys tended to dominate certain classroom interactions, while girls participated more in teacher–student interactions that supported learning. Boys received more negative attention and asked fewer questions to solicit teachers' help; girls asked more academic questions, focusing on subject content and knowledge.

In line with what has already been said, Streitmatter (1994) in an ethnographic study found that even teachers committed to gender equality tended to have difficulties in practice – with some seeking to equalize their treatment of boys and girls, and others using differential treatment to seek to redress imbalances in interactions and gender-based attitudes. Similarly, a US study of three primary school teachers (Garrahy, 2001, in Stromquist, 2007) found that although teachers believed they were not influenced by gender, and thought that they responded to male and female students in the same way, they in fact favoured boys in some behaviours (e.g., the provision of examples in class) and girls in others (e.g., reading sessions). Class projects tended to reinforce gender expectations, and boys were permitted to speak out of turn, but not girls.

Myhill, Jones and Hopper (2007) found that girls, like high achievers, were more positively participatory in class – they were more likely to put their hands up and they were more likely to join in a collective response and less likely to be off task. Boys, on the other hand, were more likely to initiate task-related talk and shout something out that was relevant to the task. It seems that boys were less likely to follow normal conventions of classroom rules about when to speak in class. Given concerns with underachieving boys nationally and internationally these patterns of participation suggest that whole-class teaching approaches might be exacerbating the problem.

By way of summing up research on gender differences in classroom interaction, Howe (1997) provided a cogent overview:

> Probably the most striking point to emerge from the research is that contributions from boys predominate during classroom interaction. In whole class sessions where the decisions about who contributes are usually made by teachers, boys make more contributions than girls, and their contributions are usually more elaborate. They achieve their higher levels of contribution partly through activities within discussion sessions, for example, hand raising and restlessness, and partly through reputations for misbehaviour which led to greater monitoring by teachers. In small group work where rights to contribute are resolved between pupils, boys usually have the upper hand. They dominate the physical context, volunteering for practical demonstrations in science and controlling the mouse and keyboard in computing. They do the same where the emphasis is on talk. Research into oral assessment suggests that boys interrupt girls more than the reverse. Although interruption has not been studied in other contexts, the assertive rather than the negotiating style reported for mixed-sex work with computers suggests a similar pattern. In addition, boys ensure their dominance by establishing themselves as sources of help, for the research shows that boys are asked for help more than girls are.
>
> *(Howe, 1997, pp. 42–43)*

A recent extensive review also by Christine Howe (with Abedin, 2013) of 225 studies of classroom dialogue published between 1972 and 2011 found little to change the conclusion drawn in the earlier review (though 'dialogue' as defined in this later review is a more restricted concept). It found that boys were more likely than girls to respond to teachers' initiations and receive feedback from teachers, especially negative feedback (but also positive). They also conclude that most research supports the view that this gender imbalance is due to both pupil self-selection (e.g., boys calling out more than girls when not invited by the teacher) and teacher selection (e.g., boys being chosen proportionately more than girls when both groups had their hands up).

Connections between classroom talk and pupil learning/attainment

The question that we now need to return to is what the implications of these differences in classroom interaction might be for learning. On the face of things, the situation is puzzling. Although boys receive more attention than girls overall, they seem in the UK to be doing less well academically. And internationally, although the gap between boys and girls in academic performance is perhaps not as marked as in the UK, it is still important, as Stromquist reminds us, to ask why girls have been improving their academic performance when classroom interactions continue to be biased against them.

This raises questions about the educational significance of the contacts children have with teachers and seems to cast doubt on the rather simplistic assumption of many so-called process-product studies (see Dunkin & Biddle, 1974; Shulman, 1986) that educational attainment is directly linked to the quantity and quality of instruction. As Arnot et al. (1998, p. 26) conclude, 'Gender differences in classroom processes are therefore present but their significance for educational performance is not self-evident.'

One possibility is that the role of teacher–pupil interaction in educational progress is easily exaggerated. Children learn in a number of ways and the experience of more or different forms of teacher contact may not be significant. On the other hand, as Stromquist points out, we should not underestimate the indirect importance of classroom interactions, e.g., because they are an important influence on the opportunity to learn, which research (e.g., Finn & Zimmer, 2011) has found to be a significant correlate of science and maths achievement. Opportunity to learn can also be expected to influence self-confidence and self-respect through the visibility and recognition provided in classrooms.

Howe and Abedin (2013) point out that the change over the past forty years in academic performance, from a higher performance of boys to comparable or even higher average performance of girls, is not easily explained by gender imbalances in classroom interaction, given these have stayed broadly similar over the same time-frame. But they also point out that this does not mean that classroom dialogue is irrelevant to attainment. It is possible, for example, that over time girls have become more adept at compensating for the imbalance in classroom interactions.

It is not only through interactions with pupils that teachers have an influence. For example, having female science teachers can increase girls' interest in science (see Leaper, 2013). It appears that teachers can act as role models, and this may be significant, given that the vast majority of teachers in primary schools in the UK are female.

Teachers may also hold gender stereotypical beliefs about girls' and boys' abilities in particular subjects which, in the same way as teacher expectations examined in Chapter 10, might be expected to affect their teaching and pupil self-perceptions.

Moss (2007) carefully develops a modern feminist perspective on gender differences in academic attainment, grounded on extensive classroom observations. Drawing on the work of Elkjaer (1992), which focused on IT lessons in Denmark, she shows that the mistake often made – and relevant to this chapter – is to conflate the public dominance of boys in classrooms with their actual subject competence. The two are not the same. In summary, boys' approaches to learning may be adversely affected by their positioning for dominance in the peer group. This line of thought also helps reconcile the apparent advantages conferred on boys, e.g., through more teacher attention, with their poorer educational outcomes, at least in the case of some boys. This explanation links pupil self-perceptions, positioning within the peer group and teaching approaches, and we return to these connections below. What it is less able to do is to address why there has been an increased gap in recent times in the achievements of boys and girls.

Other factors related to gender differences

We now consider other processes that might help an understanding of differences in classroom interaction and educational attainment. There is a host of possible factors, many of which have been reviewed by Arnot et al. (1998), DfES (2007), Howe (1997), Powney (1996) and Stromquist (2007). They include curriculum content, the way subjects are taught, changes to assessment arrangements, school organization changes, biological and school peer cultural influences, school subject choices, and home influences.

One explanation, already alluded to, is the changing school workforce. In primary schools in the UK, there are now far more female teachers than male teachers and so boys do not have a male role model in their schools. The growing number of paraprofessionals in schools, who often have the role of supporting low-attaining pupils and those with SEN (often male), are almost exclusively female (Blatchford et al., 2012). It has also been pointed out that a larger proportion of boys in more recent years come from single-parent families and may not have male models in their home lives either.

Another possible explanation is the types of assessments in schools and the broader curriculum context. It might be argued that in the UK improvements in girls' performance coincided with the introduction of the National Curriculum in the late 1980s, as well as more emphasis on coursework. But this explanation has been disputed (e.g., in Arnot et al., 1998; DCSF, 2009b).

In this section we concentrate more on child factors such as self-perceptions and attitudes, self-concept and motivational processes because recent research has provided insights into connections between gender and academic interactions and performance. The choice of within-child factors also reflects our conceptualization of context: children and their surroundings influence each other. By examining individual differences we sharpen understanding of the effects that children have on their environments.

This chapter will not make much of biological differences between boys and girls. One reason for this is because Leaper (2013) has concluded that research on biological influences on gender-related variations in cognitive abilities is 'complicated, inconclusive, and often speculative'. But more importantly, biological differences are unlikely to be able to explain relatively recent changes in the gap between boys and girls and it seems we need to look elsewhere for an explanation.

Different ways of learning and knowing

One possibility, sometimes advanced to explain differential gender achievements, is that girls develop alternative and compensatory strategies that aid their learning and their measured attainments. So although boys may get more of a teacher's attention, girls find other ways to get information and learn.

At a general level, boys and girls seem to respond differently to school, with girls valuing the teacher's opinion of them, enjoying school more and spending more time improving what they produce (see review in DfES, 2007, p. 102). Boys and girls seem to respond differently to the materials and tasks given to them (Sukhnandan et al., 2000 in DfES, 2007), e.g., boys prefer non-fiction with pictorial representations and diagrams while girls prefer fiction, and it may be that this experience of narrative structure better equips girls for extended writing, and work in English. Boys' level of motivation in a topic also seems, more than girls', to relate to their engagement in and understanding of the work (Oakhill & Petrides, 2007, in DfES, 2007).

Arnot et al. (1998) review studies that indicate that girls and boys may have different 'ways of knowing'. They cite a study by Boaler (1997) of a year group of pupils in each of two schools over the period Year 9 to Year 11. The schools were in similar locations and had similar scores on tests of cognitive ability at the beginning of Year 9. However, the schools had different approaches, with one more traditional and textbook-led and the other more open and project-based, with an emphasis on process. Boys and girls had similar achievements in maths in terms of grades A–C in the more open school but girls significantly underachieved in the school with the traditional approach, particularly the girls in the top set. Interviews with pupils indicated that these girls were disaffected by the pace and competitiveness and wanted to understand and discuss things more. This is a study of only two schools but it seems consistent with the view that boys and girls prefer different ways of knowing, with girls preferring 'connected knowing' which builds on personal experience and integrates a wide range of understandings, while boys favour 'separate knowing' which is based more on impersonal procedures to establish truths. Arnot et al. (1998, p. 28) conclude that:

> Boys show greater adaptability to more traditional approaches to learning which require memorising abstract, unambiguous facts and rules that have to be acquired quickly. They also appear to be more willing to sacrifice deep understanding, which requires sustained effort, for correct answers achieved at speed.

Powney (1996) wonders whether students learn that only some kinds of responses are likely to succeed in achievement and assessment situations and that these favour conformity, being 'good' pupils, and not taking risks. Although alternative strategies may in other circumstances be more a sign of creativity, in school they can disadvantage children in achievement situations, and this may be more likely in the case of boys.

Fennema and her colleagues (e.g., Fennema, 1996) have argued that males and females learn differently and perform differently in mathematics. She argues that gender differences in the amount and type of interaction are not a major driving force so much as symptoms of existing and more fundamental gender differences. She concludes that classroom organization and instruction favour boys in maths. Competitive activities are more common in maths classes than cooperative activities, but the former encourages boys' learning while the latter encourages girls'. Fennema takes the view that 'autonomous learning behaviour' is important to success in maths but girls are less likely to be encouraged in this, partly because of their own preferences and partly because of social and teacher influences. In suggestions that are similar to the findings of Stanworth, Fennema argues that teachers' knowledge about boys who are successful is more accurate than girls who are successful, and that teachers think more about boys during instruction because they pressure teachers more.

However, the research evidence base for claims about different ways of knowing and learning appears rather slight. As Powney (1996) has said, we need more understanding about how boys and girls learn and the kind of peer pressure and supports that influence their approaches to learning. Psychologists have been studying for many years possible differences in a number of relevant areas. One topic has been cognitive style, with perhaps the most well-known distinction being between field-dependent and independent (Witkin et al., 1962), and impulsive/reflective styles, but the link between cognitive style and gender is not clear-cut. There has also been a lot of attention in recent years to the importance of pupils' different learning styles, and the implications this can have for teaching.

It is quite possible however that this line of enquiry is likely to be unproductive. Younger et al. (2005) found no evidence to support the notion that the dominant learning style of boys differs from that of girls, e.g., that more boys than girls favour kinaesthetic learning. Moreover, work on preferred learning styles is misconceived if it simply seeks to identify and teach to student dominant styles and in the process risks narrowing opportunities for learning. At heart is the questionable assumption that gender differences as expressed in classrooms are innate rather than learned, and still worse, then taking steps to help boys (or girls) in ways that simply reinforce these differences.

There are therefore clear dangers in exaggerating fixed, presumably intrinsic differences between boys and girls. Often cited claims like those of the Australian author and speaker Steve Biddulph that 'Girls are able to connect directly with subjects, but a boy can only connect with a subject via a teacher' (in Ontario Ministry of Education, 2004, in Moss, 2011) are not based on any credible research evidence and, as Moss (2007) points out, are a curious basis for professional practice.

Pupil attentiveness

We have seen that pupil attentiveness and engagement in class is a strong correlate of academic performance (e.g., Finn & Zimmer, 2011). In an Australian study, Hill et al. (1993, in Arnot et al., 1998) found that girls were rated as more attentive in class and this was positively related to achievement and progress. This has been found in other studies as well. So here attention and concentration are a likely explanation for differences in achievement.

Results from a large-scale study of pupils' progress in Key Stage 1 in England (part of the CSPAR class-size project, described in Chapter 8) found that girls in the first, reception, year were rated by teachers as more likely to concentrate in class, and, in findings which support the Australian research, this was highly related to attainment at the end of the reception year, and progress over it (Blatchford, unpublished). This research suggests one reason why achievement levels may differ, but it is less clear why differences have become more marked recently.

One possible overlap is between attentiveness and compliance. In this regard, one possible factor that might help explain the gender difference in teacher–pupil interaction stems from girls' experience of more adult structured activities at home and school (Huston et al., 1986, in Leaper, 2013), as a result of which they engage in more compliant behaviour. This kind of compliance may be connected to behaviours like listening and attentiveness that help girls perform better in school subjects. Interestingly, although teachers might favour this kind of compliant behaviour in class, research, as we have seen, in fact suggests that boys receive more attention than girls. It may therefore be that compliance can lead to girls being more likely to be ignored by teachers, perhaps because they are seen as of less potential concern, behaviourally and academically.

Pupil self-perceptions and attitudes to school

Research on self-concept and motivation has made a number of advances over the past twenty years (Pintrich & Schunk, 1996). It is widely recognized that earlier more general measures of self-concept and self-esteem were too global to be helpful. Hattie and McInman (1991), in a meta-analysis, found few differences in average self-concept scores for males and females. However, specific dimensions on which males scored higher were mathematics and physical ability self-concepts, and for females, verbal self-concept. The weak and inconsistent results from earlier studies on general self-concept measures may well have masked differences on sub-scales within global measures of self-concept. Marsh and colleagues found that pre-adolescent boys (grades 2–5) have higher self-concepts than girls in the areas of maths, general self, physical appearance and physical abilities, while girls have higher self-concepts in areas of reading and general school (see Crain, 1991). During adolescence (grades 6–10) girls tend to have higher scores on verbal, honesty/truthworthiness and same-sex relations areas, while boys have higher scores on physical abilities, physical appearance and maths areas. Hattie and Marsh (in Bracken, 1991) argue that males tend to be more inclined to be 'self-enhancers', while females are more likely to attribute negative concerns to themselves (they are 'self-verifiers'), though these differences may not be particularly evident until adulthood. Crain (1991) reminds us that these differences should not be overstated. Gender effects are actually quite small and account for little of the variation. She also concludes that it would not be warranted to intervene in educational settings in order to affect boys' and girls' self-concept, for example, to improve adolescent girls' physical appearance and ability self-concepts. By and large, boys and girls are more similar than different with regard to self-concept.

In a more recent meta-analysis of sex differences in specific self-concept domains, O'Mara (2008) found that results generally followed a-priori predictions about gender differences, i.e., maths, physical appearance, physical ability, emotional and in particular power/potency and leadership self-concepts favoured males, while verbal, behavioural conduct and in particular moral/honesty/trustworthiness self-concepts favoured females. Against expectation, social self-concept favoured males and creativity/artistic self-concepts were gender neutral. Males had slightly higher global self-esteem scores. Several specific self-concept domains became more significant with age for males: global self-esteem, emotional stability and power/potency; domains which became less significant with age were verbal, physical ability and creativity.

At a general level, it is often reported that there are well-established differences in boys' and girls' attitudes to schooling, especially in literacy. Sainsbury and Clarkson (2008, in DCSF, 2009b) found that girls were more positive about reading, more likely to see themselves as readers, and more likely to see readers as clever/intelligent, while boys were more likely to see readers as 'geeky nerds'. Girls were also more likely than boys to indicate that their friends were readers. These findings indicate that girls are more motivated to read than boys.

It is known that children's academic expectations and values predict their academic achievement and occupational aspirations (Eccles & Wigfield, 2002, in Leaper, 2013), e.g., beliefs about one's own ability are correlated with academic outcomes such as classroom participation and engagement in class and later career choices, and interest in academic subjects tends to predict performance in exams. Any gender differences in academic self-concepts therefore have important implications for girls' and boys' achievement.

Leaper (2013) reviews various meta-analyses to show that average differences in academic self-concepts tend to occur in different subjects, along predictable lines, with, e.g., higher scores amongst boys in maths. Else-Quest, Hyde and Linn (2010, in Leaper, 2013) found in their meta-analysis that boys had higher maths-related self-concepts in confidence, self-efficacy, perceived value and intrinsic motivation, with girls higher on maths anxiety. Leaper also reviews theories that might account for the development of these self-perceptions including gender schemas, gender goals and values.

Motivational processes

Motivational processes have been linked to gender differences in classroom processes and academic achievement. One view is that motivational styles can be seen as differing in main ways. One well-used distinction is between 'mastery' and 'performance' orientation. The argument is that students differ in the extent to which failure and success in academic work is attributed to external causes (e.g., teachers' explanations or classroom equipment) and internal factors such as their own effort. Girls are thought more likely to attribute success to external causes and failure to their own efforts.

Dweck's research has been influential in showing ways that teachers' feedback can affect pupils' feelings of 'learned helplessness'. Dweck et al. (1978) analysed types of feedback to girls and boys from teachers in elementary school. Negative and positive feedback to boys focused on conduct rather than academic aspects of their work. In contrast, girls received little criticism for their conduct and so most of the criticism was on the intellectual quality of their work. When teachers criticized children for the quality of work they were eight times more likely to attribute boys' problems to lack of effort – typically not making any overt attribution for girls' performance. Dweck et al. suggest that these differences in feedback might mean boys and girls develop different attributional patterns. If boys receive criticism focusing on their behaviour they may see negative feedback as about them rather than their academic ability. In addition, the emphasis on lack of effort in teachers' feedback may encourage boys to blame their academic failures on lack of effort. In contrast, if girls are criticized less, they may be less likely to attribute their failures to lack of effort and may come to attribute failures to lack of ability. Dweck et al. (1978) manipulated teacher feedback in a laboratory situation and found, as expected, that children who received a boy-type feedback had higher expectations for success and attributed failures to external factors and lack of effort than did children who received a girl-type pattern.

These results are described at length because of the wide currency they have in debates on gender differences. However, serious questions have been raised about the findings and interpretation. One factor concerns the often low frequencies of overt teacher attributions about quality of work. More fundamentally, as we alluded to in the last chapter, Eccles and her colleagues, as well as others, have not found that girls are more prone to learned helpless behaviours than boys (see Eccles & Wigfield, 1985). Also, observational studies have found that teachers give more work-related criticism to boys, rather than girls, and that the proportion of criticism given to work versus conduct is the same for boys and girls (Parsons et al., 1982, in Eccles & Wigfield, 1985). Kelly's meta-analysis of observation studies also showed that boys receive higher criticism for work and behaviour, and that boys did not get a higher proportion of praise for academic work than girls. These studies indicate that teacher feedback does not vary as would be predicted by Dweck, and that learned helplessness may not be gender-specific. Eccles and Wigfield (1985) conclude that 'we now believe that the typical experiences that children have with affective feedback and teacher attributions are not powerful determinants of their classroom motivation'.

Peer pressure

The attitudes that children have towards school work, and their self-perceptions, will develop in social and educational contexts. One significant context will be the peer group, and this is likely to become more influential in the secondary years. There is not space here to review this topic in depth. It is often said that within many schools there is peer pressure against seeming to be too good at schoolwork, and it can be difficult to persuade boys in particular that it is cool to want to learn at school.

In general, there is a good deal of research to suggest that it is more acceptable for girls to work hard at school and yet still be a part of the popular peer group, whereas boys have more pressure to adopt a 'cool' masculine image and this can conflict with working hard on academic work at school (Warrington et al., 2000, in Stromquist, 2007). It is commonly accepted that girls do not experience the same conflict of loyalty between friends and school (Forde et al., 2006, in DfES, 2007). Adherence to the traditional masculine peer culture may contribute to some boys' difficulties in school adjustment and overall school achievement (Renold, 2001 and Van Houtte, 2004, in Leaper, 2013).

Forde et al. (2006) review work to show that boys' sense of masculinity conceptualizes school work as feminine and therefore boys' sense of self-worth can become estranged from school success, and result in strategies like avoidance of work, disruptive behaviour, withdrawal of effort, and procrastination. This can serve to protect a boy's status in the peer group and also serve to deflect attention from failure to achieve (which in attributional terms might then be put down to lack of effort rather than lack of ability). But it can also serve to adversely affect academic performance. These defensive processes on the part of boys are reflected in their classroom behaviour and may well be a contributory factor behind the patterns of teacher–pupil interactions (e.g., in terms of more attention and more criticism of behaviour) that we saw earlier in this chapter. One problem with this, as already seen with other possible explanations of gender differences, is that they would need to account for changes over time in gender differences in attainment.

There is an interesting distinction made by Harris et al. (1993) between boys' and girls' perceptions of what schoolwork meant in terms of freedom and autonomy during lesson time. More girls than boys were found to interpret 'freedom' as an opportunity for self-expression and developing confidence in managing their work, while boys tended to see freedom as an opportunity to talk about things unrelated to work. There also appeared to be differences in perceptions of peer pressures. Girls tended to refer to the ability to ignore peers when they wanted to get on with their work and were more likely to do as the teacher wanted. It is likely that boys' attitudes, supported by peer group pressure, will be harder to change. If it is the case that they are implicated in male under-achievement at school then a main challenge of school improvement efforts will be to find ways of understanding and affecting peer group pressures. In this respect it has been found that gender-role conformity may be less evident when girls and boys receive peer support for academic achievement (Leaper, 2013).

There may be however a danger in oversimplifying effects of peer pressure by considering boys and girls as groups; it would be helpful to have more information on individual differences in the susceptibility to peer pressure, for example by considering a connection to temperament.

There is an obvious danger in over-simple accounts of gender differences in motivation, self-perceptions, academic achievement and classroom interaction. Insights into some of the subtleties of the forces at work, and into the important connections with peer relationships, classroom interaction and teaching approaches, have been provided by Gemma Moss (2007). Based on a two-year ethnographic study in four schools in London and Hampshire, the study examined gender and reading in the 7–9 years age range. Pupils were classified into three categories of readers: first, those who could read and did, second, those who could read but didn't, and third, those who couldn't yet read and didn't. Boys were under-represented in the first group, as might be expected, given the results on reading progress at school examined above. One common explanation for boys' relative lack of progress in reading, as we have seen, is that their preferences in reading are not represented in school texts and that they see too few men aspiring to be readers themselves. Moss found little support for either of these explanations. Instead, the explanation seemed to have far more to do with boys' reactions to proficiency judgements made about them as readers. These judgements are highly visible, e.g., through ability groupings in class, procedures for monitoring and tracking progress in reading, and the more limited use of resources accorded less able readers. The result of a low estimate of reading ability was often a restricted range of texts and less opportunity to develop their own reading preferences. These judgements will be made on boys as well as girls but boys far more than girls were likely to seek to escape the consequences of this categorization; girls seemed happier to go along with teacher judgements. The status accorded to children in class in relation to reading mattered differently for boys and girls: weaker girl readers seemed to find less contradiction between their teachers' judgement of their proficiency in reading and their sense of self-worth, while weaker boy readers would chose non-fiction books, not, as might be expected, as a rejection of 'feminine' narrative forms found in fiction books but because non-fiction texts allowed them still to claim expertise without requiring them to show proficiency in reading the text. Boys are more likely to demonstrate what they know about a subject, e.g., football, while the text itself is not given close attention. There are here subtle connections between peer relationships and the role for literacy that differ for boys and girls.

Younger et al. (2005) in a similar way concluded that some boys at primary as well as secondary schools will go to considerable lengths to protect their macho image and their sense of self-worth by indulging in non-conformist behaviours which hinders them, and often others in the class, from achieving at school work. They argue that it is crucial to understand how important it is for many boys to be accepted by other boys and to act in line with peer group norms, and this depends on a process of negotiation and the adoption of 'laddishness' in their behaviour as well as risk. This is expressed through behaviour, speech, dress and body language, often revolves around football culture, and often runs counter to the expectations and ethos of the school. Younger et al. point out that this is found again and again in very different parts of England, in urban and rural, poor and wealthy areas. Some boys, particularly those in the higher sets, can exist outside this peer culture, but others risk being marginalized or excluded.

Intriguingly they also argue that such disaffected boys are often 'key players' in affecting the 'tone and engagement of the whole year group' and can have significant influence on their peers, both male and female. This is an intriguing link with the idea of the 'key player' role introduced in Chapter 3, and suggests an interesting and important avenue for further enquiry into peer group status, learning and school academic achievement.

Homework

The peer group context may also be related to one out-of-school activity that is likely to impact in a direct way on school progress. It has often been said that girls are more likely to engage in more homework and do this more conscientiously than boys. If so, this matters because the Longitudinal Study of Young People (reported in DfES, 2007) found that pupils who did regular homework have higher attainments. Though we cannot impute causal direction from these findings, we also know that girls tend to do more homework. In the Families and Children Survey (FACS) of over 7000 11–16-year-olds, 78% of parents of girls, but only 61% of the parents of boys, said they did homework.

One study (Harris et al., 1993) looked at female and male student attitudes in three schools in traditional working-class areas. There appeared to be differences with regard to homework, and these appeared to be connected to attitudes in the wider community. There was a strong sense of men upholding a traditional distinction between work and time off work, and this was reflected in the attitudes of boys at school who maintained a similar distinction, spending time out of school with larger groups of friends, on sport, etc. Women were more likely to be seen as organizers, and even when holding a job as well were still likely to have a domestic role, and in this sense 'work', at home. Girls were also more likely to be with one other friend, do homework together and work at homework every night and at weekends.

Wider social and cultural influences

We have hinted in this section at the wider social and cultural influences that will condition pupil attitudes and self-perceptions. We have seen that it is necessary to explain what appear to be fairly recent changes in gender differences in school attainments.

The complexities involved can be seen when we see that social structural influences on gender differences in mathematics-related outcomes vary greatly between countries. Ekse-Quest at al. (2010, in Leaper, 2013) found in a meta-analysis that gender differences in maths achievement varied, with boys scoring higher in Saudi Arabia while in other countries, e.g., Sweden, there was no difference or girls scored higher. These differences seemed attributable to social structural moderators like the representation of women in higher education and representation in science professions.

One factor that might explain the historical changes in gender differences in school attainment is wider changes in employment which have been associated with problems faced by males. Whereas boys in traditional working-class areas in particular would once have moved as a matter of course into traditional manual employment when they left school at 16 years, these jobs may not now be available. They are then forced to compete for alternative employment, for example in the public sector, where they can be less successful than girls, who may be more attractive as employees. So the collapse of manufacturing industry may be one factor which has conspired to make working-class boys feel useless and unwanted. This line of reasoning is consistent with early sociological research (e.g., Hargreaves, 1967; Willis, 1977) which showed that children grouped in lower groups or sets could respond by reacting negatively to school and adopting anti-school activities. But while the older account accommodated employment patterns, sociological research suggests a worrying isolation of male culture from wider society. Connell (1989, in Arnot et al., 1998) and Mac an Ghaill (1994, in Arnot et al., 1998), for example, reach similar conclusions about the way that working-class boys who have been denied traditional male employment and forms of power reacted by adopting a kind of heightened masculinity and challenging of authority. In an attempt to regain control of their situation they took pride in sporting prowess, physical aggression and sexual conquest.

In more recent years it may also be that girls are changing their attitudes to future careers and becoming more confident and less inclined to adopt a domestic role and marriage, though this may well vary between girls (Arnot et al., 1998). Francis (2000, in Stromquist, 2007) found that there was more awareness of equal opportunities and more availability of jobs for females. There was also more awareness of the efforts girls have to make to succeed in the workplace and therefore more awareness of educational performance as a way of combating the inequalities that girls face.

We have clearly come a long way from pupil self-perceptions and concentration in class. But enough has been said to indicate that such self-perceptions are likely to be supported by powerful and entrenched social, cultural and structural factors, and this is why simplistic solutions are unlikely to be useful.

Interactions between gender and other group differences

The search for group differences in school achievement and classroom interaction is clearly a complex task, with many potentially confounding factors. In the case of group differences, as Connolly (2006, in DfES, 2007) argues, an 'interactions effects model' might be more appropriate, i.e., where differences between boys and girls are not the same across different social class and ethnic groups but there are particular (and complex) combinations of gender, social class and ethnicity that need to be taken into account when looking at differences in attainment. In a similar way, Strand (2008, in DCSF 2009b) indicates that the interplay between gender, social class and ethnicity is important when examining public exam results at 16 years in England.

An interaction effects model might also be important when examining classroom interactions. Mac an Ghaill (1988, in DfES, 2007) argued that black boys and girls may respond differently to racism, with black girls complying with formal rules but not withholding real engagement with the organization, while black boys are more likely to challenge the school culture directly and can therefore become excluded from school.

An interesting example of interactions between gender and ethnicity in relation to classroom interactions was found in an early detailed systematic observation study of London infant schools, based at the Institute of Education Thomas Coram Research Unit (TCRU). Four groups were studied throughout their schooling, from pre-school to 16 years – black boys and girls whose parents were of Afro-Caribbean origin, and white boys and girls whose parents were white indigenous. In terms of classroom interactions, there were no systematic differences in the total amount of academic interactions teachers had with boys and girls, or black and white children (Blatchford et al., 1987; Tizard et al., 1988), but in line with other research, boys received more criticism/disapproval (boys 55%, girls 45%) and more praise (boys 56%, girls 44%).

In this study of multicultural schools, the importance of examining ethnic and gender groups together was highlighted. White boys had the most academic interactions with their teachers, black boys least. Black boys engaged more in some 'task avoidant' behaviours: they showed more 'fooling around' with other children when the expectation was that they should be working (these differences were statistically significant). As we saw in Chapter 10, white girls seemed to be more 'invisible' to teachers, receiving the least disapproval/criticism and the least praise from teachers, while engaging in more 'procedural' matters, like getting materials or sharpening pencils when on their own (these results were statistically significant) – behaviour that can be a sign of avoiding work (without overtly avoiding the task) and also the teacher.

In this study (Tizard et al., 1988), pupil self-perceptions and attitudes to school were also studied and the importance of considering gender and ethnicity together was again indicated. A main concern was with pupils' perceptions of their own attainments, which can be considered to be one part of academic self-concept. There were differences between the two girl groups. To take the black girls first: at 11 years they had by far the highest self-ratings of their own attainments in English/reading, and at 16 years they showed a continued confidence in their attainments (Blatchford, 1997). Black girls had the highest Marsh SDQII general self-esteem scores, and also tended to have higher SDQII verbal self-concepts. More detailed analyses of individual items from the SDQII showed that black girls were also less likely than the other groups to say that nothing that they did turned out well, less likely to say that they were not good at reading, more likely to agree that things they did turned out well, more likely to disagree that nothing they did turned out well, and more likely to agree that they did most things well. So although there were important main effects for ethnic groups (Blatchford, 1997), results concerning some items reinforce the view that the black girls were the most confident group, and most positive about their performance in school work.

These results are consistent with those from ethnographic research in the UK. In a well-known study of a small group of black girls in a London secondary school (Fuller, 1984), they were found to be strongly committed to doing well at school, despite appearing disaffected from school in some respects.

But as we saw in Chapter 10, the results concerning white girls were quite different. They were the least likely of the four groups to consider themselves better than others at reading, likely to underestimate themselves in reading and maths, and were not pleased with their work because of their ability. These kinds of results have been reported for girls generally but here we found them only for the white girls.

These results, although intriguing, are rather dated now and indicate that one line of enquiry would be further exploration of pupil ability assessments and classroom interactions in relation to gender and ethnic group differences. The white sample in the TCRU study were also predominantly working class and relatively disadvantaged, and so social class may be a factor as well. It may be that underestimation by white girls is a form of defensive strategy used to preserve self-regulation. Further research could be directed at the links between group differences in underestimation and other motivational measures (see Blatchford, 1997).

More generally, these results on pupil self-perceptions indicate the complexity of attempts to explain gender differences in achievement in school. Reviews have pointed to the complex interconnections of gender, race and achievement (Powney, 1996); the present discussion indicates the value of an accompanying and more fine-grained analysis of self-perceptions and classroom interactions.

Conclusions

In this chapter we have looked at two main questions. In the first place we asked if there were differences in academic interactions at school involving boys and girls and their teachers. To sum up, the evidence from studies that have used systematic observation methods and numerical analysis shows a clear tendency for girls to receive less interaction than boys, though this is not true of all studies or classrooms. There is a suggestion that after the age of about 9 years girls receive progressively less instruction from teachers. These differences between boys and girls are not huge, and some of the claims made in the past about gender differences in teacher–child interaction do seem exaggerated. However, as Kelly (1988) reminds us, if these differences are added up over a child's school career – say 15,000 hours – this would mean something like 1,800 more hours will have been spent with boys than girls. She estimates that the average girl will end up with 30 hours less individual attention than the average boy.

If the interaction results are relatively clear, answers to the second main question addressed in this chapter are far less so. This concerns what effect these differences have on learning and educational progress. We have seen that there does not appear to be a direct link between gender differences in classroom interaction and gender differences in school progress. Indeed there is something of a puzzle. If the bias in favour of males in classroom interactions were mirrored in educational progress, we would expect girls to be at a disadvantage. This was indeed the background for much early research on this issue. But we have seen that recent changes make this linkage much more problematic. Gemma Moss has approached this dilemma in this way: 'Is the anomaly that of girls' success in a system weighted against them, or of boys' failure in a system which should work in their favour?' (Moss, 2007, p. 14). At the very least, it does seem to cast doubt on any simple linear connection between educational attainment and the quantity and even quality of instruction.

However, we have also argued that this is not to say that differences in classroom interactions are insignificant. They may be significant in ways that are not yet clear. There may also be an indirect link. It is possible that differences in classroom interaction between boys and girls are more likely to affect pupil attitudes – for example, in the science laboratory and when using computers the physical control by boys of apparatus and equipment may still disadvantage girls by putting them off and affecting their school subject choices and involvement in class lessons (Howe, 1997; Powney, 1996). It is also possible, though more speculative, that the different contributions of boys and girls to classroom conversations may have long-term implications for future careers. If it is true that boys are more likely to take part in classroom talk, are responded to more in public and have more experience of public speaking and claiming turns in classroom discourse, and that girls are more likely to listen, and to talk in more private contexts, then this might create the pattern for similar gender differences in the work place and possibly have a negative effect on career advancement.

We also need to be mindful of the argument that the relative improvements in girls' performance relative to those of boys does not mean that somehow pro-female perspectives have triumphed in schools. Following the recognition of the growing gender gap in measured performance there was something of a backlash – a moral panic even – with the blame for boys' relatively poor performance being placed on a feminized curriculum, a predominantly female teacher workforce, and so on. It is important not to approach the issue of boys' underachievement in terms of claims for female advantages. On the contrary, many of the targets of feminist concern have not changed, and girls may suffer inequalities in more subtle ways and at other stages in their education and employment.

One key theme to emerge from this chapter and the literature on boys' underachievement in schools is the importance of finding ways of addressing the commonly found conflict between prevalent masculine peer cultures and attitudes to school work. This requires us to challenge notions of gender itself at the whole-school levels. But it also seems to be best approached by educational strategies that benefit both boys and girls. Strategies to help address boys' underachievement in literacy have been found to be: well-targeted support for low-attaining groups that offers challenge while still maintaining self-esteem; classroom practice that helps children develop and share independent reading; support for writing that allows time to reflect with peers to ensure meaningful engagement with the task; and a collaborative environment in which pupils have opportunities to take responsibility as learners (DCSF, 2009b).

This chapter has also looked, albeit briefly, at two other types of group difference: attainment and ethnicity. Enough has been written to show that the influence of gender and other group differences, and potential interconnections between the categories, is clearly a complex area. Some examples of a statistical interaction between gender and ethnicity have been considered but this has barely scratched the surface of the background influences on gender and ethnic differences in school attainment; one would also need to address, for example, historical trends on immigration, cultural belief about education, parental support, family structures, and so on. Nevertheless, further examination of these interactions between groups is important, as results will inform strategies and approaches to tackle underachievement in schools.

With apologies for the predictability of the conclusion, it is clear that much more research is needed on a wide range of topics connected to gender differences in school interactions. Given the wide recognition of the scale of the problem of male underachievement in schools, there is some urgency to this task. Howe and Abedin (2013) point out that very little attention has been paid to pupil factors that might be influential on classroom interaction, including personality, but also that very little attention has been paid to the role of curriculum areas as a potentially influential contextual factor (though this has been addressed in insightful ways by Moss's ethnographic research on literacy). Another avenue for future research is more comparative studies of factors linked to gender differences, particularly connected to classroom interactions and pupil self-perceptions. Stromquist (2007) found no studies of this sort in the field.

References

Arnot, M., Gray, J., James, M., Ruddock, J. & Duveen, G. (1998). *Recent Research on Gender and Educational Performance.* Office for Standards in Education (OFSTED) Reviews of Research. London: Stationery Office.

Blatchford, P. (1997). Pupils' self-assessments of academic attainment at 7, 11 and 16 years: effects of sex and ethnic group. *British Journal of Educational Psychology, 67,* 169–184.

Blatchford, P., Burke, J., Farquhar, C., Plewis, I. & Tizard, B. (1987b). A systematic observation study of children's behaviour at infant school. *Research Papers in Education,* 2(1), 47–62.

Boaler, J. (1997). *Experiencing School Mathematics: Teaching Styles, Sex and Setting.* Milton Keynes: Open University Press.

Bracken, B.A. (Ed.) (1991). *Handbook of Self-Concept: Developmental, Social and Clinical Considerations.* New York and Chichester: Wiley.

Crain, R. (1991). The influence of age, race, and gender on child and adolescent multi-dimensional self-concept. In Bracken, B.A. (Ed.), *Handbook of Self-Concept: Developmental, Social and Clinical Considerations.* New York and Chichester: Wiley.

Croll. P. & Moses, D. (1990). Sex roles in the primary classroom. In Rogers, C. & Kutnick, P. (Eds), *Social Psychology of the Primary School.* London: Routledge.

Department for Children, Schools and Families (DCSF) (2009a). *Gender and Education: Mythbusters.* Nottingham: DCSF Publications.

Department for Children, Schools and Families (DCSF) (2009b). *The Gender Agenda Final Report.* Nottingham: DCSF Publications.

Department for Education and Skills (DfES) (2007). *Gender and Education: The Evidence on Pupils in England.* Nottingham: DfES Publications.

Dunkin, M.J. & Biddle, B.J. (1974). *The Study of Teaching.* Lanham, MD: Holt, Rinehart & Winston.

Dweck, C.S., Davidson, W., Nelson, S. & Enna, B. (1978). Sex differences in learned helplessness: the contingencies of evaluative feedback in the classroom: an experimental analysis. *Developmental Psychology, 124,* 268–276.

Eccles, J. & Wigfield, A. (1985). Teacher expectations and student motivation. In Dusek, J.B. (Ed.), *Teacher Expectancies* (pp. 185–226). London: Erlbaum.

Elkjaer, B. (1992). Girls and Information Technology in Denmark: an account of a socially constructed problem. *Gender and Education,* 4(1/2), 25–40.

Fennema, E. (1996). Scholarship, gender and mathematics. In Murphy, P.F. and Gipps, C.G. (Eds), *Equity in the Classroom: Towards Effective Pedagogy for Girls and Boys.* London: Falmer and UNESCO.

Finn, J.D. & Zimmer, K. (2011). Student engagement: What is it? Why does it matter? In Christenson, S.L., Reschly, A.L. & Wylie, C. (Eds), *The Handbook of Research on Student Engagement*. New York: Springer Science.

French, J. & French, P. (1984). Gender imbalances in the primary classroom: an interactional account. *Educational Research, 26*(2), 127–136.

Fuller, M. (1984). Black girls in a London comprehensive school. In Hammersley, M. & Woods, P. (Eds), *Life in School*. Milton Keynes: Open University.

Galton, M., Simon, B. & Croll. P. (1980). *Inside the Primary Classroom*. London: Routledge & Kegan Paul.

Hargreaves, D.H. (1967). *Social Relations in a Secondary School*. London: Routledge.

Harris, S., Nixon, J. & Ruddock, J. (1993). Schoolwork, homework and gender. *Gender and Education, 3*, 3–14.

Hattie, J.A. & McInman, A.D. (1991). Gender differences in self-concept: a meta-analytic review. Unpublished manuscript, University of Western Australia.

Howe, C. (1997). *Gender and Classroom Interaction: A Research Review.* Edinburgh: Scottish Council for Research in Education.

Howe, C. & Abedin, M. (2013). Classroom dialogue: a systematic review across four decades of research. *Cambridge Journal of Education, 43*(3), 325–356.

Jones, S. & Dindia, K. (2004). A meta-analytic perspective on sex equity in the classroom. *Review of Education Research, 74*(4), 443–471.

Kelly, A. (1988). Gender differences in teacher–pupil interactions: a meta-analytic review. *Research in Education, 39*, 1–23.

Leaper, C. (2013). Gender development during childhood. In Zelazo, P.D. (Ed.), *The Oxford Handbook of Developmental Psychology, Vol. 2: Self and Other*. Oxford: Oxford University Press.

McIntyre, D. & Macleod, G. (1986). The characteristics and uses of systematic observation. In Hammersley, M. (Ed.), *Controversies in Classroom Research*. Milton Keynes: Open University Press.

Meece, J.L. & Courtney, D.P. (1992). Gender differences in students' perceptions: consequences for achievement-related choices. In Schunk, D.H. & Meece, J.L. (Eds) *Student Perceptions in the Classroom*. Hillsdale, NJ: Lawrence Erlbaum.

Merritt, F. & Wheldall, K. (1992). Teachers' use of praise and reprimands to boys and girls. *Educational Review, 44*(1), 73–79.

Mortimore, P., Sammons, P., Stioll, L. & Ecob, R. (1988). *School Matters: The Junior Years.* Wells, UK: Open Books.

Moss, G. (2007). *Literacy and Gender: Researching Texts, Contexts and Readers*. Abingdon, UK: Routledge.

Moss, G. (2011). Policy and the search for explanations for the gender gap in literacy attainment. *Literacy, 45*(3), 111–118.

Myhill, D., Jones, S. & Hopper, R. (2007). *Talking, Listening, Learning: Effective Talk in the Primary Classroom*. Maidenhead, UK: Open University Press.

O'Mara, A.J. (2008). Methodological and substantive applications of meta-analysis: multilevel modelling, simulation, and the construct validation of self-concept. Unpublished thesis submitted to the University of Oxford for the degree of D.Phil.

Pintrich, P.R. & Schunk, D.H. (1996). *Motivation in Education: Theory, Research and Applications*. Englewood Cliffs, NJ: Prentice-Hall.

Powney, J. (1996). *Gender and Attainment: A Review.* Edinburgh: Scottish Council for Research in Education.

Shulman, L.S. (1986). Paradigms and research programs in the study of teaching. In Wittrock, M.C. (Ed.), *Handbook of Research on Teaching* (Third edn). New York: Macmillan.

Stanworth, M. (1981). *Gender and Schooling: A Study of Sexual Divisions in the Classroom.* London: Unwin Hyman.

Streitmatter, J. (1994). *Toward Gender Equity in the Classroom: Everyday Teachers' Beliefs and Practices.* Albany, NY: State University of New York Press.

Stromquist, N. (2007). The gender socialization process in schools: a cross-national comparison. Background paper commissioned for the *EFA Global Monitoring Report 2008, Education for All by 2015: Will We Make It?* Paris: UNESCO.

Swann, J. & Graddol, D. (1988). Gender inequalities in classroom talk. *English in Education,* 22, 48–65.

Tizard, B., Blatchford, P., Burke, J., Farquhar, C. & Plewis, I. (1988). *Young Children at School in the Inner City.* Hove, UK: Lawrence Erlbaum.

Warrington, M., Younger, M. & Williams, J. (2000). Student attitudes, image and gender gap. *British Journal of Sociology of Education,* 26(3), 393–407.

Willis. P. (1977). *Learning to Labour.* Farnborough, UK: Saxon House.

Witkin, H.A., Dyk, R.B., Faterson, H.F., Goodenough, D. & Karp, S.A. (1962). *Psychological Differentiation.* New York: Wiley.

Younger, M. & Warrington, M., with Gray, J., Ruddock, J., McLellan, R., Bearner, E., Kershner, R. & Bricheno, P. (2005). *Raising Boys' Achievement.* Department for Education and Skills Research Report (RR636 ISBN 1 84478 458 4). London: DfES.

Younger, M., Warrington, M. & Williams, J. (1999). The gender gap and classroom interactions: reality and rhetoric? *British Journal of Sociology of Education,* 20(3), 393–407.

12

A CONCLUDING NOTE

The developmental and social world of children in school

Writing this book about children's social lives in school has been a very rewarding task. It has enabled us to think about and present much of what we've been studying and teaching for a number of years, and it has given us opportunities to re-think what may have become familiar. These sorts of efforts are especially productive when they involve a collaboration between scholars. As we have argued throughout the book, when peers interact with each other around an interesting task, both learn a great deal. The conflicts and resolutions that are the inevitable product of these interactions lead to deeper and broader understanding.

Our joint efforts in this volume, as we outlined in the first chapter, were guided by a common orientation. Basically, we took a developmental perspective towards our study of children in schools. Correspondingly, we considered children's social and academic lives in schools to be inextricably linked. We have spelt out the implications of this position for schools. Most basically, schools for young children should be different places to schools for adolescents. What gets taught and how it gets evaluated should vary.

A second consequence of writing this book was the clearer recognition that it has real implications for public and educational policy. Schools, after all, are public places which are typically supported by the public through rates or taxes. Further, the end result of schooling – young adults taking their places in society – has an important societal impact, as the American philosopher John Dewey noted a hundred years ago.

Our concern in this book may appear at odds with some aspects of current education policy in many countries, with their concern with league tables of school exam results and accountability. But this may be looked at a different way. Specifically, psychologists and educational researchers have reasonably good knowledge about what works in schools and what does not. Rate and tax payers, parents and children deserve those educational programmes and policies which have withstood the rigours of empirical testing. These stakeholders in the educational process should demand no less, and they should hold educational policy makers and politicians accountable for their choice of programmes and policies. The case of breaktime is a good example of educational policy not being guided by data. Other aspects of children's educational experiences, such as the practice of discouraging peer or friendship interaction during academic lessons, is another practice not rooted in theory or data.

In this concluding note, we draw out a few key conclusions from what we have learned about, first, peer relations, and then teacher–pupil interactions.

Peer relations

The importance of children's social lives has been a central focus – and what we think is unique about our discussion of children in schools. One instance of this was framing children's social worlds in terms of a broader construct, social competence, and noting the differing demands and hallmarks of social competence as children develop from infancy to adolescence. Most broadly, social competence is expressed as children's adaptation to an environment. In schools, this includes interacting with peers (both friends and non-friends alike) and teachers, and the demands of the school curriculum. These social factors affect and are affected by more traditional measures of school performance, such as achievement. That we included separate chapters on social competence, friendships, teacher expect-ations, and teacher–student interaction highlights the depth and breadth of the issues involved here. A couple of examples of the interrelations between these social processes and achievement will highlight our argument.

Take the case of friendships. Friendships are relationships that provide mutual support and challenges for youngsters. Friends are very important to children, as they (and their parents) will readily tell us, yet they are typically not considered in traditional discussions of schooling. Not only do friendships relate (both posi-tively and negatively) to children's adjustment, but they also provide an effective context in which academic subjects get learned. As we noted in the chapter on friendship (Chapter 3), and also Chapter 7, when children interact with friends, compared to acquaintances, more productive learning can go on. This typically happens by friends interacting around a subject, disagreeing about their interpre-tation and resolving the disagreement. This process enables youngsters to reflect upon the processes constitutive of the subject matter at hand.

Social relationships between peers also interconnect with academic aspects in other ways. As we noted in the discussion of aggression, youngsters who are having trouble academically often affiliate with others like them. Affiliation with low achievers often leads to an anti-school orientation, further academic decline and affiliation with anti-social youngsters. This process can end with these youngsters dropping out of school. Less dramatically there are a number of ways in which aspects of peer relations, e.g., social networks and status in the peer group, correlate with academic performance.

But in this book we have also shown a positive way in which peer interactions and academic aspects are interconnected. As we saw in Chapter 7, pupils working together in collaborative ways in classrooms can lead to positive results in terms of learning and productive forms of interaction. The evidence for this in the results from the SPRinG study, described in the chapter, is compelling. Even though teachers were at first worried that introducing group work would interfere with pressures on them to cover the curriculum, it was found that a carefully developed programme of group work significantly improved achievement.

We have also identified some ways in which there is likely to be overlap between informal peer relations, e.g., as expressed during play activities at break-time and out-of-school activities, and peer relationships within the classroom. We have argued that skills revealed in informal peer activities – such as turn-taking, reciprocity, mutual engagement – are similar to skills that underpin successful collaborative group work. It seems to us that this possibility is relatively underexplored and needs more research, both theoretical and empirical.

We are, of course, aware that not all peer relationships and interactions are positive. The occurrence of bullying in schools is a testament to this problem. Indeed, the occurrence of bullying is one frequently cited reason for the marginalizing of breaktime in schools in both the UK and the USA. We suggest, however, that a lack of opportunities for peer interaction may actually be contributing to the problem. By this we mean that children learn the social skills necessary to get along with each other, and the consequences of anti-social behaviour, by having repeated and sustained opportunities to interact with peers, relatively free from adult control. Consequently, breaktime should be viewed as an important venue in which children learn social skills. The current practice, at least in many American schools, of implementing 'character education programs' seems to miss the point. Children, as Piaget noted, develop social understanding and morality through peer interaction. We do not mean to imply that breaktime should be a time when children are unsupervised and allowed to interact in any way they please. It needs to be supervised in such a way that real aggression is not tolerated and cooperative interaction is encouraged.

A theme of this chapter has therefore been a tension between positive and negative features of peer relations. Though children value peer relations and friendships, we should not overlook ways in which friendship groups can support rejection and stereotyping, and how they can lead to insecurity, jealousy and resentment. Many pupils love breaktime in schools, but the school playground can be a cruel place for some children, and victims of bullying can suffer enormously.

This reflects an important feature of peer relations: any given aspect can present opportunities and difficulties for children. As Hartup and Laursen (1993) have argued, there is a longstanding tradition of work in psychology which stresses the importance to interpersonal relationships of both 'affirmations' and 'conflict', and children necessarily have to learn to manage both these facets of social relations. One line of research, in fact, has shown ways in which conflict has a central and productive role in children's social development (see chapters in Shantz & Hartup, 1992). Brown (1990) has shown that it is not whether peer influences are basically positive or negative that is the point; they are both mixed blessings. The challenge for research, and by implication for schools, is to clarify how and under what circumstances peer groups benefit development.

A theme underpinning much research and comment on peer relations is the degree of importance of peer relations in development. We have seen that some have assigned a primary, necessary role to peer relations, while some see peer relations as only helpful or an advantage. But the attempt to identify a specific role for peer relations in development is unlikely to be successful. In this book we have stressed a contextual approach, and have seen a number of ways in which contextual factors are important in understanding peer relations in school. We have seen differences between contexts within schools, e.g., classroom and playground and between primary and secondary schools. There are a number of ways in which the classroom context and organization can affect peer relations, sometimes encouraging and sometimes inhibiting school learning.

In the Spencer project we also found a number of ways in which whole schools differed in, and affected, pupils' breaktime experience and peer relations (Blatchford & Baines, 2010). Schools are likely to differ in the extent of inter-peer group rivalries and conflicts. We have also suggested ways in which contexts affect sociometric status in complex ways, e.g., that in some schools children who want to learn and do well feel they should keep their heads down, and may be classified as average or neglected.

Pupil culture and peer relations in schools are therefore likely to be best conceived as something emerging in context and affected by the school culture and environment. Epstein (1989, p. 183) has said:

> It is no longer feasible to study or explain the selection of friends with attention only to psychological constructs and child development terms. It is also necessary to give attention to the designs of the school, classroom, family, and other environments in which peer relations and the selection and influence of friends take place.

But in fact very little is known about ways in which schools differently affect breaktime experiences and pupil peer relations, and this is an important area of future research.

We feel that our own research and our review of work on peer relations have important implications for school management and the wider approach to young people. A main problem arises out of a tendency towards growing restrictions on pupils' peer relations, friendships and unsupervised activities, on the one hand, and the likely benefits of these activities for their social development, on the other hand. There is a tension, in other words, between a greater control of pupil behaviour, and the likely value of pupil independence. The move to greater control, which is probably gaining dominance, risks overrunning pupils' freedoms and the positive aspects identified above, while a more non-interventionist stance risks allowing anti-school cultures to develop and dominate, and have a destructive effect on school learning. An important challenge facing schools, therefore, is getting the balance between the two polarities right.

It is understandable if difficulties found as a result of anti-social behaviour lead to adult-led solutions. Reports from the Institute of Public Policy Research indicate that the behaviour of teenagers in the UK is worse than in other countries, and suggest that we should seek to increase time spent with parents and adults and time spent in adult structured and supervised clubs in and out of schools (Margo & Dixon, with Pearce & Reed, 2006).

But we query the view that the solution is yet more adult structure and control. Just as important, we feel, is dealing with peer relations in everyday school contexts (e.g., during breaktimes). Whilst schools and teachers can be effective in teaching children about moral understanding, children also learn from their own experiences, mistakes and reflections. We sympathize with a submission to the Children's Society national inquiry (2007) which suggested that teacher training might include more on the ability to promote cooperation and friendship between students. It is clearly difficult to get the balance right, but a coherent approach to peer relations in schools, within which there is attention to informal and class-based co-learning, could do much to improve learning and also school ethos. School breaktimes can again play a role here. The difficulties that staff know arise at breaktime can be viewed positively in the sense that they can be the basis for discussion with pupils and greater involvement of pupils in school decisions and management (Blatchford, 1998), within a moral framework provided by the school.

Teacher–pupil interactions

One of the key points to emerge from our review of research on teacher–pupil interactions was a tension between teachers' talk designed to maintain control, enhance classroom management and coverage of the curriculum, on the one hand, and classroom talk that encourages a higher cognitive content, challenging pupils to think and advance conceptually, on the other. It was concluded that despite the differences between quantitative and qualitative approaches to research on teaching, a common theme to emerge is agreement about the primary importance of teaching interactions and in particular a more interactive form of teacher-to-pupil talk.

There is much that we have learned from careful observational studies of classrooms, going back thirty or forty years, but, worryingly, there are signs that research on classroom talk is having less and less effect on initial teacher education, and this is likely to get worse in England at least as the preparation of new teachers is handed over more and more to schools, with progressively less input from higher education or local authorities. This is not helped in the UK by the strong political control of education planning.

It is a depressing fact that the accounts of teaching as reviewed in this book come to very different conclusions to those of government ministers in charge of education. When working on this book the authors had the opportunity to immerse themselves in many years' scholarship and research on teacher–pupil talk and classroom interaction, and a hugely impressive body of work it is. At the same time (2014) the then UK Secretary of State for Education Mr Gove gave a widely reported speech on teaching. Mr Gove dismissed 'education academics' as out-of-touch ideologues, and caricatured their views as 'progressive' and that they felt teachers do not matter. The sad thing is that much of the research and comment that is dismissed or unread by politicians and their advisers in fact strongly supports the view that teaching is the most important thing in education, but in addition it offers profound insights into why this is the case and what is worth developing. An overriding and central agreement across studies from different traditions is in relation to the power of teacher's talk to develop children's thinking.

It is therefore vital that we support research which seeks to better understand effective modes of classroom interaction. We suggested in Chapter 9 the value of descriptive research on classroom teaching, within which teacher–pupil interactions are studied at different levels of analysis, with embedded methods of observation at different levels of specificity and detail. This would then combine elements of, for example, ratings of classroom practice, supplemented by ongoing codings of categories of teacher–pupil interaction and talk, and a more detailed 'micro' analysis of a strategic selection of teacher–pupil interaction sequences. This integration of coding methods promises to provide a rich analysis of key aspects of effective teaching.

But we also agree with Howe and Abedin (2013) and Mercer (2014) that a judicious combination of quantitative and qualitative approaches to research effective teaching practices is long overdue. This could, for example, systematically evaluate the consequences of teacher–pupil dialogue on pupil learning, e.g., whether scaffolding approaches are better than dialogic approaches.

A consistent theme through several chapters has been the way that different approaches – for example, psychological and sociological/ethnographical – have developed quite separately from each other, even when the processes and relationships they study are similar. We believe that there is much potential in combining approaches from different disciplines – to link, for example, psychological research on self-perceptions and motivation, research on classroom interaction and classroom discourse, ethnographic research on peer cultures and employment patterns. For the long term we feel that research will be successful in informing policy on underachievement when it combines research on classroom interactions, pupil attitudes and perceptions, and wider social, cultural and structural factors.

The chapter on teacher expectations showed that they are an important component underpinning classroom teaching and organization and one main way in which differences and inequalities between pupils can become magnified or appropriately handled. It was concluded that a main task for future research is to clarify the conditions under which expectancies are heightened or minimized and to address the qualities of teachers, schools and students that predict susceptibility to expectancy effects. The implications for education policy are profound in that the research suggests that we need to rethink the common belief systems of teachers about pupil capabilities. In line with recent motivational research we need to encourage teachers and pupils to adopt 'incremental' over 'entity' views of children's abilities, and encourage school systems within which students are encouraged to develop effort-based beliefs about intelligence and their own abilities; we need to shift to school cultures that emphasize perception of potential over ability.

We finish by returning to the key theme of contextual influences, this time in relation to classroom learning. The chapter on classroom environments (Chapter 8) sought to show that teaching and learning needs to be understood and researched in context, and showed ways in which aspects of the classroom environment, like class size, and also at the within-class level, like groupings, are important contexts for teaching and learning. Classrooms are complex and multifaceted and we need to recognize the multidimensional nature of grouping in classrooms in terms of group composition (e.g., in relation to ability, sex and friendship mix), the size and number of groups in the class, but also the interconnections with classroom-level factors like class size, and classroom layout. All of these need to be considered in relation to the curriculum, task and activity type, as well as the role of adults and support of groups. This, then, is another way in which the context is vital when considering the nature and effects of interactions in school. But we also argued that the social pedagogic potential for learning in classroom groups is not often considered by teachers. There is often little relationship in practice, for example, between the size of groups and the learning tasks or types of interaction assigned to them by the teacher.

We therefore suggested in Chapter 8 the value of developing a 'social pedagogy' of classroom learning, in which group size and composition, teaching roles, learning tasks, perceptions of different curriculum and pedagogy come together in a dynamic relationship. Better understanding of effective teaching requires an understanding of separate and interconnecting influences, and this is a key task for future research and theory.

References

Blatchford, P. (1998). *Social Life in School: Pupils' Experience of Breaktime and Recess from 7 to 16 years.* London: Falmer Press.

Blatchford, P. & Baines, E. (2010). Peer relations in school. In K. Littleton, C. Wood & J. Kleine-Staarman (Eds), *International Handbook of Psychology in Education.* Bingley, UK: Emerald.

Brown, B.B. (1990). Peer groups and cultures. In Feldman, S.S. & Elliott, G.R. (Eds) *At the Threshold: The Developing Adolescent.* Cambridge, MA: Harvard University Press.

The Children's Society (2007). *The Good Childhood National Enquiry: Evidence Summary One – Friends.* Retrieved 10 September 2007, from www.childrenssociety.org.uk/resources/documents/good%20childhood/Friends%20evidence%20summary_2721_full.pdf.

Epstein, J.L. (1989). The selection of friends: changes across the grades and the different school environments. In Berndt, T.J. & Ladd, G.W. (Eds), *Peer Relationships in Child Development.* New York: Wiley.

Hartup, W.W. & Laursen, B. (1993). Conflict and context in peer relations. In C.H. Hart (Ed.) *Children on Playgrounds: Research Perspectives and Applications.* Albany, NY: State University of New York Press.

Howe, C. & Abedin, M. (2013). Classroom dialogue: a systematic review across four decades of research. *Cambridge Journal of Education, 43,* 325–356.

Margo, J. & Dixon, M., with Pearce, N. & Reed, H. (2006). *Freedom's Orphans: Raising Youth in a Changing World.* London: Institute for Public Policy Research.

Mercer, N. (2014). 40 years on: research into teacher–student talk. *Research Intelligence,* 123, Spring, 16–17.

Shantz, C.U. & Hartup, W.W. (1992). *Conflict in Child and Adolescent Development.* Cambridge: Cambridge University Press.

INDEX